THE
INKBLOTS

HERMANN
RORSCHACH,
HIS ICONIC TEST,
AND THE POWER
OF SEEING

CROWN
NEW YORK

THE INKBLOTS

DAMION SEARLS

Grateful acknowledgment is made to Hogrefe Verlag Bern for permission to
translate the essay *Leben und Wesensart* by Olga Rorschach, from "Gesammelte
Aufsätze," Verlag Hans Huber, Bern, 1965. All rights reserved. Used with kind
permission of the Hogrefe Verlag Bern.

Library of Congress Cataloging-in-Publication Data
Names: Searls, Damion, author.
Title: The inkblots : Hermann Rorschach, his iconic test, and the power of seeing /
Damion Searls.
Description: New York : Crown Publishing, [2017] | Includes bibliographical
references and index.
Identifiers: LCCN 2016028995 (print) | LCCN 2016042118 (ebook) |
ISBN 9780804136549 (hardcover) | ISBN 9780804136563 (pbk.) |
ISBN 9780804136556 (ebook)
Subjects: LCSH: Rorschach, Hermann, 1884–1922. | Psychiatrists—Switzerland. |
Rorschach Test.
Classification: LCC RC438.6.R667 S43 2017 (print) | LCC RC438.6.R667 (ebook) |
DDC 616.890092 [B]—dc23
LC record available at https://lccn.loc.gov/2016028995

ISBN 978-0-8041-3654-9
Ebook ISBN 978-0-8041-3655-6

Printed in the United States of America

Book design: Lauren Dong
Jacket design: Elena Giavaldi
Jacket photographs: (inkblot) Spencer Grant/Science Source/Getty Images; (Rorschach
and handwriting) Archiv und Sammlung Hermann Rorschach, University Library of
Bern, Switzerland

10 9 8 7 6 5 4 3 2 1

First Edition

The *soul of the mind* requires marvelously little to make it produce all that it envisages and employ all its reserve forces *in order to be itself*. . . . A few drops of ink and a sheet of paper, as material allowing for the accumulation and co-ordination of moments and acts, are enough.

—PAUL VALÉRY, *Degas Dance Drawing*

In Eternity All is Vision.

—WILLIAM BLAKE

CONTENTS

———

AUTHOR'S NOTE

THE RORSCHACH TEST USES TEN AND ONLY TEN INKBLOTS, ORIGI-
nally created by Hermann Rorschach and reproduced on cardboard cards. Whatever else they are, they are probably the ten most
interpreted and analyzed paintings of the twentieth century. Millions
of people have been shown the real cards; most of the rest of us have
seen versions of the inkblots in advertising, fashion, or art. The blots
are everywhere—and at the same time a closely guarded secret.

The Ethics Code of the American Psychological Association requires that psychologists keep test materials "secure." Many psychologists who use the Rorschach feel that revealing the images ruins the
test, even harms the general public by depriving it of a valuable diagnostic technique. Most of the Rorschach blots we see in everyday life
are imitations or remakes, in deference to the psychology community.
Even in academic articles or museum exhibitions, the blots are usually
reproduced in outline, blurred, or modified to reveal something about
the images but not everything.

The publisher of this book and I had to decide whether or not to
reproduce the real inkblots: which choice would be most respectful
to clinical psychologists, potential patients, and readers. There is no
clear consensus among Rorschach researchers—about almost anything
to do with the test—but the manual for the most state-of-the-art Rorschach testing system in use today states that "simply having previous
exposure to the inkblots does not compromise an assessment." In any
case, the question is largely moot now that the images are out of copyright and up on the internet. They are easily available already—a fact
that many of the psychologists opposed to publicizing the images seem

to want to ignore. We eventually chose to include some of the inkblots in this book, but not all.

It has to be emphasized, though, that seeing the images reproduced online—or here—is *not* the same as taking the actual test. The size of the cards matters (about 9.5" × 6.5"), the white space, the horizontal format, the fact that you can hold them in your hand and turn them around. The situation matters: the experience of taking a test with real stakes, having to say your answers out loud to someone you either trust or don't trust. And the test is too subtle and technical to score without extensive training. There is no Do-It-Yourself Rorschach, and you can't try it out on a friend, even apart from the ethical problem of possibly discovering sides of their personality that they may not want to reveal.

It has always been tempting to use the inkblots as a parlor game. But every expert on the test since Rorschach himself has insisted it isn't one. They're right. The reverse is true, too: the parlor game, online or elsewhere, is not the test. You can see for yourself how the inkblots look, but you can't, on your own, feel how they work.

Tea Leaves

V ICTOR NORRIS[*] HAD REACHED THE FINAL ROUND OF APPLYING for a job working with young children, but, this being America at the turn of the twenty-first century, he still had to undergo a psychological evaluation. Over two long November afternoons, he spent eight hours at the office of Caroline Hill, an assessment psychologist working in Chicago.

Norris had seemed an ideal candidate in interviews, charming and friendly with a suitable résumé and unimpeachable references. Hill liked him. His scores were normal to high on the cognitive tests she gave him, including an IQ well above average. On the most common personality test in America, a series of 567 yes-or-no questions called the Minnesota Multiphasic Personality Inventory, or MMPI, he was cooperative and in good spirits. Those results, too, came back normal.

When Hill showed him a series of pictures with no captions and asked him to tell her a story about what was happening in each one— another standard assessment called the Thematic Apperception Test, or TAT—Norris gave answers that were a bit obvious, but harmless enough. The stories were pleasant, with no inappropriate ideas, and he had no anxiety or other signs of discomfort in the telling.

As early Chicago darkness set in at the end of the second afternoon, Hill asked Norris to move from the desk to a low chair near the couch in her office. She pulled her chair in front of his, took out a yellow legal pad and a thick folder, and handed him, one by one, a series of ten cardboard cards from the folder, each with a symmetrical blot on it. As she handed him each card, she said: "What might this be?" or "What do you see?"

---

[*] Names and identifying details in this story have been changed.

Five of the cards were in black and white, two had red shapes as well, and three were multicolored. For this test, Norris was asked not to tell a story, not to describe what he felt, but simply to say what he saw. No time limit, no instructions about how many responses he should give. Hill stayed out of the picture as much as possible, letting Norris reveal not just what he saw in the inkblots but how he approached the task. He was free to pick up each card, turn it around, hold it at arm's length or up close. Any questions he asked were deflected:

Can I turn it around?
It's up to you.

Should I try to use all of it?
Whatever you like. Different people see different things.

Is that the right answer?
There are all sorts of answers.

After he had responded to all ten cards, Hill went back for a second pass: "Now I'm going to read back what you said, and I want you to show me where you saw it."

Norris's answers were shocking: elaborate, violent sexual scenes with children; parts of the inkblots seen as female being punished or destroyed. Hill politely sent him on his way—he left her office with a firm handshake and a smile, looking her straight in the eye—then she turned to the legal pad facedown on her desk, with the record of his responses. She systematically assigned Norris's responses the various codes of the standard method and categorized his answers as typical or unusual using the long lists in the manual. She then calculated the formulas that would turn all those scores into psychological judgments: dominant personality style, Egocentricity Index, Flexibility of Thinking Index, the Suicide Constellation. As Hill expected, her calculations showed Norris's scores to be as extreme as his answers.

If nothing else, the Rorschach test had prompted Norris to show a side of himself he didn't otherwise let show. He was perfectly aware

---

Previous pages: Rorschach Test, Cards I and II

that he was undergoing an evaluation, for a job he wanted. He knew how he wanted to come across in interviews and what kind of bland answers to give on the other tests. On the Rorschach, his persona broke down. Even more revealing than the specific things he had seen in the inkblots was the fact that he had felt free to say them.

This was why Hill used the Rorschach. It's a strange and open-ended task, where it is not at all clear what the inkblots are supposed to be or how you're expected to respond to them. Crucially, it's a visual task, so it gets around your defenses and conscious strategies of self-presentation. You can manage what you want to say but you can't manage what you want to see. Victor Norris couldn't even manage what he wanted to say *about* what he'd seen. In that he was typical. Hill had learned a rule of thumb in grad school that she had repeatedly seen confirmed in practice: a troubled personality can often keep it together on an IQ test and an MMPI, do pretty well on a TAT, then fall apart when faced with the inkblots. When someone is faking health or sickness, or intentionally or unintentionally suppressing other sides of their personality, the Rorschach might be the only assessment to raise a red flag.

Hill didn't put in her report that Norris was a past or future child molester—no psychological test has the power to determine that. She did conclude that Norris's "hold on reality was extremely vulnerable." She couldn't recommend him for a job working with children and advised the employers not to hire him. They didn't.

Norris's disturbing results and the contrast between his charming surface and hidden dark side stayed with Hill. Eleven years after giving that test, she got a phone call from a therapist who was working with a patient named Victor Norris and had a few questions he wanted to ask her. He didn't have to say the patient's name twice. Hill was not at liberty to share the details of Norris's results, but she laid out the main findings. The therapist gasped. "You got that from a Rorschach test? It took me two years of sessions to get to that stuff! I thought the Rorschach was tea leaves!"

DESPITE DECADES OF controversy, the Rorschach test today is admissible in court, reimbursed by medical insurance companies, and administered around the world in job evaluations, custody battles, and psychiatric clinics. To the test's supporters, these ten inkblots are a marvelously sensitive and accurate tool for showing how the mind works and detecting a range of mental conditions, including latent problems that other tests or direct observation can't reveal. To the test's critics, both within and outside the psychology community, its continued use is a scandal, an embarrassing vestige of pseudoscience that should have been written off years ago along with truth serum and primal-scream therapy. In their view, the test's amazing power is its ability to brainwash otherwise sensible people into believing in it.

Partly because of this lack of professional consensus, and more because of a suspicion of psychological testing in general, the public tends to be skeptical about the Rorschach. The father in a recent well-publicized "shaken baby" case, who was eventually found innocent in the death of his infant son, thought the assessments he was subjected to were "perverse" and particularly "resented" being given the Rorschach. "I was looking at pictures, abstract art, and telling them what I was seeing. Do I see a butterfly here? Does that mean I'm aggressive and abusive? It's insane." He insisted that while he "put stock in science," which he called an "essentially male" worldview, the social services agency evaluating him had an "essentially female" worldview that "privileged relationships and feelings." The Rorschach test is in fact neither essentially female nor an exercise in art interpretation, but such attitudes are typical. It doesn't yield a cut-and-dried number like an IQ test or a blood test. But then nothing that tries to grasp the human mind could.

The Rorschach's holistic ambitions are one reason why it is so well known beyond the doctor's office or courtroom. Social Security is a Rorschach test, according to *Bloomberg*, as is the year's Georgia Bulldogs football schedule (*Sports Blog Nation*) and Spanish bond yields: "a sort of financial-market Rorschach test, in which analysts see whatever is on their own minds at the time" (*Wall Street Journal*). The latest Supreme Court decision, the latest shooting, the latest celebrity wardrobe malfunction. "The controversial impeachment of Paraguay's president, Fernando Lugo, is quickly turning into a kind of Rorschach test of Latin American politics," in which "the reactions to it say more than the event does itself," says a *New York Times* blog. One movie reviewer impatient with art-house pretension called *Sexual Chronicles of a French Family* a Rorschach test that he'd failed.

This last joke trades on the essence of the Rorschach in the popular imagination: It's the test you can't fail. There are no right or wrong answers. You can see whatever you want. This is what has made the test perfect shorthand, since the sixties, for a culture suspicious of authority, committed to respecting all opinions. Why should a news outlet say whether an impeachment or a budget proposal is good or bad, and risk alienating half of its readers or viewers? Just call it a Rorschach test.

The underlying message is always the same: You are entitled to your own take, irrespective of the truth; your reaction is what matters, whether expressed in a like, a poll, or a purchase. This metaphor for freedom of interpretation coexists in a kind of alternate universe from the literal test given to actual patients, defendants, and job applicants by actual psychologists. In those situations, there are very real right and wrong answers.

The Rorschach is a useful metaphor, but the inkblots also just look good. They're in style for reasons having nothing to do with psychology or journalism— maybe it's the sixty-year fashion cycle since the last burst of Rorschach fever in the fifties, maybe it's a fondness for forceful black-and-white color schemes that look good with midcentury modern furniture. A few years ago, Bergdorf Goodman filled its Fifth Avenue windows with Rorschach displays. Rorschach-style T-shirts were recently on sale at Saks, only $98. "MY STRATEGY," proclaimed a full-page splash

Bergdorf Goodman window, Fifth Avenue, New York City, spring 2011 in *InStyle*: "This season I'm finding myself very attracted to clothes and accessories that have a sense of symmetry. MY INSPIRATION: The patterns of Rorschach inkblots are spellbinding." The horror-thriller *Hemlock Grove,* the science fiction cloning thriller *Orphan Black,* and a Harlem-based tattoo-shop reality show called *Black Ink Crew* debuted on TV with Rorschachy credit sequences. The video for *Rolling Stone*'s #1 Best Song of the 2000s and the first single ever to hit the top of the charts from internet sales, Gnarls Barkley's "Crazy," was a mesmerizing animation of morphing black-and-white blots. Rorschach mugs and plates, aprons and party games are available everywhere.

Most of these are imitation inkblots, but the ten originals, now approaching their hundredth birthday, endure. They have what Hermann Rorschach called the "spatial rhythm" necessary to give the images a "pictorial quality." Created in the birthplace of modern abstract art, their precursors go back to the nineteenth-century brew that gave rise to both modern psychology and abstraction, and their influence reaches across twentieth- and twenty-first-century art and design.

In other words: three different histories spill together into the story of the Rorschach test.

First, there is the rise, fall, and reinvention of psychological testing, with all its uses and abuses. Experts in anthropology, education, business, law, and the military have also long tried to gain access to the mysteries of unknown minds. The Rorschach is not the only personality test, but for decades it was the ultimate one: as defining of the profession as the stethoscope was for general medicine. Throughout its history, how psychologists use the Rorschach has been emblematic of what we, as a society, expect psychology to do.

Then there is art and design, from Surrealist paintings to "Crazy" to Jay-Z, who put a gold Andy Warhol blot painting called *Rorschach* on the cover of his memoir. This visual history seems unrelated to medical diagnosis—there's not much psychology in those Saks shirts—but the iconic look is inseparable from the real test. The agency that pitched a Rorschach-themed video for "Crazy" got the job because singer CeeLo Green remembered having been given the test as a troubled child. Controversy gathers around the Rorschach because of its prominence. It's impossible to draw a hard and fast line between the psychological assessment and the inkblots' place in the culture.

Finally, there is the cultural history that has led to all those metaphorical "Rorschach tests" in the news: the rise of an individualistic culture of personality in the early twentieth century; widespread suspicion of authority beginning in the sixties; intractable polarization today, with even facts seeming to depend on the eye of the beholder. From the Nuremberg Trials to the jungles of Vietnam, from Hollywood to Google, from the community-centered social fabric of nineteenth-century life to the longing for connection in the socially fragmented twenty-first, Rorschach's ten blots have run alongside, or anticipated, much of our history. When yet another journalist calls something a Rorschach test, it may be just a handy cliché, the same way it is perfectly natural for artists and designers to turn to striking, symmetrical patterns of black on white. No single instance of the Rorschach in everyday life requires any explanation. But its lasting presence in our collective imagination does.

For many years, the test was hyped as an X-ray of the soul. It's not, and it wasn't originally meant to be, but it is a uniquely revealing window on the ways we understand our world.

ALL OF THESE STRANDS—psychology, art, and cultural history—lead back to the creator of the inkblots. "The method and the personality of its creator are inextricably interwoven," as the editor wrote in the preface to *Psychodiagnostics,* the 1921 book that introduced the inkblots to the world. It was a young Swiss psychiatrist and amateur artist, tinkering with a children's game, working alone, who managed to create not only an enormously influential psychological test but a visual and cultural touchstone.

Hermann Rorschach, born in 1884, was "a tall, lean, blond man, swift of motion, gestures, and speech, with an expressive and vivid physiognomy." (See photographs in the insert.) If you think he looks like Brad Pitt, maybe with a little Robert Redford thrown in, you are not the first. His patients tended to fall for him too. He was openhearted and sympathetic, talented but modest, sturdy and handsome in his white doctor's robe, his short life filled with tragedy, passion, and discovery.

Modernity was erupting around him, from the Europe of World War I and the Russian Revolution and from within the mind itself. In

Switzerland alone, during Rorschach's career there, Albert Einstein invented modern physics and Vladimir Lenin invented modern communism while working with the labor organizers in Swiss watch factories. Lenin's next-door neighbors in Zurich, the Dadaists, invented modern art, Le Corbusier modern architecture, Rudolf von Laban modern dance. Rainer Maria Rilke finished his *Duino Elegies,* Rudolf Steiner created Waldorf schools, an artist named Johannes Itten invented seasonal colors ("Are you a spring or a winter?"). In psychiatry, Carl Jung and his colleagues created the modern psychological test. Jung's and Sigmund Freud's explorations of the unconscious mind were battling for dominance, both among a wealthy neurotic clientele and in the real world of Swiss hospitals filled far past capacity.

These revolutions crossed paths in Hermann Rorschach's life and career, but despite tens of thousands of studies of the test, no full-length biography of Rorschach has ever been written. A historian of psychiatry named Henri Ellenberger published a sketchily sourced forty-page biographical article in 1954, and that has been the basis for nearly every account of Rorschach since: as pioneering genius, bumbling dilettante, megalomaniac visionary, responsible scientist, and just about everything in between. Speculation has swirled around Rorschach's life for decades. People could see in it whatever they wanted to see.

The true story deserves to be told, not least because it helps to explain the test's enduring relevance despite the controversies that have surrounded it. Rorschach predicted most of the controversies himself. This double biography of the doctor and his inkblots begins in Switzerland but reaches around the globe, and down into the core of what we are doing every time we look and see.

All Becomes Movement and Life

ONE LATE DECEMBER MORNING IN 1910, HERMANN RORSCHACH, twenty-six years old, woke up early. He walked across the cold room and pushed the bedroom curtain aside, letting in the pale white light that comes before a late northern sunrise—not enough to wake his wife, just enough to reveal her face and the thick black hair spilling out from under their comforter. It had snowed in the night, as he'd thought it would. Lake Constance had been gray for weeks; the water's blue was months away, but the world was beautiful like this, too, with no one in sight along the shore or on the little path in front of their tidy two-room apartment. The scene was not just empty of human movement but drained of color, like a penny postcard, a landscape in black and white.

He lit his first cigarette of the morning, boiled some coffee, dressed, and left quietly as Olga slept. It was a busier week than usual at the clinic, with Christmas around the corner. There were only three doctors to look after four hundred patients, so he and the others were responsible for everything: staff meetings, visiting the patients on twice-daily rounds, organizing special events. Still, Rorschach let himself enjoy the morning's solitary walk through the clinic grounds. The notebook he always carried with him stayed in his pocket. It was cold, though nothing compared to the Christmas he'd spent in Moscow four years earlier.

Rorschach was especially looking forward to the holiday this year: he and Olga were reunited; they would be sharing a tree as husband and wife for the first time. The clinic celebration would be on the twenty-third; on the twenty-fourth, the doctors would carry a small tree lit with candles from one building to another, for the patients who couldn't join in the communal ceremony. On the twenty-fifth the Ror-schachs would be free to go back to his childhood home and pay a visit to his stepmother. This he tried to put out of his mind.

Christmas season at the asylum meant group singing three times a week, and dance classes run by a male nurse who played a guitar, a harmonica, and a triangle with his foot, all at the same time. Ror-schach didn't like to dance, but for Olga's sake he forced himself to take lessons. One Christmastime duty he truly enjoyed was direct-ing the holiday plays. They were staging three this year, including one with projected images—photographs of landscapes and people from the clinic. What a surprise it would be for the patients to suddenly see faces they knew on the screen, larger than life.

Many of the patients were too far gone to thank their relatives for Christmas presents, so Rorschach wrote little notes on their behalf, sometimes fifteen a day. On the whole, though, his patients liked the holidays as much as their troubled souls allowed. Rorschach's adviser used to tell the story of a patient so dangerous and unruly she had been kept in a cell for years. Her hostility was understandable in the restrictive, coercive clinical environment, but when she was taken to a Christmas celebration she behaved perfectly, reciting the poems she had memorized especially for January 2, Berchtold Day. Two weeks later she was released.

He tried to apply his teacher's lessons here. He took photos of his patients, not only for his own sake and for the patient files, but because they liked posing for the camera. He gave them art supplies: pencil and paper, papier-mâché, modeling clay.

As Rorschach's feet crunched the snow on the clinic's grounds, his thoughts on new ways to give his patients something to enjoy, he would naturally have mused on the holidays of his own childhood and the games he had played then: sled races, capture the castle, hare and hounds, hide-and-seek, and the game where you spill some ink on a sheet of paper, fold it in half, and see what it looks like.

HERMANN RORSCHACH WAS born in November of 1884, a light-bringing year. The Statue of Liberty, officially titled *Liberty Enlighten-ing the World,* was presented to the US ambassador in Paris on America's

Independence Day. Temesvár in Austria-Hungary became the first city in continental Europe with electric streetlights, put up not long after those in Newcastle, England, and Wabash, Indiana. George Eastman patented the first workable roll of photographic film, which would soon let anyone make pictures with "the Pencil of Nature" by capturing light itself.

Those years, of early photography and primitive movies, are probably the hardest era in history for us, today, to *see*: in our mind's eye, everything then looks stiff and rickety, black and white. But Zurich, where Rorschach was born, was a modern, dynamic city, the largest in Switzerland. Its railway station dates from 1871, the famous main shopping street from 1867, the quays along the Limmat River from midcentury. And November in Zurich is shocks of orange and yellow under a gray sky: oak and elm leaves, fire-red maples rustling in the wind. Back then, too, the people of Zurich lived under pale blue skies, hiked through bright alpine meadows dotted with deep blue gentian and edelweiss.

Rorschach was not born where his family had been rooted for centuries: Arbon, a town on Lake Constance some fifty miles east. A small town called Rorschach is four miles past Arbon down the coast of the lake, and that must have been the family's place of origin, but the Rorschachs could trace their ancestors in Arbon back to 1437, and the history of the "Roschachs" there reaches back another thousand years, to A.D. 496. This was not so unusual in a place where people stayed put for generations, where you were a citizen of your canton (state) and city as well as country. A few ancestors roamed—one great-great-uncle, Hans Jakob Roschach (1764–1837), known as "the Lisboner," made it as far as Portugal, where he worked as a designer and perhaps created some of the mesmerizing, repeating patterns for the tiles that cover the capital city. But it was Hermann's parents who truly broke away.

Hermann's father, Ulrich, a painter, was born on April 11, 1853, twelve days after another future painter, Vincent van Gogh. The son of a weaver, Ulrich left home at age fifteen to study art in Germany, traveling as far as the Netherlands. He returned to Arbon to open a painter's studio and in 1882 married a woman named Philippine Wiedenkeller (born February 9, 1854), from a line of carpenters and boatmen with a long history of marrying Rorschachs.

The couple's first child, Klara, born in 1883, died at six weeks old, and Philippine's twin sister died four months later. After these hard blows the couple sold the studio and moved to Zurich, where Ulrich enrolled at the School of Applied Arts in the fall of 1884. For Ulrich to move to the city at age thirty-one, with no stable income, was unusual in staid Switzerland, but he and Philippine must have been eager to have their next child in happier surroundings. Hermann was born at 278 Haldenstrasse, in Wiedikon (Zurich), at 10 p.m. on November 8. Ulrich did well in art school and got a good job as a middle school drawing and painting teacher in Schaffhausen, a city some thirty miles north. By Hermann's second birthday, the family was settled where he would grow up.

Schaffhausen is a small, picturesque city full of Renaissance buildings and fountains, situated on the Rhine, the river that forms the northern border of Switzerland. "On the banks of the Rhine, meadows alternate with forests whose trees are reflected, dreamlike, in the dark green water," says a guidebook from the time. House numbers had not been introduced yet, so each building had a name—the Palm Branch, the Knight's House, the Fountain—and distinctive decorations: stone lions, painted facades, bay windows jutting out like giant cuckoo clocks, gargoyles, cupids.

The city was not stuck in the past. The Munot, an imposing circular fortress on a vineyard-covered hill with a moat and a grand view, dating from the sixteenth century, had been restored for tourism in the nineteenth. The railroad had arrived, and a new electricity plant was exploiting the river's plentiful water power. The Rhine poured out of Lake Constance at the Rhine Falls nearby, low but wide enough to be the largest waterfall in Europe. The English painter J. M. W. Turner drew and painted the falls for forty years, showing the water massive like a mountain and the mountains themselves dissolving in whirlpools of paint and light; Mary Shelley described standing on the lowest platform while "the spray fell thickly on us . . . looking up, we saw wave, and rock, and cloud, and the clear heavens through its glittering ever-moving veil. This was a new sight, exceeding anything I had ever before seen." As the guidebook put it: "A heavy mountain of water hurls itself at you like a dark fate; it plummets, and all that was solid becomes movement and life."

After Hermann's sister Anna was born in Schaffhausen, on August 10, 1888, the growing family rented a new house on the Geissberg, a steep twenty-minute hike uphill out of town to the west, where Hermann's brother, Paul, would be born (December 10, 1891). The house was roomier, with larger windows and a mansard roof, more French château than Swiss chalet, and with forests and fields to explore nearby. The landlord's children became Hermann's playmates. Inspired by James Fenimore Cooper's Leatherstocking adventures, they played pioneers and Indians, with Hermann and his friends slinking through the trees around a nearby gravel quarry and making off with Anna, the only "white woman" they had.

This was the setting of the children's happiest memories. Hermann liked to listen to the roar of the ocean he had never seen, in a seashell a missionary relative of their landlord had brought back from abroad. He built wooden mazes for his pet white mice to run through. When he came down with the measles at age eight or nine, his father cut out enchanting tissue-paper puppets and Hermann made them dance in a glass-lid box. On walks, Ulrich told his children the history of the city's beautiful old buildings and fountains and the meaning of the images they bore; he took them butterfly hunting, read to them, taught them the names of the flowers and trees. Paul was growing into a lively, chubby little boy, while Hermann, according to a cousin, "could look at something for a very long time, absorbed in his thoughts. He was a well-behaved child, quiet like his father." This cousin told the nine-year-old Hermann fairy tales—Hansel and Gretel, Rapunzel, Rumpelstiltskin—"which he liked because he was a dreamer."

Philippine Rorschach, warm and energetic, liked to entertain her children with old folk songs and was an excellent cook: pudding with cream and fruit was a favorite with the children, and every year she would throw a pig roast for all of her husband's colleagues. Ulrich's own parents had fought bitterly, to the point where Ulrich felt they had never loved each other; it was important to him to create a loving home for his children, the kind he had never had. With Philippine he did. You could joke with her—light a firecracker under her wide skirts, as Hermann's cousin remembered having happened once—and she would join in the laughter.

Ulrich, too, was respected and genuinely liked among colleagues and students. He had a minor speech impediment, probably a lisp, "which he could, however, overcome when he tried." It made him unusually reserved, but he was kindhearted to students during exams, giving hand and head signals and whispered encouragement. "I can still see this modest man, so ready to help, before my eyes more than half a century later," one student would recall. Or else he would spend half an hour correcting a student's drawing, patiently making line after line, erasing the student's wrong efforts, "until finally the picture stood before me, not differing from the model in any way. His memory for forms was astonishing; his lines were absolutely sure and true."

Though artists in Switzerland were not trained at universities or given a liberal arts education, Ulrich was a broadly cultured man. In his twenties he had published a small compilation of poetry, *Wildflowers: Poems for Heart and Mind,* writing many of the poems himself. His daughter Anna claimed he knew Sanskrit—and whether he had somehow learned it or spoke fake Sanskrit to fool the kids and amuse himself says much the same thing about him.

In his spare time, he wrote a hundred-page "Outline of a Theory of Form, by Ulr. Rorschach, Drawing Teacher." This was not a collection of middle school lecture notes or exercises but a treatise, opening with "Space and Spatial Apportionment" and "Time and Temporal Divisions." "Light and Color" eventually moved into "the primary forms, created by concentration, rotation, and crystallization," and then Ulrich set out on "an orienting stroll through the realm of Form": thirty pages of a kind of encyclopedia of the visual world. Part II covered "The Laws of Form"—rhythm, direction, and proportion—which Ulrich found in everything from music, leaves, and the human body to Greek sculpture, modern turbines, and armies. "Who among us," Ulrich mused, "has not often and with pleasure turned our eyes and imagination to the ever-changing shapes and movements of the clouds and the mist?" The manuscript ended by discussing human psychology: our consciousness, too, Ulrich wrote, is ruled by the basic laws of form. It was a deep and thoughtful work, not of much practical use.

After three or four years in the house on the Geissberg, the Rorschachs moved back into the city, to a new residential area near the Munot fortress, closer to the children's school. Hermann was active, a good ice skater, and there were sledding parties where the children would link their sleds together in a long line and ride down the hill around the Munot on wide streets into the city, before there were too many cars. Ulrich wrote a play that was performed on the roof terrace of the Munot with Anna and Hermann as actors; another time, he was commissioned to design a new flag for a Schaffhausen club, and the children looked for wildflowers for him to use as models. Afterward they were delighted to look up at the flag embroidered with his design in the colors of their poppies and cornflowers. Hermann, for his part, showed skill from an early age in drawing landscapes, plants, and people. From woodcarving, cutouts, and sewing to novels, plays, and architecture, his childhood was a creative one.

Charcoal drawings by Ulrich Rorschach (*left*) and Hermann, ca. 1903 (*right*)

In the summer of 1897, when Hermann was twelve, his mother Philippine came down with diabetes. In an age before insulin treatments, she died after four bedridden weeks of terrible, constant thirst. The family was devastated. A series of housekeepers moved in to help, but none fit in. The children especially despised one ostentatiously religious woman who spent all her time proselytizing.

On an evening a little before Christmas in 1898, Ulrich walked into the children's playroom with an announcement to make: they would soon have a new mother. And no stranger, but Aunt Regina. Ulrich had chosen to marry one of Philippine's younger half sisters,

Hermann's godmother; Hermann and Anna had spent vacations with her in Arbon, where she had a little store selling fabrics and textiles. She would be coming to Schaffhausen over Christmas, Ulrich said, for a visit. Anna started screaming; young Paul burst into tears. Fourteen-year-old Hermann stayed calm and reasoned with his siblings: they should think of Father, this was no life for him, with no happy home to return to at the end of the day. Naturally he didn't want these house-keepers turning his children into sanctimonious little hypocrites. Everything, Hermann said, would be fine.

The marriage took place in April 1899, and a new child was born less than a year later. She was named Regina, the same as her mother, and called Regineli. The siblings welcomed their new half sister "and had several peaceful, lovely, harmonious months together," in Anna's words—"but alas only months."

Ulrich may already have had symptoms more severe than a lisp: his hand shaking at school when he took off his hat, to the point where his students made fun of his palsy. After Regineli's birth, he began suf-fering from fatigue and dizzy spells, diagnosed as a neurological dis-ease resulting from lead poisoning when he was a journeyman painter. Within months, he had to give up his teaching, and the family moved one last time, to Säntisstrasse 5, where Regina opened a store in the building so she could support the family while staying home to care for Ulrich. Hermann started tutoring Latin to bring in some extra money and hurried home from school every day to help his stepmother look after his father.

Ulrich's last years were filled with what his obituary called "un-speakable torments": depression, delusions, and bitter, senseless self-recriminations. Hermann was with his father much of the time toward the end and came down with a severe lung infection exacerbated by the stress and strain. When Ulrich died, at four in the morning on June 8, 1903, Hermann was too sick to attend the funeral. His father was bur-ied in the cemetery between the Munot and Hermann's school, a few steps away from their house down a pretty, tree-lined path. He was fifty; Hermann was eighteen, his siblings fourteen, eleven, and three. Helplessly watching his father's illness and death made Hermann want to become a doctor, a neurologist. But for now he was an orphan, his stepmother widowed, without a pension, a single mother of four.

Anna's fears of a wicked stepmother soon proved justified. Regina was rigid, strict to the point of cruelty. Hermann's cousin later described her as "all work and no ideals," thinking only about how to make a living: she had married late, at age thirty-seven, "because she was a shop girl for thirty years and knew nothing else." Whereas Philippine Rorschach had been a firstborn child and her husband's first wife, Regina was a stepmother's daughter, a second wife, and a stepmother to three willful children with personalities very different from her own.

She fought often with Paul and made life miserable for curious, outgoing Anna, who now felt the family home was "narrow and constraining, with almost no air to breathe." Anna later described Regina as "like a chicken with short wings that cannot fly. She had no wings of imagination." The house under her miserly regime was kept cold, with the children's hands sometimes literally turning blue. They had no time to play, their free time devoted to working or doing chores.

Hermann, still in high school, had to grow up fast. When Anna looked back on her childhood, she remembered Hermann as being "father and mother both" to her. At the same time, he was Regina's main support, the man of the house, who would sit and talk to her for hours in the kitchen. He understood Regina and her inability to show more love—"I am afraid that, in her timid pride, she has never been able to make an attachment to anyone"—and he urged Anna and Paul not to be too critical of her. They should forgive what they could and think of little Regineli.

All of this left Hermann little time for his own grief. He would later admit to Anna, "I think back about Father and Mother—our real mother—much more than before; I maybe didn't feel Father's early death six years ago as deeply as I feel it now." It also made him eager to get away. Hermann would come to think of "all this scrambling and clawing and sweeping the floors, everything that sucks away so much life and kills off so infinitely much vitality," as "the Schaffhausen mind-set." As he wrote to Anna, "None of us can even consider living with Mother for any length of time. She has great and good qualities, and deserves the highest praise, but—life with her demands too much silence, it's not for people like us who need freedom to move."

All three of Ulrich and Philippine's children would eventually travel far more widely than their parents, and Hermann was the first to set out. "We have a talent for living, you and me," Hermann continued to Anna: "We inherited it from Father . . . and all we have to do is keep it, we have to. In Schaffhausen that kind of talent is completely strangled, it struggles and thrashes around for a moment and then it's dead. But, God knows, that's why we have the world! So that there's somewhere to let our talents unfold."

By the time he wrote this, Hermann had escaped. But his years in Schaffhausen, though full of upheaval, were important ones for Hermann's development as a thinker—and an artist.

2

Klex

IN A TWIST OF FATE THAT SEEMS TOO GOOD TO BE TRUE, ROR-schach's nickname in school was "Klex," the German word for "inkblot." Was young Blot Rorschach already tinkering with ink, his destiny foretold?

Nicknames were important in German and Swiss-German fraternities, which students joined while attending the six-year elite academic high school called the *Gymnasium*. A fraternity brother swore an oath of friendship and fidelity and was a member for life, with the connections he made there often greasing the wheels of his whole career. In Schaffhausen, social life was dominated by the fraternity of Scaphusia (the city's Roman name). Scaphusia members, Rorschach included, wore blue and white with pride on the school grounds, in the bars, and on the hiking trails. They also bore the new name they had received to mark their new identity.

Scaphusia initiations took place at a local bar, in total darkness except for a single candle mounted on a human skull. The initiate, known as the Fox, a fourth-year student sixteen or seventeen years old, stood on a crate filled with the club's fencing equipment, a mug of beer in each hand, and answered a tough round of questions. In Switzerland the hazing was no worse than that; at German universities the fencing was with real blades, resulting in the famous Heidelberg dueling scars that marked the faces of the German elite for life. When the Scaphusia Fox passed the test, he got his "beer baptism"—the two mugs poured over his head, or disposed of as usual—and a name: some obvious in-joke about his physical appearance or proclivities. Rorschach's fraternity sponsor was "Chimney" Müller, because he smoked like one; Chimney's sponsor was "Baal," a womanizing rich devil.

Hermann's new name Klex meant he was handy with pen and ink, someone who drew quickly and well. *Klexen* or *klecksen* also means "to daub, to paint mediocre paintings"—one of Rorschach's favorite artists, Wilhelm Busch, was the author of an illustrated children's book called *Maler Klecksel,* something like "Smudgy the Painter"—but Rorschach was being praised as a good artist, not teased as a bad one. Another Fox nicknamed Klex, in a different fraternity at around the same time, was also good at drawing and later became an architect.

So "Klex" did not mean "inkblot" in Scaphusia, though maybe it made an inkblot slightly more likely to come to mind as Rorschach strolled through the grounds of his asylum a decade later, trying to dream up ways to establish a connection with his schizophrenic patients. Either way, what mattered was Klex Rorschach being a Klex at all: an artist, with a visual sensibility.

RORSCHACH ATTENDED THE Schaffhausen *Gymnasium* from 1898 to 1904—from the year after his mother's death until the year after his father's. There were 170 students, fourteen in Rorschach's class, and the school was known as the best in the region, attracting students from other parts of Switzerland, even Italy, along with liberal-minded, democratically inclined professors from authoritarian Germany. The curriculum was demanding, including analytic geometry, spherical trigonometry, and advanced courses in qualitative analysis and physics. Students read Sophocles, Thucydides, Tacitus, Horace, Catullus, Molière, Hugo, Goethe, Lessing, and Dickens in the original, and the Russian masters in translation: Turgenev, Tolstoy, Dostoyevsky, Chekhov.

Rorschach did well in school without ever seeming to try very hard. He was ranked near the top of his class across all subjects; he learned English, French, and Latin in addition to his native Swiss dialect and standard German and would later teach himself Italian and fluent Russian. Socially he was reserved, a wallflower at school dances, preferring to hand out his visiting card and look on rather than risk the complex figures and maneuvers of the popular dance of the time, the Munot Tower ("Right hand, left hand, one, two, three"). He liked to work in a quiet environment and resented interruptions. Hermann's best friend in school, an extraverted future lawyer named Walter Im Hof, felt "it was my role to bring him out a little"; others agreed that socializing and drinking parties with his classmates did Hermann good. But Hermann and his more outgoing brother Paul also played pranks, which Hermann would remember with delight long afterward. He got out into nature whenever he could—hiking in the mountains, rowing in the lakes, swimming nude.

Financial worries were a constant preoccupation. Most of Rorschach's classmates came from wealthy and, in some cases, quite prominent families. The International Watch Company, still well known today as IWC Schaffhausen, had been founded in the city by an already wealthy manufacturer, and the founder's daughter, Emma Rauschenbach—Carl Jung's future wife—was one of the richest heiresses in Switzerland. In that prosperous milieu, Hermann Rorschach was noticeably poor. One classmate wrongly thought Rorschach's stepmother was a "washerwoman" who "must have had to work very, very hard to put the boy through school"; the classmate's patrician mother looked down on Rorschach and his family as lower class. Another schoolmate said Rorschach looked like a country bumpkin, "but" was intelligent anyway. Still, Rorschach refused to let his circumstances interfere with his independence. He was excused from fraternity dues and got himself appointed the group's librarian so he could buy new books when needed.

He also had access to at least one subject for scientific experiments: himself. Having read that mood can make your pupils grow bigger or smaller, the teenaged Rorschach found he could contract and dilate his pupils at will. In a dark room, he imagined looking for the light switch and his pupils would get noticeably smaller; outside, in bright afternoon sunlight, he could make them bigger. In another experiment in mind over matter, he tried to transpose the discomfort from a toothache into music, turning the "throbbing" pains into low notes and "sharp" pains into high notes. Once, curious to see how long it was possible to go without food and still work, he fasted for twenty-four hours, sawing and splitting wood all day. He found that if he didn't work he could fast longer. This was around the time of his father's remarriage.

There is no payoff from being able to dilate your pupils at will, except the knowledge that you can. These exercises were explorations: Rorschach exerting his will on himself, like his father, who could overcome his lisp or tremor "when he tried." He was testing his limits, investigating how his different "systems"—food and work, pain and music, mind and eye—fit together and could be put under conscious control. Another experience he found thought provoking:

> I have a rather bad musical memory, so when I am learning a tune I can rely very little on auditory memory images. I often use the optical image of the notes as a way to remember the melody; other times, when I was younger, taking violin lessons, it often happened that I could not imagine the sound of a passage but could still play it from memory, or in other words, the movement memory was more reliable than the auditory one. I have also often used imitation finger movements as a way to awaken auditory memories.

Rorschach was immensely interested in these transformations from one kind of experience into another.

He was also interested in putting himself in others' shoes, making their experiences his own. On July 4, 1903, at age eighteen, Rorschach gave the talk that Scaphusia members were expected to give to their peers: his was called "Women's Emancipation," a full-throated plea for full gender equality. Women, he argued, were "neither physically, intellectually, or morally inferior by nature to men," were no less logical and at least as brave. They did not exist to "manufacture children" any more than men were merely "a pension fund to pay women's bills." Making reference to the century-long history of the women's movement and to laws and social structures in other countries, including the United States, he advocated for full voting rights and access to university and professions, particularly medicine, since "women would rather reveal their intimate illnesses to another woman." He strengthened his arguments with wit and empathy, pointing out that while bluestockings horrified the older generation, "a male intellectual show-off is a sour and repellent figure too." As for women's alleged gossipy talkativeness, "The question is whether there is more chit-chat at a coffee klatsch or at a bar," that is, among women or men. He wondered if "we" weren't as ridiculous as "they" were—trying, as he often did, to see himself from the outside.

Naturally, Ulrich's son contributed numerous artworks to the Scaphusia scrapbook. A page of violin sheet music with klexy cats frolicking up and down the staff in place of notes was a pun, since cacophonous, screechy music is called "cat music" in German. A face-off between two people in silhouette, captioned *A Picture Without Words,* was also signed "Klex." Rorschach's artworks outside the Scaphusia scrapbook included a finely detailed charcoal drawing of his maternal grandfather, dated 1903 and copied from a small photograph (see page 17). Expressive faces and gestures interested him more than static objects or textures. In one picture, a student's clothes and furniture are less convincing than his posture; his cigar smoke doesn't look like smoke but it curls like smoke.

From the Scaphusia scrapbook, signed "Klex," a modified copy of *Cat Symphony,* by Austrian artist Moritz von Schwind. Rorschach simplified the image, removing many of the cats/notes. While some of the cats look a bit mousier, the picture as a whole has a livelier movement.

Another of Rorschach's Scaphusia lectures, "Poetry and Painting," called for better training in how to see. In the timeless fashion of teenagers everywhere, he criticized his school: "There is a lack of understanding of visual art among the people, even among the educated class, a shortcoming that can be traced to our education. . . . One looks in vain for art history courses in our *Gymnasium* curriculum, yet the child can think artistically as much as some adults." He also gave three talks on Darwin and our relationship to nature. Darwin was not studied in school, so the lectures were doing real educational work, and again

Rorschach focused on seeing. Addressing the question of whether Darwinism should be taught to children, Klex answered, according to the minutes of the meeting, "decidedly in the affirmative. For only through accurate treatment of these themes, adapted to the child's understanding, does the young person learn 'to see nature.' Only in this way will his motivation for observing be stimulated. Only in this way will a genuine joy of nature be awakened in the eyes of the young." What mattered was how to see, and see with joy. Rorschach ended his talk with an appreciation of another artist: "Darwin's great disciple on German soil, Haeckel." Illustrating his talk with pictures from Haeckel's *Art Forms in Nature,* he "drew particular attention to how Haeckel, with his method of natural observation, possessed a sharp eye for the art forms in Nature."

Ernst Haeckel (1834–1919) was one of the most famous scientists in the world. A recent biographer writes that "more people learned of evolutionary theory through his voluminous publications than through any other source," including Darwin's own work; *The Origin of Species* sold fewer than forty thousand copies in thirty years, while Haeckel's popularization *The Riddle of the Universe* sold more than six hundred thousand in German alone, as well as being translated into languages from Sanskrit to Esperanto. Gandhi himself wanted to translate it into Gujarati, believing it "the scientific antidote to the deadly wars of religion plaguing India." Aside from popularizing Darwin, Haeckel's scientific accomplishments included naming thousands of species—3,500 after just one of his polar expeditions—correctly predicting where fossils of the "missing link" between man and ape would be found, formulating the concept of ecology, and pioneering embryology. His theory that the development of the individual retraces the development of the species—"Ontogeny recapitulates phylogeny"—was enormously influential in both biology and popular culture.

Haeckel was also an artist. An aspiring landscape painter in his youth, he eventually combined art and science in luxuriously illustrated works. Darwin praised Haeckel on both counts, calling his breakthrough two-volume book "the most magnificent works which I have ever seen" and his *Natural History of Creation* "one of the most remarkable books of our time."

Art Forms in Nature, which Rorschach used to illustrate his Scaphu-

sia talk, was a visual compendium of structure and symmetry throughout the natural world, suggesting harmonies between amoebae, jellyfish,
crystals, and all sorts of higher forms. Published in book form in 1904,
though the hundred illustrations were originally published in ten sets
of ten between 1899 and 1904, it was popular and influential in both
science and art, creating a kind of visual vocabulary for Art Nouveau
while superimposing that vision onto nature. The fact that horizontally symmetrical forms look "organic" to us is partly a legacy of his way
of seeing. *Art Forms in Nature* was a household showpiece in German-
speaking Europe and beyond; the Rorschachs surely owned at least
some of the illustrations. Ulrich's "Outline of a Theory of Form,"
though it doesn't mention Haeckel by name, is practically a prose ana-
logue to Haeckel's book, filled with his vocabulary of "forms."

Top: Two of the black-and-white images from Ernst Haeckel, *Art Forms in Nature*:
"Brittle Stars" and "Moths," engraved by Adolf Giltsch after Haeckel's drawings.
Bottom: Ulrich Rorschach, design.

Also central to Haeckel's reputation was his crusade against religion. It was likely due in large part to Haeckel's personal antireligious activism that Darwinism became the ultimate atheistic science, at the heart of the feud between science and religion, even though geology and astronomy and other fields of knowledge contain equally nonbiblical facts. This, too, Hermann admired. Like his father, he was a tolerant freethinker on matters of faith but refused to see the natural world through religious eyes. In one of his Darwin talks, according to the Scaphusia secretary, "Klex tried to dismiss completely the argument against Darwinism that it undermines Christian morality and the meaning of the Bible."

Already working as a tutor, Rorschach was considering becoming a teacher like his father but was uneasy about being required to teach religion. He took the unusual step of writing to Haeckel for advice, and the eminent anti-Christian wrote back, "Your misgivings seem misplaced to me. . . . Read my *Monistic Religion,* a compromise with the official church. Hundreds of my students do this. One *must* diplomatically make one's peace with the reigning orthodoxy (*unfortunately!*)."

The seventeen-year-old's bold overture was later exaggerated into something more. In the recollections of several people close to Rorschach, he had asked Haeckel whether to study drawing in Munich or pursue a career in medicine, and the great man advised science. It is unlikely that Rorschach would have put his whole future in a stranger's hands, and there seems to have been only the one letter to Haeckel. Yet a founding myth for Rorschach's career was born. A practical question about teaching had been turned into a symbolic choice between art and science, and the most influential artist-scientist of the older generation had passed the baton to the artist-psychologist of the new one.

3

I Want to Read People

As far as I'm concerned, that whole blister on the mountainside could slide into the lake with a crash and the smell of brimstone, as Sodom and Gomorrah did in olden times"—Rorschach was not a fan of Neuchâtel, in French-speaking western Switzerland, where he spent several months after graduating from high school in March 1904. Many German-speaking Swiss took a semester before starting university to improve their French; Rorschach wanted to be able to give French lessons as well as tutor in Latin, to send money home to his family. He was desperate to go straight to Paris, but his rigid stepmother refused to let him. Compared to Schaffhausen, where Rorschach had felt like "a real 'scholar,'" the Académie de Neuchâtel was tedious: "There was nowhere stupider I could have ended up than that dreary mish-mash of Germany and France."

The Académie's one advantage was its two-month language course in Dijon, France. There, Rorschach made occasional trips to the legal French brothels, which he was mostly too poor to make use of. "Aug. 30," he scribbled in his private diary, with key passages further concealed in shorthand: "Visit to the Maison de tolérance: red lanterns in the narrow alley, dark, nice house . . . the whores all around, [*illegible*]; tu me paye un bock? Tu vas coucher avec moi? [Buy me a beer? Are you going to sleep with me?]."

It was also in Dijon that Rorschach's interests took a decisive turn. Inspired by the Russian writers he had read in Schaffhausen, he sought out Russians for company: "Everyone knows the Russians learn foreign languages easily," he reported to Anna, and, more important to a young man abroad on his own, "They like to talk and they make friends easily." He soon grew interested in one man in particular, a political reformer and "personal friend" of Tolstoy's. "This good fellow has gray hair already," Rorschach wrote, "and not for nothing."

Ivan Mikhailovich Tregubov, born in 1858, had been exiled from Russia and, like Rorschach, was in Dijon for the French course. Rorschach called him "a very deep soul" and wrote, "I hope to profit further from my acquaintance with him." Tregubov was not just a personal friend of Tolstoy's but at the heart of his inner circle, as a leader of the Dukhobors, the extreme pacifist sect that Tolstoy had been involved with for decades. This was Rorschach's first encounter with such a traditionalist spiritual movement. Russia had long been swept by them—from Old Believers, Flagellants, Hermits, and Wanderers to Jumpers, Milk-Drinkers, and Self-Castrators—all without civil rights until the 1905 Revolution and more or less harassed or suppressed by the tsarist church and state. The Dukhobors were one of the most venerable of these groups, dating back at least to the mid-eighteenth century.

In 1895, Tolstoy called the Dukhobors "a phenomenon of extraordinary importance," so advanced that they were "people of the 25th century"; he compared their influence with the appearance of Jesus on earth. In 1897, four years before the awarding of the first Nobel Peace Prize, Tolstoy wrote an open letter to a Swedish editor arguing that Nobel's money should go to the Dukhobors, and he came out of self-imposed retirement to write his last novel, *Resurrection,* so that he could give all of the proceeds to the sect. By that point, Tolstoy was not merely the author of *Anna Karenina* and *War and Peace* but a spiritual leader advocating "the purification of the soul." He inspired people around the world to wear simple white robes, turn vegetarian, and work for peace—to become Tolstoyans. What he represented, to Rorschach and millions of others, was not merely literature but a moral crusade to heal the world.

Tregubov opened Rorschach's eyes. "It is finally becoming clear to this young Swiss man," he wrote from Dijon, describing himself in the third person, "to someone who in general couldn't care less about politics, what politics really means—especially thanks to the Russians, who have to study so far away from home in order to find the freedom they need." Before long Rorschach would write, "I think we will see it turn out that Russia will be the freest country in the world, freer than our Switzerland." He started to learn Russian, apparently mastering the language in two years without taking classes.

It was in this context that Rorschach found his calling. He already wanted to be a doctor if he could—"I want to know if it wouldn't have been possible to help Father," Anna recalled him saying. But in Dijon he learned that "I never again want to read just books, the way I did in Schaffhausen. I want to read people. . . . What I want is to work at a madhouse. That is no reason not to get a complete training as a doctor, but the most interesting thing in nature is the human soul, and the greatest thing a person can do is to heal these souls, sick souls." His pursuit of psychology was rooted not mainly in professional or intellectual ambitions but in a Tolstoyan impulse to heal souls and an affinity with Russians such as Tregubov. When Rorschach left the blister on the mountainside, it was to pursue his studies at a world-class school of psychiatric medicine with one of the largest communities of Russians in Europe.

RORSCHACH HAD FINALLY been able to scrape together enough money to go to university. Because his father had been a citizen of two Swiss cities, Arbon and Schaffhausen, Hermann could apply for financial aid from both: in concrete terms, this was the greatest gift his parents' mobility would ever give him. In the fall of 1904, a few weeks shy of his twentieth birthday, Hermann showed up in Zurich with a handcart of belongings and less than a thousand francs to his name.

He was five foot ten, slim and athletic. He tended to walk quickly and purposefully, hands clasped behind his back, and to talk quietly and calmly; he was lively, serious, nimble with his fingers whether sketching out quick drawings or making meticulous cutouts or wood carvings. His eyes were light blue, almost gray, though the color is listed as "brown" or "brown-gray" in some official documents, such as his military-service record, the booklet that every Swiss male keeps for life. Hermann would be declared unfit to serve, like many young men superfluous in a country with universal military service. The reason given was poor eyesight: 20/200 in his left eye.

Rorschach had left his birthplace of Zurich too young to remember living there, but he had returned on visits with his parents. In his first letter to Anna after arriving in 1904, Rorschach wrote that he "went to two art exhibits yesterday, thinking again about our dear father. A few days ago, I also went looking for a little bench I used to sit on with him, and I found it." But a new life replaced the memories soon enough.

He had planned to stay at an inn run by a family friend, helping out with chores in exchange for rent, but took a classmate's advice and moved in to more independent lodgings. A dentist and his wife were renting out two bright and spacious spare rooms on the fourth floor of Weinplatz 3, steps away from the Limmat River running through the center of Zurich (and, as it happens, on the site of ancient Roman baths from Zurich's previous life as "Turicum"). Rorschach rented the rooms with a fellow medical student from Schaffhausen and a music student. They set up a common bedroom and a workspace and shared books—which "I get more out of than they do," Rorschach admitted. The medical student, Franz Schwerz, woke up at 4 a.m. to go to anatomy class and was asleep by nine at night, while the musician was out on evenings and weekends; Rorschach could do his work later in the mornings and at night. His only complaint was that his bedroom window was right under the tower of St. Peter's Church, with the largest church clock in Europe; the bells woke him up.

But it was cheap, seventy-seven francs a month including two meals a day, which Schwerz remembered as delicious and enormous and which Rorschach told his stepmother were "very good, almost exactly like your home cooking." (Zurich housing generally ran four francs a day at least, and an affordable restaurant lunch was one franc.) The students were responsible for their own lunch on Sundays, so on Saturday night they would buy *Schübling* sausages from the butcher shop around the corner and roast them in the apartment the next morning, filling the building's stairway with a smell that worked up their appetite. There was little to do on weekends but walk the city streets, good weather or bad—they could afford no bars, no movies, no theater. The roommates would often "return home bored and frozen, to dig into sausage number two."

Every opportunity to earn some extra money was welcome. When Rorschach, an extra in the student theater, remembered that the student union was sponsoring a contest for theater posters, he dashed off a caricature of a professor, adding a rhyming couplet underneath from

Wilhelm Busch's children's book about a mole; two weeks later, ten much-needed francs arrived in the mail: Third Prize.

Despite a punishing schedule at one of the best medical schools in the world—ten courses in his first winter semester (October 1904 to April 1905) and another twelve his first summer semester (April to August 1905)—Rorschach did not keep his nose entirely to the grindstone. His best friend at the university, Walter von Wyss, remembered Rorschach as a voracious reader, curious about everything. There was time for art, conversation, and browsing at the excellent used bookstores in "Athens on the Limmat," as Zurich was called.

Rorschach often spent the long Saturday afternoons at the Künstlergütli, Zurich's only public art museum, across the river and up the short hill toward the university. He and his friends explored the galleries of mostly Swiss and not yet modern art: peasant scenes by nineteenth-century Switzerland's Norman Rockwell, a genre painter named Albert Anker; nature scenes by the neo-Romantic Paul Robert; sentimental works like *Old Monk of the Hermitage* by Carl Spitzweg. The collection included realist master Rudolf Koller's most famous painting, the exceptionally dynamic *St. Gotthard Mail Coach,* and a *River Scene* by Zurich's greatest writer and Rorschach's favorite poet, Gottfried Keller. A few works pointed the way to the future: Ferdinand Hodler's *Procession of Gymnasts,* a nightmarish *War* by Art Nouveau pioneer and proto-Surrealist Arnold Böcklin, who had been one of the subjects of Rorschach's high school "Poetry and Painting" talk.

In the conversations afterward, Rorschach took the lead and asked his friends about how they saw the art. He liked to compare the different effects each piece had on each person. Böcklin's outrageously psychosexual *Spring Awakening,* with its hairy, pipe-playing, goat-footed satyr, a topless woman in a red skirt towering over the landscape, and a river of blood between them: What might this be?

Rorschach was starting to categorize people while priding himself on remaining individual. After passing his preliminary exams with flying colors in April 1906—"I was the only one who took them after four semesters," he bragged to Anna, "the others had five, six, seven, eight, but two five-semester students and I got the best results"—he cast a cold eye over his classmates:

I was especially happy because I'd been doing quite a lot "different" before and during the exams, although I did work a lot. There is a very common type among medical students, you know: someone who drinks beer, almost never reads the newspaper, and whenever he wants to say anything respectable talks only about illnesses and professors; who prides himself on frightfully much, especially the job he is planning to land, who thinks fondly in advance about a rich wife and a fancy car and a walking stick with a silver handle; this type finds it very unpleasant when someone else does things "differently" and can pass his exams anyway.

Many sensitive twenty-one-year-olds have had such thoughts, but this was not a letter Rorschach would have written without his Dijon experiences.

The most obvious sign of his "difference" was the time he spent with the exotic foreigners in the city. Zurich was full of Russians, with Switzerland's political freedom attracting countless anarchists and revolutionaries. Vladimir Lenin lived there in exile between 1900 and 1917, and preferred Zurich to Bern because of "the large number of revolutionary-minded young foreigners in Zurich," not to mention the excellent libraries, with "no red tape, fine catalogues, open stacks, and the exceptional interest taken in the reader": a model for the future Soviet society. There was a "Little Russia" neighborhood near the University of Zurich, with Russian boardinghouses, bars, and restaurants: as the respectable Swiss put it, the debates in Little Russia ran hot and the meals were served cold.

In Rorschach's time, half of the more than a thousand university students were foreign, many of them women. Two Swiss women had studied philosophy in Zurich in the 1840s, paving the way for women to study medicine there as early as the 1860s. The first woman ever to get a doctorate in medicine, in 1867, was a Russian in Zurich: Nadezhda Suslova. Meanwhile, Russian universities continued to exclude women until 1914, German universities until 1908.

These foreigners were, in turn, the majority of female students in Zurich, because Swiss fathers wouldn't let their well-bred daughters mingle with the riffraff. Emma Rauschenberg, the Schaffhausen heiress and Carl Jung's future wife, had graduated first in her high school class but was not allowed to study science at the University of Zurich: "It was simply unthinkable for the daughter of a Rauschenbach even to contemplate mingling with the great variety of students who enrolled in the university," according to a recent biographer of Carl Jung. "Who could predict what ideas a girl like Emma would assimilate from being in such company. . . . A university education would make her unfit for marriage to a social equal." Russian women flocked to Zurich, though, braving not only the sexism of male Swiss students and professors but also protests from the few Swiss women students that this "wave" of "semi-Asian invaders" was stealing spots from more deserving locals and turning the university into a "Slavic finishing school."

When not being caricatured as bluestockings or wild-eyed revolutionaries, Russian women in Zurich were often worshipped as beauties. One raven-haired Russian named Braunstein was known around Zurich as "the Christmas angel"; strangers came up to her on the street to ask to take her photograph, but she always refused. When some chemistry students invited her to the annual department party, they addressed the envelope with a street name and "MnO_2"—the chemical formula for manganese dioxide, or in German, *Braunstein*—and the zealous mailmen did not rest until they found her. She still declined. Rorschach, who wanted to draw her portrait, succeeded where others had failed by inviting her and a friend up to his rooms with the promise to show them a handwritten letter from Leo Tolstoy. He spoke passable Russian, respected Russian women in a hostile environment, and presumably his looks didn't hurt. That Saturday afternoon, the art at the museum was neglected and an easel was set up at Weinplatz 3 instead.

The Russians in Zurich were a diverse group. Some were young, some older; some truly were revolutionaries, like one female classmate who had been forced to flee through Siberia to Japan, eventually returning by ship to Europe the long way around, while others were "thoroughly bourgeois, modest, hardworking, and anxious to avoid politics." Some were rich, like Jung's patient, student, colleague, and mistress Sabina Spielrein, who came to Zurich in 1904, like Rorschach. Some were poor, including a pharmacist's daughter from Kazan named Olga Vasilyevna Shtempelin.

LIKE HERMANN, OLGA was the oldest of three children, forced by circumstances into the role of head of the family. She was born to Wilhelm Karlovitch and Yelizaveta Matveyevna Shtempelin on June 8,
1878, in Buinsk, near Kazan, a center for trade on the Volga River and
the Russian empire's "gateway to the East." Although girls' schools in
Russia were for the daughters of the wealthy, she had been able to study
for free at Kazan's Rodionov Institute for Girls, a perk stemming from
her great-grandfather's services in the military. She arrived in Berlin in
1902, took time off to work and support her family, and transferred to
the Zürich medical school in 1905. She would be remembered by those
who knew her in Zurich as by far the smartest in her class.

In early September 1906, Rorschach gave his sister Anna a striking
description of Olga's background and character. "My Russian friends
have mostly gone home" after the summer semester, but

> one woman I met recently, around two months ago, is leaving now.
> I have often thought that she in particular is someone you should
> meet: she is all alone on her path through life, and once, when she
> was twenty, she had to support her whole family for a year and a
> half, with tutoring and copying documents: a sick father, her
> mother, and two siblings. Now she is in her last year of medical
> school, about to turn twenty-six, full of life and high spirits, and
> when she graduates she wants to go be a doctor in a peasant vil-
> lage, far away from all higher-class people, and cure sick peasants
> until maybe some of them beat her to death. Would you have ever
> imagined there are lives like these?—This pride, this courage, that
> is what distinguishes Russian women.

Noble-minded, talented, histrionic: Hermann captured Olga's personality from the first. And also not entirely reliable—she was six years
older than Hermann, so actually about to turn twenty-eight.

Olga embodied for Rorschach the image of Russia he had formed
in Dijon. When Tregubov had returned to Russia and Rorschach lost
contact with him, the young student took steps to track him down:
"Dear Count Tolstoy," he wrote in January 1906. "A young man who is
worried about a friend of yours hopes you will grant him a few minutes
of your time." Tolstoy's secretary answered, and contact with Tregubov

was reestablished. In the meantime, Rorschach had opened his heart to the great writer:

> I have learned to love the Russian people, ... their contradictory spirit and genuine feelings. .... I envy them for being so cheerful, and also that they can cry when they are sad. .... The ability to see and shape the world, like the Mediterranean peoples; to think the world, like the Germans; but to feel the world, like the Slavs—will these powers ever be brought together?

Russianness, for Rorschach, meant *feeling*: being in touch with strong, genuine emotions, and being able to share them. And "to be understood, from the heart, without formalities and tricks and heaps of erudite words," he wrote to Tolstoy: "that is what we are all looking for."

He was far from alone in casting the Russians in this role. Russian novels and plays were astonishing readers from Virginia Woolf to Knut Hamsun to Freud; the Russian ballet was the toast of Paris; the physical immensity of Russia, its combination of semi-European civilization and epic otherness, spiritual depth and political backwardness, inspired awe and anxiety across the Continent. However accurate this vision of a land roiling with passions was or wasn't, it framed Rorschach's lifelong desire to be, in his words, understood from the heart.

It was Zurich that made Rorschach's increasingly intimate cultural and personal connection to Russia possible. At the same time, the question of what it meant to be understood was being investigated all around him. Rorschach's professors were fighting a battle over the very meaning of the human mind and its desires. Psychiatry was blazing new trails in the first decade of the twentieth century, and Zurich was at the crossroads.

4

Extraordinary Discoveries and Warring Worlds

THE PROFESSOR'S COMPACT SILHOUETTE WAS RECOGNIZABLE FROM a distance. He came hurrying from the hospital at the last minute to arrive at the podium, where he stood five foot three, robustly bearded, intense, bent slightly forward. His movements were angular and jerky, and when he spoke his face was unnaturally lively, almost startling. The lectures covered clinical and laboratory techniques in workmanlike fashion, with frequent recourse to statistics, but also emphasized again and again the importance of emotional rapport with patients. Conscientious, professional, sometimes fussy, he was also unassuming and obviously kind. It was sometimes hard to remember that this was Eugen Bleuler, one of the most highly respected psychiatrists in the world, his methods taught in classrooms throughout Europe and debated by eager students afterward.

Another lecturer in the same department was anything but modest. Tall, impeccably dressed, aristocratic in voice and manner, he was the grandson of an illustrious doctor rumored to be an illegitimate child of the great Goethe. He exuded a seductive mix of confidence and sensitivity, even vulnerability, and arrived early to sit on a bench in the hall where anyone who wanted could come over and talk. His lectures were open to students and nonstudents alike, and their high caliber and broad, engaging range made them so popular that they had to be moved to a bigger auditorium. Before long, he "acquired a devoted, highly visible female following" known as the Zürichberg Fur-Coat Ladies, named after the richest neighborhood in the city, who "marched with poise and self-assurance into his every lecture, commandeering the best seats and thereby earning the enmity of the students, who had to stand at the rear." And that was before the Ladies started inviting him to private discussion groups in their homes. The daughter of one such Lady dismissed the professor's fan base as "sex-starved groupies or postmenopausal hysterics."

Instead of offering dry statistics and instructing future practitioners in laboratory techniques, Carl Jung talked about family dynamics and human stories, often cases of women like the ones in his audience. He implied, even said outright, that their own "secret stories" held the key to more truth than the doctors could find on their own. The message was thrilling; his penetrating insight at times seemed almost magical.

These were Rorschach's teachers, shaping not only his own trajectory but the future of psychology.

ZURICH IN THE first decade of the twentieth century was at the center of an enormous transformation in the understanding and treatment of mental illness. As the century began, the field was deeply split between respect for subjective inner experience and an effort to achieve scientific respectability by focusing on objective data and general laws. There were scientists known as "psychopathologists," often French, who set out to explore the mind, and others, often German, pursuing so-called "psychophysics," preferring to dissect the brain. This professional and geographical divide overlapped, but not entirely, with an institutional divide between psychiatrists, usually based in hospitals or clinics, and psychologists, in university labs. Psychiatrists tried to cure patients, psychologists studied subjects. There was crossover, and the greatest advances in psychology often came from practicing psychiatrists—Freud and Jung, for example, were psychiatrists and medical doctors. But psychiatrists were doctors, with an MD; psychologists were research scientists, with a PhD.

Despite advances in neurology and disease classification, a nineteenth-century psychiatrist could do almost nothing to help people. This was somewhat true of medicine in general—no antibiotics, no anesthesia, no insulin. Describing a slightly earlier doctor, Janet Malcolm points out that "medicine in Chekhov's day did not have the power to cure that it has only recently begun to wield. Doctors understood diseases they were helpless to cure. An honest doctor would have found his work largely depressing." Psychiatry was in even worse shape.

Outside of medicine, the very borders between science and the humanities were being redrawn. Should the goal of psychology be to scientifically *define* a condition, with lists of symptoms and laws of how diseases progress, or to more humanistically *understand* a unique individual and his or her suffering? In practical terms: Was an aspiring young psychologist supposed to study science or philosophy? In the early days—before Freud, before modern neuroscience—psychology was generally classified as a branch of philosophy. There was simply no other way to grasp the mind. Medical doctrines, too, largely coincided with religious teachings about virtue and sin, character and self-restraint. Psychiatrists tried to cure cases of demonic possession. Their most advanced technology was mesmerism.

Rorschach was a student when all that was starting to change. Freud had synthesized a theory of the unconscious mind and sexual drives that brought together psychopathology, psychophysics, and a new and effective psychotherapy, at the same time reintegrating the humanities into natural science and redefining the distinction between normality and illness. The apparently meaningless fantasies of psychotic patients were being deciphered, and healed, with methods based on assumptions that seemed incredible to materialistic brain scientists.

When Rorschach entered medical school, though, all Freud had was a couch in Vienna and a narrow range of upper-class neurotics for clients. *The Interpretation of Dreams,* published in 1899, sold 351 copies, total, in its first six years in print. In terms of scientific and institutional respectability, and the resources and international reputation needed to establish psychoanalysis as a lasting movement, the place that mattered was Zurich.

The University of Zurich medical school was a hybrid institution connected to the Burghölzli: a laboratory, university psychiatric clinic, and teaching hospital opened in 1870 and by Rorschach's time widely considered the best in the world. It was a large facility run by the canton of Zurich, housing mostly uneducated, lower-class patients suffering from schizophrenia, tertiary syphilis, or other dementias with physical causes. But its directorship was tied to the newly founded chair of psychiatry at the university.

At most universities, prestigious psychiatry professors were brain researchers, with small clinics and a few short-term cases to teach from. But any professor of psychiatry at Zurich, as the historian John Kerr writes, would be in charge of more than a hundred patients, mostly incurable. And they were locals, speaking Low German or the Zurich dialect of Swiss German: the professor literally could not understand their language. Not surprisingly, a series of clinic directors quickly jumped ship, and while the university professorship gained in stature, the Burghölzli was soon "better known locally for the brothel situated on the far side of its grounds" than for its hospital. It started to improve under director Auguste Forel, but even he took early retirement. In 1898, he passed the position to a man named Eugen Bleuler (1857–1939, Freud's exact contemporary).

Bleuler was from Zollikon, a farming village outside Zurich adjacent to the Burghölzli. His father and grandfather had been part of the struggle in the 1830s to win equal rights for farmers and establish the University of Zurich in the first place. Bleuler was the second person from his village ever to graduate university and the first to attend medical school. Throughout his life, he remained deeply conscious of his rustic appearance and background, and also of the class struggle and political organizing that had made his career possible. Crucially, he spoke the local language, so he could understand what his patients were saying.

The prevailing wisdom was that the kind of people under Bleuler's care were hopeless. In the words of Emil Kraepelin, the psychiatrist who had given the name *dementia praecox* to what is now called schizophrenia: "We know now that the fate of our patient is determined mainly by the development of the disease; we can rarely alter the course of the disease. We must openly admit that the vast majority of the patients placed in our institutions are forever lost." Even more brutally: "The great mass of uncured patients piling up in our mental institutions belongs to *dementia praecox,* whose clinical picture is marked above all by the more or less far-reaching collapse of the personality." They "belonged to" the disease. Freud, too, had said that these patients were unreachable. But Bleuler, down in the trenches, learned otherwise. The line between mental illness and health was not as hard and fast as his university colleagues believed, and seeing patients as a "great mass" "piling up" was part of the problem.

Before becoming director of the Burghölzli, Bleuler had lived for twelve years at the largest asylum in Switzerland, an island monastery-hospital (originally a twelfth-century basilica) called Rheinau, with six to eight hundred patients. There and at the Burghölzli, Bleuler immersed himself in the world of the seriously psychotic, visiting the wards up to six times a day and talking to unresponsive catatonics for hours. He gave his assistants enormous workloads, typically eighty-hour weeks—morning rounds before 8:30, writing up case histories after the evening rounds, often until 10:00 or 11:00—and enforced monastic celibacy and abstinence from alcohol. The doctors and staff slept in large shared bedrooms, with very few exceptions. They couldn't complain, since Bleuler worked harder than any of them.

By living in such close contact with his patients, Bleuler realized that they had more nuanced, less compulsive reactions to their environments than had been thought. For instance, they behaved differently with different relatives, or with members of the opposite sex. Biological determinism could not completely explain their symptoms. Nor were they doomed, at least not necessarily—even the progression of the most severe cases could sometimes be halted, or reversed, if doctors developed good personal relationships with patients. Bleuler would suddenly discharge patients who seemed severely ill, or invite a particularly violent patient to a formal dinner at his house. He pioneered work therapy and other "reality-oriented tasks"—chopping firewood, caring for fellow patients who had typhus—for chronic cases long thought hopeless, resulting in cures that seemed little short of miraculous. When his schizophrenic patients were working the fields he would join them, doing work familiar to him from his youth in Zollikon. Bleuler devoted his life to establishing an emotional connection with everyone in his care. Both the patients and the staff tended to call him "Father."

It was Bleuler who named the disease *schizophrenia*—his most well-known contribution to science, along with inventing the terms *autism*, *depth psychology,* and *ambivalence*. He did this because Kraepelin's earlier label, *dementia praecox,* means "early-onset loss of mind," something biological and irreversible, whereas "a split mind" (the meaning of *schizophrenia*) is not hopelessly lost: it may still have functioning, living powers. Bleuler also wrote that he wanted a new term because there is no way to use *dementia praecox* as an adjective. In his view, illness should not be a medical object—a noun in Latin—but one way among many to describe a particular, human sufferer.

This empathy for patients had personal roots: when Bleuler was seventeen, his sister had developed catatonia and was hospitalized near their village at the Burghölzli. The family was outraged at brain doctors who seemed, as the locals said, more interested in microscopes than people and who couldn't even speak her language. Bleuler decided, or in some versions of the story his mother inspired him, to become a psychiatrist who could truly understand his patients. While he never wrote or spoke publicly about his sister Anna-Paulina's illness, her decisive influence on him is undeniable. One of Bleuler's assistants at the Burghölzli in 1907 and 1908 recalled: "Bleuler often told us that even the most serious catatonics can be influenced by verbal persuasion. He gave his own sister as an example. . . . One time, Bleuler had to get her to leave the building while she was in a state of acute excitement. He refused to use force and . . . talked to her for hours and hours, until eventually she put on her clothes and left with him. Bleuler used this example as proof that verbal persuasion was *possible*."

She lived with him in his apartment at the Burghölzli for almost thirty years, from their parents' death in 1898 until her death in 1926. His assistant recalled: "I could see her monotonously pacing back and forth all day long from my room across the hall. Bleuler's children were very young at the time, and they did not seem to notice his sister. Whenever they wanted to climb up anywhere, they simply used her like an inanimate object, like a chair. She showed no reaction whatsoever, no emotional relationship at all with the children." Bleuler had lived face to face with extreme schizophrenia for decades before the term existed, and during his entire career at the Burghölzli he had a living example of the schizophrenic's humanity right there in the room. His pioneering efforts began at home.

Of course, every generation sets out to correct the mistakes of the previous one; psychiatrists regularly accuse their predecessors of being heartless or at least misguided. In fact, psychiatrists before Bleuler, from Forel to Kraepelin to the father of brain-centered psychiatry, Wilhelm Griesinger, were by all accounts sympathetic and caring doctors too. But the Burghölzli truly was different. Bleuler's assistant recalls: "The way they looked at the patient, the way they examined him, was almost like a revelation. They did not simply classify the patient. They took his hallucinations, one by one, and tried to determine what each meant, and just why the patient had these particular delusions. . . . To me, that was altogether new and revealing." The transformation toward patient-centered care didn't start at the Burghölzli, or end there, but Bleuler mentored generations of psychiatrists, both students and assistants—including his son Manfred, Carl Jung and Sabina Spielrein, two of Rorschach's later bosses, and Rorschach himself. If it is unthinkable today that a psychiatrist would be unable to speak his patient's language, that is largely thanks to Eugen Bleuler.

CARL JUNG ARRIVED at the Burghölzli in December 1900, to work as Bleuler's assistant. He set about becoming the prominent, then preeminent, figure who would repeatedly transform the field of psychology in the decades to come.

Starting in 1902, Jung and the Burghölzli's other assistant doctor, Franz Riklin, developed the first experimental method to reveal patterns in the unconscious: the word association test. Subjects were read a list of a hundred prompt-words and were asked to say the first thing that came into their heads, while the doctor timed their responses with a stopwatch; then they went through the list again and were asked to remember their initial responses. Any aberrations—long delays, memory lapses during the second round, surprising non sequiturs, getting "stuck" and repeating responses—could be explained only by unconscious acts of memory and repression, a kind of hidden black hole pulling and warping the person's answers toward concealed desires, or prompting feints in the opposite direction. Jung called these hidden centers "complexes." The test found, empirically, that most of them were sexual.

With this, the Burghölzli doctors had made an "unprecedented and extraordinary" discovery. Independent of Freud—and doing something entirely unlike letting a neurotic ramble on a couch—they had succeeded in producing concrete proof of unconscious processes at work, in "normal" people no less than in the mentally ill. They immediately recognized that their results had confirmed Freud, and before long the word association test was being incorporated into psychoanalysis, as doctors improvised stimulus-words to pursue certain lines of thought or used the complexes they found as starting points for therapy. The method had tremendous potential in criminology. Jung and Riklin had created the modern psychological test.

What erupted next at the Burghölzli was nothing less than an orgy of testing, with doctors stopwatching, dream-interpreting, and psychoanalyzing their patients, their wives, their children, one another, themselves. They jumped on every sign of the unconscious they could find: every slip of the tongue or pen, lapse of memory, absentmindedly hummed tune. For years, "that was how we got to know one another," Bleuler wrote. His oldest child, Manfred (born in 1903), and Jung's oldest, Agathe (born a year later), both recalled feeling under total psychoanalytic observation as children. Publications on the word association experiment included anonymized results from Bleuler, Bleuler's wife, her mother and sister, and Jung himself.

Bleuler was thrilled by Freud's discoveries and immediately wanted to use them to help the deeply psychotic, not merely private patients suffering from sexual complexes. Before long, he found the results compelling enough that he reached out to Freud. He took the occasion of a 1904 book review to speak out as forcefully as he could, saying that Freud's *Studies on Hysteria* and *Interpretation of Dreams* had "opened up a new world"—a powerful endorsement from one of the leading psychiatrists in Europe. Then he wrote to Freud personally: "Dear Honored Colleague! We here in the Burghölzli are fervent admirers of the Freudian theories in psychology and pathology." As part of the rampaging self-analysis at the Burghölzli, he even mailed Freud several of his own dreams, asking for tips on how to interpret them.

The news of Bleuler's fervent admiration was one of the most heartening letters Freud would ever get, and the first sign Freud saw of his theory's acceptance in academic circles. It may have been what inspired him to end his multiyear hiatus from writing and produce the three great works he would publish in 1905 (*Three Essays on the Theory of Sexuality, Jokes and Their Relation to the Unconscious*, and *An Analysis of a Case of Hysteria*). Freud crowed to his friends: "An absolutely stunning acknowledgment of my point of view. . . . Just think: an official Full Professor of Psychiatry and my † † † Hysteria and Dream studies, always invoked with disgust and loathing up until now!" (Three crosses were chalked on the front doors of peasant houses to ward off danger and evil—Freud used them in his letters to ironically indicate horrifying, devilish things.) He wrote to Bleuler: "I am confident we will soon conquer psychiatry."

That "we" skimmed over something Freud knew perfectly well: Bleuler, at the pinnacle of professional psychiatry in Zurich, was far more important for Freudian ideas than vice versa. By making the Burghölzli the first university psychiatric clinic in the world to use psychoanalytic treatment methods, Bleuler and his assistants were the ones who brought Freud into professional medicine. Zurich, where Rorschach was studying, had replaced Vienna as the epicenter of the Freudian revolution.

By 1906, the Burghölzli was fully embroiled in the controversies around Freud's ideas—what Freud called the "two warring worlds" of academic psychiatry and psychoanalysis. With the Jung-Riklin word association studies offering apparently ironclad proof of Freud's theories, the anti-Freudians attacked. Gustav Aschaffenburg, the German psychiatrist who had taught Riklin how to perform the word association tests, delivered a fierce denunciation of Freud at a psychiatric convention and then published it.

Bleuler had spoken up for Freud in 1904, two years earlier, but since then he had dared to ask some tough questions. Freud's theory seemed extreme, Bleuler wrote—was *everything* rooted in sexuality? Where was the evidence Freud's earlier work was so rich in? Surely Freud wasn't unscientifically generalizing about human nature from a single case? Bleuler found it productive to have one's views challenged; not so Freud, who dismissed all of Bleuler's reasonable doubts as resistance to the great truth and turned his attention to Bleuler's younger colleague.

It was Jung, not Bleuler, who responded to Aschaffenburg in 1906—a devastating critique that did much to advance Freud's reputation. Jung had already gone over Bleuler's head to write to Freud, slipping into his first letter that he had "published the case that first drew Bleuler's attention to the existence of your principles, though at that time with vigorous resistance on his part." The opposite was closer to the truth. Jung took the opportunity of his first personal meeting with Freud in 1907 to drive another wedge between the two older men and persuade Freud that he was Freud's man in Zurich.

Jung's letters to Freud increasingly ranged from catty to outright backstabbing, harping on his boss's pedantic, small-minded spirit and utter incompetence at psychoanalysis: "Bleuler's virtues are distorted by his vices and nothing comes from the heart"; Bleuler's lecture "was dreadfully superficial and schematic"; "*the real and only reason*" for Bleuler's objections "*is my defection from the abstinence crowd*"; "I admire the way you put up with Bleuler. His lecture was pretty awful, don't you think? Have you received his big book?" This was the book on schizophrenia—Bleuler's lifework. "He has done some really bad things in it."

If Bleuler is unjustly forgotten today, it is largely because Jung wrote him out of history—never once mentioning him by name in his memoirs, going so far as to say that the Burghölzli psychiatrists cared only about labels, with "the psychology of the mental patient playing no role whatsoever." It was Jung, said Jung, who was driven to uncover his patients' individual stories: Why did one patient believe one thing and the other something else, and where did these particular, specific beliefs come from? If one patient thought he was Jesus and another said, "I am the city of Naples and I must supply the world with noodles," then what was the point of lumping them both under the label "delusional"? Jung's accusation that Bleuler "preferred to make diagnoses by comparing symptoms and compiling statistics" over "learning each patient's language" was a particularly low blow, given the history of Swiss dialect at the Burghölzli.

What has often been seen as a duet of attraction, repulsion, and self-interest between Freud and Jung was actually a triangle: Jung sold himself hard to Freud because he wanted to displace Bleuler; as Bleuler became less reliable, Freud's need for Jung intensified; Jung's bristling under Bleuler's authority set up the power struggle with Freud to come. Bleuler comes off best in these squabbles, sometimes dithering and unimaginative but with the least ego and the most willingness to learn from others. Yet Bleuler's star fell as Jung's rose.

Beneath the intellectual differences was a basic class conflict: while the Bleulers lived modestly, ate meals in the hospital dining room, and shared their lives with Eugen's catatonic sister, Jung in 1903 had married one of the richest women in Switzerland. The Jungs moved out of their apartment at the Burghölzli directly downstairs from the

Bleulers' and had private meals cooked by their servants when not out enjoying one of Zurich's fine restaurants. Jung asked for a string of unpaid leaves to pursue his own work or travel—he could now afford them—and Bleuler approved them all, more and more grudgingly as the years went by and the obligations of running a large hospital kept him from his own work. Jung's increasing disdain for the hardworking Bleuler was a sign of his own rising fortunes.

Both men fell out with Freud within a few years and continued to feud with each other for decades—"twenty years of active enmity" that, "while both were still at the Burghölzli, varied from the occasional veiled remark to openly hostile invective, often before shocked doctors or frightened patients." Any Zurich psychiatrist had to navigate an ever-changing minefield of "warring worlds," where even the refusal to take sides would be felt as betrayal by both parties. This was the dilemma Bleuler now had to face. He felt that absolute authority was inimical to scientific debate and progress: "This 'you're either with us or against us' is in my opinion necessary for religious communities and useful for political parties, but I consider it harmful for science," he told Freud directly. Seeking plurality, he joined organizations set up in opposition to Freud's closed camp. Freud disagreed, while most research scientists criticized Bleuler for having supported Freud at all.

RORSCHACH WOULD NATURALLY not have known about the intrigues revealed only in Freud's, Jung's, and Bleuler's private letters. In early 1906, while Freud was transferring his allegiance from Bleuler to Jung, Rorschach was a second-year university student taking his preliminary exams and attending lectures by Jung, who later said he never met Rorschach personally. Still, Rorschach could not help being aware of the feuds among these pioneers and the issues at stake.

As a student and for the rest of his life, Rorschach both respected Freud's ideas and preserved a certain skepticism toward them. He would continue to use psychoanalysis while remaining clear about its limitations. In a later lecture to a general audience of doctors far from Zurich, he offered authoritative explanations of how psychoanalysis worked and what it could and couldn't do; meanwhile, he also joked that "in Vienna, they're going to be explaining the rotation of the earth psychoanalytically before long."

Rorschach used the word association test on patients and in criminal cases for years, even after Jung had largely left it behind, and he was inspired by Jung's later work as well. Jung's 1912 book *Transformations and Symbols of the Libido* would come to define the "Zurich School," which extended psychoanalytic explorations to an enormous range of cultural phenomena, from Gnostic myths and religions to art and what would come to be called the collective unconscious. Jung had rejected Freud's literalistic understanding of sex drives, seeing them instead more mythically and symbolically as the "life-energy" shared by sexuality, fire, the Sun. Rorschach, too, was "fascinated by archaic thought, myths, and the construction of mythologies," according to Olga. "He pursued the traces of these ancient ideas in various patients, looked for analogies, and found, in the delusions of a sick Swiss farmer leading a hermit's life, astounding allusions to the world of the Egyptian gods."

As with Freud's ideas, Rorschach used Jung's without falling entirely under their sway. Jung took sides: while he recognized that there were certainly physiological causes of mental illness, he was soon pointing out that most of his patients had unimpaired brains, or at least that there was no way to connect their psychological disturbances to the brain. "For this reason," Jung said in January 1908 in a lecture at the Zurich Town Hall, "we have entirely abandoned the anatomical approach in our Zurich Clinic and have turned to the psychological investigation of mental disease." Whether or not Rorschach attended this particular lecture, he absorbed its message. He paid his dues in hard science, doing solid anatomical research on the pineal gland in the brain, but he agreed that the future of psychiatry lay in finding ways to interpret the mind, not merely dissect the brain.

But Rorschach was closest in spirit to the third great pioneer, who was constitutionally unable to "entirely abandon" either the interpretative or the anatomical approach. If a disease is biological, Bleuler argued, then perhaps it should be treated irrespective of what the patient's particular delusions or "secret story" might be. Rorschach, too, would continue to believe that psychology rested on a physiological basis—in his case, the nature of perception.

Rorschach shared Bleuler's modest social background, his human interest in sufferers of serious mental illness, and an ability, which their colleagues often lacked, to respect and learn from others even while finding one's own path. While Freud saw women as beings with mysterious psychologies very different from "ours," and Jung often wrote about women's predominant interest in domesticity and tendency to use emotion over intellect, Rorschach—the high school champion of women's rights—and Bleuler shared none of these prejudices and, more important, never built their theories around them.

They also both matter-of-factly rejected paranormal psychology. Freud and Jung—as well as William James, Pierre Janet, Théodore Flournoy, and the other preeminent psychologists of the time—frequented séances and studied spiritual mediums, not as a hobby but because that was where they hoped to get access to the "subliminal" realm soon to be called the unconscious. Rorschach, like Bleuler, understood these practices in terms we would use today. When his sister Anna had mocked their grandmother for turning to spiritualism, Hermann, in medical school, responded that "if an old person is upset and turns to spirits, she does so only because people don't want her anymore. She tries to communicate with ghosts because she no longer has anyone alive who's close to her. That is a situation of real, deep tragedy, and nothing to get angry about."

Rorschach never worked at the Burghölzli himself, but because of the symbiotic nature of the University of Zurich and the Burghölzli hospital he was able to have a world-class clinician as an academic adviser. He became enough of a Bleulerian to take the pledge of abstinence from alcohol, in January 1906, and to keep it for the rest of his life. Bleuler was the exception among the university psychiatrists of his era in supporting, applying, and teaching Freud's ideas, yet Zurich's independence from Vienna was crucial: Rorschach was in the only place in the world where psychoanalysis was both taken seriously and open to further refinement and exploration. He studied with the inventors of the world's first psychological test of the unconscious. It would prove to be an ideal background.

IN 1914, WHEN Rorschach was a practicing psychiatrist, Johannes Neuwirth, a soldier in a bicycle battalion in the Swiss Army, was sent to Rorschach's clinic for evaluation. Neuwirth had gone on a ten-day leave, paid off 2,900 francs in debts for his stepfather's business, and on Thursday, December 3, two days before he was due to return to duty, suddenly disappeared. The police found him in a tavern six days later, bent low over a plate of food with a large beer in front of him, eating slowly and calmly. After a while, the policeman said, "Neuwirth, why didn't you go back into service on Saturday?" Neuwirth looked up and said, hesitant and embarrassed, "I have to go now."

He went with the policeman willingly and wanted to rejoin his troop at once—he liked serving in the army. When asked what day it was, he said "Thursday" and refused to believe it was already Wednesday the ninth; he seemed confused in general. Transferred to the hospital, Neuwirth said his bicycle had flipped in the snow on the evening of the third and he had fallen by the bridge near the train station. He remembered nothing further until the policeman spoke to him in the tavern. "It was like I was waking up from a dream. They accused me of wanting to run away, but if I'd wanted to do that, I would have done it with 2,900 francs in my pocket, not after I'd paid it all out in bills."

After taking a lengthy history of Neuwirth's background, physical health, and family circumstances, Rorschach used the Jung-Riklin word association experiment, Freudian free association, and hypnosis—one of Bleuler's specialties—to help Neuwirth remember what had happened. The word association test turned up nothing that had happened in the incident itself but revealed complexes explaining *why* Neuwirth's attack had taken the form it had (hostility to his stepfather, wishing that his father were still alive so that "everything would be the way it was"). Freudian free association took the patient back into a dissociated state, which demonstrated *how* he had acted: he immediately started hallucinating and afterward could not remember anything but the first thing he had seen. Hypnosis worked best to uncover the facts of *what* had happened, as Rorschach had expected it would; he had saved it for last so he could compare the results of the different methods. Under hypnosis, Neuwirth revealed that he had left the bicycle lying by the station, sat on a bench in the park, walked back to his stepfather's business, couldn't find his way home, had what sounded like an epileptic fit. His story was always consistent, but he remembered it all taking place on one single day.

After the hypnosis, Rorschach was able to interpret the free-associated visions and word association results to piece much of the story together. "It was especially important to me," he summed up, "to show, using the material retrieved in the hypnosis afterward, that *so-called 'free associations' are actually determined,*" not random but rather the products of "unconscious memories." Each technique had an important function. Rorschach concluded that a full analysis would have been the best of all, to give further details not revealed under hypnosis and to prove that all the aspects of the case, in his words, "coalesced into a unified picture."

But there hadn't been time for a full analysis. What he needed was a method that could work in a single session, producing "a unified picture" immediately. It would have to be structured, with specific things to respond to, like the prompts in a word association test; unstructured, like the task of saying whatever comes into one's head; and, like hypnosis, able to get around our conscious defenses to reveal what we don't know we know, or don't want to know. Rorschach had three valuable techniques at his disposal, from his three main influences, but the test of the future would have to combine them all.

5

A Path of One's Own

I N THE SPRING OF 1906, AS A STUDENT-DOCTOR IN ZURICH HAV-
ing just passed his preliminary exams, Rorschach was in no position to imagine such a synthesis, much less create it. He was hungry
for experience but not allowed to do much on his own beyond eye
exams, physicals, and autopsies. As he wrote to Anna, though, he was
thrilled to be practicing medicine at last: "Real work with real patients, a glimpse of my future career!" He could "mostly only look on.
But there's a lot to see." After two weeks of his first residency, working
more than fifty hours a week: "I don't think I will ever forget these
fourteen days."

He had so many stories to tell. A sixteen-year-old boy had fallen
through a glass roof and the doctors thought he could be saved, "but
three days later his brain was on the anatomical demonstration table."

An old woman with a waxy yellow face was shown to us; she did not
open her eyes once, and two days later I personally saw her body
being dissected. A young man with a terribly swollen hand was
doped up and operated on, and when he woke up he noticed, with
a groan I will never forget, that he no longer had a right hand. A
twenty-one-year-old student was put on display: he had made inci-
sions into the place on his forearm where you feel for a pulse—he
had wanted to kill himself. A girl, around eighteen, who had a
severe venereal disease, had to show herself in front of 150 of us
students, and so on, so it goes every day, and all because the poor
people don't have enough money to have themselves admitted as
pensioners. That is the tragedy of the clinics.

He was appalled at how his beer-drinking, silver-handled-walking-stick classmates responded to the show: "Just think how the student types I described before react to all that. We have to be cold about it, that's the way things are; but to be crude about it, to turn into moral idiots, no, physicians don't have to do that."

These experiences, however gripping, certainly did not make him feel understood from the heart. The reality of seeing dozens of patients a day plus endless hours of consultation "exposed all kinds of ideals to the cold light of day," he wrote to Anna. "The doctor meets with more mistrust than gratitude, more rudeness than understanding." That spring, he had put a little book in his Zurich room for visitors to write their name in; six months later, and with thirty names in the book—"nowhere near all" his visitors—the only thing it had to tell him was that he needed to get away. This pattern was a constant in Rorschach's life. Years later, after "two months busy being extraverted," he would write to a friend that he had "had his fill of it and was hungry for something more inward. Man does not live by extraversion alone."

"I know too many people here already," he wrote to Anna from Zurich in the 1906 letter first describing Olga Shtempelin. "Do you know what that means? They come and invite you out and come by again and take up the only time you have to be alone the way you need to be. They cast a shadow over your freedom." Olga was off to Russia, and, for all his interest in people, Rorschach was "ready to move away and let the dispensable ones go."

He spent the rest of medical school alternating study abroad, travel, and a series of short-term jobs across Switzerland with his time in Zurich. Advanced medical students often spent semesters at different universities with different specialties and substituted for doctors in private practice over the summers, but Rorschach ended up with a broader range of experience than most—partly because of his personal determination to be "different" from his more privileged classmates and partly because he needed the money from any job he could find.

He initially went to Berlin for a semester, his first escape from Switzerland since Dijon. "Berlin with its millions of people will let me be more alone than Zurich," he wrote to Anna. At first he found what he thought he wanted: "I'm in total solitude here. . . . I was entirely alone for all of the first few days, and still am most of the time—luckily." He lived in a typical Berlin room, on the fourth floor, with one window and a view into many others, overlooking a small courtyard—"a little stone and a little grass"—with a tree "that gives *me* a lot of pleasure," if not the other city-types crowded into the building. Nights were spent at home or wandering the streets, always full of people until almost dawn. He enjoyed the theater, the circus, the cinema.

But the chaos of the modern metropolis was not for him. In the early 1900s, Berlin was one of the world's biggest and fastest-growing cities, its population having quintupled in sixty years to two million people, not counting another million and a half in the new suburbs ringing the city. Streetcars ran until 3 a.m.—some lines ran all night on weekends—and bars stayed open until dawn. The perpetual construction only added to the noise and confusion: to walk just a hundred steps down busy Friedrichstrasse at the turn of the century was to face what one chronicler described as a "cacophonous blowing of horns in the traffic, melodies of organ grinders, cries of newspaper vendors, bells of Bolle's milkmen, voices of fruit and vegetable sellers, hoarse pleas of beggars, whispers of easy women, the low roar of streetcars and their screech against the old iron tracks, and millions of steps dragging, tripping, pounding. At the same time, a kaleidoscope of color . . . neon lights, bright electric lights of offices and factories . . . lanterns hanging from horse-drawn carts and automobiles, arc-lighting, light bulbs, carbide lamps." Even compared to Vienna, Paris, and London, Berlin was seen as especially fluid, indeterminate, and unstable, somewhere that was "always becoming and never is." As one of its leading dailies, which called itself "the fastest newspaper in the world," said of Potsdamer Platz in 1905: "Every second a new picture."

Many newcomers found freedom and possibility in Berlin, but Rorschach's heart was back in Switzerland, or maybe already with Olga. His perceptions of Berlin were distinctly uncharitable: "In a few years, Berlin will have many more inhabitants than our whole country, but it's quality that matters, not quantity," he wrote to his fifteen-year-old brother Paul. "Just be glad you're not a Berliner. There are old men here who have probably never seen a cherry tree in their lives. I haven't seen a cat or a cow in two months." He encouraged Paul to "enjoy our good Swiss air and our mountains and I hope you become true and free and honest, with real experience of life, not like the types I see here every day." He found the people "cold" and "boring," the society "despicable," the whole experience "idiotic."

Worst of all was the conformity of the Germans, who Rorschach felt were less free than even the Russians under the tsar. He happened to turn up in Berlin during one of the most famous incidents of unthinking obedience to authority in German history: On October 16, 1906, four days before Rorschach's arrival, a drifter who had bought different pieces of a Prussian Guard captain's uniform at different stores around the city put the clothes on and became a new man. He commandeered soldiers, arrested the mayor of the town of Köpenick, and confiscated the town's treasury, claiming to act on the Kaiser's orders, while everyone obeyed his uniform without question. Stories about the "Captain of Köpenick" filled the press before and after his arrest on October 26; he became a folk hero. Germans "worship the uniform and the Kaiser," Rorschach wrote Anna from Berlin, "and think they are the greatest people in the universe when actually they're only the best bureaucrats."

Russia continued to attract Rorschach. Anna Semenoff, another Russian studying medicine in Berlin and Zurich, had invited him to visit Moscow in July 1906, before his Berlin semester started, but politics had intervened. Russia was convulsed by its first twentieth-century revolution, sparked by a disastrous war with Japan, and Rorschach did not feel comfortable putting himself in harm's way, since he was still the main support for his family. When Semenoff made it back to Berlin and renewed her invitation for the Christmas holidays, Rorschach accepted. In December 1906, he traveled from Berlin to Moscow.

It was the most exciting month of his life. He would see the place he called "the land of unlimited possibilities" for the first time with his own eyes. The expansive, glowing report he·sent his sister after his return was full of wonderfully sensory descriptions of Moscow—the panorama from the Kremlin tower, the total silence of twenty-five-thousand sleighs moving around the city, frozen sleigh-drivers "thawing the glaciers from their beards" at bonfires in the middle of the streets. He attended cultural events, from the Moscow Art Theater, "which people say is the best in the world," to the Grand Opera, to lectures, sect meetings, political meetings; he saw his old friend Tregubov again. The Russians helped him get outside of himself. A common saying held that St. Petersburg was Russia's head, Moscow its heart, and Rorschach agreed: "You can see and understand more about Russian life in two weeks in Moscow than in a year in Petersburg."

The trip to Russia was also when Rorschach self-consciously reached adulthood. He had originally wanted to set off from Berlin "retracing our father's steps," he wrote in his report to Anna: "But it's better to seek out a path of one's own; if the son doesn't have enough courage to find his own way, he can always follow someone else's later." From this point on, Hermann mentioned his father only rarely in his letters, except around crucial family milestones. He mourned the loss of his father in productive ways, becoming a doctor for him while continuing to pursue the passions for travel and art he had inherited from Ulrich.

Russia satisfied a need for broader horizons that Rorschach doubtless would have found some other way to fulfill even if he had never met Tregubov in Dijon. No one rereads *War and Peace* during the grueling, two-month-long period of final medical school exams, as Rorschach would do in 1909, merely out of interest in Russian culture—that is what someone does who refuses to be defined by his immediate environment, who is seeking an intellectual and emotional life elsewhere.

AFTER RUSSIA, WESTERN Europe was a letdown. Rorschach left Berlin in early 1907 "disappointed and a bit depressed," and his next semester was not much better. "Bern isn't bad," he wrote to Anna, "if a bit lowbrow and washed-up, and the people here are mostly quite coarse and crude, to the point where even I, not the most refined person in the world after all, am taken aback." He spent the rest of 1907 and all of 1908 in Zurich or working as a substitute doctor elsewhere, but clearly felt that student life and Switzerland had little more to offer him.

At least his sister got out. In early 1908, after she had spent two years as a governess in French-speaking western Switzerland, Hermann helped find her a job as a governess in Russia, and Anna jumped at the chance to see the "land of unlimited possibilities" she had heard so much about. For the next few months his letters were almost giddy with excitement on her behalf: page after page helping Anna with

Russian grammar, train routes and schedules, how much luggage to take and how to get it through customs.

Anna's journey was a vicarious second visit to Russia for Hermann. Stuck in Switzerland, he could see the sights she described, transposing the written pictures into movement: "When I read your first letter, I actually wandered around Moscow with you in a very visual way." Memories of his own trip resurfaced as he gave her advice, plying her with questions and suggestions that she see the Moscow theater, the opera, the Bolshoi Theater, Tregubov, Tolstoy, everyone and everything. Rorschach asked her to send him reproductions of Russian paintings and encouraged her to buy a camera to help her see: "Do it. Even if it costs a month's salary, you will get so much pleasure from it that it will definitely be worth the price. In your later, sedentary days, it is truly wonderful to have pictures of the places from your earlier life—everything stays much more alive in your memory. Aside from that, you look at places better when you have a camera." He started by advising her—"I can easily send you a few instructions, but you'll only learn it after you take your fiftieth picture"—but before long he was asking her for advice: "I'm enclosing one of my photos, but it has problems. It's so brown and airless. What's wrong with it, do you know? Underexposed or overexposed? Underdeveloped or overdeveloped?"

After being "father and mother both" to Anna after the death of their parents, he was settling into the role of a big brother. "I could come to him with any and every question," Anna felt. "As a medical student and a young doctor, he introduced me to the secrets of where life comes from, and gave my hungering soul endlessly much to feed upon." Among all sorts of other advice and instruction, Hermann had sent his eighteen-year-old sister a description of the "meat market" of Berlin streetwalkers: "Elegant from top to toe, in velvet and silk, with makeup, powder, penciled eyebrows and mascara, red eyeliner.— They walk around like that, but the men looking them over with their shameless, mocking, lustful eyes are even sadder to see, and the whole thing is their fault."

Once Anna started having sexual experiences of her own, he remained supportive: "Shockingly many men see women as sex objects. I don't know how much you've thought about this last issue, but I hope you have thought about it on your own. Hold tight to the conviction that a woman is a human being too, who can be independent, and who can and must improve herself and complete herself on her own. Also realize that equality must exist between men and women. Not in political tussles but in the domestic sphere, and above all in sex life." He thought his sister had as much right to know about sex as he did.

As everyone did, for that matter: "The stork question is the most delicate in the child's life," he advised her when she was a governess. "Of course you should *never* say anything about a stork!" She should show the child flowers being fertilized, a pregnant animal, the birth of a calf or kittens. "It's not a big step from there."

Anna craved knowledge of the wider world, and he was happy to give it to her, while expecting to learn at least as much from her. "You will probably know more about Russian conditions than I do soon," he wrote. Men "see a country only when other people are around, where social intercourse and lies and traditions and customs etc. are dams that block our view into real life," but it is women who "have it much better," because they have access to private, family life. "You're right in the middle of a very different environment now. That's how someone gets to know a country, truly know it. Take advantage of it and really look at the people there. And write to me about it. It's you who need to tell *me* about Russian officer families, I don't know anything about them."

Rorschach burned with curiosity about what he could not see directly, and was convinced from the first that different people— especially those of different sexes—have distinct but communicable perspectives. Knowledge required both closeness and distance: "You only learn to love your own homeland when you go abroad," he wrote to her once. He wanted to explore every aspect of human nature he could, so he needed Anna. "You have to write me as much as you can squeeze out of your head and your pen, okay? . . . What are the people like? How does the countryside look, and the people? Write me lots and lots!"

He also wanted to sustain his bond with his sister. "You know, Annali," he wrote in 1908, "what I really want is for us to write to each other a lot, that we'll stay close across all the many countries and mountains and borders that separate us, or grow even closer, I think we will." They did. Except for a short return to Switzerland in 1911, Anna stayed in Russia until mid-1918, living through war and revolution and losing most of her belongings in the chaos. Hermann's letters to her after 1911 are lost, but his heart doubtless remained in Russia with his sister—and with Olga.

THE YEARS AFTER Olga met Hermann in the summer of 1906 had been a time of study and travel for her, too, but by early 1908 the beautiful Russian and the handsome Russophile were a couple. He had strong opinions, strong feelings, but kept them strongly in check; he lived through other people's outbursts of emotion, and in Olga he found someone who supplied him with plenty. He later said that she showed him the world—gave him a way to live in it. She was even synesthetic, an ability that fascinated Hermann—at age four, she had drawn seven pictures of archways in different colors so that she could see and remember the days of the week. For her part, she was less than enraptured with Switzerland and Swiss ways but accepted them well enough and was as eager as Hermann to find some stability.

Olga returned to Russia at the end of July 1908, with Hermann accompanying her as far as Lindau, an attractive German border town at the eastern edge of Lake Constance. She was thirty, he was twenty-four. If Rorschach was eager to hear back from Anna, his surviving letters to Lola, as Olga was called by family and friends, were desperate: "My love, my darling Lolyusha, it's been so long since I've gotten anything from you, more than 24 hours already. Write Lola write. It's horribly boring and empty here for me. . . . I'm sitting here after lunch, smoking and thinking about you. The afternoon mail will be here in an hour. But nothing came in the morning mail, will there be anything at all today? I want to know how my girl is doing!!" Later, with a different pencil: "Now it's four and I didn't get any mail today!"

Olga was busy working with cholera patients in her hometown of Kazan, and by late November she had moved to a smaller and poorer town more than three hundred miles farther east. "She doesn't feel well there at all," Hermann reported. "All she sees everywhere is dirt and roughness. . . . She is all alone." Left behind in Zurich, Rorschach spent another summer working, at Kriens near Lucerne and at Thalwil on Lake Zurich, and continued to collect stories to share with Anna:

Four people died on me, but they were all old derelicts, dilapidated to the point of, well, dying. The doctor couldn't have saved them either. On the other hand, I was able to bring a difficult birth to a happy ending, a very difficult breech delivery where I had to pull out the baby with a noose. The midwife stood there and talked about the "rare, miraculous cases" where such children were brought into the world alive. She was already prepared to give him an emergency baptism on the rear end, since the people were Catholic, but I was able to get the baby out alive after all, so now it's alive and doesn't need a baptism on the rear end anymore.

Otherwise he plowed through the rest of his academic work, studying every night through the fall and winter with a friend. "I've had it up to here with all this school and practically have bedsores from sitting around so much," he wrote; he couldn't wait to "finally, finally! be done with school-stuff." On January 25, 1909, he declared, "There is nothing keeping me in Switzerland but our mountains." Exactly one month later, he passed his final exams.

Rorschach could now practice medicine, but his professional options were limited. He could either work at a university clinic for low pay—impossible in his financial situation—or else work in a more isolated asylum, with a slightly better salary and more practical psychiatric experience but no university career. He lined up a job at the asylum in Münsterlingen, having met its director in 1907 while interning at the hospital nearby. It would start in August. First, though, he wanted to reunite with Olga, meet her family, and lay the groundwork for a permanent move to Russia. He hoped he could earn enough in a year in Russia to pay off his debts, which would take six years or more in Switzerland.

Immediately after his final exams, he set out to visit Anna in Moscow, then traveled on to Kazan. Hermann was able to perfect his spoken Russian and to work. He observed cases at a neurological clinic and then spent four weeks navigating the red tape to get permission to visit the large Kazan asylum, which housed more than eleven hundred patients and mountains of unexplored case material. "If science is not very far advanced here," he told Anna, "at least the files are in order." He saw "a strange mix of peoples among the patients: Russians, Jews,

German colonists, Siberian heathens," although "the doctors here are not concerned about the interesting questions of racial psychiatry," by which he seems to have meant the heredity of mental illness as well as racial or ethnic differences in psychology. He felt confident that he could easily find a job in Russia, and found himself "very tempted to work at the Kazan asylum later," or in one of the many in Russia like it. He appreciated "how infinitely freer, more open, more natural, more honest people are with each other here." Elsewhere, he wrote, "I like Russian life. People are straightforward and you can get ahead quickly (if you don't need to deal with the authorities)."

Unfortunately, he did need to, and the maddeningly opaque and arbitrary bureaucracy he encountered made it impossible for him to get credentialed to practice in Russia. "This waiting! In Russia, you simply have to learn to wait. . . . The main unpleasantness is that it's so hard to get a clear answer. . . . I will need to go through the same detours" as another Swiss colleague, who had spent eight months in St. Petersburg in vain. He would also need to return to the schoolwork he had been so glad to leave behind: literature, geography, and history, this time in Russian. While he understood the need to jump through these hoops—if a delusional patient believed he was Tsar X or Count Y, the doctor had to know what the patient was talking about—he still didn't relish the prospect.

It was a trying time personally as well. "Kazan is not a large city like Moscow, but only a very large small town, and you feel it in everything, including the people," Hermann wrote. It was larger than Zurich but provincial, though it did have a park known as Russian Switzerland, a kind of mirror image of Zurich's Little Russia. Hermann helped Olga study for her own exams, all twenty-three of them, while Olga's mother reminded him rather too much of his own stepmother: oppressive to be around and "lacking in understanding." He and Olga had planned to get married in Russia but in the end didn't have enough money, "and obviously we didn't want to get married on credit. I really wanted to have the ceremony, since Olga is off to another job for another five months or so and you never know what might happen. I wanted to give her that at least."

Rorschach stayed five months in Russia before returning to Switzerland, no longer as an intern to a string of doctors or an applicant struggling with the authorities but as an experienced psychiatrist. By that point he had soured somewhat on Olga's homeland. He was amazed to find Otto Weininger's deeply misogynist book *Sex and Character* translated into Russian and widely read there, since, as he had earlier written to Anna,

> no human society treats women with as much respect as in Russia. . . . With us, it's enough for the man in most cases if a woman is not too stupid, not terribly ugly, and not as poor as a church mouse; as for what she *really is,* he doesn't bother much about that. That is not the case in Russia, at least not among the intelligentsia. . . . In Russia, women, especially the most intellectual women, are a force that wants to help society as a whole, and can help, and *do* help, they don't just sweep the floors and do the children's laundry.

He expected that a book "trying to prove that Woman is worth absolutely nothing and Man is everything" would "only be laughed at" there—he himself dismissed it as "the most outlandish nonsense," by someone "soon declared insane." Instead it was a hit.

Like his early experiences as a student-doctor, which had exposed all kinds of ideals to the cold light of day, Rorschach's 1909 journey brought his romanticized picture of Russia down to earth. He started to insist, even more snappish than he was in Berlin, that the principle of equal rights for all had arisen in Swiss families, and that "it *is* true and it *remains* true that we Western people are on a much higher cultural level" than the "half-Asiatic masses" in Russia. When Anna considered marrying a Russian officer, Hermann was strongly opposed: aside from the fact that she was interested in an officer, not "a doctor or engineer or something like that," he warned her that "you would have to become a Russian, and that is not good. . . . Think about it: You are the citizen of a free country, the oldest republic in the world! And Russia is the only absolute monarchy in the world, except for a couple of African states. . . . You would be bringing children into the most reactionary state anywhere, instead of the most advanced, and your children might even end up in the most reactionary of armies, the Russian one."

As for himself, "I will go back to Russia myself someday, but my fatherland will remain Switzerland, and I can tell you, the events of the last few years have made me more of a patriot than I was before. If our Switzerland was ever endangered, I would fight alongside everyone else for our ancient freedom, our mountains." In July 1909, he returned to take up his new job in Münsterlingen, Switzerland—but not before one last maddening incident: being stopped at the border and forced to pay a bribe to get out of Russia.

Rorschach kept a sketchbook while in Russia, with charcoal drawings and color scenes of whatever caught his eye. On one page, after an onion dome church along the Volga River, is this shape, possibly smoke from a smokestack. The caption in Russian says "Steamship *Trigorye*." On the left, though, he wrote: "A cookie? A mountain? A cloud?"

6

Little Inkblots Full of Shapes

A TWENTY-FOUR-YEAR-OLD PAINTER, WHENEVER HE SEES CHURCH towers, has the obsessive thought that a similarly sharp object exists inside his body. He has an intense dislike of Gothic-style pointed arches and feels soothed by the Rococo style, but he also thinks that looking at the airily flowing Rococo lines makes his nerve cells take on corresponding twists and turns. When he walks on a patterned carpet, he feels each geometric shape he steps on pressing down on a hemisphere of his brain.

J.E., a forty-year-old schizophrenic, feels himself transformed into pictures he sees in books. He adopts the poses of the people depicted, turns into the animals, or even becomes inanimate objects like the large letters on the title page. When he looks at the lightbulb above his bed, he sometimes feels he has been turned into the bulb's filament: miniaturized, rigid, inserted in the bulb, and glowing.

L.B. draws one of the spirits she often hallucinates, a human figure, but forgets to draw any arms. When Dr. Rorschach points this out to her, she puts the paper in front of her, says "Upsy!" and raises her arms, staring at the spirit the whole time. Then she says: "Look now, the arms are there now."

These were a few of Rorschach's patients in Münsterlingen. When he himself put together a collection of psychiatric cases, he did so visually, taking photographs of hundreds of his patients and binding them into booklets that he organized by diagnosis: "Nervous Ailments," "Imbecility," "Manic Depression," "Hysteria," "Dementia Praecox: Hebephrenia" (now called disorganized schizophrenia), "Dementia Praecox: Catatonia," "Dementia Praecox: Paranoia," and "Forensic Cases." Rorschach understood by looking and seeing, connected to people by photographing and drawing them. Some of his sketches of patients in the clinic files captured their characteristic gestures so perfectly that the patients who were still alive were recognizable from the sketches decades later. The faces in the photographs occasionally scream or stare blankly into the camera, some heads even sticking out of locked boxes restraining their bodies, but many of the patients show signs of rapport with the young doctor taking their picture.

MÜNSTERLINGEN CLINIC, WHERE Rorschach worked from August 1, 1909, until April 1913, is a peaceful complex of buildings on the shores of Lake Constance, built on the site of a monastery founded in 986 by the daughter of Edward I of England. The monastery was torn down in the seventeenth century and rebuilt as a baroque church a quarter mile up the hill, later repurposed as a hospital. Some of the old cloister walls still stand, down near the lake, a low stone line separating nothing from nothing in a circle of nineteenth- and twentieth-century buildings. An attractive 1913 brochure for a new wing for women retirees promised a building "in manor style, surrounded by a pretty garden, located directly on the lake with a magnificent view of our beautiful surroundings." Patients "not in a position to afford the naturally expensive private facilities for an illness of long duration" would receive an "appropriate level of treatment and care in accordance with the modern requirements of psychiatry."

Buried in the clinic's century-old annual reports is a world of details from the mundane to the heartbreaking: cures, deaths, escape attempts (one in 1909, out a window along the ivy then over the outer wall into the lake; four in 1910), forced feedings (972 times total, for ten patients). The number of hours of work therapy over the course of the year: farming, carrying coal, woodwork, housework, gardening, and basket weaving for the men; cooking, laundry, ironing, field work, housework, and "women's crafts" for the women. The price of beef (rising). "Last year too," the management reported in 1911, "we were unable to avoid the use of mechanical restraint equipment": leather gloves for patients who otherwise would systematically pull apart everything they touched, and in some cases, covered bathtubs. "When we see that such patients, despite large doses of sedatives, disturb others' sleep in the dormitories with their noise and constant thrashing, annoy their fellow patients while awake, and are so rowdy that they smash everything they can reach in their isolation rooms to pieces, and smear themselves and the room with leftover food, excrement, and the like, we can no longer avoid the conclusion that forced stays in a bath are a true blessing for such patients and those around them." The official report for 1909 listed four hundred patients, 60 percent women, not quite half with schizophrenia and a significant number with manic depression, among a variety of other diagnoses. These were Rorschach's patients described en masse, not seen as individuals.

The medical staff at Münsterlingen consisted of the director, Ulrich Brauchli, and two assistants: Rorschach and a Russian, Dr. Paul Sokolov, who spoke German and Russian with Rorschach in alternating weeks for language practice while Olga remained abroad. The staff also included a clinic manager, an assistant manager, and a housemistress, but no other social workers, therapists, assistants, or secretaries, so the three doctors were responsible for everything. Or rather, Rorschach and Sokolov were. "The director is very lazy," Rorschach griped, "and actually very crude and tactless, but at least he's easy to get along with." Brauchli was a former assistant of Eugen Bleuler's and director of Münsterlingen since 1905; Rorschach had met him in 1907, while working at the hospital up the hill. They were never deeply close, but their relations were cordial, and Rorschach's view of his boss was basically positive. "It's totally natural: he's lazy, we do all the work for him, and he sits around in the sun, or in other words, he's the director; when he's away, we all get what we deserve, in other words, we're the directors and get to sit around in the sun ourselves."

Rorschach moved in to a small apartment while Olga remained in Russia, treating typhus and cholera outbreaks. "At last," he wrote, "for the first time, I am in a position where I'm earning money and have a steady job—all my wishes fulfilled, except that Olga isn't here." She arrived six months later, and the Rorschachs were finally married in a civil ceremony in Zurich on April 21, 1910. They pasted three photographs into a photo album—a wedding photo and two pictures of their apartment overlooking the lake—and wrote "May 1, 1910" underneath. Olga described Münsterlingen as "a very nice little town. We have two attractive rooms right on the lake with many flowers." Hermann worked until seven; then, in the evening, they took walks, or read, or went for a boat ride on the lake, with day trips on Sundays. "Our life here has little diversion, this is an out of the way little town, but Hermann and I don't need any."

Six months after appearing in front of a Zurich magistrate, Hermann and Lola were married again in a Russian Orthodox church ceremony in Geneva. After three days of sightseeing, they traveled onward by boat to Montreux and by train and on foot to Spiez, Lake Thun, and Meiringen: the same route that Rorschach's beloved Leo Tolstoy had walked at age twenty-eight in 1857, a crucial journey in Tolstoy's path as a writer and person. The itinerary was popular—that's why Tolstoy had taken it—but the Rorschachs almost certainly chose it so that they could extend their Russian-Swiss wedding into a Russian-Swiss pilgrimage. On their return, they were "rather relieved" that Brauchli was leaving on vacation. "Lola and I are doing well, very well, we're in love,"

Hermann wrote to Anna a few weeks later. "It's almost like we're living on an island, just for ourselves, completely undisturbed."

Lake Constance had dramatically receded, he went on, and would soon be inky black from the winter sky. Rorschach had been living a few steps from its shore for over a year. He had just turned twenty-six.

Scenes from Münsterlingen.
(photographs on pages 68–70 by Hermann Rorschach, ca. 1911–1912)

THE RORSCHACHS' CIRCLE of activities gradually widened. "There is a fair for the patients today, some of them Hermann's patients," Olga wrote to Anna one August: "All kinds of carousels, puppet theaters, shooting galleries, and so on." Hermann added, "A carousel, a dance floor, a menagerie, all kinds of things. The patients liked it very much. It's too bad that these things have to end in the evening." In other years there would be visiting players from the Güttingen Music Society and, starting in 1913, a large cargo ship rigged specially to take more than a hundred patients on a trip across the lake; it proved so popular that they hoped to be able to repeat the occasion every year.

The same photo album that holds the Rorschachs' wedding picture contains dozens of pictures of these asylum events. Hermann was an avid photographer and seemed to like the challenge of candid photography as much as the festivities he wanted to document. He was a generalist, and curious; to follow just his scientific trajectory would be to miss much of what made his work possible. Again and again, he took pictures of his house and of boat rides just off Münsterlingen, the land from the lake and the lake from the land, the reflections of light and shadow on sky and water. He gave his patients art supplies—not cameras, but paper, paint, clay. Maybe you couldn't have a conversation with a schizophrenic, but there were other ways to draw a person out.

After their first Christmas reunited in snowy Münsterlingen, Hermann and Lola filled their days playing chess, playing music— Hermann on his fiddle brought back from Schaffhausen, Lola on a guitar Hermann gave her for Christmas. Hermann thanked Anna for her

In the background is the building where the Rorschachs lived.

"perfect" gift of a book by Gogol. The Rorschachs had sent her an Alpine calendar "to give her something of her homeland every day"—Olga's idea; she knew what homesickness felt like. The previous year, Hermann without Olga had more pedantically

The Rorschachs' building seen from the lake.

sent his sister Goethe's *Faust*, "which you probably haven't read yet. It is the most magnificent thing that has ever been written in the world."

After New Year's came Carnival. Rorschach designed a program of songs, plays, masked balls, and dancing. As the years went on and demands on his time grew greater, the holiday parties would start to feel like more of a chore, but at first he threw himself into taking part.

While art therapy, drama therapy, and the like were not unknown, the diversions Rorschach staged seemed to Olga and others more like entertainment than treatment. Still, the way Rorschach described how he hoped his patients would react to the larger-than-life slide projections at the Christmas party suggests that he thought it would bring them some benefit. He even got hold of a monkey, from a troupe of traveling players, and brought it along on his rounds for a few months in another such effort. Some of the severe cases, usually totally nonresponsive, loved the monkey's grimaces and reacted when it mischievously jumped on their heads and played with their hair. Even if not directly healing, such activities gave Rorschach at least indirect access to his patients' minds.

Rorschach's monkey. He named it Fipps, after *Fipps the Monkey*, a book by Wilhelm Busch.

When not busy experimenting with monkeys and photography, Rorschach published eleven articles based on his work at Münsterlingen: some were Freudian, some Jungian, and some revealed interests of his own. As a later director of Münsterlingen summarized: "For a period of three years, this scientific output is astonishing, especially when you consider that Rorschach also reviewed a large number of books, wrote voluminous case histories, put in a lot of time-consuming work organizing activities for the patients, wrote humorous songs and rhymes for Carnival, got hold of a monkey, went bowling in the village, and, not least, completed a rigorous scientific monograph on a case of pineal gland tumors, giving up his holidays to investigate the tumors microscopically at the Brain Anatomy Institute in Zurich."

One of Rorschach's articles analyzed a patient's drawing that, "while seemingly so simple, actually has a very complicated meaning."

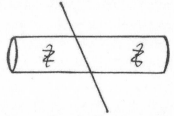

Schizophrenic's drawing. Rorschach's interpretation of this drawing mentions a phallic pipe, magnetic needles, and one male Z and one female Z intersected by question marks; the Z's were the patient's initial, the initial of the place where his earlier psychiatrist had lived, the first letter of the word "doubt" in German, and more.

Another was about a wall painter with artistic ambitions. Among the twenty-four handwritten pages of Rorschach's case notes in the Münsterlingen files, there is a photograph of the man: wearing a flowing smock, ascot, and beret, with a small flower sticking out of his mouth, and staring eyes. He had copied a small Bible-story woodcut of the Last Supper, except that in his version John cuddles up with Christ; they are all given long, feminine hair except Judas; and Christ is given a strange halo in the form of the bonnet worn by women in the typical local folk costume. The patient probably made his painting on Rorschach's instigation, Rorschach having recognized that, given his reduced capacities, it was impossible to psychoanalyze him using talk therapy, dream interpretation, or the word association test. Only something visual could be analyzed.

Those who knew Rorschach said he had a wonderful ability to connect with his patients, helping them by whatever means to re-emerge from their shells of paranoia or catatonic madness. Not a few female patients fell for their handsome doctor, and Rorschach was adept at freeing himself from their grasp without hurting their feelings. He would take the patient's hand, distract her, and slip out from under her arm. And so, Carnival to Summer Fair to Christmas and New Year's and around again, Rorschach's Münsterlingen calendar rolled on.

HERMANN'S TIME BY the lake with Olga was, for him, an apprenticeship in vision. In a birthday letter to Paul, who was thriving in Zurich now that he had left home, Hermann wrote: "I'm glad that you and I are so much closer this year than five birthdays ago, don't you think? Since you got out you've turned into a real man and a good friend remarkably quickly. It wasn't so fast for me. I had to get married to learn how to see the world properly." Hermann always gave Olga credit for his own development.

There was still bad blood between Hermann and his stepmother. "Mother gave me nothing, *nothing!* as a wedding present, a custom that exists all over the world! Olga was especially stung: 'It's not the present that matters to me, it's the love!'" Hermann and Olga avoided visits to Schaffhausen whenever they could. But they invited his half sister Regineli, ten years old, to visit Münsterlingen for two weeks, where she ran wild—a welcome break from the regime back home. They saw a lot of Paul, who, "despite everything he went through in Schaffhausen, is still so good-natured that for a while he was even homesick." Paul "naturally feels very free" now, Hermann reported, "though he isn't misusing his freedom"—he even asked his older brother's advice about pledging lifetime abstinence from alcohol. (Not yet, Hermann said, offering as a reason only that it was unsafe to drink the water in many countries.) Hermann and Olga also visited Rorschach's extended family in Arbon, only fifteen miles from Münsterlingen, where Olga was warmly received; she was curious to see how the "peasants" lived in Switzerland compared to Russia.

Rorschach was also writing for Swiss and German newspapers. Having tested the waters while in Russia—getting one piece published in Frankfurt and another in Munich—he now wrote short essays on alcoholism or on "Russian Transformations." He entered the arena of literature, serializing his translation of Leonid Andreyev's psychological novella *The Thought* over the course of a month in a Swiss newspaper. Andreyev was considered one of the leading contemporary Russian writers, and *The Thought,* as widely read in psychiatric circles as it was by the general public, was a genuinely creepy mix of Poe and Dostoyevsky, drawing on both psychology and Andreyev's experience as a court reporter. The story is cast as the first-person confession by a remorseless murderer, Kerzhentsev, who has killed his best friend. He describes his plans to get away with the crime by pleading insanity, but there are more than a few hints that he is crazier than he thinks. The thought of the title, which the narrator reveals in the third person, is that maybe *"Dr. Kerzhentsev is really insane. He thought that he was simulating madness, but he is really insane. He is insane now."* Andreyev shows us Kerzhentsev's unreliability to himself and re-creates the same uncertainty in us; the killer confesses in the desperate hope that doctors or judges can solve his existential crisis for him.

Why was Rorschach—unique among his psychiatrist peers—writing for newspapers? To make a little extra money, for one thing, a strategy he soon gave up on. "This writing for the papers doesn't bring in much," he griped to Anna. "I have no real desire to write for the German papers and no real opportunity to write for the Russian ones." More than income, such articles gave Rorschach an outlet for creative interests outside the bounds of psychology.

Olga would later say that the secret of her husband's success was "his constantly moving between different activities. He never worked for hours at a time at one thing. . . . Long conversations on a single topic tired him, even if it was one he found interesting." Then again, this cannot be the whole story. Rorschach was a "fanatical" note taker, for one thing, with his handwritten excerpts of others' books, written in a lightning-fast scrawl, sometimes adding up to 240 pages *per book*. He could not afford to buy books and lived far from central libraries; he also seemed to understand and retain material better by physically copying out a book's words. (The pages are nearly illegible—the process of transcribing was likely more useful to him than rereading the pages.) Whatever his motivations, it is nearly impossible to imagine Hermann doing this work in the half-hour bursts Olga seems to be describing.

Rorschach pursued another sideline with Konrad Gehring, a close friend from Schaffhausen three years older than Rorschach who was working as a schoolteacher in Altnau, the next village over from Münsterlingen. He and his wife often came to visit Hermann and Olga. It was with Konrad Gehring, in 1911, that Rorschach conducted his first experiments with inkblots.

THE INKBLOTTER USUALLY considered Rorschach's main predecessor is Justinus Kerner (1786–1862), a German Romantic poet and a doctor. Some of his wide-ranging accomplishments were in what we would now call medicine: he was the first to describe botulism, the bacterial food poisoning, and the first to suggest its therapeutic properties for muscles—botox. He was also an important figure in a Romantic tradition of psychiatry. His autobiography describes growing up next door to an insane asylum he could see from his window, in a small town that boasted the tower where the historical Doctor Faust practiced black magic. He treated cases of demonic possession with a mix of magnetism and exorcism; was the first biographer of Franz Anton Mesmer, the inventor of mesmerism; and wrote the enormously influential *Seeress of Prevorst: Revelations About Our Inner Life and the Incursions of the Spirit World into Ours* (1829), describing his experiments on a woman who had mystical visions, saw the future, and spoke secret languages. *The Seeress of Prevorst* has been called the first book-length psychiatric case study, and Jung's dissertation was about a spirit medium who claimed to be the reincarnation of Kerner's Seeress. Jung also discovered that Nietzsche had unconsciously plagiarized Kerner in *Thus Spake Zarathustra*; Hermann Hesse called Kerner "curiously gifted, the author of a book in his youth that seems to have caught and gathered up all the radiant beams of the Romantic spirit."

Later in life, Kerner assembled a series of what he called *Klecksographien* ("blotograms"), which he then captioned or paired with decidedly gloomy poems—three "Messenger of Death" poems, twenty-five "Hades Images," eleven more "Hell Images," and so on. Inkblot making was a kind of spiritual and spiritualist practice for Kerner. He felt that the images were "incursions of the spirit world," like the Seeress's powers. The blots made themselves—magically, unconsciously, inevitably—while he merely "tempted them over" from the hidden

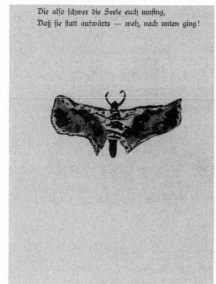

Die alfo ſchwer die Seele euch umfing,
Daß ſie ſtatt aufwärts — weh, nach unten ging!

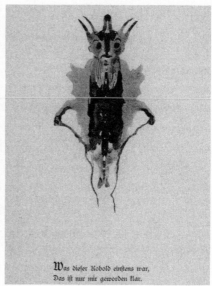

Was dieſer Kobold einſtens war,
Das iſt nur mir geworden klar.

"Two souls tempted over from the other world," by Justinus Kerner, from his "klexographies"

world into our own, where they then inspired his poems. At one point, he called his inkblots "daguerreotypes of the invisible world."

The geographical proximity between Kerner and Rorschach and their common background in psychiatry have made many historians of psychiatry, and art, unable to resist assuming a connection between them. But well after developing his test, Rorschach was asked if he had heard of Kerner, who "apparently did experiments with blots, obviously of a necromantic not scientific sort," and he answered: "I have heard of Kerner's experiments but I would be very grateful if you could find me the relevant book. Perhaps some substantive things lie behind the necromancy after all." He was aware of Kerner's work in a general sense, but it did not influence his own.

In any case, "klexography" was a common enough child's game. Kerner himself had played at inkblots as a child; young Carl Jung had "filled a whole exercise book with ink blots and amused myself giving them fantastic interpretations." Thoreau tried it too. A Russian woman in Rorschach's circle recalled a game she had often played when young, where you write your first and last name in ink, fold the paper in half, and "see what your soul says," and speculated that maybe this game had given him his idea.

In psychology proper, inkblots had occasionally been used before as a way to measure the amount of imagination someone had, especially schoolchildren. A French psychiatrist named Alfred Binet was the first to have had the idea, in 1895. For Binet, a person's psychology consisted of ten capacities, including memory, attention, force of will, moral sentiments, suggestibility, and imagination. Each capacity could be measured with its own test—for example, someone's ability to reproduce a complicated geometric shape tested how good or bad their memory was. As for imagination: "After asking about the number of novels the person usually reads, the kind of pleasure he takes from them, his taste in theater, music, games, etc., one can proceed to direct experiments. Take a strange-shaped blot of ink on a white sheet of paper: some people will see nothing there; for others with a lively visual imagination (Leonardo da Vinci for example), the little inkblot will be full of shapes, and one can note down the kind and number of shapes the person sees." If a subject saw one or two things, he didn't have much imagination; if he saw twenty, he had a lot. The question was how many things you could find in a random blot, not what a carefully designed blot could find in you.

From Binet, the idea of measuring imagination with inkblots spread to a string of American intelligence-testing pioneers and educators— Dearborn, Sharp, Whipple, Kirkpatrick. It reached Russia as well, where a psychology professor named Fyodor Rybakov, unaware of the Americans' work, included a series of eight blots in his *Atlas of the Experimental-Psychology Study of Personality* (1910). It was an American, Guy Montrose Whipple, who called his version an "ink-blot test" in his *Manual of Mental and Physical Tests* (also 1910)—this is why the Rorschach cards would come to be called "inkblots" when American psychologists took them up, even though Rorschach's final images would use paint, not just ink, and would not be simply blotted.

Rorschach knew Binet's work and was familiar with Binet's own inspiration—Leonardo da Vinci, who in his "Treatise on Painting" described throwing paint at a wall and looking at the stains for inspiration. But he was unaware of Binet's Russian and American followers. Still, Rorschach's early inkblot testing was similar to these efforts in some ways. The specific shapes were not really the point, with Dearborn cranking out 120 blots for one study, 100 for another. In the latter, he laid them out in a ten-by-ten grid and asked subjects to spend fifteen minutes choosing and ranking which ten blots were most like a 101st blot. He was studying pattern recognition, not interpretation.

Likewise, Rorschach's early blots were not standardized: new ones were made fresh each time, with fountain-pen ink on normal white paper, several blots per page, sometimes as many as a dozen (see Color Plate 4). Patients, and Gehring's schoolchildren aged twelve to fifteen, were shown the blots, then Rorschach and Gehring would mark them up with notes of what was seen where, or else the patients and students themselves would draw pictures of what they saw. This was not so different from the other visual expressions Rorschach encouraged his patients to make: the drawings, the paintings. Sometimes they chewed or wetted newspapers, scrunched them into heads with buttons for eyes, and gave the heads to Dr. Rorschach, who lacquered and kept them. One of these paper heads, with a large Cyclopian button in the middle, made an especially powerful impression on Gehring's wife. She was skeptical about inkblots at first, until she saw the insightful analysis Hermann was able to give of people's answers. When Gehring tried the blots out on his students, he got no great results—his country boys didn't see much. Rorschach's patients saw much more.

These early experiments were simply one more avenue of exploration among many, and Rorschach abandoned them without hesitation when the Gehrings moved away. They were not the Rorschach test to come, though one wonders about those insightful interpretations that so impressed Mrs. Gehring. Still, Rorschach was showing people inkblots in connection with research on the nature of perception, not the measuring of imagination; he was already interested in what people saw, and how, not just how much. But in 1912 crucial pieces in Rorschach's thinking were still missing, and other approaches to studying perception seemed far more promising.

7

Hermann Rorschach Feels His Brain Being Sliced Apart

F RAU B.G., A SCHIZOPHRENIC PATIENT AT MÜNSTERLINGEN IN love with one of the male nurses, thought he was trying to attack her sex organs with a little knife. Sometimes she saw floaters as little knives twirling through the air before her eyes, and when she did, she felt a violent slash below the waist. She also extended these ideas to other kinds of hallucination. Whenever she looked out the window and saw a workman mowing the lawn, she felt the swipes of the scythe in her own neck, something she found infuriating, since she knew perfectly well that the scythe couldn't reach her.

Her case reminded Rorschach of a dream he had had himself, back in Zurich. Years later, the dream remained vivid in his mind:

In my first clinical semester, I was present at an autopsy for the first time, and I looked on with all the well-known eagerness of a young student. I was especially interested in the dissection of the brain, connecting it to all sorts of reflections about where thoughts and feelings were located, slicing up the soul, etc. The deceased had been a stroke victim, and the brain was dissected in transverse slices. That night I had a dream in which I felt my own brain being cut in transverse slices. One slice after the other was detached from the mass of the hemispheres and fell forward, exactly as had happened at the autopsy. This bodily sensation (unfortunately, I have no more precise expression at my disposal) was very clear, and the image of this dream experience in my memory is even today quite vivid; it has the quality—weak, but nonetheless clear and perceivable through the senses—of a lived, experienced perception.

It would certainly be possible to ask Freudian questions about this dream's content, but Rorschach's interests lay elsewhere. No one, he pointed out, could ever feel his own brain being sliced apart; Frau B.G. had never actually been scythed in the neck either. And yet the "lived, experienced perception" was real. And the feeling in the dream didn't merely come after seeing the autopsy—they had, he felt, "a much closer and more intimate relationship, almost as if the visual perception had been translated, transposed, or turned into a bodily sensation." The marvelous fact was that seeing something could make a person feel something, even something impossible to feel. One sensation could turn into another.

Rorschach had been paying attention to such experiences for years. There were the toothache pains he had transposed into high and low notes as a teenager, and the muscle memory that let him remember a violin melody by moving his fingers. As a child, he had played a game where a group of kids told a boy they were going to pull out one of his teeth, then grabbed the tooth and unexpectedly pinched the boy's calf, which made him scream and think they had pulled out a tooth. The boy felt the pain not where it was but where he expected to feel it. As a doctor, Rorschach had noticed how hard it was to get a child to say exactly where he or she was hurt, because the pain had no precise location. And at Münsterlingen, there were the same kinds of experience all around, if you knew where to look for them: "We who live on Lake Constance have, for a long time now, localized any humming noise we hear in the air, expecting to see Zeppelin's airship come into view."

Rorschach realized that one fact about perception underlay all these experiences. Sensations could be detached from their original location and felt somewhere else, a process called relocalization. We have never flown like a bird, but we can dream of flying because we have done headstands, or jumped from a hayloft into a haystack. The slicing off of his brain in the dream "felt like getting a haircut, the slices fell forward the way a tired arm falls to a person's side, in other words these were known qualities localized in an unusual place." Relocalization was what made impossible sensations possible.

Sensations could also change in kind, not just in location. A pinch in the calf could be felt as a pain in the tooth, but a purely visual experience—B.G. seeing floaters or H.R. watching an autopsy—could turn into a nonvisual bodily sensation. Rorschach had a long history of looking at paintings and paying attention to what he felt, and as an artist he had experienced the reverse: bodily sensations turning back into visual perceptions. "If I try to call up in my mind a given image," he wrote, "my visual memory is often unable to do it, but if I have ever drawn the object and I remember one single stroke of the pen from the drawing, even the tiniest line, the memory image I am looking for appears at once."

Rorschach's body could activate his vision: "When, for example, I am unable to call up Schwind's painting *Falkenstein's Ride* as a memory image but I know how the knight is holding his right arm ('knowing' here as a nonperceptual mental image), I can voluntarily copy the position of this arm, in my imagination or in reality, and this immediately gives me a visual memory of the picture that is much better than without this aid." This was, he reiterated, precisely the same as what happened in his schizophrenic patients: by holding his arm the right way, he had "hallucinatorily called forth, so to speak, the perceptual components of the visual image."

What Freud had described in dreams actually took place across all of our perceptions, awake or asleep, sane or insane. In Freud's theory, the bizarre images in dreams are "condensed" or combined together out of various experiences. Someone in a dream can look like my boss, remind me of my mother, talk like my lover, and say something I overheard a stranger say at a café while I was talking to a friend, and the dream is about all these relationships at once. Rorschach realized that our bodies do the same as our dreaming minds: blend things together, the calf and the tooth, the arm and the memory of the painting, the man on the lawn and the slash in the neck. "Just as the psyche can separate, combine, and condense various visual elements under certain circumstances (primarily under the influence of unconscious desires)," Rorschach wrote, "it must be able to similarly redefine other sense perceptions under the same circumstances." Sensations "can be 'condensed' in the same way as visual perceptions are condensed in dreams."

Faced with a patient such as B.G., Rorschach was drawn not so much to decipher her "secret story," as Jung would have put it, as to share her way of seeing and feeling. What made these unreal sensations possible, whether a hallucinated scythe in the neck, shapes from a carpet pressing into the brain, or turning into what you saw in a book?

It was while studying the transformations of perception that Rorschach first used inkblots.

RORSCHACH WAS FAR from the first psychologist to explore the connection between seeing and feeling. In the nineteenth century, "aesthetics" was a branch of psychology and *aesthetic* was a science word—meaning "related to sensation or perception"—along with its siblings *anesthetic* (a substance we take so we won't feel), *synesthetic* (combining the senses), and *kinesthetic* (the sensation of motion). There was a tradition of psychological aesthetics in this sense, quite separate from Freud's or Bleuler's psychiatry—until Rorschach, with his Zurich training, hallucinating patients, and interest in visual experience, brought the two together.

The key figure in this tradition was Robert Vischer (1847–1933), who in 1871 wrote a philosophy dissertation that set out to explain how we can respond to abstract forms. Why do we feel elegance in two arcing lines, or balance, or converging forces—how can we feel anything at all when faced with seemingly empty and inanimate shapes? "What do a resplendent rainbow, the firmament above, or the earth below have to do with the dignity of my humanity? I can love all that lives, all that creeps and flies; such things are akin to me; but my kinship with the elements is too remote to require any kind of compassion on my part." One possible answer is that when we hear music or see abstract shapes we are reminded of something else: our reactions rest on an association of ideas. But Vischer rejected this line of thought because it reduced works of art to their content, theme, or message. Music doesn't just remind us of our mother putting us to sleep, or some other such concrete image or event—we respond to it as music.

The only viable explanation, Vischer argued, is that we can feel emotion from a lifeless thing because we put the emotion into it first. "With an intuitive investment on our part," he wrote, "we involuntarily read our emotions into" these inhuman forms. Not just our emotions, our very selves: "We have the wonderful ability to project and incorporate our own physical form" into those rainbows, those harmonious or battling lines. We lose our fixed identity but gain the ability to connect with the world: "I seem merely to adapt and attach myself to the object as one hand clasps another, and yet I am mysteriously transplanted and magically transformed into this Other." Our selves, refound in the world, are what we respond to, feeling outward things as parts of us.

Vischer's idea of a back and forth between projecting the self and internalizing the world—what he called a "direct continuation of the external sensation into an internal one"—influenced generations of philosophers, psychologists, and aesthetic theorists. To describe his radical new concept, he used the German word *Einfühlung,* literally "feeling-in." When psychological works influenced by Vischer began to be translated into English in the early twentieth century, the language needed a new term for this new idea, and translators invented the word *empathy.*

It is pretty shocking to realize that empathy is barely a hundred years old, about the same age as X-rays and lie-detector tests. Talk of an "empathy gene" feels exciting because of the friction between timeless aspects of the human condition and cutting-edge science, but in fact, "empathy" is the newfangled part of the term: genes were discovered first. What the word *empathy* described was not new, of course, and the ideas of "sympathy" and "sensibility" had long and closely related histories, but "empathy" recast the relationship between self and world in a new way. It also comes as a surprise that the term was invented not to talk about altruism or acts of kindness, but to explain how we can enjoy a sonata or a sunset. Empathy, for Vischer, was creative seeing, reshaping the world so as to find ourselves reflected in it.

In the English tradition, the exemplary empathizer in this sense was the Romantic poet John Keats, who could even enter into the lives of things. One recent critic summarizes Keats's "gift for entering imaginatively into physical objects":

> The way he hoisted himself up, looking "burly and dominant" when he first met Spenser's description of "*sea-shouldering whales*"; or mimed the "pawing" of a dancing bear, or the rapid flurry of a boxer's punches like "fingers tapping" on a windowpane. Or those famous moments of imaginative attention and empathy. "If a Sparrow come before my Window I take part in its existence and pick

about the Gravel." Or simply eating a ripe nectarine: "It went down soft pulpy, slushy, oozy—all its delicious embonpoint melted down my throat like a large beatified Strawberry." Or even entering into the spirit of a billiard ball, so he could feel "a sense of delight from its own roundness, smoothness, volubility, & the rapidity of its motions."

These examples would fit seamlessly among Rorschach's experiences. Keats, incidentally, was a medical student, followed the latest advances in neurology, and even on occasion integrated neuroscience into his poetry. The Swiss psychiatrist may have been far less effusive than the English Romantic, but underneath Hermann's reserve lay a John Keats, delighting in the world's volubility & the rapidity of its motions—"the golden overflow of the world," as Rorschach would often say, quoting his favorite line of poetry.

Vischer had the same kind of experiences, likewise anticipating Rorschach's. "When I observe a stationary object," Vischer wrote, "I can without difficulty place myself within its inner structure, at its center of gravity. I can think my way into it," feel "compressed and modest" when I see a star or flower, and "experience a feeling of mental grandeur and breadth" from a building, water, or air. "We can often observe in ourselves the curious fact that a visual stimulus is experienced not so much with our eyes as with a different sense in another part of our body. When I cross a hot street in the glaring sun and put on a pair of dark blue glasses, I have the momentary impression that my skin is being cooled off." There is no ironclad evidence that Rorschach read Vischer, but he almost certainly did, undoubtedly read works influenced by him, and in any case perceived the world in a similar way.

Decades before Freud's *Interpretation of Dreams*, Vischer was tracing the same creative activity of the mind that Freud would describe, but in the opposite direction. Since Freud wanted to get at the underlying psychological content of dreams, starting from their bizarre, seemingly meaningless surface, he needed to know how that underlying content was being "condensed" or otherwise transformed. Then he could follow the dream upstream, so to speak, to the source. Vischer, in contrast, valued these transformations in their own right, as the basis for empathy, creativity, and love. Freud cared about how the process worked, Vischer about the beautiful forms it could create: "Every work of art reveals itself to us as a person harmoniously feeling himself into a kindred object."

That is why Freud led to modern psychology and Vischer led to modern art. The psychology of the unconscious and abstract art, two groundbreaking ideas of the early twentieth century, were actually close cousins, with a common ancestor in philosopher Karl Albert Scherner, whom both Vischer and Freud credited as the source of their key idea. Vischer called Scherner's 1861 book *The Life of the Dream* a "profound work, feverishly probing hidden depths . . . from which I derived the notion that I call 'empathy' or 'feeling-into'"; in *The Interpretation of Dreams,* Freud cited Scherner at length, praising the "essential correctness" of his ideas and describing his book as "the most original and far-reaching attempt to explain dreaming as a special activity of the mind."

Vischer led to abstract art via Wilhelm Worringer (1881–1965), whose 1906 art history dissertation *Abstraction and Empathy* had an argument as simple as its title: empathy is only half the story. Worringer argued that Vischer-style empathy produces realistic art, the product of striving to correspond with the external world. An artist may feel at home in the world, feel-into things, put himself into them, and then find himself out there through his connection to them. Certain vigorous, confident cultures, in Worringer's view, were particularly likely to produce such artists, such as classical Greece and Rome, or the Renaissance.

Other individuals or cultures, though, find the world dangerous and frightening, and their deep psychic need is to find a place of refuge. Such an artist's "most powerful urge," Worringer wrote, is "to wrest the object of the external world out of its natural context" of chaos and confusion. These artists might depict a goat as a triangle with two curved lines for horns, ignoring its actual complex shape, or portray an ocean wave in the timeless geometry of a zigzag line, not by trying to copy the arbitrary details of its real appearance. This is the opposite of classic realism: abstraction.

For Worringer, then, empathy had a "counter-pole" in the urge to abstraction; empathy was but *"one* pole of human artistic feeling," no more valid or more aesthetic than the other. Some artists create by reaching out, feeling-into the world, and others by turning their backs, pulling away (the word *abstraction* is from Latin *ab-trahere*, to pull away). Different people have different needs, and their art must satisfy those needs, almost by definition—otherwise there would have been no reason to make it.

While early twentieth-century artists saw Worringer's ideas as important vindication, Carl Jung recognized the insight in Worringer's psychological theory. In his first essay advancing a theory of psychological types, Jung cited Worringer as a "valuable parallel" to his own theory of introversion and extraversion: abstraction is introverted, turning away from the world; empathy is extraverted, entering into the world. But it would take Rorschach—an artist and psychiatrist studying the psychology of perception—to fully bring the strands together.

RORSCHACH COULD PRACTICE medicine in Münsterlingen, but he needed to write a dissertation to receive his MD. Students were usually assigned dissertation topics by their professors, but when the time came, Rorschach proposed five ideas of his own to his adviser, Bleuler.

The mix was typical of his Zurich School background: heredity, criminology, psychoanalysis, literature. He thought he might study whether a predisposition to psychosis could be traced through a patient's family history, using archival material in Münsterlingen or his hometown of Arbon; he proposed a psychoanalytical study of a teacher accused of offenses against morality, and another of a catatonic patient who heard voices. He was interested in working on Dostoyevsky and epilepsy but hoped to pursue the topic more thoroughly in Moscow. In the end, he chose his most original idea, telling Bleuler he "would be very pleased if something could come of it."

Rorschach's dissertation, which he finished in 1912, set out to define the physiological pathways that make empathy in Vischer's sense possible. "On 'Reflex Hallucinations' and Related Phenomena" may be a brain-numbing title in English, but the subject was nothing less than the connection between what we see and how we feel.

Reflexhalluzination was a technical psychiatric term invented in the 1860s for precisely the class of phenomena that Rorschach found fascinating in his patients and himself, along with synesthesia, Proustian memories unlocked by certain smells, and any other instance of involuntary perception induced by a stimulus. John Keats feeling himself pick about the gravel when he looked at a sparrow was a reflex hallucination, if you want to put it that way, although "cross-sensory perception" or "induced hallucination" might be a more vivid translation.

After opening his dissertation with the mandatory dry review of the literature, Rorschach presented forty-three vivid, numbered examples of crossovers between vision and hearing, between seeing or hearing and bodily sensations, and between other pairs of senses, starting with the dream of his sliced brain as Example 1. He quickly dismissed the simple associations that happen all the time (when you hear your cat meow, you picture him in your mind), much as Vischer had dismissed associations. While reflex hallucinations did involve associations— Rorschach acknowledged that there was a reason B.G. felt the workman's scythe in her neck, not in a less symbolic part of her body—such associations were secondary. What made the case interesting was the transformation from one kind of perception into a different one.

Rorschach's main examples were not crossovers between seeing and hearing, the focus of most studies of synesthesia; instead they linked outward perception to inward bodily perception. They involved kinesthesia, our sensation of *movement*. He described how, "when I move my finger back and forth at arm's length in total darkness and look in that direction, I believe I can see my finger moving even though this is completely impossible," so the perception of movement must trigger a weak visual perception, parallel to one known from experience. Learning a song or a foreign language—or learning a word as a young child— he likewise described as creating a link between sound and movement, "an acoustic-kinesthetic parallel," until the learner felt herself move her mouth to say the word whenever she heard it and vice versa.

These parallels could operate in both directions. One schizophrenic patient in Solothurn, A. von A., used to look out the window and see himself standing in the street. His double "copied" every movement he made—that is, the patient's movements turned into a visual perception of his double, "traveling backwards along the same reflex hallucination path" as that of a schizophrenic who felt others' movements in her own body.

In linking vision and movement along the pathway of empathy,

Rorschach used the work of an obscure Norwegian psychophysicist, John Mourly Vold, whose two-volume treatise on dreams had bypassed Freud altogether and focused on kinesthesia. Mourly Vold described endless experiments where parts of a sleeper's body were tied or taped down, and the resulting dreams analyzed for how much movement they contained and what kind. Rorschach tried some of these experiments on himself. (One resulting dream was about stepping on the foot of a patient with the same last name as his boss.) It is hard to imagine two theories more completely alien to each other than Freud's and Mourly Vold's, but Rorschach integrated them: "Mourly Vold's analysis of dreams in no way excludes psychoanalytic dream interpretation. . . . The Mourly-Vold aspects are part of the building material, the symbols are the workers, the complexes are the construction supervisors, and the dreaming psyche is the architect of the structure we call a dream."

Rorschach was straining to cast these mechanisms as universal. Only at the end of his dissertation did he acknowledge that perhaps not everyone had the abilities he had: "My account of reflex-hallucinatory processes may seem subjective to some readers, for example auditory types, since it is written by someone who is primarily a motor type, secondarily a visual type." He didn't define what he meant by these "types" but clearly realized, however uneasily, that different people tended to experience different kinds of "parallels." Because his own gifts of mimicry, realistic artistic ability, and empathy were the foundation for his new psychological ideas, he was reluctant to admit that they might be particular to him.

Like many dissertations, Rorschach's ended up being less than definitive. He was forced to drastically shorten the final product, and he admitted in the dissertation itself, twice, that given "the relatively small collection of examples" it was "naturally impossible" to reach any final conclusions. But by paying such close attention to specific perceptions, in all their slippery transformations, he was starting to see the processes underlying them—laying the groundwork for a much deeper synthesis of psychology and seeing.

8

The Darkest and Most Elaborate Delusions

IN 1895, UNSETTLING RUMORS WERE BEGINNING TO GO AROUND Schwarzenburg, a mountain village in central Switzerland. A man named Johannes Binggeli, married, sixty-one years old, was the head of a community of true believers called the Forest Brotherhood. He was a mystic, a preacher, and the author of various pamphlets dictated to him by the Holy Spirit. A tailor by trade, he would sometimes be hired by locals, but usually only to predict winning lottery numbers. The Brotherhood, ninety-three members strong, kept largely to itself.

Then a woman in the Brotherhood was arrested for concealing the birth of her child and named Binggeli as the father. Two years earlier, she had been unable to urinate for eight days and Binggeli had said that her Water Gate was under a spell, which he removed by having sex with her. She was cured, but their sexual relationship continued. Other members of the congregation began to come forward with stories about Binggeli using intercourse to expel demons from women and young girls. The authorities discovered that there was an esoteric sect within the Forest Brotherhood, one that worshipped Binggeli as "the Word of God made flesh once more." Binggeli's penis was the "Shaft of Christ," and his urine, "Heaven's Drops" or "Heaven's Balm," had healing properties: his worshippers drank it or applied it externally to fight illness or temptations. He was said to be able to pass red, blue, or green urine at will, and he sometimes used it as Communion wine.

Binggeli was found to have committed incest with his daughter repeatedly between 1892 and 1895: of her three illegitimate children, at least one, probably two, were his. After his arrest, he claimed at various times that he hadn't done it; that he had, but only in a dream, to protect her from cat-shaped and mouse-shaped demons; that the law did not apply to him because he was not constituted like other human beings. Binggeli was found insane and sent to the nearby Münsingen asylum for four and a half years, from July 1896 to February 1901.

In April 1913, Rorschach transferred to Münsingen. Ulrich Brauchli, Rorschach's boss in Münsterlingen, had been promoted to director of the new, larger, more prestigious institution near Bern, and Brauchli's replacement, one Hermann Wille, was less than pleasant to work with. Rorschach followed Brauchli, while Olga, earning money and pursuing her own career as a doctor, had to stay at Münsterlingen for three months until her position ended. They were separated again, although by only 120 miles this time.

Rorschach stumbled onto Binggeli's patient file in Münsingen and was fascinated. Researching further, he discovered that Binggeli's Forest Brotherhood had grown out of an earlier, more widespread movement, the Antonianers, founded by Antoni Unternährer in the Napoleonic era and surviving into the twentieth century in both Europe and America. These religious movements likely reawakened his interest in the Dukhobor sect, which he had discovered through Ivan Tregubov. Rorschach tracked down Binggeli in person and went to visit him in his mountain retreat, where he now lived with a small core of believers including his second wife, his daughter, and the son who was also his grandson. Binggeli "was in his eightieth year by then," Rorschach wrote, "senile and asthmatic. He was a dwarfish little man with a large head, large torso, and short arms and legs" who "always wore the traditional Schwarzenburg folk costume with brightly polished metal buttons, seven on each side"—these shiny metal objects, along with his watch chain, played a key role in his delusions. Rorschach was able "to convince him without much trouble to let himself be photographed."

This was the start of a project on Swiss sect activity that, by 1915 at the latest, Rorschach was sure would be his lifework. He had taken his physiological studies of perception as far as he then could, so he broadened his focus to cultural ways of seeing—and gave his broad curiosity free rein. When not busy treating patients, he gathered material on other archaic phallic cults in Switzerland and gradually assembled an astonishing body of research, synthesizing the psychology of religion with sociology, psychiatry, folklore, history, and psychoanalysis.

He found that sect activity always appeared in the same regions, along frontiers of race or political sympathies—that is, in earlier war zones. He made a hand-colored map showing that areas of sect activity corresponded with high concentrations of weavers, and speculated about why. Historically, he traced sect activity in these regions back through earlier Protestant cults to the twelfth-century Waldensians and thirteenth-century Brethren of the Free Spirit, to still earlier heresies and separatist movements, all leaving clear traces in the region down to the present day. Psychologically, he argued along Jungian lines that schizophrenic delusions tap into the same psychic sources as ancient belief systems, and he noted similarities between the images and ideas of this entire history of sects to those of myths and philosophies reaching back to the ancient Gnostics. He showed, for instance, that the eighteenth-century Antonianers' teachings matched, in detail, those of first-century Adamites.

Sociologically, he argued that in founding a sect a charismatic leader was less important than a receptive group of followers—a community can manufacture a leader out of almost anyone, if the need is strong enough, and when sects were imported from elsewhere, they tended to die out quickly unless the community was already primed. He distinguished between active and passive followers, as well as between hysterical leaders, whose messages were determined by personal complexes, and the more powerful schizophrenic leaders, whose doctrines tapped deeply into archetypal mythologies.

His lectures and essays on the topic of sects, both academic and nonacademic, were some of his liveliest writing—equally interesting as biography, case study, history, theology, and psychology. He had plans for "a thick book" to address a range of questions:

Why can one schizophrenic found a community and another can't? Why does a schizophrenic retrace primitive man's ideas while a neurotic follows local superstitions? And how do these various things relate to the respective populations? Why are sects always where there are textile industries? Which races are the carriers of the local indigenous sects, and which join only the imported ones? All with numerous mythological, ethnological, religious, historical, and other parallels!

This was Rorschach the thinker, not Rorschach the doctor. Like Freud, Jung, and the other pioneers of his time, he wanted to do more than treat patients: he wanted to bring culture and psychology together to explore the nature and meaning of individual and communal belief.

As part of the Zurich School, Rorschach believed in an interplay between individual psychology and culture, and he resisted claiming that one universal psychology applied to everyone. What may look like a radical detour in Rorschach's career was part of his lifelong effort to understand the particular ways that different people see things differently.

As he widened the focus of his work, Rorschach was once again restless to leave Switzerland. He had tackled the Moscow bureaucracy again, this time with more success: the Swiss ambassador confirmed that Rorschach would be able to take the first Russian state medical exam offered in 1914. In December 1913, he and Olga left Münsingen for a cosmopolitan environment where it was common knowledge that psychology and art were inextricable: Russia.

It was an exhilarating time to go. Russian culture was in its so-called Silver Age, saturated with reciprocal influences of art, science, and occult belief. Russian science, especially in an era of revolutionary turmoil and sweeping cultural movements, was less specialized and segregated than in the West. As Alexander Etkind, the major historian of psychoanalysis in Russia, has written: "Decadent poets, moral philosophers, and professional revolutionaries have played as great a role in the history of psychoanalysis in Russia as have physicians and psychologists"; from the other side, in the words of John Bowlt, a leading cultural historian of modernist Russia, "No appreciation of that 'hysterical, spiritually tormented time' can be complete" without reference both to the artistic figures—Chekhov and Akhmatova, Fabergé and Chagall, Diaghilev and Nijinsky, Kandinsky and Malevich, Stravinsky and Mayakovsky—and to the "extraordinary progress in the Russian sciences," from rocket engineering to Pavlov's behaviorist psychology.

Rorschach was offered a job at an elite private clinic just outside of Moscow, the Kryukovo, run by the leading psychoanalysts in Russia and full of writers and artists. In many ways, this was an ideal setting for Rorschach. It was a private clinic for voluntary patients of nervous illnesses, as was typical in Russia at the time, and quite a change from the packed hospitals he was used to. Founded by doctors without salaries from universities or state hospitals, such institutions became partly commercial enterprises, which meant they paid well—and at least they concentrated on selling their services to the patients, not, as with English "madhouses," to families who simply wanted patients locked away. The clinic was in a rural setting, to take advantage of the healing properties of "natural, healthy living," and patients were treated humanely and well. The psychiatrists were free to combine theories, experiment with new therapies, and take a holistic approach: "to heal by the intimate and supportive psychological atmosphere, and by the physician's 'personality,' rather than relying on any given theory," in the words of one doctor there, Nikolai Osipov.

The Kryukovo doctors were generalists and public intellectuals. Osipov, for instance, would later become a well-known Tolstoy expert and a lecturer on Dostoyevsky and Turgenev as well. As for the patients, they included leading cultural figures, among them the preeminent Russian Symbolist poet Alexander Blok and the great actor Mikhail Chekhov, nephew of the playwright—the sanatorium gave preferential treatment to writers, doctors, and relatives of the late Anton Chekhov. After years of putting on amateur plays in a Swiss backwater and translating Andreyev in his spare time, Rorschach found himself in a cultural center.

Coursing through the Russian Silver Age were a number of themes close to Rorschach's heart: synesthesia, madness, visual art as self-expression. Movement, the key element in the reflex hallucinations Rorschach had studied, was here seen as "the basic feature of reality," in the words of modern novelist Andrei Bely; theorists of the Russian ballet called movement the most important aspect of all great art.

Within psychology, the sectarian distinctions that seemed so important in far-off western Europe largely fell away. A 1909 advertising brochure for the Kryukovo proclaimed that patients would receive "hypnosis, suggestion, and psychoanalysis," as well as "psychotherapy in its proper sense"—meaning so-called rational therapy, a technique pioneered by another Swiss, Paul Dubois, which for a time was more prominent and popular than Freud's method (much as a similar approach, now called cognitive-behavioral therapy, is today). No battle lines were drawn between the different camps.

And the inspiration for Russian psychiatry was Tolstoy, the wise, humanistic soul-healer who had inspired Rorschach too. One reason psychoanalysis was so well received in Russia was that it meshed with homegrown traditions of introspection, "purification of the soul," existential reflections on the deep questions of human life, and respect for people's inner worlds. If Rorschach's mix of ideals and intellectual interests—generalist, nonsectarian, broadly humanist, literary, visual—seemed idiosyncratic in a western European context, it was standard for Russian psychiatrists.

Freud had joked in a 1912 letter to Jung that "there seems to be a local epidemic of psychoanalysis" in Russia, but it was not in fact a one-way relationship, an "epidemic" spreading from Europe to the hinterlands. Russians were prominent psychoanalysts in both Russia and the West. Osipov, Rorschach's Kryukovo colleague, published the first journal of psychoanalysis anywhere and sat on the board of Freud's journal. Even supposedly "European" ideas were not themselves un-Russian. Freud called the psychic mechanism of repressing unacceptable psychological material "censorship," an explicit allusion to Russian political censorship: in his definition, the "imperfect instrument of the Tsarist regime for preventing penetration of alien Western influences." Many of Freud's patients were Slavic, often Russian, including the "Wolf Man," the exemplary patient whose case he chose as the subject of his most important case study. Jung's first psychoanalytic patient, who exerted the greatest influence on his own life and work, was the Russian Sabina Spielrein. The list goes on. If the history of psychiatry is the story not only of its doctors and theorists but also of its patients, then it is largely a tale of Russian culture.

Rorschach's own psychoanalytic approach grew out of his experience treating Russians, most obviously because the Kryukovo was where he had patients he could psychoanalyze—unlike the psychotics in the Swiss asylums, or criminal cases needing quick evaluation, such as Johannes Neuwirth. But he also came to see psychoanalysis as intrinsically linked to aspects of Russian culture. In a lecture he later gave to a general audience on the subject, he said that Russian and Swiss neuroses worked in more or less the same way, although there were certain "quantitative differences" between the populations, but that psychoanalysis was more effective on Slavic patients than those of German background. Not only were "most of them good self-observers (or self-devourers, as their saying goes, since this self-observation often grows into a truly tormenting, devouring addiction)," but they could express themselves more freely, "not inhibited by all kinds of prejudices." Russians were "much more tolerant of illness than other peoples," without "the contempt that we Swiss so often feel along with our pity." Those with nervous illnesses could seek treatment in an institution without fear of "damaging stigma" upon their release. The idea of Russia he had fallen in love with through Olga—the "Russian" ability to express one's feelings—now carried over to his sense of his patients and shaped his psychiatric practice.

RORSCHACH'S MONTHS AT the Kryukovo in early 1914 came at a watershed moment in Russian art, one that redefined the power of visual images. Russian Futurism was in full force, and Rorschach witnessed it firsthand. Probably in 1915, he drafted an essay called "The Psychology of Futurism," whose journalistic opening set the scene nicely: "Futurism, as it presents itself today to an astonished world, appears at first to be a colorful jumble of incomprehensible images and sculptures, of high-sounding manifestos and inarticulate sounds, of noisy art and artistic noise, of a will to power and a will to illogicality. Only one common theme is distinct: An unbounded self-confidence and a perhaps even more boundless condemnation of everything that came before, a battle-cry against all of the concepts that until today have shaped the course of culture, art, and daily life."

Futurism was a modernist pressure cooker in which everything seemed to be shattering or dissolving at once. An explosion of energy in literature, painting, theater, and music, its Russian version contained a swarm of submovements, cliques, and branding strategies, including Cubo-Futurism, Ego-Futurism, Everythingism, Centrifuge, and the excellently named Mezzanine of Poetry. These were discussed in the press almost daily while Rorschach was in Russia, and in January and February 1914 the leading Italian Futurist, F. T. Marinetti, gave well-publicized and well-attended lectures in Moscow. The movement took to the streets with parades in which artists would "walk with painted faces among the crowds, reciting futurist poetry." When a little girl gave one parading poet an orange, he began to eat it. "He's eating, he's eating," the astonished crowd whispered, as if the Futurists were Martians; a nationwide tour soon followed.

The Futurists' explorations resonated with many of Rorschach's interests. The composer and painter Mikhail Matyushin, a follower of Ernst Haeckel, studied chance forms of driftwood, wrote theories of color, and tried to expand human visual capacity, in part with exercises meant to regenerate lost optical nerves in the back of the head and the soles of the feet. Nikolai Kulbin, whom Rorschach heard lecture, was an artist and medical doctor who published books and scientific articles on sensory perception and psychological testing. He had this psychological slogan as his motto: "The self does not know anything except its own feelings, and while projecting these feelings it creates its own world." Poet Aleksei Kruchenykh championed "seeing things on both sides" and "subjective objectivity": "Let a book be small, but . . . everything the writer's own, to the last ink blot." Futurists published synesthetic works such as *Intuitive Colors* and tables of correspondences between colors and musical notes; manifestos on how neologisms and mistakes "bring about movement and the new perception of the word"; a poem where the poet is in a movie theater and, making a special effort, begins to see the image upside down. These and other key figures are mentioned or quoted in Rorschach's Futurism essay.

He acknowledged that Futurism seemed crazy and illogical but affirmed that "the time has now passed when any movement, any action, can be dismissed as 'crazy.' . . . There is no such thing as absolute nonsense. Even in the darkest and most elaborate delusions of our dementia praecox patients, there exists a hidden meaning." He drew the parallel between Futurism and schizophrenia in Zurich School terms, justifying the wider applicability of psychoanalytic theory: "Connections unimaginable until now have been forged with the elaboration of the depth psychology that Freud has pioneered. . . . Not only neurotic symptoms and delusional systems and dreams but also myths, fairy tales, poems, musical works, paintings—all have proved to be accessible to psychoanalytical research." As a result, "Even if we decide to

describe Futurism as madness and nonsense, we still have the obliga-
tion to find sense in that nonsense."

Rorschach took Futurism seriously and found sense in it specific
enough to criticize. In the most original analysis in his Futurism essay,
he argued that the Futurists misunderstood how images generate a
feeling of movement. He pointed out that usually only cartoonists,
like his old favorite Wilhelm Busch, try to present motion by showing an object in multiple states at once, for instance by giving a vigorous pianist numerous arms and hands. Michelangelo's sculptures or
paintings, in contrast, are themselves dynamic—they make you *feel* the
movement. The Futurists, with their dozen-legged dogs, made the mistake of trying an approach like Busch's, but Rorschach was unusually
firm: for an artist aspiring to more than cartoons, "there is no other
way to handle motion" than Michelangelo's way; "The only serious
way to represent motion in an object is by influencing the kinesthetic
sense of the beholder." The Futurist strategy is "impossible" because
it misunderstands the relationship between empathy—Vischer's term
hineinfühlen—and vision: "There is no need to consult the philosophers
and psychologists, but simply the physiologists. Multiple legs next to
each other do not awaken an idea of movement, or only in a very abstract way, just as a human being cannot empathize with a millipede
along kinesthetic pathways."

Visual images, at least if they're good, produce mental states—they
"awaken an idea" in the viewer. At one point in his essay draft, between
X's, Rorschach inserted without explanation a Russian quotation:

X

A picture—The rails on which the viewer's imagination must roll,
according to the artist's representation.

X

In Switzerland, Rorschach and Gehring had used inkblots to gauge the
viewer's imagination, treating it as a measurable quantity. Here was a
vision of pictures *changing* the viewer's imagination—leading it, as on
rails, in a new direction.

Regardless of his specific arguments, a psychiatrist writing about
"the psychology of Futurism" in 1915, engaging with avant-garde art in

Forte vivace

Fortissimo vivacissimo

Wilhelm Busch, from "The Virtuoso" (1865); Giacomo Balla's Futurist *Dynamism of a Dog on a Leash* (1912), using the strategy Rorschach thought suitable only for comics. Rorschach had already mocked "Expressionism!" in a high school yearbook drawing; later, in this and other series of small paintings, he explored how to capture movement more effectively.

ways entirely consistent with his psychiatric theory and practice, was ahead of his time. Freud would freely admit that he was a philistine about modern art; Jung would write one essay on Joyce and one on Picasso, both superficial and dismissive, and would be widely mocked, never going near the subject again. There were other psychiatrists more attentive to art, and artists who studied psychology, even outside of Russia—the German surrealist Max Ernst, for instance, had extensive university training in psychiatry. But Rorschach was a uniquely knowledgeable figure to straddle the disciplinary divide.

Beyond Futurism, western European and Russian ideas were coming together in the nineteen-tens to create abstract art. The figures usually credited as the first purely abstract modern artists are the Dutchman Piet Mondrian, the Russian Kazimir Malevich, the Russian émigré in Munich Wassily Kandinsky, and the Swiss Sophie Taeuber. Worringer's *Abstraction and Empathy* was a shared point of reference. Rorschach's Futurism essay just predated the defining event in the birth of modern art in Switzerland: the creation of Dadaism in a Zurich cabaret in February 1916. Sophie Taeuber took part, along with her future husband Hans (Jean) Arp; at the Zurich School of Arts and Crafts, where Ulrich Rorschach had studied a generation before, Taeuber taught what Arp called "bevies of girls hastening to Zurich from all the cantons of Switzerland, with the burning desire to neverendingly embroider floral wreaths on cushions," and "managed to bring most of them to embrace the square."

There is no record of any direct contact between Rorschach and the Dadaists, but he certainly followed developments in western European modern art. He had made a cartoon satirizing Expressionism in high school; he would later use the Austrian Expressionist artist Alfred Kubin to illustrate his theories about introversion and extraversion. More generally, he would bring his insights about art and psychology back from Russia to his psychiatric practice in Switzerland.

HERMANN AND OLGA's "chronic question" of where to settle down had continued to pull the couple in opposite directions. Hermann found in 1914, as he had in 1909, that however drawn he was to Russian culture, the reality of life there was a different matter. Olga liked the unpredictability of life in Russia; Hermann experienced it as chaotic. Olga dismissed Hermann's ambitions as "a European longing for 'achievement,'" saying "he had a kind of fear of succumbing to Russia's magic." And what she perceived as warm companionship sometimes felt too intrusive to the introverted Hermann, who had already complained to Anna about the overly social Russian culture—"It's very hard to work at home here; open doors and visits all day long." Anna later recalled that the endless conversations one found oneself having in Russia left Hermann with "a great longing to be alone": for all the interesting patients at Kryukovo, they took up so much of his time and energy that "he had no free time to write down his observations or work on them.

He told me that he felt like a painter standing in front of a wonderful landscape without paper or paint." She did not think that Hermann ever wanted to live abroad again after that experience.

A long string of late-night family fights finally ended at 2 a.m. one May morning in 1914. Hermann had prevailed. It was impossible to get a job at the world-famous Burghölzli, but he found a job at the Waldau, in Bolligen on the outskirts of Bern, one of the only two other university-based psychiatric hospitals in German-speaking Switzerland. He wrote from Russia to a colleague at the Waldau, saying that "after our endless gypsy wanderings, we feel a strong need to finally settle down." It was an anxious letter: "Would you be so kind as to give me some information about the rooms we are being offered in Waldau? How big are they—how many paces? How many windows? What about the entrance, how many stairs and hallways? Are the rooms all together? Would a comfortable married life be possible there?" The answer he received must have been reassuring enough. He left Russia for Switzerland on June 24, 1914, never to return.

Olga planned to stay in Kazan about six weeks before following her husband, but no sooner had he returned to the West than Archduke Franz Ferdinand was shot in Sarajevo, on June 28, and by the end of Olga's six weeks the Great War had begun. She remained in Russia for ten more months, until the spring of 1915. This long separation—their fourth at least—was by choice as well as by circumstance. Olga was not ready to give up on her dream of staying in Russia and could not bring herself to leave her homeland just yet, especially in its time of need. Without her, Hermann's worries about the apartment were moot, and the "small but nice new three-room apartment on the fourth floor of the central clinic building" was fine—Rorschach called it "my dovecote," a perfect garret for solitude and hard work.

The future colleague Rorschach had written to from Russia was Walter Morgenthaler (1882–1965), whom Rorschach knew from his Münsterlingen days. When Rorschach arrived at the Waldau, Morgenthaler was busy searching through the case histories to find patients' drawings for his growing collection, encouraging patients to draw as much as they wanted, and systematically promoting their artistic activity by giving them paper, asking them to draw, and assigning specific topics (a man, woman, and child; a house; a garden). Morgenthaler recalled Rorschach's rapport with patients along just these lines: "The son of a drawing teacher and a very good draftsman himself, he was vitally interested in patients' drawings. He had an amazing gift for getting patients to draw."

Rorschach found out, for instance, that one catatonic patient, who spent most of every day lying or sitting stiffly in bed, had been a good draftsman before falling ill. Rorschach laid out on his blanket not just a sketch pad and a handful of colored pencils but a large maple leaf with a crawling maybug tethered to it with tape. Not just art supplies, but something to look at; not just an object, but life in motion. The next day, beaming with delight, Rorschach showed Morgenthaler and their boss the patient's extremely accurate colored drawing of the beetle on the leaf. Although this patient had not moved for months, he now slowly started to draw more, then took painting classes, improved further, and was eventually discharged.

Rorschach was enthusiastic about Morgenthaler's research into art and mental illness, and with reason: Morgenthaler was working on a pioneering study of art and mental illness. One of his patients was a schizophrenic named Adolf Wölfli, hospitalized since 1895, who had developed into a visual artist, writer, and composer, producing a large body of drawings by 1914. In 1921, Morgenthaler would publish the groundbreaking *A Mental Patient as Artist* (1921), which would influence everyone from the Surrealists—André Breton grouped Wölfli with Picasso and the Russian mystic Gurdjieff as important inspirations, calling Wölfli's art "one of the three or four most important bodies of work in the twentieth century"—to Rainer Maria Rilke, who thought his case "will help us someday gain new insights into the origins of creativity." Wölfli would become the paradigmatic outsider artist of the century.

Rorschach likely saw Wölfli on his rounds and helped Morgenthaler treat him. He looked for visually interesting material in the Waldau files for Morgenthaler and promised that "one of the first things he would do" after leaving the Waldau was start a collection of patients' drawings like Morgenthaler's. This departure was looming: when Olga eventually did return to Switzerland, the Rorschachs decided that the apartment was too small after all, as was the salary. They moved again, to Herisau in northeastern Switzerland.

Hermann's years of wandering from 1913 through 1915 had helped him envision a more holistic, humanistic psychology. Discovering Binggeli had taken his interest in perception in an anthropological direction, showing him a way into the dark core of individual and collective belief, where psychology meets culture. Russian culture gave him a model for linking art and science. And the Futurists and Wölfli showed him how closely psychological explorations could be tied to art. This deeper understanding of the power of visual images would soon lead to his breakthrough.

9

Pebbles in a Riverbed

H ERISAU LIES IN A LANDSCAPE OF HIGH ROLLING HILLS, SUNNY *Sound of Music* summers with Alpine rambles and wildflowers dotting the meadows giving way to early autumns, bleak cold winters of heavy snows, and long, wet springs. It has one of the highest elevations of any town in Switzerland, and "even when St. Gallen"—the glorious monastery town about five miles away—"is under a deep fog, we often have sunshine and clear air here," Rorschach wrote to his brother. His relatives in Arbon were nearby, about fifteen miles to the north; on a clear day, Rorschach could see Lake Constance from the hill where he lived. The Säntis, the highest peak in the region and his destination for hikes, was the same distance away to the south, visible out Rorschach's second-floor window—he always seemed to choose upstairs apartments. "It is especially beautiful here in winter, late spring, and late fall," Rorschach wrote of his new home. "Fall is probably our most beautiful time, with a clear view into the distance."

Rorschach lived in Herisau longer than anywhere else except Schaffhausen. It was where he raised his family, pursued his career and his calling. The Krombach, the canton psychiatric hospital, was on a hill to the west of town. Opened in 1908, not long before Rorschach's arrival in 1915, it was the first asylum in Switzerland built using the pavilion system: buildings in parklike surroundings, separated to limit the spread of infections as well as for therapeutic benefits. Behind the administration building there were three buildings for men and three for women, and a chapel in the middle. By Rorschach's time, the hospital built for 250 patients held about 400, most of them severely psychotic. It was primarily a custodial institution—less politely, a holding facility—rather than a place of treatment.

The doctors and staff lived at the Krombach alongside the patients, relatively isolated in the picturesque surroundings. The population of Herisau was around fifteen thousand, increasingly from outside the canton and the country, predominantly textile workers; St. Gallen produced half of the world's embroidery in 1910. Herisau had a movie theater and a few amenities but not much to offer, especially after the textile industry's collapse following World War I. The canton, Appenzell Ausserrhoden, was rural and largely conservative, with a population famously reserved toward outsiders. Rorschach identified more closely with the stereotypically slow and introverted Bernese than with the Appenzellers but got along with the locals, respecting them without trying to be one of them.

It was an enormous relief to Hermann and Olga that their "gypsy wanderings" had come to an end. They had a large apartment at last, about a hundred feet long and full of windows, arcing around the front of the administration building; a painting Hermann made later showed the airy rooms with a view in summer (see Color Plate 5). When the moving van arrived it was almost empty, yet Hermann could write to his brother, soon after, "We are sitting on some of our own furniture, can you imagine? It's a real experience."

The asylum director was Arnold Koller, an uninspiring doctor but diligent administrator. He had efficiently managed the Krombach's construction—in retrospect, the high point of his career—and his handwritten reminiscences describe life there. "Once the institution was running smoothly," he admitted, "its direction did not require too much work." As another student of Bleuler's, Koller championed a personal understanding of patients' physical and mental well-being, but he was an uptight man, rigid and moralistic: his son remembers telling a lie and his father responding, "I would rather you die than keep doing that."

Koller also cared deeply about budgets and costs; Rorschach called him "somewhat small-minded and a born statistician," and every year like clockwork he was driven slightly insane by having to write up and analyze the year's numbers—"Statistics Week," he called it. January 1920: "I have only just finished the most unpleasant work in the institutional year: the statistics for 1919. After days and days of absolute imbecility, I am slowly returning to consciousness." January 1921: "I am still suffering from a case of statistical dementia, able only to address the most necessary matters. . . . I am looking forward to Freud's forthcoming book, but is there anything Beyond the Pleasure Principle that makes life worth living? What will Freud say? I know one thing that lies beyond the pleasure principle—statistics!"

Rorschach kept up appearances, writing Welcome Back notes whenever the director and his family returned from their trips, with charming drawings and little poems describing what had happened during the four weeks they were away. Koller's son Rudi remembered the notes vividly forty years later and recalled Rorschach as extraordinarily gifted but modest, never putting himself forward, "the soul of the entire institution"—this according to the son of its director. The boy was six or seven when he had a severe appendix pain while his father was away; Rorschach sat down next to him, took off his wedding ring, and hypnotized Rudi with it: talked to him, put him to sleep, and when the boy woke up his pain was gone.

Rorschach's workdays began with a morning meeting with Koller, after which he was off on his rounds, handling the acute male and female patients. Terrible screaming filled the halls; one day, Hermann turned up at his apartment with his clothes ripped open from top to bottom by a patient. New Year's Day 1920 was not auspicious: "More or less exactly at midnight, a patient tried to strangle himself." The main treatments were daylong baths, which the patients liked, and sedatives, along with work therapy such as making paper bags or separating coffee beans; if a catatonic wanted to leave the assigned task "to stand against the wall," he or she was free to do so. There was manual labor for those who could do it—gardening, carpentry, and bookbinding. The doctors ate their meals with their families. Olga often stayed in bed reading until noon or one o'clock; she sometimes did the cooking, less often when they eventually had the money to hire a maid. Hospital staff did the laundry. Hermann worked late.

His salary was still low, and the clinic was in desperate need of a third doctor—in 1916, Rorschach was personally responsible for 300 patients; later, for 320. But permission for an unpaid volunteer assistant was granted only in 1919; Rorschach himself was almost not hired, because Olga was a doctor and Koller was afraid that his superiors, who had steadily refused another hire, would think he was trying to present

them with a fait accompli. An unmistakably irritated Rorschach wrote
to Morgenthaler back in Bern:

> As you can see from the long reading period I needed for the books
> you loaned me, I still have very little time for myself. I have just
> sent off an epic poem to the oversight committee, which, using co-
> pious statistical material—the Appenzeller's *locus minoris resistentiae*
> [place of least resistance to invasion by toxins or bacteria]—proves
> that Herisau is in last place, far and wide, perhaps in all of Europe,
> re: number of doctors, and that the addition of a third doctor is
> simply indispensable. I have many votes in favor, but one member
> of the council apparently came to the bizarre conclusion that "we
> were *artificially* forcing up the number of patients so high in order
> to *extort* a third doctor." What insight!

Rorschach had little intellectual stimulation. He helped found the
Swiss Psychoanalytic Society and served as vice president, but the occasional meetings were hardly enough. "It's too bad I live so far away,
or we could have talked it over in person a long time ago," he wrote
to Morgenthaler about one topic; to another friend and colleague in
Zurich: "Here in the provinces I get a glimpse of new publications only
by accident, if at all." While his friends said they were jealous of Herisau's rural peace and quiet, Rorschach envied his colleagues who dealt
with "interesting people, not like the Appenzellers here, worn smooth
as pebbles in a riverbed."

Rorschach could continue work on his earlier projects, especially his
sect studies, and stay professionally connected to Switzerland's other
psychiatrists and psychoanalysts, at least by mail. But what would come
next? Having promised Morgenthaler that he would collect patient
drawings, Rorschach found it impossible to do so. He attributed the
failure to cultural variation, writing regretfully to Morgenthaler that
"if you put a piece of paper in front of a Bernese, he will start to draw
after a while, without saying a word, but an Appenzeller will sit there in
front of a blank sheet of paper and blab his head off about all the things
one could draw there, without making a single mark!" Rorschach's new
patients were better at talking about pictures than making them.

THE GREAT WAR was raging during the Rorschachs' first years in Herisau, and even neutral Switzerland felt the effects: nationalistic rivalry between Swiss French and Swiss Germans, military service as noncombatants, rampant inflation. Having just returned to Switzerland when the war broke out, Rorschach had tried to volunteer at a military hospital with Morgenthaler. To no avail: "What are you thinking?" their superior at the Waldau had snapped. "Don't you understand that it is your duty to stay right here?" Morgenthaler recalled Rorschach's dark reaction: hanging his head in a bad mood for days, even quieter than usual, then mournfully observing that "now it's the Germans' duty to kill as many Frenchmen as possible, and the Frenchmen's duty to kill as many Germans, while it's our duty to sit here right in the middle and say 'Good morning' to our schizophrenic patients every day."

After moving to Herisau, Rorschach was able to serve. He and Olga volunteered for six weeks, helping to transport 2,800 mental patients from the French asylums in German-occupied territories to France, among other noncombat duties. He also followed the events of the war from his usual analytic distance. Contemptuous of the need to avoid anti-German sentiment by writing to his brother in French, he was equally repelled by the pro-German Swiss who opportunistically changed their tune at the end of the war: "There was a sudden reversal among the Germans in Switzerland as early as October [1918]: the more Kaiser-crazy they were before, the more they heaped curses on him afterward. . . . It was worse than all their earlier arrogance. I will never forget the disgusting impression this crowd psychology made as long as I live."

Of greatest concern were the events in Russia. Shocking stories were reaching Switzerland in 1918, of shootings in Russia, executions, starvation, the entire intelligentsia being killed off. The Rorschachs were desperate to get news of Anna, still in Moscow, and Olga's relatives. Anna returned to Switzerland in July, but it took two more years to get news of Olga's family in Kazan, and the news was not good: Olga's brother had "barely survived" a typhus outbreak, after which there was no further word.

The pro-Bolshevik propaganda, "in defiance of all truth and humanity and common sense," disgusted Rorschach equally in Switzerland and in Russia, and he turned his occasional newspaper writing in a more political direction, with articles railing against Western procommunist naïveté. He vented still more openly in his letters: "Have you read or heard about the pamphlet by Gorky where he condemns both Tolstoy and Dostoyevsky for their petit-bourgeois message that the people should 'merely suffer'? Have you ever seen such a fetid swamp! At least Judas Iscariot went off and hanged himself. I wonder what dreams Gorky has at night!"

As always, he directed his sharpest attention to questions of perception:

> I'm only just beginning to see how it's possible to get so many contradictory eyewitness reports out of Russia. . . . The main thing is that it makes a huge difference whether an observer is seeing Russia for the first time or knew it in earlier days, and then also whether he knows anyone who can describe earlier Russia or only sees the amorphous mass of the people, who are actually not a people, just a mass. . . . Whoever arrives in Russia for the first time now and didn't know it before simply won't *see* anything.

The emphasis on the key term is Rorschach's. A few months later: "What do you think of these communist parties springing up everywhere? Is there something here that I'm blind to, or are they the blind ones? As much as I try to use psychology and history to approach the question, I can't answer it."

The Rorschachs' financial situation was worse during the war, too. They continued to send whatever they could to the relatives in Russia, including such basics as soap; on one occasion, their gift to a loved one in Herisau was a candle. "At least we have always gotten enough coal during these years," he wrote to Paul in 1919, "and this year it shouldn't be any worse. Hopefully when you visit, you won't have to freeze with us. In any case, we froze more during our winters in Schaffhausen."

As at other times, Rorschach made the best of his financial troubles. He didn't care about clothes or drink alcohol; his only vice was cigarettes. Without money for a personal library, or support from Koller, he borrowed most of his books and journals, taking his extensive notes and making his endless excerpts. He transcribed furniture, too: when he had to go to Zurich on business, he would go into the city, spend a long time looking closely at the furniture and toy shops, then go back to Herisau and re-create what he had seen. "I am constantly in the woodworking shop, so that we get at least something new coming into the house," he wrote to Paul. "I'll soon graduate to more impressive looking things," such as bookshelves, but for now he was building "a whole set for the little one: a table, three chairs, and a wash table built, painted in farmhouse style."

For Rorschach was now a father. His great joy in Herisau was the birth of his two children, Elisabeth (Lisa) on June 18, 1917, and Ulrich Wadim (the German spelling of "Vadim") on May 1, 1919: "one genuine Swiss name and one genuine Russian name," he told Paul, "for various reasons that you can easily imagine." The boy was called Wadim, but he would hopefully not turn out too Russian: since his birthday, May 1, was the Russian Revolution's holiday, Hermann joked to his brother, "I hope he won't become too much of a rabid Bolshevik, though we do have to realize that our children will someday think of world struggles from completely different points of view than ours."

Anna made it out of Russia in August 1918 and married soon afterward; Hermann would see Paul again in 1920, on a visit from Brazil where he had escaped the war and become a successful coffee merchant. Paul was married, too, and brought his new wife, a Frenchwoman named Reine Simonne, on his visit to Herisau. Hermann found it deeply rewarding to see his siblings settled with partners they loved.

As in the Münsterlingen years, Hermann and Lola visited Arbon when they could and Schaffhausen when they had to. Regineli continued to live with her mother in Schaffhausen, but Hermann invited her to Herisau for extended stays. She later remembered Hermann reading to her a lot at Herisau; it was at the foot of the Säntis, on a trip with her brother, that she once heard the sound of a church bell ringing through the clear air—her first great experience, she said decades later, the only time in her life she felt in contact with the infinite, the eternal.

Rorschach's study became the children's playroom, when he was not seeing patients in it or writing. His cousin remembered him as an "excellent father" who "helped a great deal with the children's upbringing, almost more than their mother." He lavished on Lisa and Wadim the physical things he so rarely gave himself, making them all sorts of toys, pictures, and picture books; Lisa remembered one little drawing of a fruit she had thought was so real that she licked it until it blurred. For Christmas one year, his plans included carving "4 hens, 1 rooster, 5 chicks, turkey and turkey hen, peacock, 4 geese, 4 ducks, 1 shed, and 2 girls" for Lisa. Art not just for but of his children: "I'm hoping to send you some drawings of Lisa," he wrote to Paul. "I'm producing a whole biography of her in pictures!" (See Color Plate 5.)

BUT NOT ALL was well in the family. The Kollers lived right downstairs with three boys, and the youngest, Rudi, only four years older than Lisa, remembered the Rorschachs' marriage as "very, very explosive." Sophie Koller, the director's wife and a good friend of Hermann's, heard loud fights upstairs and was afraid of Olga. She thought Hermann was afraid of Olga too. Hermann's staying up to work, typing late into the night, would lead to repeated arguments: "There he goes clattering away again," Olga would rage. Regineli witnessed fights, tears, accusations, fits—one day, not long after Lisa was born, he got home late and Olga lost her temper. "It was terrible." During fights, Olga was known to throw plates, cups, and coffeepots, to the point where the Rorschachs' kitchen wall was permanently mottled with coffee stains.

These outside impressions of Olga, negative though they are, reveal more than her own later reminiscences, which consistently idealized her marriage. What others recalled was a tempestuous, impulsive, voluptuous, dominating woman, and that was what Hermann loved about her. Descriptions of Olga as a "half-Asiatic" Russian—"Scratch a Russian and you'll find a barbarian," a common catchphrase, was applied to Olga—only show that the Swiss were largely unable to respect the outsider Hermann had married and loved. As a doctor stuck in Herisau without permission to practice, she must have felt far more isolated than he did. And for all her supposed stubbornness, the pair did end up back in Switzerland; their children were baptized Protestant, not Russian Orthodox as she had wanted.

If Hermann felt it was a bad marriage, he never let it show. He always spoke well of Olga to Regineli, for example, and tried to explain

Olga's behavior, much as he had his stepmother's. He loved Olga for drawing him out of his shell, for "giving him children," for the life he felt he lived fully through her. The wallflower from Schaffhausen and event planner in Münsterlingen and Herisau almost never danced, even at parties where Olga in her black dress danced close with one patient after another. After fights, Hermann and Olga would ostentatiously walk arm in arm through the asylum.

Their arguments about Hermann's working hours must have had two sides too. He did work an enormous amount, which Olga saw as "Western" ambition, antisocial and misguided; one of their maids later said she felt Hermann did things for the children, such as making them toys and presents, more often than with them.

At times, Rorschach found his job at the asylum satisfying. On a boat ride with family, after some years at Herisau, he said he felt that he meant something to his patients—he was not just a doctor but a real emotional and spiritual help for them, and that was rewarding. He and Olga gave slide-show lectures about Russia on winter evenings, and along with other personal development opportunities for the staff (sewing and embroidery classes for the female attendants, woodworking for the men), Rorschach pioneered medical training courses for the nursing personnel, with "Lessons on the Nature and Treatment of Mental Illness" in 1916. Nothing of the kind had ever taken place in a Swiss clinic.

He was active again staging plays, for which he designed and built props, most notably some forty-five puppets for a Carnival shadow-play in February 1920. These whimsical creations—about ten to twenty inches tall, made of gray hinged cardboard—depicted the doctors, staff, and patients, including Rorschach himself. They were a hit with everyone in the audience, according to Rorschach's diary, and they showed his ability to see and capture movement: "He could instantly cut out a cardboard silhouette and give it moving joints that enabled an astonishing reproduction of the figure's characteristic movement, such as that of someone playing the violin" or doffing his baroque hat, a friend recalled. Still, having seen the Moscow theater and worked with some of the century's greatest actors in Kryukovo, Rorschach knew full well that the asylum productions hardly measured up. Unlike in Münsterlingen, most of the patients at Herisau were too incapacitated even to watch the performances, much less take part. In a letter to a friend, he wrote: "My wife would like to see what a real theater looks like again—she has almost entirely forgotten."

Rorschach tried to put a positive face on his overtime duties, but he increasingly resented their demands on his time and the little artistic satisfaction they gave. As early as September one year, he would write: "My extra winter work is starting up again soon: theater, etc., not exactly fun. I will have to go to the woodworking shop to make up for it"; "As the years go by, it gets a bit tiresome."

The Rorschachs could not take vacations, because of money and work demands. Not until 1920 would he and Olga and the children enjoy their first real family holiday, at Risch on the Lake of Zug. "It's very good for us," Hermann wrote: "I drew a lot during the vacation, so at least Lisa will be able to remember the experience better." Otherwise Hermann took hikes around the Säntis for a few days or traveled on business to give lectures in Zurich and elsewhere. One of these trips proved fateful.

Hinged cardboard shadow figures
made for Krombach Carnival:
back showing construction; asylum
administrator with account book,
patient carrying buckets, night
watchman with signal horn.
Two drawings: girls playing.

↭

IN MID-1917, WHILE visiting the University Clinic in Zurich, Rorschach met a twenty-five-year-old Polish medical student named Szymon Hens for around fifteen minutes; they met briefly once more, later that year. Eugen Bleuler was Hens's adviser, too, and had given him thirty dissertation topics to choose from. Hens had picked inkblots.

Hens used eight crude black blots to measure his subjects' imagination—how much they had or how little. Although he did connect certain responses to the subject's background or individual personality, he did so superficially, purely by content: a hairdresser saw "*a woman's head, wearing a wig*," an eleven-year-old tailor's son saw "*a tailor's dummy for fitting vests*," and this showed that jobs or parents' jobs "had a strong influence on the imagination." Mostly Hens just counted the number of answers, which the subjects had to write out themselves (twenty blots, one-hour time limit). There was not much more he could do, since he was testing a thousand schoolchildren, a hundred normal adults, and a hundred mental patients in the Burghölzli—an enormous undertaking. Hens later said that "his girlfriends" had helped him collect the results. While his dissertation ended with some suggestive ideas for future research, his own conclusions were very limited, for instance: "The mentally ill do not interpret the blots differently from healthy subjects in such a way as to permit diagnosis (at least at this time)."

Rorschach had been in Herisau for two years, with his hard-to-treat patients worn smooth as pebbles. His article on Johannes Neuwirth, the deserter he had analyzed in 1914, was published in August 1917, with its clear implication that an ideal test would somehow combine and supersede the word association test, Freudian free association, and hypnosis. Hens's dissertation, *A Test of Imagination on Schoolchildren, Normal Adults, and the Mentally Ill Using Formless Blots*, was published in December 1917, though Rorschach surely saw the text or heard about the experiment earlier, through Bleuler or from Hens himself. Everything came together.

10

A Very Simple Experiment

RORSCHACH REALIZED HOW MUCH DEEPER AN INKBLOT EXPERI-
ment could go, but the first thing he needed was better images. He
knew that there were some pictures you could feel your way into, that
produced psychological and even physical reactions in the viewer, and
others that didn't. He started to make dozens, probably hundreds, of
inkblots of his own, trying the good ones out on everyone he could find.

Even Rorschach's first efforts at Herisau were more accomplished
than they might seem, with relatively complex compositions and an
Art Nouveau–ish sense of design. Successive drafts (see Color Plates 2
and 3) then simplified and clarified the blots, at the same time making them increasingly hard to pin down. The images hovered between
meaninglessness and meaning, right on the borderline between all too
obvious and not obvious enough.

The comparison with Hens's and Kerner's blots makes the quality of Rorschach's easier to see. Trying to interpret one of Hens's blots
feels forced: Well, you *could* say it looks like an owl, but it doesn't *really* . . . Hens himself wrote, on his dissertation's first page: "The normal subject knows as well as the experimenter that the blot can have
no claim to be anything but a blot, and that the requested answers can
only depend on vague analogies and more or less imaginative 'interpretations' of the images." A Rorschach blot, though, really *might* be two
waiters pouring out pots of soup, with a bowtie in the middle. You can
feel answers coming at you from the image. There's something there.

At the other extreme, Justinus Kerner's klexography is unambigu-
ous. He even added captions. Compared to his blots, Rorschach's are
suggestive—some more so, others less—and richly open to interpretation. They have unclear foreground/background relationships, poten-

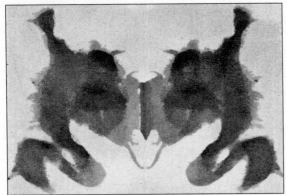

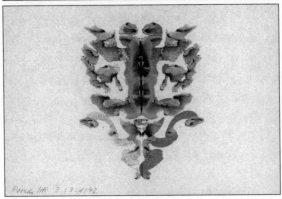

Top: Plate 8 from Szymon Hens's dissertation. *Bottom:* Rorschach, early inkblot, no date and possibly not used in any test or experiment.

tially meaningful white spaces, questionable coherence so that a viewer has to integrate the image into a whole (or not); they can be seen as human or inhuman, animal or nonanimal, skeletal or nonskeletal, organic or inorganic. They have a mystery about them as they strain at the edge of the intelligible.

While crafting the blots, Rorschach worked to eliminate any sign of craftsmanship and artistry. The blots had to not look "made" at all; their impersonality was crucial to how they worked. In his early drafts, it was still obvious where Rorschach had used a brush, how thick the brush was, and so on, but soon he had shapes that seemed to have made themselves. His images were clearly symmetrical, but too detailed to be mere folded smears. The colors added to the mystery: how did *they* get into an inkblot? Rorschach's images increasingly looked unlike anything seen before, in life or art. After "spending a long time using images that were more complicated and structured, more pleasing and aesthetically refined," he later wrote, "I dropped them" in the interest of producing better, more revealing results.

It was especially important that they not seem like a puzzle, a test, because Rorschach's paranoid patients had hair-trigger reactions to any hint of ulterior motives. There couldn't be names or numbers on an image, since patients would pay too much attention to what they might mean, ignoring the picture itself. The cards couldn't have a border, because in Switzerland that was likely to remind a schizophrenic of a black-edged death notice. Rorschach knew from Münsterlingen how to get around patients' suspicions; a great advantage of the inkblot method, he realized early on, was that it could be "conducted either like a game or like an experiment, without affecting the results. Often, even unresponsive schizophrenics unwilling to undergo any other experiment will willingly perform this task." It was fun! Rorschach did not originally conceive of the blots as a "test" at all: he called it an *experiment,* a nonjudgmental and open-ended investigation into people's ways of seeing.

The choice to make the blots symmetrical might seem inevitable, but it was one of Rorschach's crucial decisions or intuitions, with all-important consequences. Earlier inkblots in psychology didn't have to be symmetrical: Alfred Binet's were merely "strange-shaped blots of ink on a white sheet of paper"; only two of Whipple's fifteen blots were symmetrical, only two of Rybakov's eight. But Rorschach's blots were, and he laid out arguments for why: "The symmetry of the images has the disadvantage that people see disproportionately many butterflies etc., but the advantages far outweigh the disadvantages. Symmetry makes the form more pleasing to the eye and thus makes the subject more willing to perform the task. The image is equally suitable for right-handed and left-handed subjects. It also encourages the seeing of whole scenes."

Rorschach could have chosen to use vertical symmetry across a horizontal center line, evoking a landscape with horizon or a reflective pool, or even symmetry across a diagonal. Instead he used horizontal or bilateral symmetry. Perhaps he remembered from Haeckel's *Art Forms in Nature* that this is what seems organic and natural, or recalled from Vischer's essay on empathy that "horizontal symmetry always presents a better effect than vertical symmetry because of its analogy with our body." Whether consciously or intuitively, he worked with the symmetry of everything we care about most: other people, their faces, ourselves. Bilateral symmetry creates images we react to emotionally, psychologically.

Another pivotal choice was to use red. Like any painter, Rorschach knew that red and other warm colors come at the viewer while blue and cool colors recede: in the inkblots, red would confront the test taker more aggressively than any other color, demanding that we react, or suppress a reaction. Red appears brighter to the human eye than other colors at the same saturation—the Helmholtz-Kohlrausch effect; it also looks more saturated than other colors at the same brightness. It interacts with the light/dark dichotomy better than any other color, looking dark in contrast to white, and light in contrast to black. (Anthropologists would discover in 1969 that some languages have only two color terms—for black and white—but that any language with a third term uses red: red is color as such.) Earlier inkblots in psychology had not used color at all, but Rorschach used the color with the most color, just as bilateral symmetry is the most meaningful kind of symmetry.

Rorschach's most definitive break with his predecessors was to stop using inkblots to measure the imagination. When Rorschach read on the first page of Hens's dissertation that seeing things in a formless inkblot "requires what we call 'imagination,'" that "the blot can have no claim to be anything but a blot" without "more or less imaginative 'interpretations' of the images," his whole life had prepared him to say: No. A blot is not just a blot, at least not if it's any good. Pictures have real meaning. The image itself constrains how you see it—as on rails—but without taking away all your freedom: different people see differently, and the differences are revealing. Rorschach had learned that from his friends at the Zurich art museum, from all his efforts to read people as a doctor and as a human being.

The most obvious problem with measuring a subject's imagination by counting answers—though it hadn't been obvious to Hens, or to Alfred Binet and his successors—was that some answers are imaginative and others are not. An answer could be perceptive, seeing something really there in the image; it could be crazy, but that's not the same as imaginative. Delusions seem real to the person who has them. No one looked at a blot and tried to see something that wasn't there, Rorschach realized; they tried "to come up with an answer that gets as close to the truth of the picture as they can. This goes for the imaginative person exactly as much as for anyone else." He found that whether or not he told a subject to "use your imagination" made no difference. A schizophrenic who was originally imaginative "would, of course, produce different, richer, more colorful delusions than a patient who was originally unimaginative," but when a psychotic took his delusions for reality, this "probably [had] nothing whatsoever to do with the function of imagination."

Two responses to his inkblots that Rorschach heard early on proved the point. In what would be Card VIII of the final test (see Color Plate 1), one thirty-six-year-old woman saw "*A fairy-tale motif: a treasure in two blue treasure chests buried under the roots of a tree, with a fire underneath, and two mythical animals guarding it.*" A man saw "*Two bears, and the whole thing is round, so it's the bear pit in Bern.*"

The imaginative person had integrated the shapes and colors into a complete picture; her answer was playful, spoken with delight. The second answer, in contrast, was what Rorschach called "confabulation": latching onto part of the image and overriding or disregarding the rest. The man saw the round shape as a bear pit not because bears were inside it—the bear shapes are actually around the edge of the card—but because his thoughts had gotten stuck on bears and everything now had to be about bears. He could no longer see the round shape in context, or connect it to anything else in the picture. (A more recent example of confabulation is seeing Card V [see page 145] as "*Barack Obama with George Bush on his back*" because "*It's a clash of two forces, and the whole picture may look like an eagle, the eagle being the symbol of the country.*" The symbolism of the eagle doesn't actually mean eagle parts look like presidents.) Rorschach described the tone of a confabulated answer as one not of creative play but of conquering a problem, and its logic is strangely literalistic, despite not really making sense. The woman's fairy-tale associations were literary and creative, her answer imaginative, but at the same time her perception was much more coherent and clearly grounded in the image than the confabulator's.

In short, one more thing found in a blot should not simply count as one more point on a person's imagination score. What mattered was *how* people saw what they saw—how they took in visual information, and how they understood it, interpreted it, felt about it. What they could do with it. How it set them dreaming.

In his dissertation, Rorschach had concentrated on the mechanics of perception in a relatively narrow physiological sense, exploring crossovers between pathways of seeing or hearing and bodily sensation. But perception included much more, all the way to interpreting what was perceived. *Interpretations of chance images are a kind of perception*—the italics are Rorschach's.

As HE WAS designing and creating the inkblots, Rorschach also had to figure out what he was designing his experiment to do. He wanted to study perception in the widest sense, but what did that mean he should ask people? And what should he pay attention to in their answers?

In keeping with his emphasis on perception over imagination, he asked people not what they *found*, or *imagined*, or *could* see, but what they *did* see. His question was: "What is this?" or "What might this be?" With images as suggestive as his, there were things that they actually might be.

People's answers started to reveal more than Rorschach had thought possible: higher or lower intelligence, character and personality, thought disorders and other psychological problems. The inkblots let him distinguish between certain kinds of mental illness that were hard to differentiate in other ways. What had started as an *experiment* looked to be, in fact, a *test*.

He would always insist he had invented the test "empirically," simply stumbling upon the fact that different kinds of patients, and nonpatients with different kinds of personality, tended to respond in certain ways. Of course he couldn't discover what a given type of response meant until he had started to notice it as distinctive in the first place. Once he got going, he must have suspected in advance at least some of the connections he would go on to find. But his talent was to notice a pattern, then pay attention to it, consider borderline cases, perhaps make new blots to bring out its distinguishing features, then try it all again.

The full-fledged test came to life in a matter of months. There are no surviving notes or dated drafts, no letters from Rorschach to anyone between early 1917 and summer 1918, so it will never be known exactly what the intermediate stages were. In his first surviving letter from 1918, on August 5, Rorschach told a colleague that he'd had "an experiment with 'klexography' in hand for a long time now. . . . Bleuler knows about it." That same month, he wrote up the experiment, describing the final ten inkblots in their final sequence with the testing process and basic scheme of interpreting results in place. This essay, which he hoped to publish in a journal, was twenty-six typewritten pages long, plus twenty-eight sample test results. He would later expand on this framework but would never change it.

Rorschach had decided that there were four important aspects of people's responses. First, he noted the total number of answers given in the test as a whole and whether the subject "rejected" any cards, refusing to answer at all. These were rough measures. He found that normal subjects never rejected cards—"At most neurotics blocked by specific complexes will reject one." The number of answers could imply a basic ability or inability to perform the task, or could suggest mania (lots of answers) or depression (few), but it revealed little about *how* a person was seeing the cards.

Second, Rorschach noted down for each response whether it described the whole inkblot or homed in on a part. Calling Card V *a bat* was a Whole response (W); seeing *bears* on either side of Card VIII, or *a woman raising her arms* in the central part of Card I, was a Detail response (D). Seeing something in a tiny detail almost never noticed or interpreted, such as saying that the outermost top corners on Card I were *apples*, was different: a Small Detail response (Dd). The rare but telling case of interpreting the white space on a card got its own code. Rorschach paid attention to rhythms of W, D, and Dd as the subject's characteristic approach or "way of grasping things": whether they tended to move from whole to part, from part to whole, or get stuck in one or the other.

Third, Rorschach categorized each answer according to what formal property of the image it was based on. Most answers, naturally, were based on shapes: seeing a bat in a blot that's bat-shaped, a bear in a part of a blot that's bear-shaped. He called these Form responses (F).

Other answers were about the color: a blue square seen as *a forget-me-not*, a red shape as *alpenglow*. To call a blue area "*the sky*" would be a

Color response, even without explicitly saying *"the blue sky,"* because such an answer was based on the color in the blot, not the shape. Such pure Color responses (C), with the shape playing no role at all, were rare among normal test takers. Still more abnormal was to detach color from form altogether, saying about a red patch, *"That's red."* More common were Color-Form responses (CF), based primarily on color but taking the shape into account somewhat (a gray blot as *"a rock,"* even if the shape was not especially bouldery, or a splash of red as *"blood"*), or Form-Color responses (FC), mainly based on shape but with color playing a secondary role (*"a purple spider,"* or *"a blue flag"* for a blue rectangular shape).

Answers that described shapes moving in the cards, such as *"bears dancing"* instead of just bears, or *"two elephants kissing,"* or *"two waiters bowing to each other,"* were Movement responses (M). This was the least obvious of Rorschach's categories—why should it make a difference whether the bears were dancing or not? But Rorschach's dissertation had been all about the interplay between seeing and feeling the movement in the world. His specialty as an artist was in perceiving and capturing movement, from his hinged shadow-puppets to his sketches of gestures in patient files. In the 1918 version of the test, Rorschach wrote that he usually saw people move or start to move when they gave a Movement response, for instance bending forward slightly as they saw the *two waiters bowing.* At this stage, he thought of the Movement response as essentially a reflex hallucination.

Almost every response to an inkblot was based on Form, Color, and/or Movement, although Rorschach did occasionally encounter an abstract answer that was none of the above, such as *"I see an evil force."*

Finally, Rorschach paid attention to the content of the answers—*what* people saw in the cards. "Anything you can imagine, of course," as Rorschach put it, "and, with schizophrenics, quite a lot you can't."

He was as fascinated and delighted as anyone else by the unexpected, creative, sometimes bizarre answers given by both patients and nonpatient test takers. But what he mainly focused on was whether an answer was "Good" or "Poor"—whether it could reasonably be said to describe the actual shape in the blot. He paid attention to *what* people saw primarily as a way of evaluating *how well* they saw. A Form response would be marked as F+ for a well-seen form, F– for the opposite, F for the unexceptionable.

And right at the start, in his August 1918 manuscript, this raised a question that would continue to dog the Rorschach: Who decides what's reasonable? "Of course there need to be many tests of normal subjects with various kinds of intelligence, in order to avoid any personal arbitrariness in judging whether an F answer is good or bad. One will then have to classify many answers as objectively good that one would not subjectively call good." Having just invented the test, Rorschach had no data that would let him objectively distinguish between good and bad—no set of norms. Establishing a quantitative baseline for which answers were common among normal test takers and which were unusual or unique would be one of his first goals, because someone's percentage of well-seen or badly seen forms (F+% and F−%) was a crucial measure of their cognitive functioning.

There were only a few content categories that Rorschach found significant in their own right, such as seeing Human figures, Animals, or Anatomy (noted down as H, A, Anat.). It mattered if a person got stuck on a certain kind of answer or had a wide range. In general, though, the content was secondary. Rorschach paid attention mostly to the formal aspects of the blots that produced the response: Detail and Whole; Movement, Color, and Form.

The written record of a subject's Rorschach test, known as a "protocol," listed every answer the person gave and assigned it codes. As answers to Card VIII, for example, *"Two polar bears"* would be coded as a well-seen Animal Form response about a commonly interpreted Detail, namely the red figures on the side, with the color irrelevant (D F+ A). *"The flames of Purgatory and two devils coming out"* would be a Movement response about a Detail (DM). *"A carpet"* would be the Whole as a poorly seen Form, since the blot doesn't really look like a carpet (W F−). *"The resurrection of the colossal coloric red and brownish and blue head vein tumors,"* an answer Rorschach heard from one overexcited forty-year-old schizophrenic patient at Herisau suffering from serious unsystematic delusions, was a Whole Color response (WC), with, needless to say, other issues.

After coding the answers, Rorschach would calculate a few basic scores, such as how many F's, C's, and M's there were, the percentage of poor answers (F− %), the percentage of animal answers (A%). That's it. The test results were these dozen or so letters and numbers.

Rorschach invented other visual tests in 1917–18 and used them to supplement or confirm his findings, but he gradually abandoned them as unnecessary as his expertise with the test grew.

Color (see Color Plate 4): A frog-colored cat—or cat-shaped frog—and a rooster/squirrel, to test whether shape or color plays a stronger role in a subject's perception. Epileptics, especially with dementia, saw frog and rooster, confirming the emphasis on color revealed in the inkblot test.

Movement: Rorschach copied, without ax or setting, Ferdinand Hodler's image of a woodcutter, which had been on fifty-franc banknotes since 1911 and was universally known in Switzerland. He then held it up to a window and traced the picture in reverse. He showed people both images and asked: "What is the man doing?" and "Which of the two do you feel is drawn correctly?" People who had given many Movement responses had no difficulty with the first question and could not answer the second, apparently able to feel into each image equally well. Those who gave few or no M responses answered both questions easily. Hodler's image shows a left-handed woodsman, like the image above right, but normal right-handed people said it matched them because they felt-into the action as a mirror image of their own (vice versa for the left-handed).

Form: According to Rorschach, a schizophrenic might call the Australia blot below "*Africa, but not the right shape*," because the blot is black and black people come from Africa. He also made a blot of Italy that schizophrenics called "*Russia*" [in German, <u>*Russland*</u>] because it was lampblack [*Lampen<u>russ</u>*].

In his 1918 essay outlining the test, Rorschach described typical results for dozens of different subvarieties of mental illness, always careful to state when he lacked a sufficient number of cases in Herisau to generalize safely. He insisted that these typical profiles, while they might seem arbitrary, had emerged in practice. A manic-depressive in a depressive phase, he wrote, will give no Movement responses or Color responses, will see no Human figures, and will tend to start with Small Details before moving to the Whole (the reverse of the normal pattern), giving few Whole responses overall. People with schizophrenic depression, on the other hand, will reject more cards, will occasionally give Color answers, will very often give Movement answers, and will see a much smaller percentage of Animals and significantly more poor forms (F–% = 30–40). Why? Rorschach refused to speculate, but pointed out that this differential diagnosis—being able to tell the difference between manic-depressive and schizophrenic depression, "in most cases with certainty"—was a real medical breakthrough.

Especially with findings of psychosis, the test results could be compelling enough to override what he had before his eyes. When someone with no psychotic symptoms produced typically psychotic results, Rorschach dug deeper and often found they had psychotic heredity, had sufferers in the immediate family, or had recently shown symptoms. Sometimes they had been in remission for years. Even if not, he might diagnose latent schizophrenia. Rorschach thought in general that the inkblots revealed quality, not quantity—the kind of psychology a person had, not the degree to which these tendencies were expressed. The test could detect a schizophrenic disposition irrespective of whether symptoms were strong, weak, or even nonexistent. Before long, he was grappling with the ethical issue of how to tell a subject that his or her test showed latent schizophrenia or psychosis—an invisible mental illness, perhaps totally unsuspected. But the payoff was worth it: "Maybe we'll soon reach the point where we can judge whether latent schizophrenia exists or not in every case. Just think how much of the fear of insanity that embitters people's lives we'll be able to free the world from if that happens!"

At no point did Rorschach try to use a single response to impose a psychological profile. He found, for example, that certain kinds of answers were given almost exclusively by either schizophrenics or people talented at drawing, but he was not tempted to conclude that drafts-manship must be correlated with, or similar to, the illness. "Naturally," he wrote, answers that seem similar "will be qualitatively very different" when coming from different kinds of people.

From the beginning, the inkblot experiment was multidimensional: it called upon, and thus tested, many different abilities and capacities at the same time. This meant, reassuringly, that the test was largely self-correcting. Rorschach found that if you retested a schizophrenic over time, there would be "very different interpretations of the cards, but the F– %, the number of Movement, Form, and Color responses, W and Dd, and so on, would remain more or less the same—assuming of course that the patient's condition has not significantly changed." With ten cards, and room for multiple answers on each card, an especially creative or bizarre answer or two was unlikely to change the overall record. One mustachioed ballet-dancing snake on the moon didn't mean you were crazy.

The scores worked together to give a picture of the subject's psychology. A lot of unusual or bizarre answers (F–) might be a sign of high intelligence and great creativity or might imply serious defects and an inability to see what everyone else sees. But the test as a whole could distinguish between the two. The first kind of person would tend to have a high number of Whole responses, Movement responses, and well-seen forms (W, M, F+), the second kind of person a low number of all three.

Similarly, Whole responses could be a good sign or a bad sign. Rorschach found one "intelligent highly educated man in a good mood" who pulled off a creative integration of every inkblot: a protocol of all well-seen Whole answers (WF+), twelve in total. Card II was "*dancing squirrels on a tree stump,*" Card VIII "*a fantastic chandelier.*" That meant something very different from the all-Whole protocol of another test taker, a twenty-five-year-old apathetic disorganized schizophrenic who gave one response per card, most of them F– (*Butterfly. Butterfly. Carpet. Animal carpet. Same thing. Carpet . . .*).

Such interactions between different kinds of response were why administering the test was not easy. There was never any simple decoder for what a given answer meant. Worse still, Rorschach could offer no explanation for why the test worked at all. He had derived his correlations as empirically or instinctively as he had made his inkblots, building on no preexisting theory of what Movement and Color meant, or why to pay attention to them in the first place. His interpretations of any single protocol were holistic and often seemed idiosyncratic. All of this was either the test's weakness or its strength: what made it subjective and arbitrary, or rich and multifaceted.

When Rorschach pitched a book publisher, he put it this way: "It concerns a very simple experiment, which—not to mention for the moment its theoretical ramifications—has a very wide range of applications. It permits not only the individual diagnosis of psychological illness profiles but also a differential diagnosis: whether someone is neurotic or psychotic or healthy. With healthy individuals, it gives very far-reaching information about the person's character and personality; with the mentally ill, the results let us see their former character, which is mostly still there behind a psychosis." It was also a new kind of intelligence test, in which "someone's level of education, or good or bad memory, never conceals their true level of intelligence." The inkblots "permitted conclusions not about a person's 'overall intelligence' but about the numerous individual psychological components which constitute the person's various intelligences, predispositions, and talents. Especially in this regard, the theoretical advance is not insignificant."

"I believe I may safely say that the experiment will arouse interest," he concluded with a touch of false modesty. "I would like to inquire if you might be inclined to publish it."

11

It Provokes Interest and Head-Shaking Everywhere

On Sunday, October 26, 1919, a lively young woman named Greti Brauchli came to visit Hermann, Olga, and the children in Herisau. She was the daughter of Ulrich Brauchli, Rorschach's former boss, and Rorschach had tried his earlier inkblots out on her in Münsterlingen back in 1911 and 1912 when she was a teenager. Now she was in her midtwenties, engaged to be married, too leftist for her father's taste. The inkblot experiment, too, had come into its own.

Rorschach had visited the Brauchlis in Münsingen earlier that October and showed Ulrich the test. "He understood it!" Rorschach noted with delight afterward: Ulrich Brauchli was one of the first people "who truly understood the experiment and had something to say about it." When Greti arrived in Herisau, Rorschach was preparing to present his experiment to a professional audience in a lecture to the Swiss Psychiatry Association in Freiburg, Germany. He arranged to meet Greti at the museum in St. Gallen, on October 29, to try the blots out on her. It was not often that he found such thoughtful subjects for his experiment.

He quickly interpreted her test and mailed her the results, and Greti was stunned. "Thank you for your report! I'm not surprised, but I am amazed to see how right you were about everything, at least as far as I can tell (we all know how often psychological self-descriptions are wrong)." She was especially struck at his discovering sides of her "that very few people know—how did you do it?" And she was full of questions, about her results and also the deeper mysteries: "Do you think psychological facts are inalterable givens that people simply have to work with their whole lives and accept for what they are? Does a person stay the same, psychologically speaking, or is it possible to change and develop through self-knowledge and will? It seems to me that we have to be able to, otherwise the person is a dead thing, a fixed fact, not a living creating being."

Rorschach wrote a warm reply explaining how he had reached his conclusions. Greti's attention to Small Details had revealed the tendency to pedantry she usually kept so well hidden; her many Movement responses showed a rich imagination she didn't know she had; the feelings of "emptiness and aridity" that she had told him about in her letter were probably a side effect of her suppressing this imagination, rather than being due to depression. She had asked what the difference was between what he had called her "easy affective adaptation" and her "strong empathetic ability," and he explained that conforming to others' emotions is not the same as empathy in the strong sense, the capacity to enter into and share others' experience: "Those with intellectual disabilities can adapt their feelings to others' too, even animals can, but only an intelligent person with an inner life of their own has empathy. . . . Under certain circumstances, it can escalate almost to a feeling of identity with the person you're empathizing with or whatever you're feeling your way into, for example with good actors who learn a great deal from others." As usual, he found the ability to feel at its best in women: "Emotional adaptability plus the capacity for empathy is a primarily feminine attribute. The combination results in an empathy charged with feeling." An even richer combination is "if the adapting psyche is capable of introversion, too—then it will be a sounding board that resonates much more strongly with everything that happens." Greti had it all.

To Greti's big question, he answered that psychological states are not permanent. "Probably the only thing impossible to change by working on oneself is how one's introversion and extraversion relate to each other, although the relationship does shift over the course of one's life because of a kind of maturation process. That process doesn't end at age twenty but continues, especially between thirty and thirty-five and again at around fifty." This was days before his own thirty-fifth birthday.

He also realized that Greti's questions were more than theoretical: her fiancé needed help. Rorschach had met him in Münsingen on November 2, on his way back from the conference, noting in his diary:

"Pastor Burri, Greti's bridegroom: unassuming, quiet, slow, but intelligent and lively for all his slowness." Now that Rorschach had told Greti people could change, she encouraged her future husband to see him for psychoanalysis. And after two nervous letters, Hans Burri, or as Rorschach liked to call him in private "my compulsive neurotic clergyman," started therapy.

Rorschach soothed Burri's fears of being "influenced" or "manipulated" in therapy by saying that that was not how it worked: "An analysis must never be a direct manipulation, and any indirect manipulation comes from the patient's own soul. Thus you are not actually being influenced, but unfolding your destiny." Worried at first about the conflict between psychoanalysis and his religious beliefs, Burri came to feel that Rorschach respected his views, and others' views as well: even when they discussed the Binggeli and Unternährer sects, Burri noted that Rorschach was never dismissive or sarcastic.

In his role as a therapist, Rorschach was nonthreatening and sympathetic. But he refused to discuss much with Burri in writing: actual therapy, unlike sharing insights with Greti, had to take place in person. He told Burri to start writing down his dreams, drawing on the insights of his dissertation to tell him how: "Here is a technique you may find useful for retaining and remembering your dreams: When you wake up, stay lying completely still and go over the dream in your mind. Only then write it down immediately. Kinesthesias are most likely the carriers of our dreams, and these are instantly thwarted by actual innervations as soon as we physically move." Rorschach's methods were not classically Freudian—the sessions were sometimes five times a week, but not always; he often spoke and interrupted, rather than sitting silent and impassive; after each session the pastor would stay for coffee or tea and a chat, joined by Olga, whom Greti thanked by mail for her hospitality. But the basic principles were Freudian. The difference was the new tool Rorschach had at his disposal.

Once Burri started traveling to Herisau for therapy, in January, Rorschach gave him an inkblot test. Burri's seventy-one responses—an enormous number—pinpointed the many problems he was suffering from: excessive self-monitoring, inability to show emotion, pedantic thoroughness, constant brooding, compulsive fantasies, tormenting doubts, a grumbling inability to finish anything, lack of warmth in his approach to life. . . . After five months, Burri took the inkblot test again, and the results showed how much he had "changed in the course of the analysis; his 'reflexive spasm' of consciously, compulsively monitoring every thought and experience has disappeared." Burri was more adaptable; his "emotional approach and rapport were steadier"; his access to his inner life was "more free and more powerful," with more original answers and more than twice as many Movement responses as before. While Burri's "kind of intelligence had changed the least," as Rorschach had reassured him it wouldn't, his compulsive suppression of inner impulses "had changed quite completely."

Greti's question had been answered in the real world—people can change, can heal—and Rorschach ended treatment, having achieved near-miraculous results that Burri and Greti would always be grateful for. Greti wrote him: "Thank you for everything. Your treatment of him was such a success, it was the best thing for him, and you can imagine how happy that makes me!" Four months later, the Burris invited the Rorschachs to their wedding.

While Rorschach was using the inkblots in the service of psychoanalysis, his therapeutic practice—and intelligent questioning from test takers like the Burris—also deepened his understanding of the test. "I have learned a lot from you," Rorschach wrote to Hans Burri when sharing the results of his second test. His advice to Burri about how to remember dreams would eventually go into his book on the experiment nearly word for word. This was possible because he had not yet been able to publish it.

By February of 1920, when he wrote his pitch about the "very simple experiment," Rorschach had been trying to publish the test for a year and a half. This pitch was not his first, nor would it be his last. There would be another year and half of delays before the test would appear in print.

The main problem was the images. And, as always, money. It was going to be expensive to print the inkblots, especially the ones in color. In Rorschach's first submission of the 1918 version to a journal, he suggested printing only one color blot and several black-and-white blots, perhaps greatly reduced in size. The editor was a longtime supporter and friend of Rorschach's, but he suggested Rorschach pay for it himself; that was impossible. Then he gave Rorschach the name of a foundation that might help fund the publication, but nothing came of that either. As publishers continued to balk, Rorschach suggested reducing the size by up to one-sixth, or printing all the blots small on a single sheet, or replacing the colors with different cross-hatching, or even producing a version where buyers would color in the pictures themselves. "Such primitive measures these all are!" he wrote.

This increasingly frustrating struggle for publication dogged Rorschach's professional life for three years. It also deepened and enriched the test. As Rorschach sent letter after letter, telegram after telegram, to his prospective publishers and better-connected colleagues—professional in tone, then pleading, then threatening, then desperate—his understanding of the inkblots continued to grow. He became more proficient in the new method and gained insight into what lay behind it. Facing pressure to change the test in various ways, he realized what he could compromise on and where he had to draw the line. By January 1920, he was "happy that it hadn't been printed in its 1918 form—the whole work has grown into a much bigger thing today, and even if the basic facts of the 1918 draft don't need to be changed, there is still a lot to add. The [wartime] paper shortage in 1918, and my desire to say as much as possible in as small a space as possible, made that version worse in many ways." Still, the time had come. "I have now been working on the experiment for years: something needs to get published already."

One effect of the delays was to give Rorschach time to collect a larger sample of results. By the fall of 1919, he had tested 150 schizophrenics and 100 nonpatients with identical images—for of course, as he pointed out, the results could be tabulated only when the same test series was used. The number soon grew to 405 cases—a good-sized sample that made the findings in his eventual book more convincing and let him define "Original" answers quantitatively, as those occurring no more than once every hundred tests. He was starting to shift from a subjective judgment of good and bad answers to a more objective measure of whether an answer was common or uncommon. As he put it at one point in a lecture—probably exaggerating slightly for effect, and invoking a local Appenzell tradition for his St. Gallen audience:

Subjectively, I feel about Plate 1 for example that the only good answer is *Two New Year's mummers with coats billowing, one on each side, and in the middle a female body without a head, or with the head bent forward.* But the most common answers are: *A butterfly, An eagle, A crow, A bat, A beetle, A crab,* and *A rib cage.* None of these answers seem well seen to me, subjectively, but since intelligent normal people have given them many times, I have to count them as Good and Normal answers—all except for the crab.

Also in 1919, Rorschach started checking the accuracy of the test's results the only way he could: by performing blind diagnoses. In fact, he is credited with having coined the term *blind diagnosis* for test evaluation in the absence of personal contact. Rorschach found people who could administer inkblot tests, send him the protocols to score and interpret without knowing anything else about the subject, and then tell him whether his interpretations were right or wrong, starting with his closest friend, Emil Oberholzer, a former assistant of Bleuler's who had gone into private practice in Zurich. He mentioned in his 1920 book pitch that "the control experiments were as follows: I diagnosed people entirely unknown to me—healthy, neurotic, and psychotic—on the basis solely of test protocols. The error rate was less than 25 percent, and by far the majority of these errors would have been avoided if I had known, for instance, the sex and age of the subject, which I had intentionally decided not to be told."

Rorschach was always a bit ambivalent about blind diagnoses. He saw them as useful only for control experiments and examiner training, and while he considered publishing several of them, he also worried that "it looks so much like a magician's sleight-of-hand parlor trick or something." At the same time, this was the only way he could significantly expand his range of test subjects beyond the schizophrenics in his asylum. "Where in Herisau am I supposed to get the material I need," he would lament at one point, "the great artists, the virtuosos, the highly productive types, etc., not to mention the balanced individuals?!!? In Herisau!"

These blind diagnoses did more than anything else to win over his peers, including Eugen Bleuler. Rorschach's lecture at the Swiss

Psychiatry Association conference in November 1919 was given to a sparse and skeptical audience. Several psychiatrists there accused him of being "too schematic," though he noted in his diary that when he was able to explain the test to them personally, they came around. Undaunted, the man who had once written Haeckel for career advice and Tolstoy for an address handed his blots over to Europe's leading psychiatrist and taught him how to use them.

Bleuler was already intrigued: he had known about Rorschach's inkblots since at least 1918, and on the train ride back from the 1919 conference he told Rorschach that "Hens really should have explored such things too, but he stayed stuck with imagination." Fifteen years after trying out Freud on everyone at the Burghölzli, Bleuler started giving inkblot tests left and right, mailed Rorschach dozens of protocols for blind diagnosis, and marveled at Rorschach's interpretations. Among these protocols were tests of all his children in June 1921—one, the future psychiatrist Manfred Bleuler, would publish an essay in 1929 investigating whether siblings produce results more similar to each other than nonsiblings (they do). As Rorschach wrote to a colleague, "You can easily imagine how eager I am to hear his report on how the blind diagnoses turned out," and Bleuler's postcard ten days later couldn't have been more encouraging: the experiment was a success. "Amazingly positive with respect to the diagnoses, and the psychological observations and concepts were perhaps even more valuable," Bleuler wrote. "The interpretations would retain their value even if the diagnostics were missing or wrong." Rorschach's mentor had "confirmed his results on every essential point."

Blind diagnoses were nearly all Rorschach had to work with aside from his asylum patients because, although he was eager to go into private practice, he was nervous about making the move with a growing family to support. He dropped hints to his brother in Brazil about "a certain plan, but it is so risky, and unfortunately still so presumptuous, that there is no way I can reveal it yet." In 1919, after his two major lectures on sects, he wrote to a colleague that "the 'klexography' story has had further developments," and "I recently gave two talks in Zurich about my sectarians. All dark things, you see! Black blots and black souls. But what's starting to seem darkest of all, despite everything, is life under the yoke of the clinic. Maybe I'll cast that off too someday." A couple of months later, he wrote in his diary: "11/8. Thirty-fifth birthday. Hopefully my last in the clinic."

As a full-time psychoanalyst he could make more money and have more free time, aside from what he saw as the intrinsic rewards. "An analysis that goes well is something so stimulating, interesting, and alive that it's hard to think of a greater intellectual and spiritual pleasure," even if "one that goes badly is comparable only to the torments of hell." But he also wanted to see a wider variety of patients "for the sake of the inkblot experiments."

As HE SLOWLY gained access to more subjects, Rorschach became fascinated by how the inkblots seemed to not just diagnose illness but reveal the personality. In his 1918 manuscript, only one of the twenty-eight protocols Rorschach presented was from a nonpatient; in his eventual book, thirteen of the twenty-eight cases would be from normal subjects. Issues of introversion and extraversion, empathy and attachment, were increasingly coming to the fore, as his letters to Greti show. The keys to the personality, Rorschach decided, were Movement and Color.

By February 1919, he had linked Movement responses to the core of the self: the more M's, the greater a person's "psychic inner life." The number of M's was proportional to the person's "introverted energy, tendency to brood, and—take it with a grain of salt—intelligence."

People who gave more M's didn't literally move more quickly and easily; on the contrary, they internalized movement, they moved on the inside, or slowly, often being awkward or clumsy in practice. Rorschach said the most M's he had ever received on an inkblot test was from a catatonic "completely sunk in his nirvana of introversion. He spent all day with his head down on the table, day after day, not moving all day; in the more than three years I've known him, he has had a grand total of two responsive days, otherwise he spoke not a word, year in and year out. To him, all the blots were full of movement." In his dissertation, Rorschach had described feeling movement from visual sensations as a natural human ability, while acknowledging that it varied in different people. Now he had found that these differences were measurable and meaningful.

As Movement responses became more crucial, Rorschach realized that coding them was "the trickiest problem in the entire experiment." The difficulty was that "*a bird in flight*" or "*a volcano erupting*" were not true Movement responses, because a bird is naturally described as being in flight, a volcano as erupting. These were just turns of phrase, "rhetorical embellishments" or associations, rather than anything actually felt. And just as "*sky*" could be a Color response even without mentioning "blue," a response could be coded M even if it didn't mention movement, as long as Rorschach thought that the answer involved feeling a movement. An example he gave later was that, "based on my experience," seeing Card I as "*Two New Year's mummers with brooms under their arms*" is a Movement response. The shape doesn't look much like these figures, Rorschach said, so a person would give that response "only if he felt himself into the shape, which always goes with a sensation of movement."

What made something an M response was empathetic identification, feeling-in: "The question is always: Is the subject actually *empathizing with the movement?*" But to answer that question, the examiner had to get around the subject's words to what he or she was feeling inside. Rorschach's initial idea, that when a person gave a Movement response you could see them move, was, he now realized, far too simplistic. A colleague who worked with Rorschach once described spending hours debating with him whether a single response to a single card should be coded as M.

Rorschach also started to give Color responses a deeper psychological meaning. He had mentioned in his 1918 manuscript that more M's typically went with fewer C's and vice versa, but his main distinction was between Movement and static Form responses. At that point, he had very little to say about Color answers, except in his lists of typical test results for different varieties of mental illness. None of his earlier work had paid color much attention of any kind. Now he came to see that the relationships between Form, Movement, and Color were much more complex.

Color responses seemed to be linked to emotion or feeling. Rorschach used the word *affect* to mean emotional reactions, whether feelings or expressions of feeling. A person's "affectivity" was their mode of feeling, how they were "affected" by things. Rorschach found that subjects with a "stable affect"—an even keel and calm reactions, or insensitivity, or in pathological cases depression—consistently gave few or no Color responses. Subjects with a "labile" or volatile affect—strong, even hysterical reactions or oversensitivity, possibly mania or dementia—gave a lot of Color responses.

Again, Rorschach failed to ground this insight in any theory, beyond the nearly universal folk wisdom that we react emotionally to color. He claimed only that he had noticed the correlation in practice. He also found surprisingly many test takers who were startled or unnerved by the color in the inkblots, especially in a colored inkblot after a number of black and white ones. Such people hesitated, "in a kind of stupor," sometimes unable to give any answer at all. Rorschach called this "color shock" and claimed it was a sign of neurosis: a tendency to repress incoming stimulation that would otherwise be too much.

Most people still gave mostly Form answers—describing the inkblot's shape was the standard response, not especially diagnostic or revealing. But these answers, too, interacted with the other kinds of response. All M responses were, after all, forms in motion. Rorschach also found that more C responses went with a worse perception of F (more F−, fewer F+), and vice versa. This made sense to him: The more a person's emotions got in the way, the less able they were to rationally see what was really there. "Color," he pointedly remarked in his diary, "is the enemy of form." Only "a single group of normals combine good form visualization with unstable emotions," he found: "neurotics and artists."

People generally integrated their emotional reactions more or less well into their conscious lives, of course, and the test yielded information about this, too, through the difference between C, CF, and FC responses. The rare pure C responses were signs of out-of-control affect, Rorschach claimed, and tended to be given only by the mentally ill "or notoriously hotheaded and hyperaggressive, irresponsible 'normals.'" CF, with the C outweighing the F, meant the same thing to a lesser degree: "emotional instability, irritability, sensitivity, and suggestibility." FC answers—based mainly on the shape but incorporating the color, such as "*a purple spider*" or "*a blue flag*"—were a kind of combined intellectual and emotional reaction. An FC answer reacted to the color but stayed in control.

Normal people's Color responses were mostly FC's with well-seen forms. A poorly seen form in an FC response, on the other hand, indicated that the person might emotionally want to connect but be intellectually unable to: "When a normal person wants to give me a present, he looks for something *I* would like; when a manic gives a present, he gives something *he* likes. When a normal person says something, he tries to adjust it to *our* interest; a manic graciously says things that interest only *him*. Both of these manic people seem egocentric because their desire for emotional rapport is frustrated by an inadequate cognitive ability."

By the end of 1919, Rorschach had brought Movement, Color, and Form together in a single psychological system. If Color responses indicated emotional instability, then Movement responses were signs of stability: thoughtful, reflective groundedness. And if M's meant introversion, C's meant extraversion. A person would react, or overreact, to the outside world—as evidenced by a Color response—if the outside world was what they cared about.

There were thus movement-predominant types, with "individualized intelligence, greater creative ability, more inner life, emotional stability, worse adaptation to reality, measured movements, physical awkwardness and clumsiness," and color-predominant types, with "stereotyped intelligence, greater ability to copy, more outward-directed life, emotional instability, better adaptation to reality, restless movements, skill and agility." Basically, introverts and extraverts. But a person giving almost all Form responses, with unusually few M's or C's, had neither set of abilities: this would be a cramped, pedantic, possibly obsessive personality. A lot of both M's and C's meant an expansive, balanced personality that Rorschach called "ambiequal."

Rorschach now had a formula: the ratio between M and C was a person's "Experience Type"—the overall way they experienced the world. Taking the test in a good or bad mood might change the number of M and C responses, but not the proportion between them, which "directly expresses the mixture of introvert and extravert tendencies united in a given person." This proportion was largely fixed, though it naturally changed over the course of one's life, as Rorschach had told Greti. Insofar as the inkblots were being used to test personality, not diagnose mental illness, the Experience Type became the test's single most important result.

Even so, Rorschach wasn't trying to classify people. Jung had previously discussed introversion and extraversion, but Rorschach modified Jung's terminology to emphasize different capacities of the psyche, not different types of person: he wrote of "intro*versive*" and "extra*tensive*" tendencies, not introvert*ed* or extravert*ed* personalities. The Movement-type person was not necessarily introverted but had the capacity to be introverted; the Color type had "the urge to live in the world outside himself," whether he acted on that urge or not. These abilities didn't cancel each other out—almost everyone could turn both inward and outward, though most people tended to use one or the other approach in most situations. Rorschach repeatedly insisted that the midline of his various charts, separating more M from more C, "does not represent a sharp boundary between two entirely different types: it is, rather, a question of more or less. . . . Psychologically, the types cannot be said to be contrasting, any more than one can speak of movement and color as opposites." Still, the Experience Type revealed "not how the person lives or what he is striving toward . . . not *what* he experiences, but *how* he experiences."

Rorschach may not have consciously remembered his youthful letter to Tolstoy, but he had fulfilled its dream. "The ability to see and shape the world, like the Mediterranean peoples; to think the world, like the Germans; to feel the world, like the Slavs—will these powers ever be brought together?" Movement responses were how we infuse life into the inkblots (seeing in them what we put in); Form responses were how we think the inkblots (process them intellectually); Color responses were how we feel the inkblots (react to them emotionally). Rorschach had found a way to bring these powers together, in ten cards.

While he admitted that "it is always daring to draw conclusions about the way a person experiences life from the results of an experiment," he was gaining in confidence and ambition, and as his publication delays dragged on through 1919 and 1920 he let himself be ever more daring. He generalized that "introversives are *cultured*; extratensives are *civilized*." He called his whole era extraverted (scientific and empiricist) but felt that the pendulum was swinging back toward "old gnostic paths of introversion," rejecting "disciplined reasoning" for anthroposophy and mysticism. The medieval bestiaries he was reading in his spare time seemed to him "beautiful examples of introverted thinking, not caring about reality—but the way people spoke about animals then, they speak about politics today!"

He quipped that "if you know an educated person's Experience Type, you can guess with some certainty his favorite philosopher: extreme introversives swear by Schopenhauer, expansive ambiequals by Nietzsche, cramped individuals by Kant, and extratensives by some fashionable authority, or Christian Science and such things." He conjectured that sensations of movement were linked with earliest childhood memories, including his own. He linked different Experience Types to particular psychoses, claiming that introverted psychotics hallucinate bodily sensations or voices from within while extraverts hear voices from without. After a missionary from the Gold Coast of Africa gave a lecture and slideshow at Herisau, the Rorschachs invited him over, and Hermann suggested that the blots could be used to investigate "the psychology of primitives." He mused on the philosophy of color, claiming that blue was "the favorite color of those who control their passions" (his own favorite color being gentian blue). And he ventured into analyzing visual art.

Rorschach had become friends with Oberholzer's cousin Emil Lüthy, a psychiatrist trained as an artist who regularly visited Herisau from Basel on weekends and was soon the man Rorschach trusted most about artistic matters. Before he left medicine and returned to art for good in 1927, Lüthy would give the inkblot test to more than fifty artists and would send Rorschach some of the most interesting protocols he would ever receive. Together they produced a table of various artistic schools and the experience types they represented—with Rorschach adding his typical caveat: "In truth, every artist represents an individuality of his own." Rorschach and Lüthy would later correspond about developing a diagnostic test based purely on color.

WHILE RORSCHACH WAS going deeper into the meaning of the inkblots, word was starting to get out about his discoveries. Rorschach was not a professor, but students, usually Bleuler's, came to Herisau as unpaid volunteers, attracted more by the possibility of working with Dr. Rorschach than by Koller's asylum. All things considered, they gave Rorschach less help and support than he was obliged to give them.

But their interests and pursuits began to influence his shaping and presentation of the test.

Hans Behn-Eschenburg started as a volunteer assistant doctor in August 1919. Rorschach introduced Behn to both Freud's ideas and his own: "Whoever wanted to work with Rorschach on his perceptodiagnostic experiment had first to submit his own person to the 'procedure,'" Behn-Eschenburg's wife recalled. "Rorschach worked out a psychogram which he would show you and discuss with you very candidly. Not until this was done would he initiate you into working with his experiment." Behn then started using the inkblots for his own dissertation.

Behn gave the Rorschach test to hundreds of children and adolescents, yielding fascinating preliminary results when analyzed by age and gender. "The fourteenth year is a remarkable time of crisis," Rorschach wrote in a synthesis of Behn's findings. Teenagers' personalities grow more extreme, girls usually more toward extraversion and boys toward introversion; then, the next year, their personalities constrict dramatically, boys more than girls, and they turn neurotic, "too lazy for it to be depression and too anxious for it to actually be laziness." Still, he concluded, "Even when these findings are derived from 250 tests, the individual differences are so great, even at that age, that there needs to be much more material before such conclusions can be taken as facts."

Rorschach's publication delays, and the simpler questions Behn was trying to answer, meant that Behn's dissertation was going to be the first published account of Rorschach's discovery, and Rorschach was concerned that it be unassailable and make a good impression. When Behn did not prove up to the task, Rorschach wrote whole sections of the dissertation himself. Despite the frustration and waste of time involved, Rorschach's work with Behn called forth stronger statements about the scientific and human value of his accomplishment than he would offer elsewhere. He wrote a long letter talking through how Behn should discuss the inkblot experiment:

The experiment is very simple, so simple that at first it provokes head-shaking everywhere—interest and head-shaking, as you yourself have seen many times over. Its simplicity stands in the starkest possible contrast to the unbelievably rich perspectives it opens up. That is itself another reason to shake one's head, and you can never take another person's head-shaking amiss. Therefore, your dissertation has to be much more complete, precise, definite, and clear than something on another topic which doesn't run these risks. . . . I feel obliged to appeal to your feelings, and hope you will take to heart that one of the very best things a person can possess is the consciousness of having given the scientific arsenal something truly new.

Through this detour, Rorschach revealed how he felt about his own work.

Pressure of a different kind was coming from Georg Roemer, who had met Rorschach in December 1918 as a volunteer in the Herisau regional hospital and was the first volunteer assistant at the Krombach, from February to May 1919. Roemer worked in the school system in Germany and was pushing for the test's adoption as a way to measure academic aptitude. Rorschach recognized that this would mean a significant intellectual triumph, and possibly real financial rewards, yet his reaction was cautious:

I too think the experiment might prove very successful as an aptitude test. But when I imagine some young person, who has maybe dreamed of going to university from an early age, being prevented from doing so as a result of failing at the experiment, I naturally feel a bit like I can't breathe. Therefore, I have to say: the experiment *may* be suitable for such testing. But to decide whether or not it is, it would first have to be thoroughly investigated by academics using a very large sample, systematically, statistically, following all the rules of variance and factoring in correlations. I think when that happens, it will probably be possible to make a differentiated aptitude test. Not: doctor or not, lawyer or not, etc., but rather, if someone decides to be a doctor, should he go into theoretical or practical medicine, if a lawyer, should he be a business lawyer or a defense attorney, etc. etc. . . .

Also, the experiment would surely need to be combined with other tests. . . .

Above all, the theoretical basis of the experiment would have to be established much more thoroughly, because it is wrong to take such decisive measures based on a test without an extremely solid theoretical foundation. . . .

Also, Dr. Behn's dissertation shows that one mustn't apply this test too early—fifteen- to sixteen-year-old boys, for example, have conspicuously poor results . . . and further studies of seventeen- to twenty-year-olds, perhaps older subjects as well, are needed to determine when their results stabilize at an adult level. . . . All this needs extensive work.

With Roemer chomping at the bit—even making inkblot series of his own in secret—Rorschach here insisted on due diligence and in the process anticipated most of the objections that his test would face in the century to come. He would acknowledge elsewhere that "the subject being taken unawares in the experiment is the basis for serious objection," especially if the test had real consequences: that would be like tricking people to testify against themselves. Still, he hoped the test would be used for the forces of good: "May the test discover more true latent talents than misguided careers and illusions; may it free more people from the fear of psychosis than it burdens with such fears; may it give more ease than hardship!"

Roemer deluged Rorschach with letters for years, prompting long responses about the theory behind the inkblot experiment and its relation to Jung, Freud, and Bleuler, and various other thinkers. Rorschach developed both new ideas and ones he had kept out of his book for simplicity's sake or because they weren't fully worked out; Roemer would later claim credit for them. Many of Hermann's late nights typing, the cause of his fights with Olga, were spent writing his lengthy replies to Roemer's questions. But Rorschach encouraged him: "I find your questions extremely interesting, please keep them coming."

The younger colleague he grew closest to was from outside his field. Martha Schwarz was a volunteer doctor at Herisau for seven months. Her dissertation had specialized in cremation—a far cry from psychiatry—but she was a cultured person, having hesitated for a long time between medicine and literature. Rorschach recognized her broad interests and not only gave her tips about adjusting to Herisau but soon started giving her psychiatric work to do; he tested her with the inkblots, and before long she was administering tests for him. He called one of them "one of the most interesting findings I have ever had" and seems to have used it as Case 1 in his book. She also did very thorough physical exams of the patients, something usually neglected at the time, and told Rorschach: "You know, a doctor has a completely different relationship to patients if he knows the patient's body."

Another student, Albert Furrer, who learned the test from Rorschach in the spring of 1921, began testing army sharpshooters. Rorschach could see the humor of the situation: "Someone I know is running the experiment in the barracks here in Herisau, testing very good and very bad marksmen!!! Such a test-hungry time we live in!" But it made sense to give sharpshooters a test of perception—how they see details, how they scan an ambiguous visual field, the degree to which they impose an interpretation on what they perceive. An elite marksman needed the ability to control his affect—suppress any physical reaction to feelings or emotions—and when Furrer tested Konrad Stäheli, a world-champion marksman (forty-four individual medals and sixty-nine total medals in world championships, including three golds and a bronze at the 1900 Olympics), his results showed this control to a truly dramatic degree. There were other findings, too: Rorschach's review of the soldiers' results made him realize "how strongly military service changes a person's Experience Type, suppressing the M and promoting the C," which "awakened some doubts about my view that the Experience Type is relatively constant." Still, Rorschach sighed, "The fact that talents were the first things to be tested, marksmanship no less, really is somewhat comical."

None of these spinoffs would matter so much if he could finally get the test published. But even as publishers balked, Rorschach was coming to appreciate the unique value of his own set of images and realizing that he needed to insist they be published, in color and in full. "The point is not to illustrate the book but to make it possible for anyone interested in the work to conduct experiments with these images. . . . and it is extremely important that they be with *my* images."

Earlier, he had modestly invited readers to make their own, and had encouraged both Behn-Eschenburg and Roemer to make series of inkblots, but theirs didn't work. Emil Lüthy was the only one he continued to encourage, but Lüthy gave up—as a real artist, he recognized that making inkblots truly suggestive of both form and movement was much harder than it looked. Rorschach had accomplished something impossible to replicate, and eventually he owned up to the fact: "Trying the experiment with new plates might take a lot of work; clearly the relationship between Movement and Color reactions in my series works especially well, and is not so easy to re-create after all."

Even after his 1918 essay and 1919 lectures, he was unable to write his final manuscript until he knew whether the book would be for a psychiatric, educational, or popular audience, and whether he would be able to publish it with images, full-sized or reduced or not at all. He turned for help to pastor and psychoanalyst Oskar Pfister, the co-founder of the Swiss Psychoanalytic Society who was also encouraging Rorschach to publish a short, popular version of his sect studies. When the publisher that Pfister recommended fell through as well, it was Rorschach's colleague from the Waldau, Walter Morgenthaler, who found a home for the book at last: with Morgenthaler's own publisher, Ernst Bircher.

By that time, the dam was full to bursting. Rorschach had outlined the book's structure in a letter to Morgenthaler four days earlier, and he wrote it fast—267 handwritten pages, a 280-page typewritten draft, between April and June of 1920, during "the long wet Herisau spring."

In late 1919, he had mused that ages thirty-three to thirty-five were "years of an all but certain disposition for deep introversion"—a time in life when people turn inward, dig deep. He mentioned Christ and Buddha and Augustine, all turning away from the world at thirty-three, along with the Swiss sect founders he had studied, Binggeli and Unternährer, both of whom had had their mystical visions at just that age. "In the Gnostic tradition," he noted, "man is ready for a true inward turn only when he turns thirty-three." It would not have escaped him that his own years thirty-three to thirty-five spanned late 1917 to 1920, just when he was developing the inkblot test. That phase was coming to an end, and it was time to make an outward mark in the world.

Yet months went by without Rorschach hearing whether Bircher could print the plates after all, then more months of contract negotiations, and more months of waiting after the contract was signed, with Rorschach expecting the book to come out any day. Bircher's first letter to Rorschach had been addressed to "Dr. O. Rohrbach"—not a good sign. Rorschach wrote to his brother in Brazil, saying how much he needed practical advice from a businessman, but to no avail.

Long after the contracted publication date, Bircher wrote to say that Rorschach's book might have to be published in a different font from the other books in the series, since Morgenthaler's volume was still being printed and the metal type was thus still in use. In other words, Bircher hadn't even started yet. Rorschach could sue, but that would only delay everything further. Two months later, Bircher said that there were so many capital "F"s in Rorschach's book that the printers had run out. ("F" is less common in German than in English, but Rorschach's book was full of them: "Form" is abbreviated "F," and "Color" in German is *Farbe,* abbreviated "Fb.") The first section of Rorschach's book would have to be printed at last for that reason alone: to free up the type.

All this delayed Rorschach's research as well, because while the inkblots were at the publisher, and the lithography firm, and the printer, neither he nor his colleagues had images to use. Just when he had access to a growing range of private patients, and colleagues who could supply protocols for blind diagnosis, his data collection was stopped in its tracks. He made do with sets of "parallel series" where he could, but needed to use the real inkblots in most cases, so his letters from the period are filled with pleas to return his one and only set. Despite begging the publisher to print the images sooner, or at least send him proofs, he didn't get a set until April 1921, and that with errors; no acceptable images arrived until May 1921.

Rorschach's letters to Bircher during the printing process reveal many aspects of the test Rorschach found important. One letter explained that if the image sizes had to be reduced, the arrangement of shapes in the overall space of the card had to exactly correspond to the relationships in the originals, because "images that do not satisfy these conditions of spatial rhythm are rejected by a large number of test subjects." Even the tiny spatters of ink on the edges of the shapes had to be included, because "there are test subjects who tend to interpret primarily these tiny details, a quality with great diagnostic significance." This was also where Rorschach insisted that there be no numbering on the front of the cards, because "the least sign of intentionality, even a number, is enough to adversely affect many mentally ill test subjects."

In correcting proofs, he remarked that a certain dark-blue color was too weak, and that the reproductions needed to show "the tiniest dissolvings of the paint and the ink"; he rejected another page with the comment: "No stippling that affects the outline too strongly."

Top: Postproduction: Rorschach's notes on the printer's proofs, editing out the extra shapes to make the bat of Card V—"Leave out the crossed-out smaller shapes; center the large bat-shape in the rectangle. Otherwise good to print. Dr. Rorschach." *Bottom:* The final Card V.

It is impossible to know how much the delays with Bircher were directly or indirectly Morgenthaler's fault, but he often gave Rorschach advice that showed a certain lack of understanding, for instance encouraging him to publish the images at reduced size. And for better or worse, when Rorschach wanted to give his major work the not exactly catchy title *Method and Results of an Experiment in Perception-Diagnosis (Interpretation of Chance Forms)*, it was Morgenthaler who talked him out of it. The inkblots were "more than a mere experiment," Morgenthaler argued in August 1920, and were about "far more than just perception-diagnosis." His suggestion: *Psychodiagnostics.*

Rorschach refused at first. Such a sweeping term would "go too far, it seems to me"; diagnosing the psyche sounded "almost mystical," especially at this early stage before extensive control experiments with normal subjects. "I would rather say too little at the outset than too much," he demurred, "and not just out of modesty." When Morgenthaler insisted he had to jazz up the title—no one would spend good money for "an experiment in perception-diagnosis"—Rorschach "unhappily" gave in, though he continued to think the new title sounded "extremely arrogant," and he used his original long, prosaic description as the subtitle. Maybe Morgenthaler was right and the book needed better marketing, but Rorschach didn't want to sound like a huckster.

PSYCHODIAGNOSTICS WAS PUBLISHED in mid-June 1921 in an edition of 1,200 copies. Rorschach's friend Emil Oberholzer had been the first to read the manuscript, and his response was immensely encouraging, especially to someone working outside a university setting and without official support: "I think that this research and your results are the most important findings since Freud's publications. . . . In psychoanalysis, the formal categories have long since been seen as inadequate, for partly intrinsic reasons, and in any case new methods are what bring progress. And every productive breakthrough is invariably amazingly simple." Oskar Pfister, who had tried to get both the book and Rorschach's sect work into print, sent another gratifying response. With its extended metaphor of Rorschach's books as his children, his letter is written with the slightly huffing-and-puffing bonhomie characteristic of the good pastor but glows with admiration:

Dear Doctor,
Having been able to render obstetrical service at the entrance into the world of your little newborn boy, I have already come to love him. He is a vigorous, bright-eyed little fellow indeed, of a

rare parentage, learned and unrattling, able to see through things both originally and profoundly. Faced with facts and unlike the compulsive neurotic theories, it is pure humanity itself, without pompous mannerisms or bombastic self-importance. The little fellow will be much talked about, and will secure attention from the large academic world for his father, who had long since earned it. My deepest, most heartfelt thanks for this precious gift, and I hope his little sister with her knowledge of the sects will pay me a visit soon too! Affectionately yours, Pfister.

After all the delays, the inkblots were out in the world. Roemer, now the head of business and career counseling for a German student organization, brought back a mountain of protocols from the organization's big shots, whose conformity amused Rorschach: "All of them future ministers, politicians, and organizers, so to speak. Every shade of the spectrum from the blandest bureaucrats to the feistiest Napoleons. And every last one of them—extravert. They must have to be, in politics?!" Roemer indefatigably tested shell-shocked ex-soldiers and pensioners adapting poorly to retirement; he had plans to test Albert Einstein that winter, and the famous World War I general Erich Ludendorff, even the heads of the Weimar Republic.

Early responses to the test were largely positive. At Rorschach's first conference presentation of the test after publication, in November 1921, Bleuler stood up in a discussion session to declare that he had confirmed Rorschach's approach with both patients and nonpatients. Rorschach walked up to Morgenthaler afterward, beaming: "Well, it's made it— we're out of the woods now!" As he saw it: "Bleuler has now expressed himself publicly and quite clearly for the value of the method. Several reviews have appeared, until now all good, only too good; I would like an occasional controversy, since I have so little opportunity for a verbal one." Anything would be better than his solitary work in Herisau.

Controversy would come soon enough. After a few reviews in psychology journals that were largely summaries, the first one that went into most detail was decidedly double-edged. Arthur Kronfeld's 1922 review opened by calling Rorschach "a resourceful spirit, a psychologist with fine intuition but truly limited experimental/methodological precision." He found Rorschach's insights into character and perception utterly convincing. But Rorschach's numerical approach to scoring the test was "necessarily too crude and approximate," while Rorschach's interpretations went far beyond the actual test results, however mightily he tried to "squeeze" his findings out of people's answers. The test was both too quantitative and too subjective. Ludwig Binswanger, an important pioneer of what would be known as existential psychology, who knew Rorschach, praised his work more highly—as clear, insightful, objective, meticulous, original. But he also strongly criticized its lack of theoretical underpinning, a lack Rorschach himself felt deeply. Eventually it would not be enough to argue that the inkblots worked without explaining how and why.

In the world of German academic psychology, the test had already met with blanket rejection. In April 1921, at the first convention of the German Society of Experimental Psychology after the war, Roemer had given a lecture on the inkblot test—as modified by him, using his own blots, intended for educational testing. The powerful and popular William Stern, who a generation earlier had been one of the first academic psychologists to review Freud's *Interpretation of Dreams* (he hated it), stood up to say that no single test could ever grasp or diagnose the human personality. Rorschach's—actually Roemer's—"approach was artificial and one-sided, his interpretations arbitrary, his statistics insufficient." Rorschach himself had never claimed that his test should be used in isolation, as Roemer knew from their correspondence, and he was deeply annoyed that Roemer had acted as his spokesman, "proposing unnecessary modifications before my book has even been published." He asked Roemer to back off: "Multiple different series of inkblots can only lead to confusion! And especially with Stern!!!" Even Stern became "more approachable" once he had read a copy of Rorschach's actual book, Rorschach thought, but the damage was done, and the inkblot test never gained wide acceptance in Germany.

Rorschach was already looking beyond Europe, though. A Chilean doctor volunteering at Herisau was planning to translate *Psychodiagnostics* into Spanish, but Rorschach knew that "North America would obviously be much more significant. They are almost as interested in depth psychology there as in vocational aptitude testing." Freud, Rorschach went on, was "doing practically nothing in Vienna anymore besides giving 'teaching analyses' to Americans" who wanted to go into practice. "Naturally it would be very advantageous if the Americans took up the thing." Meanwhile, "both the English *Psychoanalytic Journal* and American psychoanalytic journals are planning long reviews."

Finally, Rorschach wanted to use the inkblot experiment in the service of the anthropological interests most apparent in his sect work. In *Psychodiagnostics*, the only racial or ethnic difference he had had material to generalize about was that between the introverted Bernese Swiss, slow of speech and good at drawing, and the extraverted, witty, more physically active Appenzellers (fewer M's, more C's). But he continued to follow ethnographic and sect-related research, reviewing it for Freud's journal, and he and Oberholzer discussed the prospect of testing Chinese populations. He talked his way into Albert Schweitzer's hotel room after a lecture and tested him—"one of the most rationalistic profiles" and "the wildest case of color repression" Rorschach ever saw—after which Schweitzer apparently agreed to have Africans in his missionary communities Rorschach-tested by a fellow African.

"There is a lot more still in the experiment," Rorschach wrote in a long letter to Roemer on the day the publisher mailed him his book at last, "not to mention the question of a more or less acceptable theoretical underpinning. And surely there are other factors hidden in the results that have just as rigorous a value, it's just up to us to find them."

By the time *Psychodiagnostics* was published in 1921, the book was not only preliminary but already a year out of date—a particular freeze-frame of Rorschach's thought from spring 1920. It would have been a very different work if written a year or two earlier or later. But one thing about it was undeniably lasting. It was published in two parts: the book and a separate box containing the inkblots. At first the images were on sheets of paper, for the purchaser to mount; in later editions, the images would be printed directly on cardboard cards. They were the same ten blots that are still used today.

The Psychology He Sees Is *His* Psychology

Rorschach was gradually building up a private practice in Herisau, giving one or two hours of psychoanalysis a day to clients with a range of issues and complexes. One patient, "impulsive and childish, even though he's over forty," almost made Rorschach wonder if it was worth it: "I'll never take on a neurotic like that again, he can practically devour you."

This was a colleague who had taken the inkblot test and found the experience powerful enough that he had asked Rorschach to accept him for therapy. Rorschach reluctantly agreed to a four-week trial period, but, he wrote, "I should have paid more attention to my experiment":

> The patient interpreted the red animal on Card VIII as *"Europa, on the bull carrying her over the Bosphorus."* That he confabulated Europa from the bull shape is already a strong sign; that there are two Color responses in his answer is an even stronger one—[the Bosphorus Strait refers to the blue, and] the "bull" is for him the reddest passion. But I had no idea at the time that a whole array of determining content was important in his answer, I realized it only later. The bull is the man himself, and there are masochistic fantasies at play, a sense of victimization, and the most insane delusions of grandeur: he is "carrying all of Europe on his back," it's all in there. Well, at least in this regard I've learned something.

In using the inkblot test on a wider range of people, he was starting to move away from what he had written in *Psychodiagnostics*: that the test "does not plumb the unconscious." He was coming to think that *what*

Hermann Rorschach, age one and a half, 1886

Age six, in Swiss folk costume, 1891

Age twenty-one, as a medical student, 1905

Hermann's parents, Ulrich and Philippine

Sister Anna, 1911

Hermann, Anna, Paul, Ulrich,
and stepmother Regina,
around the time of Ulrich's
remarriage, 1899

Life in Scaphusia (1901): Hermann is second from right, with hand on stein.

Horns, steins, swords, and sashes: Hermann is third from right, in dark bow tie, holding a book.

Top: Olga in Zurich, ca. 1905, age twenty-seven
Bottom: Zurich (?), ca. 1906–8

Top: Wedding photo, May 1, 1910
Bottom: Paul, Hermann, Regineli, and Regine in Münsterlingen, ca. 1911

Olga and Hermann in gypsy costume, with
Olga's new guitar, Christmas 1910

Hermann holding daughter Lisa, 1918

Hermann in his office in the Herisau apartment, cigarette in hand, 1920

Rowing on Lake Constance, ca. 1920

On a hiking trip in the Säntis, September 1918

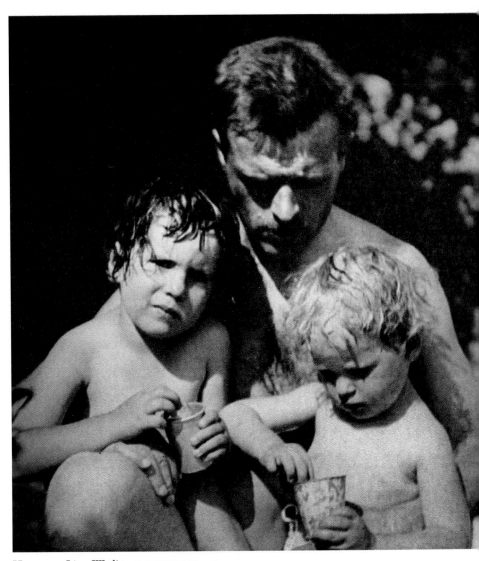

Hermann, Lisa, Wadim: summer 1921

people saw in the blots, not just *how* they saw, could be revealing: "The content of answers, too, can be meaningful."

Rorschach seems to have realized that if he wanted his insights to be part of the main line of twentieth-century thinking about psychology, he needed to lay out the connections between the inkblot experiment and psychoanalysis. Bringing the two together would give the test at least something of a theoretical underpinning, while also extending its significance beyond his idiosyncratic "psychodiagnostics," and it would enrich Freudian thought with new formal and visual insights.

Models of the mind like Freud's model are known as "dynamic psychiatry" because they focus on emotional processes and mental mechanisms, the underlying "movements" of the mind, rather than observable symptoms and behavior. By 1922, Hermann Rorschach was practicing a truly dynamic psychiatry, tracing the subtle movements of a perceiving mind. He had mastered his instrument.

That year, Rorschach set one of these virtuosic performances down on paper. Oberholzer had sent him a protocol for blind diagnosis, telling him only the patient's sex and age (male, forty). Rorschach's analysis, written up as a lecture for the Swiss Psychoanalytical Society titled "The Form Interpretation Test Applied to Psychoanalysis," first moved through the patient's protocol in great detail for twenty pages, giving advice about how to code each response and how to go about reaching an interpretation. This advice was hardly easy to follow, since Rorschach was finely attuned to how the rhythms of a patient's answers revealed their approach to the world: what they paid attention to, what they ignored, what they repressed, how they moved. He demanded a certain balanced rhythm in his own analysis, too: "Hitherto we have paid too much attention to the introverted features in our patient and have neglected the extraverted side."

Oberholzer's patient had given Movement responses later than usual in the sequence of ten cards. Therefore, Rorschach concluded, the man had a capacity for empathy (he could give M responses) but was neurotically suppressing it (he initially avoided M responses, even on cards that were conducive to them). The patient's initially bold and vigorous Color responses were followed by equivocal ones, which to Rorschach indicated a conscious struggle to control his own emotional reactions, rather than unconscious repression of them. Rorschach also noticed that the man's first answers to each card were unoriginal and often vague but that he eventually arrived at genuinely original, "definite and convincing" responses. In Card II he saw *"Two clowns,"* then *"But it may also be a wide parkway lined by beautiful dark trees,"* then *"Here's red: it's a well of fire giving off smoke."* This was someone who "reasoned inductively better than deductively, concretely better than abstractly," and kept trying until he found something he was satisfied with. At the same time, the man never seemed to notice common, normal Details, indicating that he lacked basic adaptability, "the quick wit of the practical man who can grasp the essentials and master any situation."

The key to the man's psychology was that he constantly looked to the middle of the cards. On Card III, he saw what many people see—two men with top hats bowing to each other—but then added: *"It is as though that red thing in the middle were a power separating the two sides, preventing them from meeting."* Another card *"gives me on the whole the impression of something powerful in the middle to which everything else clings."* Another: *"This white line in the middle is interesting; it is a line of force around which everything else is arranged."* These responses, while impossible to classify, were at the core of Rorschach's interpretation. He not only noticed the pattern but dug into it—what was the *relationship* with the midline in each answer? Did the center hold on to the other parts, or did the surrounding parts grasp the center?

The patient was an introverted neurotic, Rorschach concluded, probably with obsessive-compulsive behaviors, and tormented by ideas of inadequacy and self-distrust; it was these feelings that made him control his emotions so firmly.

> This patient typically nags at himself, dissatisfied with his accomplishments; he is easily thrown off balance, but then recovers, because of his need to apply himself. He has little full, free emotional rapport with the world around him, and shows a rather strong tendency to go his own way. His dominant mood, his habitual underlying affect, is rather anxious, depressed, and passively resigned, though all this can be and is controlled wherever possible, due to his good intellectual capacity and adaptability.
>
> His intelligence is, on the whole, good, keen, original, more concrete than abstract, more inductive than deductive. Still, there

is a contradiction here, in that the subject exhibits a rather weak sense for the obvious and the practical. He thus gets stuck on and trapped in trifling and subordinate details. Emotional and intellectual self-discipline and mastery are apparent, however.

All this from the inkblots. Oberholzer confirmed both Rorschach's specific descriptions of the patient's personality and his larger speculations: the patient's relation to the "central line of power," for example, matched what analysis had revealed about his relation to his father. "I could not have given a better characterization of the patient myself, even though I had him under analysis for months," Oberholzer wrote.

Rorschach's 1922 essay went on to propose how his trinity of Form, Movement, and Color might be integrated with Freudian theory. Which kinds of answers shed light on the unconscious? Rorschach argued that Form responses showed conscious powers at work: accuracy, clarity, attention, concentration. Movement responses, on the other hand, furnished "a deep insight into the unconscious," as did Color responses in a different way. Abstract answers, like "*Something powerful in the middle*," emerged from deep in the person's psychology, much like the manifest content of dreams, which can reveal the inner workings of the mind when interpreted and analyzed properly.

In other words, it *did* make a difference "whether a patient interprets the red part of a card as an open wound or sees it as rose petals, syrup, or slices of ham." But there was no formula for how much difference it made—"how much the content of such interpretations belongs to the conscious and how much to the unconscious." Sometimes a splash of blood is just a splash of blood. And sometimes Europa on a bull was not just Europa on a bull. Rorschach insisted that the significance of the content was "determined primarily by relationships which exist between *formal properties* and content"—the prevalence of Movement or Color, Whole or Detail, answers responding to one or another part of the visual field. Rorschach suspected another patient of having "ideas of remaking the world" not simply because the man saw gigantic gods in the inkblots, but because he "gave several abstract interpretations in which the center line and middle of the image prompted responses that are variations of the same theme."

No one else who used the test brought form and content together the way Rorschach did. Georg Roemer, for example, felt that "the Rorschach test must be liberated from its formal rigidity and reconstructed as a content-based, symbolic test." He made several series of his own images—the "more complicated and structured, more pleasing and aesthetically refined" kind that Rorschach specifically rejected (see Color Plate 7)—but while Rorschach granted that they were valuable to a certain extent, he insisted that they were no substitute for the real thing:

> My images look clumsy next to yours, but I had to make them that way, after being forced to discard many earlier images that were less useful. . . . It is really too bad you did not gather data with my cards. It just doesn't work to simply assume the M possibilities of my cards are double those of yours, or what have you. There are so many nuances. . . . There is no way around testing with my series first, to get a secure foundation of the Experience Type and the number of M and C responses. Afterwards, a test with your series would feel like an aesthetic relief, so to speak, and probably be more revealing of complexes.

In other words, Roemer's "content-based, symbolic test" would be much like Freudian free association, with the psychiatrist able to pay attention to what people said, irrespective of the visual, formal properties of the inkblots. People could free-associate to Roemer's images just as they could to anything else. But if Rorschach wanted free associations from his patients, he could just talk to them. If he wanted to uncover unconscious complexes, he could give a word association test. The ten inkblots, with their unique balance of movement, color, and form, did more; Roemer's blots, notably lacking in movement, did not.

First and last, what mattered in Rorschach's dynamic psychiatry was movement. In his 1922 essay, he described his ideal of mental health in explicitly dynamic terms: "a *free mixing* of Movement, Form, and Color responses appears to be characteristic of people who are free of 'complexes.'" Again: "The essential thing is a quick transition from Movement to Color, as motley a mix as possible of intuitive, combinatory, constructed, and abstracted interpretations of the whole, easily plucking the first colored flower and then returning as quickly as possible to movements . . . and playful or at least easy diction, welcoming all these things with as it were open arms."

Rorschach even pointed out that insights are dynamic. To have an insight, a person needs "to both have the intuition and then grasp and hold it as a whole; that is to say, he must be *able to shift quickly* from expansiveness to constriction" (emphasis added). Without focus, any flash of intuition would remain "sketchy, aphoristic, a castle in the air impossible to adapt to real life"; an overly rational or rigid personality paralyzes intuition altogether. These well-known truths were "obviously no new contribution," Rorschach remarked. "What is new is that we can follow the conflict between repressing conscious and repressed unconscious by means of the test," seeing in action how a patient's compulsive hypercriticism stifled his productive intuitions and free inner life. The inkblot test gave more than static results—it let Rorschach track the dynamic processes of the mind.

His OWN INIMITABLE interpretations, along with the ham-fisted efforts by followers such as Behn-Eschenburg and Roemer, must have made Rorschach wonder if anyone else would be able to use the inkblots properly. At the same time, a major new work by Carl Jung left him no choice but to confront head-on how his own vision could be generalized to a universally applicable test—or not.

Jung's *Psychological Types,* published in 1921 a month before *Psychodiagnostics*, posited two basic human attitudes, introversion and extraversion. Jung added four main psychological functions: judging the world through *thinking* versus *feeling*, and perceiving the world through *sensation* versus *intuition*. These categories may sound familiar—Jung's approach would later be popularized as the Myers-Briggs test. Questions of how we judge and perceive the world were also, obviously, central to the inkblot experiment. But the significance of Jung's *Psychological Types* for Rorschach ran deeper than that.

Jung had been writing about introversion and extraversion since 1911, and while Rorschach had adopted and modified the terms for the inkblot test, Jung's ideas had been changing too. After reading *Psychological Types*, Rorschach complained that "Jung is now on his fourth version of introversion—any time he writes anything, the concept changes again!" In the end, their definitions converged, and Rorschach's statement in *Psychodiagnostics* that his concept of introversion had "hardly anything in common with Jung's except the name" was misleading, because it referred only to the versions of Jung's theory published before 1920, when Rorschach was writing his book.

Like Rorschach, Jung rejected static pigeonholing and insisted that real people are always a mix of types. Jung described how parts of the self compensated for other parts—consciously introverted or thinking types, for instance, would have an unconscious marked by extraversion or feeling. In long, insightful descriptions of real-world interactions, he showed how people of one type behave in ways that are interpreted or misinterpreted by others through the lens of their own types. Jung's categories were not meant to label behavior but to help understand the complexity of real human situations.

The bottom line, though, was that people are different. When Jung was asked why he had said there were four types, precisely these four, each in extraverted or introverted form, he said that the schema was the result of many years of personal, psychiatric experience: that's just the way people are.

The problem, Jung wrote in the epilogue to *Psychological Types*, was that any theory of the mind "presupposes a uniform human psychology, just as scientific theories in general presuppose that nature is fundamentally one and the same." Unfortunately, it's just not true: there *is* no uniform human psychology. After referring to "Liberté, Égalité, Fraternité" and alluding to socialism and the Communist Revolution in Russia—allusions that certainly attracted Rorschach's notice—Jung raised the decisive objection that equal opportunity for all, equal liberty, equal income, even total justice of every kind would make some people happy and other people unhappy. If I ran the world, should I give Mr. X twice as much money as Mr. Y, since money means so much more to him? Or not, since the principle of equality matters to Mr. Z? What about people who need to put other people down to feel good about themselves—how should their needs be satisfied? Nothing we legislate "will ever be able to overcome the psychological differences between men." So too in science, and in any difference of opinion: "The partisans of either side attack each other purely externally, always seeking out the chinks in their opponent's armor. Squabbles of this kind are usually fruitless. It would be of considerably greater value if the dispute were transferred to the psychological realm, from which it arose in the first place. The shift of position would soon show a diversity of psychological attitudes, each with its own right to existence." Every worldview "depends on a personal psychological premise." No theorist "realizes that the psychology he sees is *his* psychology, and on top of that is the psychology of his type. He therefore supposes that there can be only one true explanation . . . namely the one that agrees with his type. All other views—I might almost say all seven other views—which, in their way, are just as true as his, are for him mere aberrations" for which he feels "a lively but very understandable distaste."

The project of *Psychological Types* had started with a case of incompatible views: while Freud thought everything was ultimately about sex, and Alfred Adler thought everything was ultimately about power, Jung's work "sprang originally from my need to define the ways in which my outlook differed from Freud's and Adler's. . . . In attempting to answer this question, I came across the problem of types; for it is one's psychological type which from the outset determines and limits a person's judgment." In the book, Jung managed a delicate dance around his own limitations. Even as his whole project implied a kind of Olympian insight into all the different types, he again and again admitted his own partiality. He said outright that the desire for a total, overarching theory was a fact of his own psychology; that Freud was as right, in his way, as Jung was in his; that it had taken Jung years to recognize the existence and value of types other than his own; that his discussion of types unlike his own was inadequate.

As Jung knew perfectly well, seeing through another person's eyes is all but impossible. "It is a fact constantly and overwhelmingly apparent in my practical work," he wrote—a fact since confirmed by every comment section on the internet, one might add—"that people are virtually incapable of understanding and accepting any point of view other than their own. . . . Every man is so imprisoned in his type that he is simply incapable of fully understanding another standpoint." The greatness of *Psychological Types* results from Jung's intuitive and analytical power combined with his decades-long effort to get outside of himself, despite everything.

Rorschach recognized the fundamental stakes of the book, and it brought him up short the way nothing else had. With his Jungian background, Rorschach was naturally asked to review the work, and in April 1921 he agreed. But the more he studied it, the less sure he was about how to incorporate its insights.

Admittedly, the book is a monster, with literally hundreds of pages on Indian Vedas, Swiss epic poetry, medieval Scholasticism, Goethe and Schiller, and whatever else could be shown to express the two poles of human experience. "I am reading Jung with mixed feelings," Rorschach wrote in June: "There is a lot that is right, definitely a lot, but embedded in a very queer architecture." Five months later:

> I am now reading Jung's *Types* for the third time and I still can't bring myself to start the review I am supposed to write. . . . In any case, I need to significantly rectify my earlier judgment about him. There really is an amazing amount in the book, and . . . for now I see no way to fault the deductive structure he lays out in contrast to Freud's thought. . . . I'm gnawing at the book, but as soon as I start to put something together, I become suspicious of my own ideas.

One of his complaints about isolation in Herisau was that "I really want to have a long conversation with someone about Jung at some point. The book has very many good things, and it is damned hard to say where the speculation goes off track." In January 1922, he was still struggling: "I have to agree with Jung, who distinguishes conscious and unconscious attitudes and says that when the conscious is extraverted, the unconscious is compensatorily introverted. This terminology is of course hideous, these formulations brutally smashed together, but clearly the idea of compensation is very significant." If nothing else, Jung had already argued for what Rorschach had thought was his own contrasting position: "Most cases have both introversive and extratensive aspects, every type is actually a mixture of the two."

Psychological Types was forcing Rorschach to rethink his ideas—and his own psychology. "I thought at first that Jung's types were purely speculative constructions," Rorschach confided to his former patient, Pastor Burri. "But when I finally tried to derive Jungian types from the results of my own experiment, I saw that it was possible. This meant that, in resisting Jung, my own type had actually prejudiced me much more than I thought."

In recognizing that his reactions revealed something about himself, Rorschach not only got to the heart of Jung's theory but also built on his own previous insights. In his dissertation, he had acknowledged that "my account of reflex-hallucinatory processes may seem subjective to some readers, for example auditory types, since it is written by someone who is primarily a motor type, secondarily a visual type." In his diary, on January 28, 1920: "Again and again we run into the fact that introverts cannot understand how extraverts think and behave, and vice versa. And they don't even realize that they are dealing with a different kind of person." Now Jung had brought the problem to a head. If ideas came from a theorist's personal psychology, then was any universal theory possible?

Jung had divided the world into eight distinct worldviews, but Rorschach's framework risked an even more thoroughgoing relativism, shattering a unitary truth into a nearly endless variety of perceptual styles. Until *Psychological Types,* Rorschach had been able to use his own balance of different qualities to paper over the troubling implications of his inkblot experiment. A brilliant intuitive reader of test protocols, he also tried to put the results on a solid numerical basis. He had written that an examiner too inclined or too disinclined to Movement responses would have a hard time scoring tests properly—but he saw himself as able to strike the right balance. He always refused to call either Movement or Color types better or worse. Jung's book confronted him with his own partiality, even the partiality of evenhandedness.

In his dissertation, Rorschach had had to admit that the psychology he described was his psychology; later, he thought that his inkblots had given him access to anyone and everyone's way of seeing. But truly accepting that everyone was different would make it harder to claim that he could bridge those differences anyway.

WHILE RORSCHACH WAS struggling with Jung, and with his neurotic patients, his ideas continued to develop, touching on many of the ways the test would evolve in the century to come. He moved away from

Experience Type and the introvert/extravert balance as the main finding of the test. He started paying closer attention to the subject's way of talking, frantic and compulsive or calm and relaxed. He raised questions that would define a century of debates: whether the examiner influenced the results; whether the test found permanent personality traits or reflected the test taker's situation and passing mood; whether standardization made the test more reliable or merely more rigid; whether responses should be scored in isolation or seen in the context of the whole protocol. "My method is still in its infancy," he wrote on March 22, 1922. "I am completely convinced that, after enough experience with the main inkblot series, ways forward to other, more specialized inkblots will open up, which will necessarily allow for significantly more differentiated conclusions."

His approach remained cautious. Examiners, he wrote, seemed able to influence the content of responses much more than formal aspects of the protocol, "but of course systematic study of this is very necessary." Even in a holistic approach, obtaining quantifiable data was essential: "A general view of the total findings must be retained to avoid being tripped up by the score for a particular variable, but even after a great deal of experience and practice, I consider it quite impossible to obtain a definite and reliable interpretation without doing the calculations." As for being free to interpret results at will or tied down to more or less crude formulas, "a dilemma that comes up unfortunately quite often in the test," Rorschach took the side of scientific objectivity: "All my work has shown me that crude systematization is better than arbitrary interpretation, if the situation is not clear in and of itself."

New discoveries continued to surprise him. When the latest volunteer assistant at Herisau started giving the inkblot test to patients at the Deaf-Mute Clinic in St. Gallen, Rorschach expected the deaf-mutes to have many kinesthetic responses, but "that turned out to be entirely false: they are purely visual Small Detail (Dd) interpreters with almost no M responses!" In retrospect, it was "a finding that is very understandable, however unexpected." He concluded from this and similar findings that it was far too soon to try to construct a theory to explain the inkblot test: only after much experience with a fuller range of subjects would the right theory "fall into place on its own."

Roemer organized a conference in Germany with Rorschach as the main speaker, to give Rorschach the chance to meet colleagues abroad and share his new ideas. It was planned for early April 1922, around Easter. On January 27, Rorschach wrote to tell Roemer he would not be attending after all: "I have thought it over again and again, and finally decided it would be better to stay home. It's very tempting, but first I want to be a bit more sure of certain points—too much is in flux at the moment. Of course there will always be something 'in progress,' even if I work on it for another hundred years, but there are a few points that are really bothering me, and I cannot free myself from these introverted hesitations no matter how much insight I have into their nature." He wanted to familiarize himself further with others' research and was especially hesitant to make any claims about vocational testing, as Roemer was pushing for. "Forgive me," Rorschach wrote, "and let us hope there will be another chance before long."

13

Right on the Threshold to a Better Future

MARCH 1922 CAME IN LIKE A LION AND WENT OUT LIKE A FREEZing lion. Spring snowstorms blanketed Switzerland, especially the high mountain country around Herisau. On Sunday, March 26, Rorschach had the day off and took Olga to see Ibsen's *Peer Gynt* in St. Gallen. The next morning, he woke up with stomach pain and a slight fever. The following week he was dead.

Olga had said that his stomach pains were nothing—friends of Hermann's still held it against her decades later. The bumbling Dr. Koller said not to worry, it was just a stomachache and would get better on its own; the doctor summoned from St. Gallen, Dr. Zollikofer, thought it was likely gallstones and recommended drinking lots of fluids. The Behn-Eschenburgs saw Rorschach walking through the halls that week bent almost double, and made a scene, saying something was seriously wrong, but Olga refused to do anything. She thought it was nicotine poisoning, which Hermann had had before, with pain so severe that he'd had to hold on to the banister to keep from falling when he climbed the stairs. The Rorschachs' maid had recently had an inflamed finger that prevented her from doing chores, and Olga had forced Hermann to lance it; the maid got an infection and had to be hospitalized, prompting the doctor to yell at Hermann about it, so now Hermann did not want to bother him again. Martha Schwarz, the competent nurse Rorschach was friends with, had left Herisau; more than forty years later, still upset, she insisted that if she had been in Herisau, Rorschach wouldn't have died.

At last Olga called Emil Oberholzer in Zurich, who hurried to Herisau with a physician: Paul von Monakov, son of the same Dr. Constantin von Monakov who had been unable to save Hermann's father Ulrich. Oberholzer saw at once that it was appendicitis and summoned a surgeon from Zurich, but snow covered everything and the surgeon got lost, driving to a town fifteen miles away instead of to Herisau. He arrived late and exhausted—a substantial delay, with Hermann in the bathroom, groaning, the snow still falling outside. The ambulance didn't get him to the hospital until 2:30 in the morning, half dead. He died in the operating room, at 10:00 a.m. on April 2, 1922, of peritonitis from a ruptured appendix.

Olga wrote to Paul in Brazil with the stunning news and details about Hermann's last days:

> He suddenly said to me, "Lola, I don't think I'm going to make it." . . . He talked about his work, his patients, about death, about me, our love, about you and Regineli, his dear ones! He said, "Say goodbye to Paul for me, I so wish I could have seen him," and sobbed when he said it, and then: "In a way it is a beautiful thing, to leave in the middle of life, but it is *bitter*." "I have done my part, now let others do theirs" (he meant his scientific work).

Even at the end, her letter makes clear, Hermann seemed to trust others' views of him more than his own.

> He said to me: "Tell me, what kind of a person was I? You know, when you're living your life you don't think much about the soul, about your self. But when you're dying, that's what you want to know about." I told him: "You were a noble, faithful, honest, gifted man." He: "Do you promise?" "I promise," I said. "If you swear it to me, then I believe it." Then I brought the children in and he kissed them, tried to laugh with them, then I took them away. . . .
>
> All the recognition he was receiving made him freer and more self-confident. But he still acted modest and ordinary. It made him look better too! Refreshed, in good spirits. I always said: "My handsome husband! Do you know what a beautiful, handsome man you are?" and he just laughed and answered, "I'm glad that's what I am in *your* eyes, I don't care what anyone else thinks."

She wrote of his joy in fatherhood, how after "so many losses when he was young, he wanted so badly to give his children a 'golden childhood,' and he could have, with his own bright mind and golden character." And whatever her earlier feelings about Hermann's work—now racked with guilt over not appreciating him enough when she could—she formed the image of her husband that she would cling to until her own death forty years later:

> Did you know that he was a rising force in science? His book caused a stir. People were already working with "the Rorschach method" and talking about the "Rorschach test," and about the first-rate brilliant ideas of a new psychology he had invented. . . . His scientist friends here said his death was an irreplaceable loss; he was the most gifted psychiatrist in Switzerland! He was genuinely highly gifted, I know it. Recently, all kinds of new ideas and trains of thought were just bubbling out of him, he wanted to take in everything. . . .
>
> I feel like we were right on the threshold to a better future—and now he's gone.

Oskar Pfister, who had remained a friend and supporter "awestruck" by Rorschach's abilities, wrote on April 3 to tell Freud that "yesterday we lost our ablest analyst, Dr Rorschach. He had a wonderfully clear and original mind, was devoted to analysis heart and soul, and his 'diagnostic test,' which would perhaps better be called analysis of form, was admirably worked out." He described Rorschach personally and tried one last time to intervene on the test's behalf: "He was a poor man all his life, and a proud, upright man of great human kindness; his death is a great loss to us. Can you not do something to verify his really magnificent testing system, which is certain to be of great service to psychoanalysis?"

At 2 p.m. on April 5, another day of nasty weather, Rorschach's funeral was held in a hurry at the Nordheim Cemetery in Zurich. Olga told Paul: "I did not want to leave him in Herisau. Zurich was 'our city' in every way. The city of our love, let him rest there now!" Pfister gave the religious service; Bleuler, never one to gush, called Rorschach "the hope of an entire generation of Swiss psychiatry." Years later, Emil Lüthy remembered looking through the window in the coffin at Hermann's "strongly suffering, pained face." There were "many wreathes, many many physicians, speeches," Olga wrote to Paul, and "a very beautiful funeral oration" from Rorschach's college friend Walter von Wyss: "I found in him a seeking after the highest things, a deep drive to understand fully the human soul and to bring himself into harmony with the world. His wonderful ability to put himself in the positions of all sorts of other people was striking. He was an individualist, precisely because he had something of his own to give, as only a rare few do." When Ludwig Binswanger published an essay on *Psychodiagnostics* in 1923, he lamented the loss of "the creative leader of a generation of Swiss psychiatrists," with his "extraordinary art of scientific experimentation, genius at human understanding, brilliant psychological dialectics, and sharp logical reasoning. . . . Where others saw only numbers or 'symptoms,' he instantly had before his eyes inner psychological connections and interrelations."

These eulogies and Olga's letters are not the only glimpse we have into the end of Rorschach's life—other views paint a darker picture. When Behn-Eschenburg came out of the operating room and told Olga and his own wife, Gertrud, that Hermann had died, Olga turned to Gertrud and said, "I hope the same thing happens to you!" The maid said that Olga "threw herself on the floor and screamed like an animal." Olga tried to throw her children out the window, and had to be physically restrained: "I can't stand to see them," she screamed. "I hate them, they remind me of him!" Lisa was four years old, Wadim almost three. Olga couldn't be left alone, and Gertrud Behn-Eschenburg stayed with her for two straight weeks, sleeping in the family apartment. It was she who later described Olga by quoting the saying "Scratch a Russian and you find a barbarian." Most cruelly of all, after Hermann's half-sister Regineli had stomach pains at the funeral and was operated on for appendicitis, and everything went well, Olga accused her of wanting appendicitis just because Hermann had it. She refused to believe that Regineli had really needed the operation.

❧❧

Rorschach's favorite quote was by the Zurich writer Gottfried Keller, whose beautiful novel *Green Henry* is the most visual of the classic nineteenth-century bildungsromans. He often recited the last two lines of Keller's most famous poem, "Evening Song." He inscribed them on the last page of the Rorschach family chronicle he made for Paul, and on gifts to the Koller boys; he put the lines on his son's birth notice and quoted them on his deathbed.

The poem celebrates the glory of the visual world and the human drive, doomed but noble, to take in as much of that glory as possible. "Eyes, my dear little windows, / Give me a little longer the fairest glows / Of vision," it opens, before describing impending death:

> Be kind, let the images in,
> For someday you too shall grow dim!

> No sooner shall the light have ceased
> And the tired lids close than the soul shall have peace;
> She will fumblingly take off her walking shoes
> And lay herself down in the coffin's gloom.

> Still, she will see two glimmering sparks,
> Like two little stars in the inner dark,
> 'Til they, too, waver and finally die,
> As though by the wing of a butterfly.

The poem ends, in the lines Rorschach loved, with a hymn to vision:

> And still will I roam in the evening field,
> With only the sinking star for a friend;
> Drink in, oh eyes, all your lashes can hold
> Of the golden abundance of the world!

"Abundance" also means "overflow"—in German, the word is an image of a cup or vessel brimming over.

In his thirty-seven years, Hermann Rorschach did drink in the overflow of the world. He created a window into the soul that we have been peering through for a century, then died before he could respond to the biggest challenge to his legacy. Was the test effective only because of Rorschach's own psychology? Were his interpretations a uniquely personal art, or could the test endure beyond him? Whatever the answers to these questions, the inkblots were now let loose on the world, without his guiding hand and eye.

14

The Inkblots Come to America

IN 1923, DAVID MORDECAI LEVY, A THIRTY-ONE-YEAR-OLD PSY-
chiatrist and psychoanalyst, was director of the first Child Guidance
clinic in the country, the Juvenile Psychopathic Institute in Chicago.
It had been opened in 1909 with the help of Jane Addams, founder of
social work in America and eventual winner of the Nobel Peace Prize;
Child Guidance, a Progressive Era crusade to address children's physical and mental health problems by listening to "the child's own story"
and looking at children in their social and family context, was a perfect
match for Levy, a perceptive observer and sensitive listener.

Now Levy was stepping down for a year abroad, during which he
planned to work on child psychoanalysis with a Swiss psychiatrist:
Rorschach's friend Emil Oberholzer. He was in the process of post-
humously publishing Rorschach's virtuosic 1922 lecture, and in 1924,
when Levy returned to Chicago to take up the directorship of the mental health clinic at Michael Reese Hospital in Chicago, he had in his
luggage a copy of Rorschach's lecture, book, and inkblots. So it was two
years after Rorschach's death—either at the Michael Reese clinic, or
at the Institute for Juvenile Research under Illinois's Department of
Criminology, or perhaps in Levy's private Chicago practice—that for
the first time in America someone was shown the ten inkblots and was
asked: "What might this be?" Before going on to have a long and successful career, in which he invented play therapy and coined the term
sibling rivalry, Levy published Rorschach's essay in English, gave the
first US seminar on the Rorschach, and taught a generation of students
what the test was and how to use it.

Hermann Rorschach's life was rooted in Switzerland, at the crossroads of Germany and France, Vienna and Russia. Rorschach's afterlife

would be global, as the inkblots spread around the world, popularized or not in various countries through very different chains of circumstance. The test's midcentury champion in Switzerland discovered antidepressants; its advocate in England was a child psychologist who published an article during the Blitz called "The Bombed Child and the Rorschach Test." In one of the first countries to introduce the Rorschach, Japan, it was popularized by the inventor of a concentration test still mandatory for close to a million employees in public transportation agencies. The Rorschach remains the most popular psychological test in Japan, while it has fallen completely out of favor in the United Kingdom; it is big in Argentina, marginal in Russia and Australia, on the rise in Turkey. All these developments have their own histories.

It was in the United States, though, that the test first came to fame, had its most dramatic rise to prominence and descent into controversy, penetrated deepest into the culture, and played a part in many of the historical milestones of the century.

The test in America was a lightning rod from the start. Which is more trustworthy, hard numbers or expert judgment? Or maybe the question is: Which should we distrust less? This has always been the key debate in American social science—indeed, in much of American life. The mainstream position, even in the early twentieth century, was to trust the numbers.

There was widespread skepticism in American psychology of anything going beyond what the hard data could prove. Especially after controversial calls to segregate or sterilize people found to be "feeble-minded," psychologists believed more than ever that it was crucial not to draw wild conclusions from tests but to use "psychometrics," the science of quantitative, objectively valid measurements. The leading theories in psychology were behaviorist, emphasizing what people actually do, not the mysterious mind allegedly behind their actions.

Yet there remained an opposed tradition, reinforced by Freudian ideas and other philosophies imported from Europe, which mistrusted what it saw as cold, hyper-rational science. Psychotherapists, having worked with real people in complex situations, often respected the truths of psychoanalysis, irrational though they were, as more powerful and convincing than the usual arguments of logic. They recognized that objective measurement had its limits when it came to human psychology.

Today it is psychiatrists who tend to be "hard scientists" while psychologists use "softer" therapies, but in the early twentieth century the poles were reversed: Freudian psychiatrists dismissed research psychologists as bean counters, while academic psychologists trumpeted their hardheaded science background against Freudian mystics and approaches resistant to objective measurement.

And now here were ten inkblots. Was a Rorschach scientific and quantitative, like a blood test, or did it yield results open to creative, humanistic interpretation, like talk therapy? Was it science or art? Rorschach himself had realized in 1921 that the inkblot test falls between two stools, too touchy-feely for the scientists and too structured for the psychoanalysts:

> It comes out of two different approaches: psychoanalysis and academic research psychology. So that means the research psychologists find it too psychoanalytical, and the analysts often don't understand it because they stay clinging to the content of the interpretations, with no sense for the formal aspect. What matters, though, is that it works: it gives amazingly correct diagnoses. And so they hate it all the more.

If anything, Rorschach understated the problem, since the test's psychiatric use—diagnosing patients—lacked any real grounding in psychology, any theory that explained why, say, introversion or extraversion produced Movement or Color responses. Psychologists couldn't help but be baffled by psychiatrists' apparently effective use of the test. But saying that the test was destined for controversy, leading even to hatred—Rorschach was right about that.

THE TWO MOST influential early Rorschachers in America personified the divide almost perfectly. In the fall of 1927, back from another year in Switzerland spent working on the Rorschach, David Levy was head of the New York Institute for Child Guidance. In its halls, he ran into a discouraged older student at a loss for a dissertation topic. Levy loaned him a copy of *Psychodiagnostics* and Rorschach's 1922 essay. It was a good tip.

That student was Samuel Beck (1896–1980), born in Romania, who had come to America in 1903 and done so well in school that by age sixteen he was on fellowship to study classics at Harvard, where he overlapped with Levy. When his father fell ill, Beck went back to Cleveland, Ohio, to support the family, working as a reporter—a psychological education in itself: "I saw some of the best murderers that a big city has, the best robbers, bootleggers, and embezzlers." After a decade of real life, he returned to Harvard, graduated in 1926, and went to Columbia to study psychology, wanting to find out "by scientific method what the human being is like."

The inkblot test would become his life's work. Beck published the first American articles on the Rorschach, starting in 1930 ("The Rorschach Test and Personality Diagnosis"); completed the first American dissertation on the Rorschach, in 1932; and went to Switzerland himself in 1934–35, where he too befriended and worked with Oberholzer. He returned and followed Levy to Chicago.

The psychoanalyst to Beck's research psychologist was Bruno Klopfer (1900–1971), a German Jew, improvisational and antiauthoritarian, the rebellious son of a banker. He had terrible eyesight at a young age from an undiagnosed condition and had been forced to "make up through his keen thinking what he could not see with the visual clarity of the other school boys." It was a perfect symbol for the man who would become America's most prominent and suspect Rorschach interpreter: he might not have seen the thing himself, but he could convince you he understood what you saw.

A PhD at twenty-two, Klopfer worked for more than a decade in the Berlin equivalent of Child Guidance and received extensive training in psychoanalytic theory and phenomenology, a philosophical approach focusing on subjective experience. For five years, he hosted a popular weekly radio program that gave listeners child-rearing advice—a pioneering show that broadcast not lectures but Klopfer sitting and discussing listeners' problems. In 1933, when his eight-year-old son came home from school in Germany and asked, "What is a Jew?"—a boy had been beaten up, and the principal had told little Klopfer it was wrong to help him because the boy was Jewish—Klopfer answered, "I'll tell you next week." By then they had left the country.

With his son safe at a boarding school in England, Bruno Klopfer got a Swiss visa sponsored by Carl Jung, which is how he ended up working at the Zurich Psychotechnic Institute, learning the Rorschach test from an assistant named Alice Grabarski so that he could administer it twice a day to Swiss job applicants. In business-friendly Switzerland, the test was being used far more in vocational counseling and industry than by serious psychologists; Klopfer found the work dull. He came to America on July 4, 1934, as a research assistant for the Columbia University anthropologist Franz Boas. For all his expertise and experience, his salary was $556 a year, roughly $10,000 in today's dollars. Finding that people in New York were hungry to learn more about the Rorschach, he saw his chance.

Klopfer, too, had brought *Psychodiagnostics* and the inkblots with him, and the chair of the Columbia Psychology Department, who had supervised Beck's dissertation, was interested in the Rorschach. But he was firmly on the side of psychometrics and behaviorism, suspicious of Klopfer's psychoanalytical and philosophical background, and he said that Klopfer could teach at Columbia only if he first got a letter of support from the more trustworthy Beck or Oberholzer. Unable to rise through official channels, Klopfer turned himself into America's leading Rorschach expert on his own.

It was an intellectually vibrant time in New York, the city full of scholars and scientists in exile from Nazi Germany who had been taken in by Princeton, Columbia, and the University in Exile at the New School for Social Research. Gatherings like the great neurologist Kurt Goldstein's informal cultural salons in basement rooms of the Montefiore Hospital in the Bronx, with voluble conversations going on simultaneously in French, German, and Italian, gave Klopfer a hospitable welcome and access to a huge and interdisciplinary range of contacts.

Despite his terrible English, Klopfer taught the Rorschach to interested grad students and staff—seven students two nights a week for six weeks, at first—in whatever space was available, from empty lecture halls to Brooklyn apartments. By 1936 he was teaching three seminars a week; in 1937, he was appointed a lecturer in the Department of Guidance, teaching one seminar a semester and continuing to offer private classes for the non-Columbia students. The first Rorschach journal grew out of the loose affiliation of Klopfer and his students: the *Rorschach Research Exchange*. Its first issue, in 1936, sixteen mimeographed pages, was funded by fourteen people chipping in three dollars each; within a year it was a respectable journal with a hundred subscribers internationally. A Rorschach Institute soon followed, with membership qualifications and an accreditation process. Beck published work in Klopfer's journal, but not for long.

Both men saw the Rorschach as an incredibly powerful tool. According to Klopfer, using a metaphor that would recur again and again throughout the test's history, it "does not reveal a behavior picture, but rather shows—like an X-ray picture—the underlying structure which makes behavior understandable." Beck synonymously described "a fluoroscope into the psyche": an "extremely sensitive" and "objective instrument having a potential for penetrating into the whole person."

Still, they saw very different things when they looked through their instruments. Klopfer, from a European philosophical tradition rather than Beck's American behaviorist one, took a holistic approach: a person's answers yielded a "configuration" to be interpreted as a whole, not scores to be added up. For Beck, configurations were secondary at best, objectivity was all. For instance, Beck felt that the decision whether to score a response as good or bad (F+ or F–) must never be based on idiosyncratic personal judgment, no matter how experienced the examiner or group of examiners: "Once the response has been finally judged plus or minus, it must always be scored plus or minus," irrespective of holistic considerations of anything else the test taker might have said. Klopfer, while he agreed that lists of good and bad responses were needed to judge common answers as F+ or F–, argued that rare and yet "keenly perceived" answers must be categorized as different from bad answers—and that meant judging them individually, because no list could contain every possible response.

Rorschach had been subjective and objective both, a personality as symmetrical as his inkblots, and both men knew it. In Klopfer's words, Rorschach "combined, to a marked degree, the sound empirical realism of a clinician with the speculative acumen of an intuitive thinker."

In Beck's: Rorschach as a psychoanalyst understood depth psychology and "knew the value of free association. Fortunately, too, he possessed an experimental bent, appreciated the advantages of objectivity, and was gifted also with creative insight."

By 1937 the battle lines had been drawn. Klopfer, improvising with eager, inquisitive students, felt free to change the test and develop new techniques based on clinical experience and instinct, not necessarily empirical research. He added a new code for responses that describe the movement of nonhuman objects, for example, even though Rorschach had insisted that M responses were about the subject's identification with human or humanlike movement. In fact, Klopfer added codes with abandon: while "Rorschach was able to handle the material of his test with the simple M, C, CF, FC, and F(C)" codes, Beck complained, "the Klopfer repertory with M, FM, m, mF, Fm, k, kF, Fk, K, KF, FK, Fc, c, cF, FC', C'F, C', F/C, C/F, C, Cn, Cdes, Csym, is bewildering."

Beck was a traditionalist, firmly committed to his lineage of teachers. He saw himself as "a student trained in the Rorschach-Oberholzer discipline." Any change to the canonical test would have to be thoroughly grounded in empirical research. He wrote that Klopfer's concept of nonhuman movement, for example, "does not seem consistent with Rorschach's, Oberholzer's, Levy's, or their close followers' understanding of the value of M. . . . If this interpretation of M is based in [Klopfer's] experience, one is naturally interested in the evidence." Beck was proud that his work showed "little influence deriving from the new idiom that has appeared in recent years, only in America, reporting studies in which the Rorschach inkblot figures were used." He disdained even to call Klopfer's studies-using-the-inkblot-figures actual Rorschach research.

Before long, Beck and Klopfer were literally not on speaking terms, and that was how it remained between America's two most prominent Rorschachers. Students at Klopfer's workshops who had studied with Beck were eyed with suspicion by their partisan classmates. In the summer of 1954, a promising graduate student named John Exner arrived in Chicago to work as Beck's assistant, soon becoming good friends with Beck and his wife. When he showed up at Beck's house one day, innocently carrying a copy of Klopfer's book on the Rorschach, Beck asked, suddenly cold: "What's that? Where did you get that book?"

"At the library," Exner nervously replied.

"*Our* library?" Beck said, as though the University of Chicago were his territory, off limits to the interloper.

In truth neither Klopfer nor Beck was as narrow or rigid as the roles they came to play representing the two contrasting approaches to the inkblots. Klopfer co-wrote his first book with a hard science psychiatrist, Dr. Douglas Kelley, and tempered his position in later years, though never to the point of being able to reconcile with his rival. Beck, for his part, would often "awe those around him" with brilliant interpretations going beyond the available data: colleagues recalled how "the phenomenologist, lurking somewhere beneath his staunch empiricist exterior, would 'out' and reveal the full expertise of the brilliant clinician." Still, the feud raged.

Every science has its feuds and backbiting, but the history of the Rorschach test has been unusually plagued by controversy, with the "squabbles," to use Jung's word from *Psychological Types*, unusually hostile. On the one side, objective scientists repelled by charismatic charlatans; on the other, subtle explorers of the mind unwilling to kneel at the altar of standardization. The test's balance—between conscious problem solving and unconscious reactions, between structure and freedom, subjectivity and objectivity—made it especially easy to see it from only one side, rejecting the other perspective.

THE KLOPFER-BECK FEUD drowned out the voices of more moderate figures, most notably Marguerite Hertz (1899–1992). Hertz had first been shown the inkblots by her Cleveland friend Sam Beck and had trained with David Levy in 1930. Her 1932 dissertation on questions of standardization was the second on the Rorschach, after Beck's, and in 1934 she published her first article, likewise using a psychometric perspective: "The Reliability of the Rorschach Ink-Blot Test." She also joined Klopfer's group in 1936.

While closer to Beck in substance, Hertz was less of an originalist in temperament, more willing than he to criticize or add to the master's system. One of her innovations was a trial blot, shown to subjects with encouraging remarks before the test proper to talk them through what they were about to do. And she was critical of both sides when necessary; she has since been called the conscience of the early Rorschach pioneers. Her first article in Klopfer's *Rorschach Research Exchange* argued that a Detail response had to be judged "normal" through empirical statistics, against Klopfer's "qualitative approach" of deciding the question as he saw fit. While she championed standardization, though, she cautioned Beck and his supporters that it must never be "rigid" or "inflexible." Elsewhere she praised Klopfer for being "far more flexible than many of his disciples," who had an "almost faddish devotion" to the Klopfer System and Klopfer himself.

Her most dramatic effort to reconcile the two sides came in 1939. Whether you liked or disliked the subjectivity involved in interpreting a Rorschach test, she pointed out, the test was worthless if different scorers and interpreters couldn't reliably reach more or less the same results, ones more or less consistent with findings from other tests or evaluations. Yet "because the Rorschach method is peculiarly different from most psychological tests," she wrote, it was hard to test its reliability in standard ways. You couldn't compare it against other series of inkblots, because there's no other series of blots that works. You couldn't use a split-half method, because the results from the first five cards and results from the last five cards are meaningless in isolation. If you retested someone after a while, their psychology might have changed, so differing results would not necessarily indicate a flawed test. How could the test be tested?

Inspired by Rorschach's own blind diagnoses, Hertz staged the first multiple blind-interpretation with the Rorschach: submitting the same test protocol for interpretation by Klopfer, Beck, and herself. The test passed the test: all three analyses agreed with each other and with the clinical conclusions of the patient's doctor, offering "the same personality picture" of the patient's intelligence, cognitive style, influence of emotions, conflicts, neuroses. There were no substantive differences, only slightly different emphases. Hertz called it "a remarkable extent of agreement." The battle royale was a win-win-win.

Hertz spent years as a researcher for the Brush Foundation at Western Reserve University (now Case Western), collecting data for an enormous normative study—more than three thousand Rorschach protocols from a variety of groups: children, adolescents, different races, healthy, pathological, superior, delinquent. By the end of the thirties, she had nearly finished her manuscript, a comprehensive textbook that would likely have changed the history of the Rorschach in America had she published it. But the Brush Foundation project was canceled, and then Hertz got a phone call: "One day it was decided to dispose of the material which was no longer in use and which the authorities felt was worthless. I was called and told that I may *have* my material. I went over at once with graduate students and a truck, but to my dismay, I learned that my material had already been burned 'by mistake.' It had been 'confused' with everything else being discarded. All the Rorschach records, all the psychological data, all the worksheets, plus my manuscript went up in smoke." The collection of data was unreproducible, the loss "irreparable," and Hertz was "unwilling to write a book without relating what I say to my own research." With that disaster, the leading moderate voice on the Rorschach—closest in tone and spirit to Rorschach's own—was lost, or at least subordinated to Klopfer's and Beck's.

Hertz wrote dozens of important articles in the years to come but never collected them into a book—apparently willing to let Klopfer take the lead after he published his own textbook in 1942, especially since her early psychometric emphasis was increasingly giving way to an approach closer to his. For half a century, she regularly wrote overview articles evaluating the state of the field as a whole, synthesizing or criticizing others rather than staking her own claims. Much of her early work focused on children and adolescents, without the emphasis on medical diagnosis that marked the early decades of the test in America outside of Chicago. It no doubt mattered that she was a woman, although as always it is hard to say precisely how the gender difference played out: directly or indirectly, through her choice of more "feminized" topics of study, through her willingness not to publish. In any case, while her approach to Rorschach administration and interpretation was importantly different from both Beck's and Klopfer's, she never presented her methodology as an integrated system of its own.

KLOPFER'S INTUITIVE INTERPRETATIONS and generally subjective approach tended to draw stronger reactions than Beck's emphasis on objectivity. At worst, Beck was dry and rigid, while Klopfer, throughout his career, would be hailed as a magician and reviled as a fraud. But no one, then or later, disputed that Klopfer's organizational brio was indispensable for the rise of the Rorschach.

By 1940, Klopfer was teaching three courses at Columbia's Teachers College and another at the New York State Psychiatric Institute, supervising eight graduate students at Columbia and New York University, and giving workshops and seminars from San Francisco, Berkeley, and Los Angeles to Denver, Minneapolis, Cleveland, and Philadelphia. Branches in Texas, Maine, Wisconsin, and Canada, Australia, England, and South America followed within a year. Hertz, too, had been teaching two graduate courses a year since 1937, along with a six-month administration and scoring course; Beck was busy in Chicago; even Emil Oberholzer, who had immigrated to New York in 1938, gave a series of lectures for the New York Psychoanalytic Society in 1938–39. Interested parties could get beginning or advanced training across the country.

At Sarah Lawrence, an elite women's college near New York with flexible instruction tailored to each student, the staff and faculty in 1937 were dissatisfied with what they could learn about their students from "observations and the general run of objective tests." So a psychologist named Ruth Munroe turned to the Rorschach. Klopfer analyzed six protocols from freshmen and gave the profiles, without names, to the students' teacher, who could identify every student correctly; other blind analyses and "various other checking devices" were equally convincing.

Satisfied that the test worked, Munroe and her Sarah Lawrence colleagues were soon "so busy using it that the projected full scientific analysis has been delayed." It seemed better than anything else they had, and if the teachers and advisers, with so much detailed personal information about every student, confirmed the test results and felt that the test in turn "confirmed and focused" what they already suspected, what else could they want? The Rorschach was "not infallible," Munroe wrote. "Neither are teacher judgments. The general correspondence is sufficiently close, however, so that we feel justified in accepting the Rorschach as a useful tool in educational planning. It is scarcely necessary to mention the qualification that we never use the test as the sole or even the major criterion of judgment in any important decision about a student." Within three years Munroe's team had Rorschach-tested over a hundred students, as well as sixteen teachers, to explore the possibility of predicting student-teacher rapport.

Rorschach results were soon being used to tailor teaching approaches to the needs of each student or to suggest whether a struggling student had "the resources from which improvement may be expected." One student, a lawyer's daughter, had narrow interests, extraordinarily stubborn ideas, and fierce resistance to anything new. When it was unclear whether these were "a superficial adolescent reaction" to be worked on further or instead "a deep-seated compulsion" unlikely to change, her rigid and intellectually undistinguished Rorschach indicated the latter. "It is difficult to know how we can best help this girl," but letting her define her own areas of study would not be the right approach. Another student, nervous and overly conscientious, revealed an original and vigorous imagination on her Rorschach. Changing her tightly structured program to one that gave her greater freedom to pursue her own interests brought excellent results.

The inkblots could also catch problems early. One freshman seemed fine, with her "lively manner," "a certain freshness and humor," "good common sense and conventionality," and "thoroughly 'collegiate'" clothes and appearance. Her weak academic performance was largely due, teachers thought, "to a somewhat excessive social life": she "made the rounds of the men's colleges with great pleasure apparently," and a recent quarrel "with the man at Princeton" had only slightly curtailed "the range of her prom trotting."

Her Rorschach, though, which she took as part of a control group and not because of any particular suspicions about her, showed her to be "the most strikingly disturbed" student in the class: "For some reason or other she is scared to death." She was extremely defensive, with signs of hostility and resentment (one of her responses was "*People spitting at each other, sticking their tongues out or something*") and severe emotional blocking that almost totally suppressed the intellectual capacities evident in her few lively and perceptive responses. A subsequent meeting with all her teachers and advisers confirmed what her performance on the test suggested: she was doing barely adequate work in all her classes, showing interest at first but staying on a superficial level before suddenly becoming disengaged or dismissive. She had once gone after her sister with a knife, "but of course was over that now." She told her adviser she had felt "suicidal all day," but then passed it off as a joke.

The problems were there, but no one had noticed them until the inkblots. Starting in 1940, the Rorschach was given to every entering student at Sarah Lawrence, with the results scanned quickly for striking problems, kept on file in case questions about the student arose later, and used as "a permanent reservoir for research material."

Within barely a dozen years of its arrival in America, the Rorschach was being taught, used, and studied furiously across the country. Scores were being refined and redefined, data collected and analyzed, techniques improved and invented, results analyzed blind and correlated with other tests and every sociocultural factor imaginable. Along with asking what about the test made it so popular, it makes sense to ask what made the country so receptive. America was in another "test-hungry time," as Rorschach had written of Switzerland in 1921, but there was more. Americans increasingly thought of themselves as having something special inside that could not be accessed with any standard tests, and the Rorschach would prove uniquely able to grasp it.

Fascinating, Stunning, Creative, Dominant

WHAT YOU DO—IN FACT, EVERYTHING YOU DO—EXPRESSES WHO you are. Your actions reveal not so much the content of your character as your personality: not conformity to recognized moral virtues, but how you stand out by being unique and special.

These familiar ideas were the product of a shift in early twentieth-century America from a culture of character to a culture of personality. "Character," an ideal of serving a higher moral and social order, was regularly invoked around the turn of the twentieth century along-side *citizenship, duty, democracy, work, building, golden deeds, outdoor life, conquest, honor, reputation, morals, manners, integrity,* and above all *manhood.* "Personality," in contrast, was invoked in the following decades together with words like *fascinating, stunning, attractive, magnetic, glowing, masterful, creative, dominant, forceful*—not nouns but adjectives, not specific kinds of behavior but hype for making an impact.

These new terms of praise were amoral: someone's character was good or bad, but a personality was appealing or unappealing. If anything, bad was better—a thrilling rebel beat an upstanding drip any day. The charm and charisma that compelled people to like you came to be seen as mattering more than integrity or honorable deeds that might earn their respect; poise took precedence over virtue, seeming sincere over being sincere. Who cared what you were like on the inside if you were too dull to be noticed in the faceless crowd at all?

The cultural shift from character to personality can be tracked in self-help books, sermons, education, advertising, politics, fiction—anything that offered an ideal of how to live. Dr. Orison Swett Marden, the Dr. Phil of his day, ended his 1899 book *Character: The Greatest Thing in the World* with a quote from US president James Garfield:

"I must succeed in making myself a man." By 1921, when he came to write *Masterful Personality*, Marden had changed with the times: "Our success in life depends upon what others think of us." Movie stars were part of the same shift: studios at first tended to conceal the identities of actors and actresses, but around 1910 the star was born, and his or her personality became the movie's main selling point. Douglas Fairbanks, the first such movie celebrity, was described this way in 1907: "He's not good looking. But he has worlds of personality." Or this slogan from one of cinema's greatest, Katharine Hepburn: "Show me an actress who isn't a personality and you'll show me a woman who isn't a star." The archetype of the jazzy new age wasn't Gatsby the Good Person, but Gatsby the incomparably Great, and how he made his money mattered infinitely less than his indescribable qualities, his sparkle, his beautiful shirts.

Since you have some control over how you come across, you can shape your destiny by improving your self-presentation—the classic American promise took on this form in the early twentieth century, echoed endlessly by style magazines and business gurus in the decades since. The downside of endless opportunities to make a masterful impression, of course, was the infinite risk of making a bad one. In a world of constant social monitoring and comparison, the demands of self-marketing never stopped: absolutely anything might reveal to watchful, judging eyes more about you than you might even know.

One classic study, Roland Marchand's *Advertising the American Dream*, reprints a truly terrifying array of early-twentieth-century ads proclaiming that your bad breath, careless shave, unfortunate clothes, or droopy socks would be noticed, dooming your chances at romance, success, and a decent life. "CRITICAL EYES ARE SIZING YOU UP RIGHT NOW," intoned the voice of Williams shaving cream. Only because she owned a Dr. West toothbrush could one woman pass "The Smile Test" when she fell off a toboggan and a handsome stranger helped her to her feet. Ads of an earlier generation had tended to actually describe their products rather than offering this combination of promise and threat.

But even if the new ads exaggerated a little, they reflected social realities. Superficial things "*were* more significant in a mobile, urban, impersonal society" than in an earlier era of more stable relationships, in Marchand's words. Especially in love and business, to have a masterful personality meant you had to "be yourself," but that also meant smiling the right smile and wearing the right sock garters. Without such external markers, you were out of luck.

Given the high stakes, the glamour and flair of "personality" paradoxically came to be essential: style *was* substance, how you came across was who you were. "As late as 1915," in the words of one leading anthropologist, "the very word still carried overtones chiefly of piquancy, unpredictability, intellectual daring: a man's personality was much like a woman's 'it'"—the sex appeal that made her, in the cliché of the time, an "It Girl." By the 1930s, though, once Freud had come to prominence, Americans had seized upon the idea that some ineffable inner force dominated our lives, and they equated that force with personality. Jung's "psychological types," which had described something more like character than style, were reimagined in America as "personality types," starting with the work of Myers and Briggs in the 1920s. And while the seething energy of the Freudian unconscious was hopelessly chaotic, personality was understood as having a "structure," something that could be analyzed, categorized, grappled with. If you described that inner force as "personality," there was more you could say about it.

This evolving sense of self was what the Rorschach test tapped into, and it in turn redefined the test. A 1939 essay called "Projective Methods for the Study of Personality," by Lawrence Frank, was nothing less than a new vision of the individual's place in the world, redefining psychology for the twentieth century and putting the Rorschach, as a test of "personality," right at the center of it.

Lawrence K. Frank (1890–1968) has been called "the Johnny Appleseed of the social sciences" for his fruitful work as a writer, lecturer, mentor, and executive in a series of leadership posts in philanthropic foundations from the twenties through the forties. Margaret Mead wrote in an obituary that he "more or less invented the social sciences" and was "one of the two or three men" who used foundations "the way the Lord meant them to be used." His greatest contribution was to promote research on childhood development and spread the results in nursery and elementary schools and treatment settings; his efforts shaped the fields of developmental child psychology, early childhood education, and pediatrics for decades to come.

In a 1939 essay, Frank explained personality in the broadest possible terms, as the way we give meaning to life. "The personality process," he wrote, "might be regarded as a sort of rubber stamp which the individual imposes upon every situation." The person "necessarily ignores or subordinates many aspects of the situation that for him are irrelevant and meaningless and selectively reacts to those aspects that are personally significant." We shape our world, which means we are not passive creatures, receiving and responding to stimuli or facts in the outside world. In Frank's view, there *are* no facts, no outside world, no external stimuli at all except insofar as a person "selectively constitutes them and responds to them." It was an idea with shades of Nikolai Kulbin, the Futurist whom Rorschach had heard in Russia: "The self does not know anything except its own feelings, and while projecting these feelings it creates its own world."

Such subjectivity posed a problem for the scientist. There was nothing replicable, no control experiments, only the unique interaction that takes place whenever "a person perceives, and imputes to what he perceives, the meaning which he himself projects upon whatever he perceives, then responds in some manner." Everything a person did was significant, but it needed to be interpreted, not simply tabulated. Standardized tests wouldn't work. The scientist needed a way to measure *how* a subject's personality organized his or her experience.

Lawrence Frank had a solution, and a new name for it: "projective methods." To Frank these were not "tests," though they were sometimes referred to as such. Instead, projective methods presented a person with something open-ended, something that meant "not what the experimenter has arbitrarily decided it should mean (as in most psychological experiments using standardized stimuli in order to be 'objective'), but rather whatever it must mean to the personality who gives it, or imposes upon it, his private, idiosyncratic meaning and organization." Subjects would then react in a way that expressed their personality. Rather than giving an "objectively" right or wrong answer, a subject would "project" his or her personality out into the world for the experimenter to see.

Frank's ultimate projective method was the Rorschach.

Other such methods for eliciting the personality already existed in

1939: Frank mentioned play therapy and art therapy, unfinished sentences and uncaptioned pictures, the Cloud Picture method, and more. The clear runner-up was the Thematic Apperception Test, or TAT, developed by two followers of Jung's at Harvard in the 1930s. In the TAT, subjects are shown pictures—a boy looking at a violin on a table, or a fully dressed man holding his arm over his eyes with a naked woman lying in bed behind him—and asked to come up with a "dramatic story" to explain the scene. But dramatic stories did not provide fixed data to measure and score, like the crucial formal features of Movement and Color, Whole and Detail, on standardized inkblots. TAT results could only be interpreted impressionistically. To psychologists looking for an objective way to measure personality, there was nothing like the Rorschach.

Seventeen years after Hermann Rorschach's death, his inkblots were reframed as the ultimate projective method and as a new paradigm of modern personality, both in psychology and in the culture at large. The Rorschach and our idea of who we are coalesced around a single symbolic situation, something like this: The world is a dark, chaotic place. It has only the meaning we give it. But do I perceive the shape of things or create that shape? Do I find a wolf in the inkblot or put one there? (Do I find Mr. Right in a handsome stranger or imagine him there?) I, too, am a dark, chaotic place, roiled by unconscious forces, and others are doing to me just what I am doing to them. Like the CRITICAL EYES SIZING YOU UP RIGHT NOW of the shaving cream ad, everyone is sizing me up, uncovering my secrets. Scientists, advertisers, handsome strangers, the inkblots themselves, are peering into me just as much as I am peering into them. (I see a wolf in the blot; the blot sees sanity or insanity in me.)

The Rorschach test, as reimagined in 1939 as a projective method, assumed that we have a creative individual self that shapes how we see, then offered a technique for uncovering and measuring that self, and a beautiful visual symbol for it.

Rorschach had not described his own test in these terms, at least not explicitly. He did not call the inkblot test a "projective method," and in fact he rarely mentioned "projection," a concept he understood in the narrower, Freudian sense of attributing something unacceptable about ourselves to other people (an angry person thinks everyone is angry at her; a repressed homosexual denies his own urges and hates what he sees as signs of gayness in others).

Yet Frank's new understanding of the test was true to what underlay Rorschach's ideas. Projection in Frank's sense was ultimately another version of empathy, putting ourselves into the world before responding to what we find there. The Movement response and Frank's idea of projection rested on the same shifts back and forth between the self and the outside world.

After 1939, both Klopfer's and Beck's camps would cast the inkblot test as a "projective method for the study of personality" in Frank's sense. If the Rorschach was an X-ray, the hidden but all-important personality was the invisible skeleton people wanted to see, and projection was what made it visible.

The broader implications of Frank's theory were there in Rorschach, too. Frank pointed out that our personality is not chosen from an infinite menu of options: we exist in a social context. "Reality" is a more or less agreed-upon public world that every individual member of a particular society has to accept and interpret within a permitted range of deviation, or else risk being excluded and considered sick. Different societies have different realities—what's crazy in one is not necessarily crazy in another. Frank's position was as relativist as Jung's: cultures, and individuals within a culture, see things their own way.

Psychology, with its new emphasis on personality differences rather than universals of human character, was crossing over into anthropology, the study of cultural differences. This was the move that Rorschach had hoped to but not lived to make himself, with his sect studies and the cross-cultural inkblot experiments he had planned.

ANTHROPOLOGY, TOO, WAS just reaching a mass American audience in its own right. Prior to 1920, it was a relatively dry pursuit: mostly descriptive and historical catalogs of artifacts and kinship structures, however exotic the subject matter might be. Anthropologists studied social institutions and entire populations, with specific people seen merely as "carriers" of the culture. The 1928 index to the first forty volumes of *American Anthropologist* contained zero mentions of the word "personality." Insofar as any psychological approach was relevant to this early anthropology, it was behaviorism, which denied universal instincts and insisted that every culture was acquired, every behavior the result of social conditioning.

Psychoanalysis, on the other hand, worked with particular people as individuals, not as representatives of a culture. Analysts could more or less ignore issues of cultural difference as long as their patients were from relatively similar social and cultural backgrounds. As psychoanalysis spread to other cultures, however, it became clear that psychological profiles were actually culturally determined. Understanding the personality, then, required seeing the individual against the background of what was fostered or downplayed by his or her culture.

The two fields came to realize that they shared common ground: anthropologists had been unwittingly collecting information about people's psychologies all along, and psychologists about people's cultures. In a way, psychoanalysis was anthropology writ small: life histories taken from individual patients. There had been forerunners of the convergence—James Frazer's *The Golden Bough* (1890) was basically psychology-oriented anthropology; William Stern, in Germany, had proposed in 1900 that individual, racial, and cultural differences should be studied by "differential psychology," in effect anthropology. As Freud gained acceptance, the pieces started to fit together. Anthropologists might take down Freud for falsely inflating Viennese-style child rearing into "natural" and "universal" family patterns, but at the same time many realized that what formed this Viennese psychology, or any other specific psychology, were precisely the social patterns they were studying.

By the 1930s, the dominant trend in anthropology was "psychological anthropology" or "Culture and Personality studies," spearheaded by figures such as Franz Boas, Ruth Benedict, Margaret Mead, and Edward Sapir. To Boas, the so-called father of American anthropology, one of the field's central problems "was the relation between the objective world and man's subjective world as it had taken form in different cultures." It was Boas who had brought Bruno Klopfer to America as his research assistant—a tight network of personal connections underlay developments across the social sciences.

Cultural relativism, a core principle in the Culture and Personality approach, was anthropology's version of Frank's and Jung's findings in psychology: we have to see each culture in its own terms, not judge it according to the standards of another. And this was the version of anthropology that, in the thirties, reached as wide an audience as Freud. Ruth Benedict recast Jung in an American context ("Psychological Types in the Cultures of the Southwest," 1930), and her bestselling 1934 *Patterns of Culture* told a generation that values are relative and that culture is "personality writ large." Just as psychology was taking an anthropological turn, anthropology was taking a psychological turn, both converging on the study of personality.

The Rorschach test held out the same promise in both fields: of being a powerful new key to the individual. The test's origins in psychiatric diagnosis had created a bias toward using it to detect mental illness, but its use in anthropology, to explore value-neutral cultural differences, increasingly detached the test from a focus on pathology. Much as Hermann Rorschach had broadened out from diagnosing patients to uncovering personalities, anthropologists now carried the inkblots out of the psychiatrist's office and around the world to investigate all the different ways of being human.

IN 1933 AND 1934, two of Eugen Bleuler's sons were in Morocco. Manfred Bleuler had followed in his father's footsteps and become a psychiatrist; as a resident at the Boston Psychopathic Hospital in 1927–28, he had been the second person to bring the Rorschach to America. Richard Bleuler was an agronomist, but he too remembered the inkblots his father had shown him in 1921. Together they showed the blots to twenty-nine rural Moroccan farmers, in an effort to "demonstrate that the Rorschach Test is applicable beyond the limits of European civilization."

The Bleulers' 1935 essay, despite its sometimes cringe-worthy tone ("For the European who lives among the natives of Morocco, there is something strange and mysterious about those human figures who, clad in their loose gowns flapping in the wind, trot indefatigably on donkeys or camels, or trudge on foot . . ."), ultimately makes the point that different cultures are different, and that these differences create both misunderstanding and fascination. A sense of "something strange and mysterious" about the Moroccans oscillated with the Bleulers' "sudden feeling of warm understanding." They quoted Lawrence of Arabia:

> In his book *Revolt in the Desert,* T. E. Lawrence writes that in the character of the Arabs there are "heights and depths beyond our reach, though not beyond our sight. . . ." Nations perceive the differences in their mental make-up, but do not comprehend them. The observed but incomprehensible differences in the character of the nations are a fascinating riddle that attracts people again and again, drives individuals and nations out of their fatherland, urges them to make friends, or drives them to hatred and war.

It was possible to see without comprehending, to honor differences that one could observe if not quite understand. In any case, the differences were real.

When the Bleulers gave Moroccans the Rorschach test, the responses were in line with those from Europeans, with two exceptions. There were many more Small Detail responses—seeing nearly invisible toothlike projections on either side of a blot as two encampments of enemy riflemen, for instance—and a tendency to give interpretations that incorporated different parts of the card without connecting them. A European might see a head and a leg on each side of a card and respond *"two waiters,"* mentally joining the parts together into whole bodies; a Moroccan would more likely see the details as a *"battlefield"* or *"cemetery,"* a heap of unconnected heads and legs (see Color Plate 6).

The Bleulers emphasized that these were perfectly reasonable responses and explained them with reference to digressive Arab literature like the *Thousand and One Nights,* fragmented and detailed mosaics, and other cultural preferences, in contrast to what they called the European predilection for broad generalizations, the "general air of order and tidiness" that Europeans value, and so on. They cited more concrete cultural differences, too, for instance that the Moroccans were much less used to looking at photographs or other pictures than Europeans were and had not internalized the conventions of such pictures. Where a European would tend to assume that every object in a picture is the same scale but at varying distances, with the bigger objects being foregrounded in importance too, Moroccan interpretations often placed differently scaled shapes side by side (a woman holding a jackal's leg as big as she is) or read significance into tiny details.

The Bleulers' goal was to "gauge the character of a foreign people," not to judge or rank it. Getting hung up on extremely small details in the inkblots might imply schizophrenia in a European, but it clearly didn't in the Moroccans. The Bleulers insisted that the test showed no mental inferiority in the Moroccans and also that it was not fine-grained enough to capture everything important about cultural difference. They argued that it was crucial to know the local language and culture, and they called for empathy (*Einfühlung*): the experimenter must "not allow himself to be guided merely by a stereotype classification of responses, but should rather 'feel himself into' every single one"—easier said than done, of course, but often not even said. Rorschach had tried to judge whether a test taker was feeling movement in the image; the Bleulers made explicit that the test giver had to feel-into the test taker as well.

In 1938, thirty-four-year-old Cora Du Bois arrived with her own Rorschach cards on the volcanic island of Alor in the Netherlands East Indies, east of Bali and just north of Timor. Some fifty miles long by thirty miles wide, the island took five days to cross, through a rugged terrain of nearly vertical cliffs and steep ravines with little arable land for corn and rice, cassava in the dry season. The population of seventy thousand, in communities relatively isolated from each other by the forbidding landscape, spoke eight different languages and countless dialects. After several trips into the interior on horseback and lengthy negotiations with the raja of Alor, Du Bois decided where she would go: the village of Atimelang, with six hundred people in a one-mile radius.

She brought with her two fundamental assumptions: that cultural differences are significant and that people are all essentially the same. We all need to eat, she wrote, and some of us satisfy this need with toast and coffee at eight, salad and dessert at midday, and a balanced three-course meal at seven, others with two handfuls of boiled corn and greens after sunrise, a calabash full of rice and meat in the late afternoon, and snacks throughout the day. These are equally reasonable responses to our human needs: everyone shares "basic similarities" and also adapts to the "repeated and standardized experiences, relationships, and values which occur in many contexts and to which most individuals are exposed" in a given culture. The interplay between the cultural setting and the basic makeup of our bodies and brains results in a "culturally determined personality structuring," which most people in a culture share, but not everyone, and not entirely.

What had sent Du Bois to far-flung Atimelang was not "an exercise in the esoteric" but the quest to understand what makes us who we are: "In its simplest form the question is: Why is an American different from an Alorese? That they are different is a common sense conclusion, but explanations, from the climatic to the racial, have proved lamentably inadequate in the past." More adequate answers would come from a nuanced approach, attuned to the interplay between cultural institutions and psychological character.

Du Bois stayed in Atimelang for eighteen months. She learned the language, in fact named it Abui and was the first to give it written form. She interviewed the people, collected information on child rearing, adolescent rituals, and family dynamics, and recorded long autobiographies from many of the villagers. She found the Alorese in her community emotionally brittle and short-tempered, with frequent verbal and physical fights inside the family and out: these qualities, among others, made up their "culturally determined personality structuring."

But she needed to put her impressions on a more solid objective basis. So, upon her return, she gave the autobiographies and other data to Abram Kardiner at Columbia, prominent at the time as a psychoanalytic theorist (author of *The Individual and His Society,* 1939). She also, without sharing Kardiner's analysis or her own observations, handed over Rorschach protocols from seventeen Alorese males and twenty females to another colleague: Emil Oberholzer.

All three reached the same conclusions about the Alorese. Oberholzer found, for instance, that "the Alorese are suspicious and distrustful. . . . This fearfulness is something that is part and parcel of their natural and normal emotional disposition. . . . They are not only easily upset and frightened, easily startled . . . but also they easily fly into a passion. There must be emotional outbursts and tempers, anger and rage, sometimes resulting in violent actions," just what Du Bois had found in person. Their analyses of specific people—whose autobiographies Du Bois had collected, whom Kardiner psychoanalyzed from afar based on the documents, and whose Rorschach tests Oberholzer scored and interpreted—converged as well.

In a letter to Ruth Benedict in February 1940, Du Bois called the overlap nothing short of stunning: "The crux of matters is whether individual data support Kardiner's analysis from institutions. The Rorschachs seem to be giving him full confirmation. . . . Oberholzer and I are still working at them and O. is gratifyingly cautious. If the individual stuff really confirms K's analysis I'm going to be permanently pie-eyed. It will be just too damned good to be true." She recognized that Kardiner's analysis was suspiciously consistent with her own impressions; perhaps she had unintentionally cherry-picked or skewed the data she had given him. "But I can't have tampered with the Rorschachs. Oberholzer, without really knowing the other implications, is as excited as I am. He knows nothing about the culture except what is necessary to explain the responses. He views it as a triumph for Rorschachs and I for the whole business of interpreting from sociology to psychology. Exciting, isn't it?"

By then Du Bois was on the faculty at Sarah Lawrence College, where Rorschach testing was already in full swing. In 1941, she finished writing her synthesis *The People of Alor*, and she published it in 1944 with extensive essays by Kardiner and Oberholzer included. She had brought anthropology and psychology together.

Like the Bleuler brothers before him, Oberholzer was testing the test. Could anything useful be learned from the Rorschach without already knowing the specific culture of the Alorese—which answers were popular or original, good or bad, which details were normal or rare, all the numerical norms that made scoring possible? The Alorese results certainly looked foreign at first sight: one woman's responses to Card V (the "bat") were:

(1) like pigs' legs (side projections)
(2) like goat's horns (top center, the "bat's" ears)
(3) like goat's horns (bottom center)
(4) like a crow (dark spot in the large portion)
(5) like black cloth (half of the large portion)

Nevertheless, Oberholzer ended up arguing that the test could see past these superficial cultural differences to the kinds of personality profile he then shared with Du Bois.

The stakes for Du Bois were higher: she wanted to find out whether it was even possible to argue that culture shapes personality. Any such argument would be circular unless there was a source of information about personality that was independent of the behavior that anthropologists studied in describing cultures. This direct access to personality was just what the Rorschach claimed to provide. An EEG had traced its first record of human brain waves onto a roll of paper in 1934, but such neurotechnology had a very long way to go. Being able to actually see through cultural differences to the person within, with inkblots, would be, as Du Bois said, "just too damned good to be true."

The figure usually credited with bringing Lawrence Frank's projective methods into the heart of American anthropology did so for just that reason. After studying with Ruth Benedict under Boas in 1922, A. Irving Hallowell (1892–1974) turned to problems of culture and personality. Between 1932 and 1940, he spent summers along the Berens, a small Canadian river flowing into Lake Winnipeg from a source almost three hundred miles to the east.

This area was one of the last in North America to be explored by Europeans, "a country of labyrinthine waterways, swamps, glacier smoothed rocks, and unbroken forests." Since the Berens linked no major lakes or rivers to Lake Winnipeg, the area had remained isolated. Nomadic hunters and fishermen, part of the Ojibwe or Chippewa group, lived in three separate communities reaching east into the wilderness: one on Lake Winnipeg at the mouth of the river, one about a hundred laborious miles inland—fifty portages if traveled by canoe, and there were no roads—and one even farther inland.

This geography put the communities at three different stages along the "culture gradient" from precontact to full assimilation. The lakeside group, with white residents in the community and a semi-weekly steamer from the city of Winnipeg during the summer, lived in European-style log houses with few obvious signs of traditional culture—no native ceremonies or dances, no sound of drums. Inland, though, where few traders or missionaries had ever gone, there were "birchbark-covered tipis . . . sharply defined against a background of the dark and stately spruces that line all horizons," and a "flavor of old Indian life remained." The Ojibwe there might wear woven clothes from the company store, cook with iron pots and pans, drink tea, chew gum, and eat candy bars, but men were still bringing moose carcasses to shore in their canoes while the women made moccasins, stitched birchbark with spruce roots, or chopped and hauled wood with babies strapped into the cradleboards on their backs. There were medicine men, conjuring lodges, midsummer *wabanówīwin* dances. "In this atmosphere," Hallowell wrote, "one could not help but feel that, despite many outward appearances, much of the core of the aboriginal thought and belief still remained." One could not help but feel, but how could one be sure?

Hallowell first heard "the strange word Rorschach" in the midthirties, uttered by Ruth Benedict in a meeting of the National Research Council's Committee on Personality in Relation to Culture. His Winnipeg fieldwork had led him into what he called the "newly emerging area of research in anthropology: the psychological interrelations of individuals and their culture," and this new technique for revealing individual psychology beneath culture was just what Hallowell was looking for. He cobbled together enough information to try his hand at it, combining elements of Beck's, Klopfer's, and Hertz's approaches and improvising a procedure to administer the test through a translator:

> "I am going to show you some cards one after another. These cards have marks"—here the interpreters inserted an Ojibwe term, *ocipie-gátewin,* which meant "picture"—"on them, something like you see on this paper (trial blot shown). I want you to take each card in your hand (trial blot given to subject). Look at it carefully and point out what you see there with this stick. (Handing an orangewood stick to the subject.) Tell me everything that the marks on the card make you think of or what they look like. They may not look like anything you have seen but if they resemble something closely, mention whatever it is."

He returned from his next summer in Canada with dozens of Ojibwe Rorschach protocols in hand.

Hallowell felt that the different stages of Ojibwe assimilation to white Canadian culture provided a perfect way to study the inter-relations of individual psychologies and culture because by definition these stages meant subjecting the same psychology to different cultural forces. "If, as has been assumed, there are intimate connections between the organization of personality and culture patterns," Hallowell wrote, "it follows that changes in culture might be expected to produce changes in personality."

Like Oberholzer with the Alorese, Hallowell claimed to detect in his Rorschachs "an Ojibwe personality constellation . . . clearly discernible through all levels of acculturation thus far studied." While outward cultural practices may have been borrowed from white Canadians, there was "no evidence at all" of changes to the "vital core of native psychology." He then argued that since the three groups along the Berens River shared the same heredity and cultural background and had been given their Rorschach tests under the same conditions, any differences between the groups' results could only be due to their different level of acculturation. The Rorschach could reveal how different Ojibwe individuals were adapting, or not, to the new cultural pressures.

What Hallowell found was the Ojibwe personality "being pushed to the limits." The tests of the inland Ojibwe showed predominantly introvert results and a significant repression of any extravert tendencies, which made sense in a culture where events were always understood with reference to an inner belief system, dreams were the most important experiences and were processed in private (there was a taboo against sharing one's dreams in most circumstances), and social relations were highly structured. The lakeside Indians, in contrast, "living in closer rapport with other persons and things in their environment," showed a greater range of personalities, especially among the women, including significantly more extraverts. People could act extraverted if so inclined, instead of repressing that side of themselves.

This greater freedom to be different, which Hallowell found especially in women, could be a good thing: 81 percent of the most well-adjusted individuals came from the lakeside group. At the same time, 75 percent of the most maladjusted came from the lakeside group as well. Hallowell concluded that white culture was more psychologically challenging, with a greater chance for failure to adapt as well as for more self-expression. "Some of these deductions might be made without the benefit of the Rorschach technique," Hallowell wrote, "but it would be difficult to demonstrate them without a method of investigation through which the actual personal adjustment of concrete individuals could be evaluated."

As with Du Bois, the overall lesson went beyond the specific findings: if the Rorschach could detect cultural norms within individuals, then it could be used to study how culture shapes personality in general. In two groundbreaking articles, "The Rorschach Method as an Aid in the Study of Personalities in Primitive Societies" written for psychologists, and "The Rorschach Technique in the Study of Personality and Culture" written for anthropologists, Hallowell laid out the test's unique advantages: it collected quantifiable, objective data; it was portable; people liked taking it; it did not require the test taker to be literate or the examiner to be a professional psychologist, since the protocol could be scored and interpreted by someone else; there was no risk that those who had already taken the test would tell their friends the right answers.

Most important: Hallowell wrote that the Rorschach was "noncultural." The norms were surprisingly stable across different populations—popular responses were almost the same among European Americans and Ojibwe, for instance, except on one card that the former often saw as *"an animal skin"* while the Ojibwe tended to see *"a turtle."* Besides, "since psychological meaning rather than statistical norms is the basis of most Rorschach interpretation," Hallowell felt that valuable insights were possible even without large samples of data. At the time of his first essay, fewer than three hundred protocols from nonliterate cultures had ever been collected, including the Bleulers', Du Bois's, and Hallowell's own. A few years later, the count had risen to more than twelve hundred, and the possibility of any future nonliterate group being un-Rorschachable, while "conceivable" to Hallowell, seemed "quite unlikely."

Even if the Rorschach could provide "non-cultural" information about personality, anthropologists using it faced another problem. Every culture had its "typical personality structure" but left room for individual variations, while cultures were assumed to be different and yet people were fundamentally the same. That meant any given result could be claimed to reveal idiosyncrasy within a society or to support a generalization about cultural differences, whichever the anthropologist wanted.

A 1942 study of Samoans, inspired by Hallowell, recognized the dilemma. The Samoans gave an unusually high number of pure Color responses, which made the Samoans test as generally extraverted. But the study's author, Philip Cook, argued that this was because of Samoan color vocabulary: the Samoan language had abstract words only for black, white, and red (*mumu*, "like fire, like flame," almost always associated with blood), with rarer color words being closely tied to specific things (the word for "blue" meant "the color of the deep sea," and referred to green or gray as the sea changed color; the word for "green" meant "the color of everything growing"). So Samoans were unlikely to describe things as colored—fewer FC responses. They also gave far more Anatomical responses, which in Europeans and Americans suggested "sex repression or morbid bodily preoccupation." But since the Samoans were sexually active from a young age, with minimal if any sexual repression in the culture, their Anatomical responses were probably perfectly normal. Cook accepted that while the Rorschach seemed to reveal aspects of Samoan culture, it was unable to distinguish or diagnose individuals. But for Cook this meant only that massive further research should be conducted on each different culture, since "the Rorschach is undoubtedly an excellent instrument for the study of cultural psychodynamics."

These were the assumptions shared by psychology and anthropology. Hallowell had proposed a full theoretical integration of the two fields and had praised the Rorschach as "one of the best available means" to that end. By 1948, Hallowell was president of both the American Anthropological Association and Klopfer's Rorschach Institute—a concrete sign of the convergence of the two disciplines. In the popular understanding as well, the Rorschach could discover the personality structure in anyone, whether in America or the most alien and exotic culture.

The Rorschach "seemed like a mental X-ray machine," recalled a graduate student at the time. "You could solve a person by showing them a picture."

16

The Queen of Tests

O N DECEMBER 7, 1941, THE JAPANESE ATTACKED PEARL HARBOR. Within three weeks, Bruno Klopfer had organized a "Rorschach volunteer unit" to coordinate between the Institute back home and its many members who had volunteered for service. He also put himself forward as the point man for information and advice about the test. By early 1942, questions and requests were trickling and then pouring in from the military, and Klopfer was soon working with the army personnel procedures division to see how the Rorschach could help in the US war effort.

This Rorschach was a very different beast from the nuanced instrument at the forefront of anthropology and personality studies. First and foremost, the military needed efficient evaluations, along the lines of its Army General Classification Test, developed in 1940 and given to twelve million soldiers and marines over the next five years. Ruth Munroe, tester of entering classes at Sarah Lawrence College, had published her Inspection Technique, designed to help examiners scan Rorschach protocols quickly for striking problems. While less subtle, such a scan produced interpretations more uniform across different scorers, and much faster.

To streamline test administration as well as scoring, Molly Harrower introduced the Group Rorschach Technique, where slides were shown in a semidarkened room and test takers wrote down their own answers. Twenty minutes were enough to test an auditorium of more than two hundred people. It was almost as hard to get the slides right as it had been for Rorschach to get his inkblots printed, especially considering "the great difficulties that arose in getting reliable film during the war years," but a photographer who could do it was eventually found.

Group Rorschach
used by the Office
of Strategic Services
for selection
purposes during
World War II

Even with these advances, the Rorschach presented two major obstacles to mass use. Though less-expert staff could administer the test, protocols still had to be scored and interpreted by trained Rorschachers. Worse, the results could still not be boiled down to a simple number for bureaucrats, punch cards, or IBM scoring sheets. So Harrower went one step further, "departing so far from the essence of what Rorschach intended" that she had, by her own admission, really invented *"an entirely different procedure,"* which she called "A Multiple-Choice Test (For Use with Rorschach Cards or Slides)."

From a list of ten responses for each card, test takers were asked to check one box for "the suggestion *you* think is the best description of the blot," and put a 2 in the box for their second choice (optional). Card I (see page 2), for instance, was:

- ☐ An army or navy emblem
- ☐ Mud and dirt
- ☐ A bat
- ☐ Nothing at all
- ☐ Two people
- ☐ A pelvis
- ☐ An x-ray picture
- ☐ Pincers of a crab
- ☐ A dirty mess
- ☐ Part of my body

Something other than the above: _____

A top-secret answer key distinguished good answers from bad, and Harrower's wartime article about the procedure described it with language out of a spy thriller: "Since it is of the utmost importance that this simple key does not fall into the wrong hands, it has not been pub-lished here. A copy will be sent immediately on request, however, to psychiatrists and psychologists in the Armed Forces." Three bad an-swers or fewer and you passed the test, four or more and you failed.

If you think this sounds a bit suspect, you're not alone. "The Group Rorschach procedure was greeted with raised eyebrows," Harrower later commented, but "the introduction of the Multiple-Choice Test met with an even colder reception." Yet the need to screen millions called for new approaches. "In the last analysis," as she had originally pointed out, a screening program is "much less interested in knowing in detail WHY the individual is unfit, provided we can spot him," and "much less interested in an extremely sensitive instrument which only few persons can handle than in a simple tool which anyone can use, anywhere."

Harrower's test seemed to work, to some extent. The results for 329 "unselected normals," 225 male prison inmates, 30 students consulting a college psychiatrist ("some of them with rather serious diagnoses, others considered much improved following psychotherapy"), and 143 institutionalized mental patients clearly categorized the groups differ-ently. The latter groups were more likely to fail, while fully 55 percent of the "superior adults" tested had no poor answers at all, and the only one with more than four turned out to have been hospitalized twice for manic depression. Harrower soon made some basic adjustments, for instance factoring in that doctors and nurses give more Anatomi-cal answers, which were otherwise scored as bad. She also found that a trained Rorschacher looking at people's results could make bet-ter judgments, especially with the borderline cases who gave three or four poor answers. But even "sticking religiously to purely quantitative terms" gave real results. She argued that her quick and dirty test had "undeniable advantages, not over and against the Rorschach but as a procedure in its own right."

The Multiple-Choice Test met with a positive reception in educa-tion and business, but several studies found it too unreliable for mili-tary screenings, and it was never adopted for mass use by the military. Still, having been reframed in 1939 as the ultimate projective method for revealing the subtleties of personality, the Rorschach was now being reinvented again as a test yielding a quick number, a yes/no. While the

Rorschach proper "remained a *method* requiring its own specialists," Harrower wrote, she had turned the inkblots into "a psychological *test* in the usual sense of the word" (emphasis added). That was what the army needed, and what Americans wanted.

Sixty million standardized tests, educational and vocational as well as psychological, were given to twenty million Americans in 1944 alone. In 1940, *The Mental Measurements Yearbook* reviewed 325 different tests and listed 200 more. Most were used by only a handful of psychologists, and only one would come to be known as "the queen of tests," for reasons having less to do with the inkblots than with the transformation of American psychology.

WORLD WAR II was the turning point in the history of mental health in America. Before the war, psychiatrists had worked in mental hospitals, psychologists—still "hard" scientists, not "soft" therapists—largely stayed confined to university labs, and the few clinical psychologists there were tended to focus on children and education. Freudian ideas had been appropriated by psychiatrists in the United States, to the point where psychoanalysis was seen almost exclusively as a way to treat mental illness—not as, say, a vehicle for scientific inquiry or personal exploration.

Most Americans had never undergone mental health treatment and didn't know what it was. Even if a psychoanalytic approach drew some psychiatrists out of the hospitals and into private practice or Child Guidance clinics in a few major cities, psychotherapy remained marginal in society as a whole. Psychiatrists treated patients, psychologists studied subjects, and most people were left for their communities to help as best they could.

With the war, and the nation's first general draft, every able-bodied man in the country was given a psychological screening along with intelligence tests and medical exams. The number of potential soldiers screened out with "intolerable psychological risk profiles" was astonishingly high: some 1,875,000 men in the army alone, or 12 percent of those tested in the years 1942–45. Even with this exclusion rate, six times the rate during World War I, war neurosis in the US Armed Forces was reported at more than twice the rate as in World War I.

There were more than a million neuropsychiatric admissions to army medical services, with another 150,000 from the navy, and so on— and these were from the soldiers who had passed the screening. Some 380,000 were discharged for psychiatric reasons (more than a third of all medical discharges), another 137,000 for "personality disorders"; 120,000 psychiatric patients had to be evacuated from the field of operations, 28,000 by air.

Whether these numbers show how badly screening was needed or that it didn't work—General George C. Marshall ordered it discontinued in 1944—there was clearly a crisis. Some people were faking, but the vast majority of cases were real, which meant two things: that mental illness affected a far greater portion of the population than anyone had dreamed of and that "healthy" people needed psychological treatment too. Only a minority of nervous breakdowns in the military took place on the front lines or even overseas. Most were caused by a variety of factors that affected people back home as well, such as "stress," a concept rapidly spreading from military psychiatry circles to the public at large.

It was a national concern. As one history of psychotherapy in America puts it, the "pitiful" physical health of America's young men was dire enough—"missing teeth, untreated abscesses and sores, uncorrected vision problems, uncorrected skeletal deformities, untreated chronic infections"—prompting efforts to increase the number of medical doctors and access to them across the country. Still, "the 12 percent rejection rate for mental illness stood alone for its shock value."

When the war started, the US Army had thirty-five psychiatrists, total. The "very great shortage of trained personnel, not only of psychiatrists and neurologists but of psychologists and psychiatric social workers," was a "revelation," according to the man in charge, Brigadier General William C. Menninger. By the end of the war, the thirty-five had become a thousand in the army and another seven hundred in the rest of the military, including "practically every member" of the American Psychiatric Association "not barred by age, disability or earmarked as essential for civilian psychiatry," as well as plenty of new recruits.

They were needed at hundreds of induction centers, basic training camps, disciplinary barracks, rehab centers, and hospitals at home and abroad. Aside from psychiatrists, military psychologists were at work on tasks such as designing complex instrument panels adapted to the mental capacities and perceptual limitations of the people using them. "Not until the war was almost over," Menninger later summed up, "did we have anywhere near enough personnel to do the job."

In fact, there weren't enough personnel anywhere in the country. Barely a third of the medical officers assigned in neuropsychiatry had had any psychiatric experience before the war. At war's end, with sixteen million returning troops to look after, the need was even greater; more than half of the postwar Veterans Administration hospitalizations would be for mental health disorders. Civilians, too, were starting to learn about the benefits of mental health treatment. In General Menninger's postwar words, "Conservatively there are at least two million people who have had direct contact or relationship with psychiatry as a result of mental sickness or personality disorders that occurred in soldiers in this war. For a large percentage of this group it is their first. They are becoming educated." Having learned his own lesson, Menninger started working aggressively to promote mental health training, preventive care, and treatment around the country. The nation had to ramp up its mental health services as much as the military just had.

Congress passed the National Mental Health Act in 1946, creating the National Institute of Mental Health with a broad public service mission. It created new standards for the field, whereby clinical psychologists were "scientist-practitioners" meant to work with the public, not just in labs. The VA set up joint programs between its hospitals and nearby medical schools to turn out the psychotherapists it needed, and before long was employing three times more clinical psychologists than had existed in the whole country in 1940. Clinical psychology was booming, heavily supported by government funding.

The Rorschach was poised to benefit on all fronts, as both a diagnostic tool with tangible benefits for practicing psychiatrists and a test compatible with the drive for quantifiable scoring in academic psychology. Psychology, meanwhile, was becoming more psychoanalytical and less quantitative anyway, with the rise of clinical psychologists and their new "scientist-practitioner" training. By an accident of timing, there were no competing assessment textbooks until the late forties, so all the new clinical psychology programs springing up had no choice but to use books on the Rorschach. In 1946, the Rorschach was the second most popular personality test, behind the simpler Goodenough Draw-a-Man Test, and the fourth most popular test overall, behind two different IQ tests. It was the most popular clinical psychology dissertation topic for years.

Within the military, the Rorschach had remained in limited use. It was still slower than other tests, and there were not enough doctors with the specialized training required to give it to all those millions of soldiers. Or even enough inkblots: one first lieutenant assigned to a psychiatric unit in Paris during the war couldn't find a set of cards anywhere and had to arrange for his wife to meet Bruno Klopfer in Manhattan to pick up a set and mail them to him. (A few weeks later, he stumbled across a hundred sets of Rorschach and TAT cards in the basement of the Eisenhower headquarters: the army had ordered and then forgotten them.) Still, despite the failure of the Multiple-Choice Test for mass screening, the Rorschach proper found many other military applications, both in psychiatry—diagnosing and treating patients—and in psychology, for instance, to study operational fatigue in air force combat pilots.

In a broader context, the new value placed on testing, and the jockeying for position between psychiatrists and psychologists, helped the Rorschach's fortunes. Case review conferences, an increasingly common practice that had started in Child Guidance clinics, brought together a psychiatrist in charge of treatment, a psychologist who gave tests, and a psychiatric social worker who participated in therapy. In the past, the psychologist would report the patient's IQ and maybe another numerical result or two; then his work was done. But if he was expert in the intricate and mysterious Rorschach, he might hold the floor with a discussion of color shock, Experience Type, or a rigid problem-solving approach, and his colleagues around the table would nod their heads, recognizing truths about their patient.

Thousands of psychiatrists and psychologists had seen what they felt were shockingly fast and exact blind diagnoses, or findings with the Rorschach that no other approach could offer. Psychoanalytic psychiatrists in particular, suspicious of "self-reporting" tests like questionnaires that in their view underestimated the power of the unconscious, felt the Rorschach was speaking their language. It was those psychiatrists, as much as the psychologists, who called the Rorschach "the queen of tests."

In other ways, both psychologists and psychiatrists were struggling to define their professional roles against a common threat. The medical officers hastily trained for military service, without degrees in psychology or psychiatry, had done a pretty good job. And what about social workers? If they could help people just as well, after less rigorous training and for less money—calling it "counseling" instead of "psychotherapy"—then what was the point of psychiatrists and clinical psychologists at all? The point, they argued, was their training and expertise, and the Rorschach was a respected and intimidating sign of that expertise. The ten inkblot cards became an important and vivid status symbol, good for the clinician's job security and self-image.

KLOPFER'S TEXTBOOK *The Rorschach Technique: A Manual for a Projective Method of Personality Diagnosis* came out in 1942, at just the right moment for it to be taken up as the bible of psychological testers and the standard textbook in graduate programs, shaping the next generation. Klopfer noted in his foreword that the book was being published "at a time of emergency when we are all called upon to make the most effective possible use of our resources, whether these be men or materials. The Rorschach method is proving its worth in helping us to avoid waste of human resources" in both the army and civilian defense, and he was grateful for the chance to do his part. Since he was an escaped German Jew, his patriotism was certainly heartfelt; it was also excellent marketing. In the words of a leading educational psychologist named Lee J. Cronbach, in the late fifties, no book "had more influence on American Rorschach technique—and therefore on clinical diagnostic practice—than the Klopfer-Kelley book of 1942."

Two women working as MA-level psychologists at New York's Bellevue, Ruth Bochner and Florence Halpern, would never become famous, but they published that same year what may have been, in real terms, the most influential Rorschach book of all. Written under the pressures of wartime, *The Clinical Application of the Rorschach Test* was pooh-poohed by Rorschach experts at the time ("a carelessly written work, replete with loose statements, contradictions, and misleading conclusions"), but it was popular—reviewed in *Time* magazine, going into a second edition in 1945. It told all those new army psychologists under orders to turn themselves into Rorschachers on the double, many of them to be plucked from analyzing rats in mazes at university labs or with no previous training in what the test was and how to use it.

Oversimplified or not, the book was straightforward. With a fold-out table of fractions in the back, you could calculate all the percentage scores without wasting time with long division or breaking out the slide rule (13/29 = 44.7 percent). Chapters were called things like "What the Symbols in Column I Mean," a level of practical clarity that the leading Rorschachers rarely descended to. Klopfer covered the same material in "Scoring Categories for Location of Responses," nearly a hundred pages into his book, while Beck's 1944 textbook would discuss it in six separate chapters, including "Scoring Problems" and "Approach and Sequence: Ap, Seq." Which do you think could teach you how to give a Rorschach?

Bochner and Halpern were well aware of the Klopfer and Beck debates, the nuances and caveats in Rorschach's own work, and the complexities of how different parts of the test could interact—but they cut to the chase. Someone giving one kind of answer "is obviously a person of ability, and social rapport will be more difficult for him"; someone giving another kind "is an egocentric person, full of demands, and inclined to irritability. Since he cannot make the necessary adjustment he expects the rest of the world to adjust to him." People who found one particular card "sinister" were "easily disturbed by concentrated darkness, and tend to be anxious and easily depressed." One woman's resistance to a certain card "is obviously of a sexual nature, and from an analysis of the contents of her responses seems linked with the question of pregnancy," which she tried to avoid by "misinterpreting or denying the symbols of male genitalia" in the inkblot. Lo and behold, her case history revealed that she and her boyfriend "went beyond the usual petting" six weeks ago, and now her period was late. A detailed report for therapy or analysis could equally well be replaced with a sentence or two, to be used for classification. The Rorschach might be harder to master than most tests, but that didn't mean it couldn't be standardized.

These sweeping assertions and others like them laid out what would become the received wisdom about the nature and meaning of the Rorschach. Bochner and Halpern firmly cast it as a projective method, not a perceptual experiment, and they downplayed the objective qualities of the actual images: "Since the blots are primarily without content, the subject must of necessity project himself into them." They declared that a test taker "must be made to think that any response he gives is a good response" and that anything else "is incompatible with the ideology of the experiment," even though responses actually were scored good or bad, and Rorschach himself had written that misleading people was unethical if the test results would have practical consequences.

Their version of the Rorschach was what entered popular culture. No right or wrong answers, you were free to say whatever you wanted, and then before you knew it you'd been categorized, your secrets revealed. Bochner and Halpern never directly reached a mass audience, like popularizations of Freud or Ruth Benedict's *Patterns of Culture* for anthropology, but what the American public thought it knew about the Rorschach was all right there.

A third book came out in 1942: Hermann Rorschach's *Psychodiagnostics,* in English at last. Here, it seemed, was the authoritative statement that could remind readers what the test was truly about, bring it back to its bearings. But too much had happened in twenty years. Badly translated, confusingly partial, and self-contradictory with its inclusion of the posthumous 1922 essay, *Psychodiagnostics* had nothing to say about projective methods, X-rays of the soul, character and personality, group testing, anthropology (beyond Bernese and Appenzeller Swiss!), or Beck's and Klopfer's dueling systems. If Rorschach had lived, he would have been only fifty-seven years old, able to weigh in on all these topics himself. On its own, the book was too little, too late, to rein in the sorcerer's apprentice.

17

Iconic as a Stethoscope

B Y THE MIDFORTIES, PRACTICALLY EVERY AMERICAN HAD A SON, brother, or other loved one who had been given psychological testing in the draft; an increasing number had taken such tests themselves. Not surprisingly, it was just then that Freudian jargon—*inferiority complex, repression,* and so forth—exploded into popular culture, along with psychotherapy in general, and the inkblots.

In October 1946, millions would have seen "Personality Tests: Ink Blots Are Used to Learn How People's Minds Work" in *Life* magazine, which in the late 1940s reached some 22.5 million readers, more than 20 percent of the entire adult and teenage US population. This article showed four "successful young New Yorkers" looking at inkblots—the Lawyer, the Executive, the Producer, and the Composer (future novelist Paul Bowles, as it happens)—along with Thomas M. Harris, "who gives a course at Harvard in adapting the Rorschach to job selection." It accurately covered details like norms and scores: "Responses are judged not so much by their actual content as by how they compare with the responses in thousands of tests previously given. . . . It belongs to a class of tests which is called projective." Readers were gently invited to give it a try themselves.

They might then have put down their magazine and gone to see *The Dark Mirror,* an Oscar-winning film noir starring Olivia de Havilland in a dual role as a pair of identical twins. The movie opened with credits rolling over inkblots and finished, after dozens of mirrors, symmetrical wallpaper patterns, and face-to-face scenes, with "The End" superimposed over another ominous inkblot. The movie's psychiatrist hero used the Rorschach test, a word association test, a polygraph, and other ultramodern methods to discover which twin had committed the murder, while falling in love with the good one. Universal Pictures considered using the universal picture of an inkblot in print ads for the film, but in the end they went with a literal dark mirror, framing two Olivia de Havillands and the scrawled word "Twins!"

The evil twin taking the Rorschach (with modified inkblot) in *The Dark Mirror:* "It might be a mask." The good twin sees "two people in costume, and they're dancing around a maypole."

Hollywood was going dark. Two years to the day after its life-affirming 1945 cover photo of a returning sailor kissing a nurse in Times Square, *Life* magazine could look back on 1946 as "the midst of Hollywood's profound postwar affection for morbid drama. From January through December deep shadows, clutching hands, exploding revolvers, sadistic villains and heroines tormented with deeply rooted diseases of the mind flashed across the screen in a panting display of psychoneurosis, unsublimated sex and murder most foul." Film noir, the cinematic art of projecting psychological shadows in black and white, brought the violent and sexual undertones of the Rorschach test to life.

Noir and the inkblots shared more than a color scheme. Expressionism was another import from the German-speaking teens and early twenties, and another new way of making mental states visual. In film noir—"dreamlike, strange, erotic, ambivalent, and cruel," as it was defined in *A Panorama of Film Noir,* the first book on the genre—émigrés to Hollywood used the visual style of *The Cabinet of Dr. Caligari* and other Expressionist classics to tackle a disorienting new world. The plot of *Stranger on the Third Floor* (1940), often cited as the first film noir, turned on perception and interpretation: whether the key witness in a murder trial was right about what he thought he had seen. The archetypal characters of a film noir were the private eye looking for truth in a world of moral ambiguity, and the femme fatale, inscrutable personality under investigation. Literal Rorschach tests naturally became a staple of movie plots.

Film was not the only midcentury art suggestive of the Rorschach. In the twenties, inkblotty images had appeared in visual art by French and German Surrealists, who were interested in the unconscious as the source of dreams and automatic writing. But Surrealism was closer to Kerner's klexography than to a Rorschach test. The Surrealists thought chance methods tempted the unconscious into view, like Kerner's self-making blots tempted over from the other world. They denied or downplayed their own conscious role in creating the poems or images, while often paradoxically insisting on a specific interpretation: in 1920, when Francis Picabia made an asymmetrical ink splash on a splattered sheet of paper, he wrote the title, *La Sainte Vierge* (The Virgin Mary), right on the image.

The art that Americans came to associate with the Rorschach was less superficially like it than the Surrealists' works, but worked more like how the inkblots worked—a new kind of painting that epitomized the culture of personality.

The *Life* headline about Jackson Pollock in 1949 was a rhetorical question: "Is He the Greatest Living Painter in the United States?" Pollock's drip paintings were pure gushing outpourings of the self: "paroxysms of passion," "ecstatic force," such vivid self-expression that the movement was named Abstract Expressionism. "Most modern painters," Pollock said, "work from within." Hans Namuth's photographs of Pollock in his studio—strewing paint, pouring sand, dripping and drizzling over a huge canvas covering the floor—were iconic, and they showed, even more clearly than the paintings, the artist in action: clad in black, cigarette dangling, performing his personality.

The paintings and the blots may have looked drastically different—in symmetry, color, rhythm, context, size—but they did similar things to the viewer (see Color Plate 7). Combined with Pollock's strong-silent-type cowboy persona and the postwar historical context of American superpower swagger, his art confronted viewers with a kind of imperious disdain: it provocatively didn't care how you would react, it didn't have an agenda about what you were supposed to see. At the same time, it engaged you, led your eyes around the dynamic canvas, often prompted you to step closer to or farther from the picture. Being confronted by a Rorschach image felt much the same way. It was around 1950, at the height of Pollock's fame, that countless articles, satires, and cartoons about modern art began to take for granted the idea that such art was nothing but a Rorschach test.

The inkblots were also being used to spice up all sorts of lighter fare in popular culture. Advertisers found the Rorschach, with its mix of expertise and mystery, known and unknown, equally evocative in a man's world of business and a woman's world of pleasure. A blot superimposed on a stock market chart in 1955 suggested an investment company whose experts knew your idiosyncrasies better than you did: "There are many kinds of analyses . . . A. G. Becker & Co. will provide an incisive review of your portfolio, with **your** particular investment goals in mind. (By the way, <u>can</u> you state your immediate and long term investment goals?—if not, all the more reason to call on A. G. Becker & Co.)" Not that business expertise had to be boring: "There's an origi-

nal way of looking at everything," and American Mutual offered "perhaps the most creative employee insurance program available." Meanwhile, in a 1956–57 series of perfume ads, some featured a photograph of a woman with an inkblot, and explained: "You are what you want to be with Bal de Tete, the ultimate complement to your personality." Others let the inkblot speak for itself.

Lowell Toy Manufacturing, publisher of family-friendly games based on TV shows (*The Price Is Right, Groucho's You Bet Your Life, Gunsmoke*), aimed a bit lower when it put out an inkblot parlor game in 1957: PERSON-ALYSIS, "a revealing psychological game for adults based on the latest psycho-scientific testing techniques," as the instruction book titillated. An ad in the *New Yorker* edged a little closer: "The newest in sophisticated parlor games," PERSON-ALYSIS "gives participants hilarious, exciting, intimate and revealing 'peeks' into the private lives of friends and family . . . even themselves." For a good time, moms and dads were turning to inkblots. Psychology meant Freud, and Freud meant sex, but Freudian ideas had no clear visual image associated with them. In the fifties, an inkblot was what the unconscious looked like, and after the Kinsey reports, published in 1948 and 1953, Americans were less embarrassed to admit what else it might look like.

In every corner of American culture, this was the Rorschach's heyday. According to Google, we hit peak Rorschach in 1954. And as an actual test given by psychologists and psychiatrists, the Rorschach was the most popular in the world in the fifties and sixties. The inkblots were shown in hospitals, clinics, and guidance centers at least a million times a year in the United States alone, "as closely identified with the clinical psychologist as the stethoscope is with the physician."

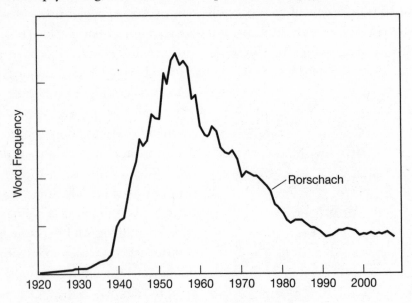

Usage of "Rorschach" in English, from Google Ngram

They were used to study everyone and everything. One German dissertation used the Rorschach to confirm evidence published elsewhere that a woman's psychology changes during menstruation. The author showed the inkblots to twenty of his female medical school colleagues, ages twenty-two to twenty-six, once during the month and once when they turned up again on the first day of their cycle. During their period, he found more sexual answers and Anatomical answers, slower response time, more fussy Small Detail answers, a more arbitrary approach overall. He couldn't help but notice twice as many *"blood"* answers, and six times as many *"fires," "caves,"* and *"gates."* The menstruating women gave fewer Movement responses and fewer answers on cards that tend to produce Movement responses, which meant repression: "mistrust of one's own inner life." More Color responses: they were highly "reactive to emotions." Conclusion: psychologists Rorschach-testing women should factor in the menstrual cycle.

Anne Roe, a Harvard professor and clinical psychologist, turned the tables, using the Rorschach and TAT to investigate the psychology of scientists. She found, for instance, that social scientists gave more responses on Rorschach tests than natural scientists (an average of 67, as opposed to 22 from biologists and 34 from physicists), were more comfortable expressing aggression, and "were more concerned with—but also more bothered by—social relations." Particularly interesting was her Rorschach test of behaviorist B. F. Skinner, who gave a staggering 196 responses, marked overall by "a contemptuous attitude toward other people." He saw few humans and showed a "lack of respect for animals' lives" as well—features that made a panel of experts, when told that the subject was a famous psychologist, speculate that it might be Skinner. He was also dismissive of the blots themselves, making remarks in his responses such as *"The symmetry is a nuisance," "Little stuff bothers me," "Bad job of painting,"* and *"Not very well organized."*

Skinner had a history with projective methods. One Sunday morning in 1934, hard at work in his basement lab at Harvard, he had heard a sound from a machine through a wall—"Di-*dah*-di-di-*dah*, di-*dah*-di-di-*dah*"—and found himself saying in his head, over and over, "You'll never get out. You'll never get out." This inspired him, not to spend more of his weekends outside the lab but to contact Henry Murray at the Harvard Psychological Clinic, who was busy developing the TAT. Skinner helped create the TAT and also created a test of his own, the Verbal Summator technique, that involved playing for subjects wordlike sounds he had collected and recorded, which he called "something like auditory inkblots." Other psychologists briefly adopted this audio Rorschach.

In the 1950s, someone else tried to take projective methods across the final frontier of the senses. It seemed a shame to Edward F. Kerman, MD, that the blind were beyond the reach of these powerful methods, so he created the Kerman Cypress Knee Projective Technique, which involved putting six rubber replicas of cypress knees into subjects' hands. ("The cypress knee," he explained, "for the information of those unfamiliar with it, is an outgrowth from the roots of the cypress tree [Taxodium distichum] that has found its place in our culture as an ornamental object, appealing to the observer because of its inherent capacity to stimulate imaginative responses to its tortuous, ambiguous form.") People were told to rank the rubber casts from favorite to least favorite, and say why; name or title each knee; tell a story using these six characters; then assign one knee the role of mother, make another the father, and another the child, and tell a story about those.

One blind eighteen-year-old high school student liked #5 best: "It kind of makes me think of one of these Grecian monsters or something that looks like it's got numerous heads. . . . Other than that I don't know, I just like it." He named it Avogadro, after the chemical law that says equal volumes of any gas at the same temperature and pressure have the same number of molecules. #4 was boring: "I don't like anything real plain." Dr. Kerman's analysis reads like self-parody—"not meant to imply" that the young man "is to be considered clinically either as a psychopathic personality or an overt homosexual, but the tendency in these directions is there." While remarking that the test's validity had not actually been proven, Kerman ended on an upbeat note: "Since validation studies are necessary, the author invites interested workers in the field of projective technics to join him."

Kerman's kind of ham-fisted Freudianism was everywhere at midcentury. A new theory held that one of the Rorschach inkblots was the "Father Card," another the "Mother Card," and that any responses to them were especially significant for the person's family psychodrama. If a woman said the arms on the Father Card looked "skinny and weak," that was an ominous sign for her love life.

As clinical psychologists drifted further toward the second half of their "scientist-practitioner" mission, becoming less quantitative and more psychoanalytical, they started to feel that it was a shame to neglect the rich verbal material turning up in the course of a Rorschach test. Specific scores might be more rigorous, and proper scoring had earlier been recognized as a delicate and difficult task, requiring long training, fine sensitivity, even art. Now, in the words of one advocate for this approach, sticking to "the standpoint of rigorous objective analysis," however "commendable," would "appear to be inadequate so far as the needs of the psychiatrist are concerned."

Robert Lindner, the popular psychologist whose nonfiction book *Rebel Without a Cause* would give the iconic movie its title, was one of the main champions of this approach to the Rorschach. He argued that "*what* the patient under Rorschach scrutiny produces is quite as important as *how* he produces it, and that occasionally it is more so." Paying attention to the content "enormously enriches the value of the Rorschach protocol for diagnostic and therapeutic purposes." According to Lindner, forty-three specific responses had been found so far that were diagnostic in and of themselves. For instance, male subjects often saw the bottom center of Card I as a fleshy female torso, but homosexuals tended to see it as a muscular male torso. Bochner and Halpern had described what it meant to find a certain card "sinister"; Lindner called it the Suicide Card: "Responses containing such projections as 'a decaying tooth,' 'a rotted tree trunk,' 'a pall of black smoke,' 'something rotten,' 'a burned and charred piece of wood' appear in severe depressive states with suicidal overtones and self-annihilative thought content. Where the response to this area frankly mentions death, however, there is a fair prospect that the patient will benefit from electroshock therapy."

Rorschach's own stance on content analysis had been ambiguous. In 1920, he had rejected it; by 1922, he had shifted to the view that "the content of answers, too, can be meaningful." Once the later lecture was included in *Psychodiagnostics,* both quotes were in the same book and proponents of either side of the debate could quote scripture in their favor.

Meanwhile, other psychologists started paying more attention to how subjects talked, irrespective of both content and formal scores. David Rapaport and Roy Schafer, the main figures in the midcentury psychoanalytic Rorschach, developed new codes for any Rorschach responses that simply sounded crazy: "Deviant Verbalizations," further classified into "Peculiar Verbalizations" ("*zebra skin, wouldn't be—no* _spots on it_"), "Queer Verbalizations" ("_psychiatric experiments, surrealistic painting, soul burning out in hell_"), "Autistic Logic" ("_another fight that takes place in South Africa_"), and a dozen other categories.

Behavior while taking a psychological test was still behavior; gibberish or violent fantasies during a Rorschach were as bad a sign there as in any other context. Why not interpret whatever turned up? And few would deny that "_a pall of black smoke_" together with other morbid answers suggested certain dark preoccupations. Yet much like Georg Roemer's attempted shift to "a content-based, symbolic test" in the 1920s, the shift away from scoring Movement, Color, and the other formal qualities of people's answers risked losing the unique value of the actual inkblots. Some felt it made the time and effort required to give a Rorschach test a bit pointless: anyone given to seeing "_surrealistic painting, soul burning out in hell_," would probably bring up something along those lines if you just talked to them for five minutes. Proponents of content analysis or verbalization analysis always hedged with disclaimers: you had to proceed with great caution; these were just suggestions or guidelines; this merely supplemented traditional scoring, never replaced it. Then out came the answer key, and smoke meant this, a male or female torso meant that.

Whatever Rorschach's intent, the content-based approach—the most seductive and Freudian but also the most controversial, prone to subjectivity and misuse—was now a viable alternative to other, more sober Rorschach methodologies. It was also increasingly widespread in the popular imagination. Seeing a happy butterfly in a meadow is good, an ax murderer is bad. It was an idea easy to popularize.

AMID THE FREE-FOR-ALL of midcentury uses and abuses of the inkblots, a few more thoughtful figures stopped to look back on what had been learned and how far there still was to go. Rorschach had thought people went through an introvert turn at thirty-three to thirty-five, retreating into themselves to emerge charged with ideas and projects for the future. Coincidentally or not, the test "born" in late 1917 went through the same kind of reflective moment in the early 1950s.

This was when Henri Ellenberger tracked down Olga Rorschach and Hermann's other surviving relatives, colleagues, and friends, writing the forty-page essay "The Life and Work of Hermann Rorschach," published in 1954. Two years earlier, in the first issue of a new journal called *Rorschachiana,* Manfred Bleuler—Eugen's son, the tester of Moroccan farmers, the second man to bring the inkblots to America—had published an essay looking back over thirty years of clinical use of the Rorschach.

He concluded, more modestly than many Americans writing on the test, that practical questions should never be decided by the Rorschach alone: it was not "by any means an infallible diagnostic instrument in the individual case." It could never replace, only complement, talking to and observing the patient in everyday situations. But beyond its use in any individual case, Bleuler argued, the test's significance was incalculable. "*What the Rorschach test can do*" (his italics) "*is this*":

> *It can give a clear picture of the great problems of psychology and of psychopathology, and can throw light on them from new angles.* . . . It is well known what role was played by a simple child's kite in the development of aviation. [Similarly,] the psychologist can prove with [the Rorschach test], search with it, almost play with it, while preparing for the difficult task of seeing the living man and his pathology as a whole and at the same time individually.
>
> I am convinced that here lies a very important cultural mission for the Rorschach, . . . following in Rorschach's personal tradition: nothing was further from his ideas than a wish to imprison man in a formula and reduce him to a mechanism that could be stamped according to measurable qualities. What he really was looking for was a picture of the man unencumbered by the veils of convention. . . . I think that future research with the Rorschach test also needs this spirit of his, which did not want to schematize the living person, but which wanted, in spite of the schematizing and formalizing spirit of our time, to help us to look deeply into the great miracle of life.

The man was "unencumbered by the veils of convention" because interpreting the blots was a task for which there were no conventions, no norms, in everyday life. As Rorschach had written to his sister in 1908, "Social intercourse and lies and traditions and customs etc. are dams that block our view into real life."

During the widespread turn to content analysis, one lone voice was calling for a turn to form. In a pair of articles from 1951 and 1953, psychologist and visual theorist Rudolf Arnheim reminded his readers that there were "objective perceptual characteristics of the blots as visual stimuli . . . in their own right." A given response was more often than not at least partly "due to properties of the inkblots themselves rather than to the personal idiosyncrasies of the respondents." In other words, it wasn't all projection. In fact, Arnheim argued, the metaphor of "projection," despite being visual, undervalued the act of seeing, of engaging with what was really there: "After paying lip service to the stimulus, we often talk as though the perceiver is hallucinating in a void," projecting whatever his or her personality dictates rather than responding to the actual, specific image.

Even the Movement response, which Rorschach had tied to the projection-like concept of "feeling-in," was not all subjective. An image can be more or less objectively dynamic, Arnheim pointed out. There *is* movement in some still images, such as a picture of a man turning his head, and not in others. These qualities were "no more 'subjective' than are shape or size." The "obliquely oriented wedges" of Card I were inherently dynamic; the "bowing waiters" of Card III had swinging curves with objectively more energy than the "climbing bears" of Card VIII, which were "pathetically short of visual pep."

Arnheim started to map out the inkblots' visual properties in detail. The central white area in Card II (see page 3) could easily be seen as a foreground figure "because of its symmetrical shape, convexity, and enclosedness," but it also "combines equally well" with the outer white area to form a background to the black shape. These were objective visual qualities that determined a person's range of responses. Arnheim spent close to ten pages on the complexities of Card I alone.

Arnheim speculated that there had never been such a visual analysis before, because the Rorschach blots were widely considered to be "unstructured," and responses to them "purely subjective." He called this a "one-sided conception." If the blots were both ambiguous and "structured enough to elicit some kind of reaction," then surely some effort should be made to say what that structure was. In any case, the images were complex enough that Arnheim suggested using them to investigate directly the way people process visual information. For instance,

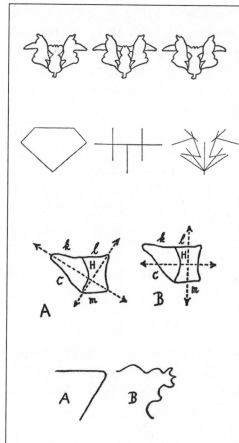

Figures from Arnheim's visual study of Card I.

(*a*) Parts can be grouped in multiple ways: for example, the triangular wings on either side can easily be seen as part of the side columns or as part of a crossbar across the top, either separate from or joined to the central column.

(*b*) "The decisive feature of visual shape is not the outer contour but what may be called the 'structural skeleton,'" and Card I conforms to multiple possible skeletons, such as these three.

(*c*) The skeletons, especially the main axes, change the perceptual dynamics. For example, the white triangle and gray rectangle in the bottom half of the card can look oblique and strongly dynamic, as A, or more static, as B.

(*d*) The contours of the image, such as the tips of the "wings," are equally amenable to perceptual smoothing or perceptual sharpening.

a psychologist could ask people outright whether they saw Card I "as a combination of three vertical blocks or as a system of soaring diagonals," instead of the roundabout detour of asking "What might this be?"

After his essays in the early fifties, as Arnheim went on to become the most influential theorist to apply neuropsychology and cognitive science in studying art, he tended to dismiss the Rorschach test, precisely because most people continued to think of it as a purely subjective exercise in projection. Only one other writer on the Rorschach took up Arnheim's call for specific visual analysis—and he too called into question the idea that the test was an exercise in "projection."

Psychologist Ernest Schachtel (1903–75) was the closest thing there ever was to a philosopher of the Rorschach. He found both Beck and

Klopfer too narrow in focus, calling Klopfer's 1942 manual vague, self-contradictory, undertheorized, and ultimately cut off from "the totality of human experience." The true goal of the inkblot experiment, Schachtel wrote, much as Bleuler would a decade later, was "adding to the understanding of the human psyche," and while Rorschach himself "never loses sight of this aim, in Klopfer's book it hardly ever comes into the field of the reader's vision."

In the debate about content analysis, Schachtel agreed examiners should use everything that turned up in the test situation. But he drew a distinction that ran deeper than the one between a formal response and a content-based response. What *are* the results of a Rorschach test, he asked: words that test takers say, or things that test takers see? Empiricists or literalists would say that we have access only to what test takers say out loud; we can't, after all, read their minds. Schachtel's view was that knowing what other people are seeing or feeling is something we do all the time and that, however hard it is to see through someone else's eyes, this is what the psychologist has to do. The Rorschach, Schachtel wrote, analyzed perceptions and perceptual processes themselves, "not the words used to communicate these perceptions or part of them, although these too are often psychologically quite significant." The point was what a person saw, and how, even if the examiner could access that way of seeing only by an unquantifiable process of imaginative empathy. Used merely to analyze spoken words, "the test will become a sterile technique rather than the ingenious instrument for the exploration of man as which it was conceived and presented by Rorschach."

Although Schachtel never created a system of Rorschach scoring and interpretation—his insights were just the kind resistant to systematization—it was he who took up Arnheim's 1951 call to give a detailed analysis of the inkblots as actual visual things, not mere screens to project onto. He analyzed the blots' unity or fragmentation, solidity or fragility, massiveness or delicacy, stability or precariousness, hardness or softness, wetness or dryness, light or darkness, emphasizing all the while the psychological resonance of these qualities.

For instance, the size of an image was an objective fact, but the meaning of its size was a fact of psychology. "No miniature portrait," he argued, "touches us with the power, profundity, and truly human quality" of an average-sized portrait by any great painter. To do so, an image had to be human scale, not literally life-sized but on "the scale within which the full range of human feelings can be spoken to and respond." The inkblots, too, while not portraits, depended on the size of the cards for how they worked—one reason why the slide-show Group Rorschach was not as effective as the real thing.

Both Schachtel and Arnheim—who late in his career wrote an entire book on balance and symmetry, *The Power of the Center*—showed how discoveries in the science of perception since Rorschach's day had backed up his insight that horizontal symmetry was crucial. For instance, vertical symmetry is less meaningful: most objects seem to change shape when we view them upside down, but not when we view them reversed. Adults reflexively turn upside-down pictures right-side up, but young children don't—they haven't yet learned spatial orientation, the fact that vertical is different from horizontal. A series of identical circles in a horizontal ring look the same size, and in a vertical ring they don't—one reason why the moon looks bigger when it's lower in the sky—but this difference does not exist for monkeys, who move through the world both horizontally and vertically, nor for babies before they learn to stand upright. These aren't laws of geometry; they are laws of human psychology.

It is only in retrospect that Schachtel, Arnheim, Bleuler, and Ellenberger, with their thoughtful reflections on the nature of the test and the life of its creator, stand out from the cypress knees, parlor games, and perfume ads. At the time, the inkblots were simply being used in too many ways, too many settings.

One of these uses, in Germany in the immediate aftermath of the Second World War, was of self-evident importance. But it was largely kept secret for a generation: it raised too many questions that the postwar world, grappling with the horrors of the Holocaust, was not yet willing to face. Another Rorschach test given in Jerusalem in 1961, at one of the defining moments of the century, would finally bring those questions to light.

18

The Nazi Rorschachs

B Y 1945, THE WORD *NAZI*—FOR A MEMBER OF THE NATIONAL SO-cialist German Workers' Party—had become shorthand around the world for a cold-blooded sadistic monster beyond the pale of humanity. Six million Jews had been killed. How could any of the Nazis not have known? There was an overwhelming desire to stage The World v. The Nazis, with the defendants all guilty and deserving to die, but there was no clear legal basis for doing so. And the truth was that not all of the Holocaust's perpetrators were party members, and vice versa. It was impossible, logistically and in principle, to condemn every single party member as a war criminal. The atrocities were unprecedented in human history, but for that very reason it was unclear what laws fit the crime.

The legal issues were resolved by negotiation among the Allies and by fiat. An international military tribunal was created. "Crimes against humanity" were prosecuted for the first time, at the Nuremberg Trials, beginning in 1945. Twenty-four prominent Nazis were chosen as the first group of defendants. But the moral quandaries remained. The defendants claimed that they had been following their own country's laws, which in this case meant whatever Hitler wanted. Could people legally be held to account on the basis of a higher law of common humanity? How deep does cultural relativity go? And if these Nazis really were deranged psychopaths, then weren't they unfit to stand trial, or even not guilty by reason of insanity? One Nuremberg defendant, Julius Streicher, was a virulent anti-Semite so obscenely perverted that he had been removed from power in 1939 and placed under house arrest by Hitler himself. In what sense was he responsible for war crimes?

The prisoners were held in solitary, on the ground floor of a three-story prison block with cells on both sides of a wide corridor. Each cell was nine by thirteen feet, with a wooden door several inches thick, a high barred window onto a courtyard, a steel cot, and a toilet, with no seat or cover, from which the prisoner's feet remained visible to the guards. Personal belongings were kept on the floor. A fifteen-inch panel in the middle of the cell door was open at all times, forming a shelf in the cell on which meals were placed and a peephole for guards to look through, one guard per prisoner at all times. The light was always on, dimmer at night but still bright enough to read by, and heads and hands had to be kept visible while the prisoner was in bed, asleep or awake. Aside from harsh corrections when any rules were broken, the guards never spoke to the prisoners, nor did the wardens who brought them their food. They had fifteen minutes a day to walk outside, separate from the other prisoners, and showers once a week, under supervision. Up to four times a week, the prisoner was stripped and the room searched so thoroughly it took four hours to straighten up afterward.

They also had medical care, to keep them healthy for the trial. A staff of doctors weaned Hermann Göring off his morphine addiction, restored some of the use of Hans Frank's hand after he had slashed his wrist in a suicide attempt, helped reduce Alfred Jodl's back pain and Joachim von Ribbentrop's neuralgia. There were dentists, chaplains— one Catholic, one Protestant—and a prison psychiatrist. This was none other than Douglas Kelley, coauthor of Bruno Klopfer's 1942 manual, *The Rorschach Technique.*

Kelley had been one of the first members of the Rorschach Institute to volunteer after Pearl Harbor, and by 1944 he was chief of psychiatry for the European theater of operations. In 1945 he was in Nuremberg, assigned to help determine whether the defendants were competent to stand trial. He saw them for five months, making the rounds every day and talking to them at length, often sitting on the edge of a prisoner's cot for three or four hours at a time. The Nazis, alone and bored, were eager to talk. Kelley said he had never had a group of patients so easy to interview. "In addition to careful medical and psychiatric examinations, I subjected the men to a series of psychological tests," Kelley wrote. "The most important technique employed was the Rorschach Test, a well-known and highly useful method of personality study."

Another American had free access to the prisoners: the Nuremberg morale officer, Gustave Gilbert. His job was to monitor prisoners' moods and gather whatever intelligence he could. He visited them almost daily, chatted casually about whatever they felt like, then left the room and wrote it all down. He happened to have a background in psychology and gave himself the title of Prison Psychologist, apparently on no real authority. In the absence of a clear chain of command, the title stuck.

Kelley needed a translator to administer the tests; Gilbert had little experience in diagnostic testing, having studied social, not clinical, psychology, but he was the only American officer on the prison staff except the chaplains who spoke German. Plus he "could hardly wait to get to work on the Nazis." Both he and Kelley knew that objective data on the personalities of these world-historical criminals were a gold mine, and both wanted to use the era's most advanced psychological technique on the captive audience, to discover the secrets of the Nazi mind.

Before the trial started, Gilbert gave the prisoners IQ tests, adjusted to eliminate questions that required an American cultural background. Some of the Nazis bristled, and at least one probably faked mistakes to mislead Gilbert, who was Jewish. (Streicher, a former teacher, claimed not to be able to figure out 100 minus 72.) But most had a good time and welcomed the distraction. Hjalmar Horace Greeley Schacht, Hitler's finance minister, found Gilbert's visits "in part exhilarating"; Wilhelm Keitel, head of the Nazi Armed Forces, praised "how much better it was than the silly nonsense that German psychologists resorted to in the Wehrmacht testing station." It was later discovered that Keitel had abolished intelligence tests in the army after his son had failed one. Hitler's former vice-chancellor, Franz von Papen, initially asked to be excused from the exercise but later came around, bragging about having placed third among the defendants (he was actually fifth). Several behaved like "bright and egotistical schoolboys"; Albert Speer said everyone "strove to do the best he could" and "see his abilities confirmed."

Hermann Göring, creator of the Gestapo and the death camps, felt particularly up to the challenge. He understood psychological testing and had installed his cousin, Matthias Göring, as head of the German Institute for Psychological Research and Psychotherapy; he loved being tested, especially with Gilbert's flattery to grease the wheels. As Gilbert's diary recorded for November 15, 1945, Göring chuckled with glee as I showed surprise at his accomplishment. . . . He could hardly contain himself for joy and swelled with pride. This pattern of rapport was maintained throughout the entire test, the examiner encouraging him with remarks of how few people are able to do the next problem, and Göring responding like a show-off schoolboy. . . .

"Maybe you should have become a professor instead of a politician," I suggested.

"Perhaps. I'm convinced that I would have done better than the average man no matter what I went into."

When Göring failed the digit-span memory test at nine numbers—anything over seven numbers is above average—he begged Gilbert: "Oh, come on, give me another crack at it; I can do it!" He was livid when later told that two other prisoners had actually done better than him, at which point he changed his mind and decided the IQ tests were unreliable.

The distasteful fact was that the Nazis did well, with IQs ranging from Julius Streicher's probably faked 106 to Schacht's truly impressive age-adjusted 143. All but three of the twenty-one Nazis tested had scores above 120, "Superior" or "Very superior," with nine being Mensa material, 130 or higher. Göring's IQ of 138 showed, in Kelley's words, "excellent intelligence bordering on the highest level."

These findings were, to say the least, not widely reported. A 1946 *New Yorker* piece on Kelley was called "No Geniuses" and in it Kelley downplayed Göring's intelligence more than he would elsewhere. The piece painted Kelley as "a lithe, agreeable chap in his early thirties, with a shock of brown hair and an authentically sardonic smile," speaking in a patter of midcentury slang straight out of J. D. Salinger. He is quoted as saying that "with the exception of Dr. Ley," who had committed suicide, "there wasn't an insane Joe in the crowd. Nor did I find any geniuses. Göring, for example, came through with an I.Q. of a hundred and thirty-eight—he's *pretty* good, but no wizard."

In any case, IQ tests were never going to solve the mystery of the Nazi mind. "With but a short time in which to work," Kelley wrote, "I took it upon myself to examine the personality patterns of these men" using the technique he had co-written the book on.

No one at Nuremberg had ordered Rorschachs. The test results were never used in the trial. Kelley and Gilbert simply decided, in the unprecedented, supercharged atmosphere of Nuremberg, to administer it themselves. The Rorschach, never as popular in Germany as in America, had been used under the Nazis but primarily in aptitude testing, or as evaluations to help "weed out disruptive social and 'racial' elements." The Nazis had not generally been interested in psychological insight, except into other countries, to try to develop effective psychological warfare. Now the test would be used to gain insight into the Nazis themselves.

Kelley gave the Rorschach to eight prisoners and Gilbert to sixteen, five of them previously tested by Kelley. Albert Speer, Rudolf Hess, racial theorist Alfred Rosenberg, Hitler's ambassador Joachim von Ribbentrop, the "Butcher of Poland" Hans Frank, the head of Nazi-occupied Netherlands—each was shown ten inkblots and asked, "What might this be?" Göring had an even better time with the Rorschach than with the IQ test. He laughed, snapped his fingers in excitement, and expressed "regret," according to Kelley, "that the Luftwaffe had not had available such excellent testing techniques."

The prisoners' results shared a few common elements—a certain lack of introspection, a propensity for chameleon-like flexibility in adapting to orders—but the differences far outweighed the similarities. Some of the defendants seemed paranoid, depressed, or clearly disturbed. Joachim von Ribbentrop was "emotionally barren" and a "markedly disturbed personality" overall; the Butcher of Poland's results were those of a cynical, antisocial madman. Others were average, and some were "particularly well adjusted." The cultured Schacht, high scorer on the IQ tests, almost seventy years old, "could call on an inner world of satisfying experiences to stand him in good stead in the stressful months prior to sentencing." He rated as an "exceptionally well-integrated personality with excellent potential" and would later look back on his Rorschach testing rather fondly: "a game that, if I remember correctly, had been used by Justinus Kerner. Through the process [of spilling ink and folding the paper], many bizarre forms are created which are to be detected. In our case this task was made even more enjoyable since inks of different colors were used on the same card."

An intelligent madman was one thing; a sane and exceptionally well-adjusted leading Nazi with excellent potential was something else. But those seemed to be the results. Gilbert refused to accept it. In his *Nuremberg Diary,* published in 1947, he described how Göring, after the guilty verdict,

> lay on his cot completely worn out and deflated ... like a child holding the torn remnants of a balloon that had burst in its hand. A few days after the verdict he asked me again what those psychological tests had shown about his personality—especially that inkblot test—as if it had been bothering him all the time. This time I told him. "Frankly, they showed that while you have an active, aggressive mind, you lack the guts to really face responsibility. You betrayed yourself with a little gesture on the ink-blot test." Göring glared apprehensively. "Do you remember the card with the red spot? Well, morbid neurotics often hesitate over that card and then say there's blood on it. You hesitated, but you didn't call it blood. *You tried to flick it off with your finger,* as though you thought you could wipe away the blood with a little gesture. You've been doing the same thing all through the trial—taking off your earphones in the courtroom, whenever the evidence of your guilt became too unbearable. And you did the same thing during the war too, drugging the atrocities out of your mind. You didn't have the courage to face it. That is your guilt.... You are a moral coward."
>
> Göring glared at me and was silent for a while. Then he said those psychological tests were meaningless.... A few days later he told me that he had given [his lawyer] a statement that anything the psychologist or anybody else in the jail had to say at this time was meaningless and prejudiced.... It had struck home.

It was a dramatic moment—a Shakespearean moment, the climax of Gilbert's book. But what did the inkblot test add, beyond confirming what Gilbert already knew from Göring's behavior and history? No double-blind study would ever prove that flicking the red was a sign of genocidal moral cowardice.

Kelley, a far more expert Rorschacher, saw the results differently. As early as 1946, even before the Nuremberg verdicts were handed down, Kelley published a paper stating that the defendants were "essentially sane," though in some cases abnormal. He didn't discuss the Rorschachs specifically, but he argued "not only that such personalities are not unique or insane, but also that they could be duplicated in any country of the world today."

He expanded on the theme in his 1947 general interest book *22 Cells in Nuremberg,* which opened by declaring:

> Since my return from Europe where I was Psychiatrist to Nuremberg Jail, I have realized that many persons—even well-informed ones—do not grasp the concept [that psychology is determined by culture]. For too many of them have said to me:
>
> "What kind of people were those Nazis really? Of course, all the top fellows weren't normal. Obviously they were insane, but what sort of insanity did they have?"
>
> Insanity is no explanation for the Nazis. They were simply creatures of their environment, as all humans are; and they were also—to a greater degree than most humans are—the makers of their environment.

Kelley insisted on going against what the postwar public strongly believed, and even more strongly wanted to believe. The Nazis were, he wrote, "not spectacular types, not personalities such as appear only once in a century," but simply "strong, dominant, aggressive, egocentric personalities" who had been given "the opportunity to seize power." Men like Göring "are not rare. They can be found anywhere in the country—behind big desks deciding big affairs as businessmen, politicians, and racketeers."

So much for American leaders. As for followers: "Shocking as it may seem to some of us, we as a people greatly resemble the Germans of two decades ago" in the twenties, before Hitler's rise to power. Both share a similar ideological background and rely on emotions rather than the intellect. "Cheap and dangerous" American politicians, Kelley wrote, were using race-baiting and white supremacy for political gain "just one year after the end of the war"—an allusion to Theodore Bilbo of Mississippi and Eugene Talmadge of Georgia; he also referred to "the power politics of Huey Long, who enforced his opinions by police control." These were "the same racial prejudices that the Nazis preached," the very "same words that rang through the corridors of Nuremberg Jail." In short, there was "little in America today which could prevent the establishment of a Nazilike state."

The Nuremberg Trials had failed to define the meaning of the war and the Holocaust, much less rebuild a shattered sense of the human community. The defendants had not been a homogeneous group of top Nazis, with the true leaders—Hitler, Himmler, Goebbels—already dead. Three of the twenty-four were even acquitted when the verdicts were handed down, including Schacht, the high performer on the psychological tests. Now Kelley was arguing that his most sophisticated technique had failed to detect a "Nazi personality."

The lesson was unacceptable. Molly Harrower, the inventor of Group and Multiple-Choice Rorschach testing, was organizing an important international congress on mental health, to be held in 1948. It would be the perfect venue in which to publicize the Nuremberg Rorschachs. She sent Gilbert's sixteen protocols to the world's eleven foremost experts on the test, including Beck and Klopfer, Hertz and Rapaport, Munroe and Schachtel. All of them were eager to see the reports, but *not one* ended up contributing to the conference. Every single one suddenly found themselves with an unexpected scheduling conflict or some other excuse.

Surely the world's leading Rorschachers could squeeze in a few hours to look at what promised to be the most significant tests in history? It is hard to believe that their unanimous refusal could be a coincidence. Perhaps they saw the implications clearly and did not want to go on the record saying so, because the public's investment in the Nazis as uniformly evil was too strong. More likely, they themselves didn't know what to make of what they were seeing and doubted Kelley's and Gilbert's competence or their own interpretations. Harrower, writing in 1976, explained the thinking of the time:

> We operated on the assumption that a sensitive clinical tool, which the Rorschach unquestionably is, must also be able to demonstrate moral purpose, or lack of it. Implicit also at that time was the belief that this test would reveal a uniform personality structure of a particularly repellent kind. We espoused a concept of evil which dealt in black and white, sheep and goats. . . . We tended to disbelieve

the evidence of our scientific senses because our concept of evil was such that it was ingrained in the personality and therefore must be a tangible, scoreable element in psychological tests.

The 1948 conference panel fell apart, while Gilbert and Kelley pressed on, each eager to get into print first with the Rorschach results.

They had had a strained relationship at Nuremberg, which soon turned into another full-blown Rorschach feud. Major Kelley tended to call Lieutenant Gilbert his "assistant," even though Gilbert was a member of the Counterintelligence Corps and not Kelley's direct subordinate. Kelley called his Rorschachs the "originals," while Gilbert called Kelley's "premature," "spoiled" (because given using an interpreter), and somehow "doctored." The insults and retaliations, legal threats and counterthreats, escalated fast. "He continually startles me by his apparent neglect of basic ethics," wrote Kelley. "I will not put up with anymore of Kelley's nonsense beyond the specific concessions I have already made," wrote Gilbert. Gilbert's publishers "probably do not realize they are publishing stolen goods," wrote Kelley.

Gilbert put out his psychological analysis *The Psychology of Dictatorship* in 1950. In the end, after requesting contributions from David Levy and Samuel Beck among others, he still didn't publish the Rorschach data or any detailed interpretations—partly under legal pressure from Kelley, partly because he was the less proficient in Rorschach interpretation of the two, and partly because the Nuremberg Rorschachs did not give him the sweeping negative results he wanted. Kelley had likewise gone to Klopfer, Beck, and others. He didn't care about their differences; he was "only interested in gaining from as many experts as possible the completest patterns of personality which can be elicited from the records." But despite receiving long and labor-intensive reports, and despite continuing to believe in the value of the Rorschach, Kelley too declined to publish the Nuremberg Rorschach results and his interpretations. He eventually stopped answering the experts' annoyed letters asking him what he was going to do with their work, and the material sat in boxes for decades.

In later years, Kelley continued to fight against demonizing criminals. He would play a part in the great midcentury artifact of sympathy for the outsider, when the director Nicholas Ray used him to vet the psychological and criminological accuracy of the *Rebel Without a Cause* screenplay. In 1957, he starred in twenty episodes of a popular and award-winning TV show called *Criminal Man,* designed to "bring about a better understanding by the public of the person who commits a crime" and to foster a shift from "simple vengeance" to rehabilitation. "No!" he shouted on camera in one episode, about whether criminals have physical features in common. "There is no such thing as a criminal type. It is simply folklore. It is like saying the world is flat. You can't tell by looking. Criminals are not born."

Kelley even refused to demonize Göring. They had developed an uncomfortably close bond at Nuremberg: "Each day when I came to his cell on my rounds," Kelley wrote in *22 Cells,* Göring "would jump up from his chair, greet me with a broad smile and outstretched hand, escort me to his cot and pat its middle with his great paw. 'Good morning, Doctor. I am so glad you have come to see me. Please sit down, Doctor. Sit here.'" Göring was "positively jovial over my daily coming and wept unashamedly when I left Nuremberg for the States." And a note of admiration, almost infatuation, crept into much of what Kelley wrote about the Nazi second-in-command, even as he was fully aware of the atrocities Göring had committed: "Göring was nobody's fool, not even Hitler's. He was a brilliant, brave, ruthless, grasping, shrewd executive."

Kelley especially praised Göring's suicide from swallowing cyanide on the eve of his execution: "At first glance his action may seem cowardly—an attempt to escape the punishment meted out to his compatriots. Careful consideration of his actions, however, reveals that here is the true Göring, contemptuous of man-made rules and regulations, taking his own life at his own convenience and in a manner of his own choosing." Having denied the tribunal's right to judge or sentence him, Göring had stoically endured the trial and now robbed the Allies of their victory, joining the other top Nazis who had already killed themselves. "His suicide, shrouded in mystery and emphasizing the impotency of the American guards, was a skillful, even brilliant, finishing touch, completing the edifice for the Germans to admire in time to come." Kelley went so far as to say that "there seems little doubt that

Hermann Göring has re-established himself in the hearts of his people. . . . History may well show that Göring won out at the end"! Here is what Gilbert had to say: "Göring died as he had lived, a psychopath trying to make a mockery of all human values and to distract attention from his guilt by a dramatic gesture." Gilbert's later essays had titles like "Hermann Göring, Amiable Psychopath."

Kelley remained a Salingeresque character to the end—like Salinger's hero Seymour Glass, Kelley too had been a prodigy, part of a landmark Stanford longitudinal study of California schoolchildren identified as geniuses with IQs over 140, and like Glass, Kelley committed suicide. He chose the exceedingly rare means of swallowing cyanide, just like his antihero. It was rumored that the pill he crushed with his teeth in front of his wife and child on New Year's Day 1958 was a souvenir from Nuremberg. Some even said that Kelley, a master prestidigitator on the side (vice-president of the Society of American Magicians), was the man responsible for smuggling the pill to Göring in the first place. He wasn't, but there is no mistaking the significance of his final gesture: an identification with Göring's "skillful, even brilliant, finishing touch."

Gilbert's fate was to end up at another trial of the century, one that would force a new reckoning with the Nuremberg Rorschachs.

IN 1960, THE NAZI who had been in charge of deporting Jews to death camps was captured in Argentina by Israeli agents. They brought him to Jerusalem to stand trial, and a court-appointed psychiatrist, Istvan Kulcsar, saw him for seven three-hour sessions and gave him a battery of seven psychological tests. These included an IQ test, a TAT, and what was by 1961 the world's leading personality test: the Rorschach.

The tests told Kulcsar that Adolf Eichmann was a psychopathic personality with an "inhuman" worldview and a sadism so extreme that it went beyond the Marquis de Sade, deserving a new name, "Eichmannism." Gustave Gilbert testified in the Eichmann trial, and his Nuremberg Rorschach material was admitted as evidence; he published "The Mentality of SS Murderous Robots" soon afterward, in the scholarly Holocaust journal *Yad Vashem Studies,* describing the Nazi personality type as a "reflection of the disease symptoms of a sick society [and] diseased elements of the German culture." Kelley was no longer around to dispute Kulcsar's and Gilbert's interpretations, but others were.

The *New Yorker* magazine sent one of the most important political philosophers of the period, Hannah Arendt, to cover the trial. In the resulting book, *Eichmann in Jerusalem,* she coined the phrase "the banality of evil." Eichmann's was a new kind of wrongdoing, she argued: bureaucratic, unmoored from both character and personality. If anything, he was the antipersonality, not standing out from the crowd at all but unquestioningly accepting the group's values. Arendt described him as an "average, 'normal' person, neither feeble-minded nor indoctrinated nor cynical," but such a person could be "perfectly incapable of telling right from wrong."

In today's terms, Eichmann was not a robot but a joiner. The problem arose when what a person decided to join was Nazi Germany—or, looked at from the other side, when Hitler found unthinking joiners rather than individuals of integrity with a moral core. Eichmann was Arendt's example of the inability "to think from the standpoint of somebody else"—even, in a sense, from an individual standpoint of his own. Such a banal failing could, in a Nazi context, "wreak more havoc than all the evil instincts taken together." But if Eichmann had no moral compass, then how could he fairly be judged?

The issue went far beyond Eichmann. When a Nazi tried to excuse his actions by saying he was only a cog in a machine, it was, Arendt provocatively argued, "as if a criminal pointed to the statistics on crime" and said "that he only did what was statistically expected, that it was mere accident that he did it and not somebody else, since after all somebody had to do it." Psychology and sociology too—any theory "from the *Zeitgeist* down to the Oedipal complex" that "explained away the responsibility of the doer for his deed in terms of this or that kind of determinism"—made it pointless to pass judgment.

Arendt called this "one of the central moral questions of all time," and it was an impossible dilemma. One might be tempted to distance oneself from an Eichmann, denying any shared humanity, but the rule of law presupposed a common humanity between the accuser and the accused, the judge and the judged. Or one might insist on common humanity, assuming that every human conscience has the same bedrock values and that there is such a thing as crimes objectively "against humanity" or orders that should never be obeyed. But the Nazis, and Eichmann in particular, showed that these universal ideals were, in Arendt's words, "truly the last thing to be taken for granted in our time." People do what they have to do, and "about nothing does public opinion everywhere seem to be in happier agreement than that no one has the right to judge somebody else." And yet Eichmann's case cried out for judgment.

While Arendt was writing about the trial, a psychologist at Yale named Stanley Milgram was responding to Eichmann differently, by designing an experiment meant to discover how ordinary people could take part in genocide. "Could it be," Milgram famously asked, "that Eichmann and his million accomplices in the Holocaust were just following orders?" Originally, Milgram planned a preliminary run in the United States before taking the experiment to Germany, where he expected to find people more prone to obedience. That turned out not to be necessary.

Starting in July 1961, American volunteers in a "teaching exercise" operated a device that delivered what they thought were extremely painful shocks to "learners" in another room. The whole thing was staged, but these volunteers, when verbally ordered by the experimenter, administered what they thought were real electric shocks, up to and including 450-volt blasts labeled "Danger: Severe Shock," even after the screams audible from the next room fell ominously silent. They told the experimenter it was wrong, and that they didn't want to do it, but they did it anyway. To find monsters willing to just follow orders, it seemed we needed only to look in the mirror.

Arendt's book and Milgram's study were both published in 1963. Their lines of argument were very different—the philosopher calling into question the meaning of personal responsibility, the experimenter showing how easy it was to compel obedience in a specific situation— but they were soon impossible to disentangle. Milgram made Arendt's reflections concrete; Arendt gave Milgram's scenario world-historical resonance. The submissive volunteers electrocuting people seemed even more horrifying given their association with Eichmann; Milgram's image of conformity overriding moral values made people read Arendt as claiming Eichmann had been forced to "just follow orders," even though she never said he was an unwilling follower.

Arendt had mischaracterized Eichmann's actual Rorschach testing—writing that "half a dozen psychiatrists had certified him as 'normal'" when in fact he was examined only by Kulcsar, who found him deranged. Her point was to scathingly dismiss "the comedy of the soul experts" altogether. And her overall philosophical argument, about what individual responsibility can mean when actions are explained by general laws, went far beyond what any test could possibly prove or refute. And yet, in a broader sense, Arendt—at least Arendt in conjunction with Milgram—was a key figure in the history of the Rorschach test. Her views, or how they were understood, took the relativism implicit in the test to its radical conclusion.

Arendt and Milgram also eventually made it possible to grapple with the Nuremberg Rorschachs. It was Molly Harrower—the organizer of the 1948 conference that had failed to publicize the results—who returned to Gilbert's protocols, though not until 1975, when asked to address an academic seminar on American civilization. She explicitly said that the reason she and her profession had previously "espoused a concept of evil which dealt in black and white, sheep and goats," was because "we had not been challenged by such startling and unpopular ideas as those of Arendt and Milgram."

Harrower had the Nuremberg protocols reanalyzed blind, with non-Nazi results as controls. The results confirmed Kelley's view that the Nazis were normal, or abnormal in typical ways: "It is an oversimplified position to look for an underlying common denominator in the Rorschach records of the Nazi prisoners," Harrower concluded. "The Nazis who went on trial at Nuremberg were as diverse a group as one might find in our government today, or for that matter, in the leadership of the PTA."

Also in 1975, the first book to specifically quote and analyze the Nazi Rorschachs was published: *The Nuremberg Mind: The Psychology of Nazi Leaders*, by Florence R. Miale (one of the experts who had backed out of the 1948 conference) and Michael Selzer, a political scientist. They unambiguously came down on the side of passing moral judgment and claiming that there was a distinctive, pathological psychology common to all the Nuremberg defendants. Selzer published an article called "The Murderous Mind" in the *New York Times Magazine*, including Eichmann's drawings from two other projective tests, the Bender-Gestalt Test and the House-Tree-Person Test, and blind diagnoses describing Eichmann as a "highly warped individual." The Kelley-Gilbert debate was being rehashed again in the media, and now about Eichmann's results as well.

Critics immediately called *The Nuremberg Mind* biased, written to prove the authors' preexisting judgments. Most psychologists felt its authors had relied too heavily on content analysis, recognized by the 1970s as the most subjective and least verifiable approach to Rorschach interpretation. Others responded by embracing subjectivity and bias. In a 1980 analysis of Eichmann's Rorschach, one psychologist unapologetically admitted that it had influenced his analysis to know whose test it was, but he argued that his goal was insight into a particular individual's complex personality—"to discover more about what this particular man may have been like"—not an objective diagnosis.

Still, a consensus had been reached. The Nuremberg Rorschachs showed, as Kelley and Harrower claimed, that there was no such thing as a "Nazi personality." In the one case where we *wanted* there to be an unbridgeable difference between people, a moral chasm between Nazis and "us," the test seemed to have reached the opposite conclusion—and seemed to imply that these differences between people could not be judged.

The case of Eichmann's Rorschach was more complex, partly because it concerned a single individual. Did the results show Eichmann to be normal or abnormal? The results as interpreted by whom? And was Eichmann actually a monster, or just an example of "the banality of evil," and what does that term mean anyway? The debates around all these interlocking questions continue.

Taken together, though, these developments dealt a devastating blow to the status of psychological tests such as the Rorschach. There was no common ground to label evil as evil, no basis for moral judgment that everyone would accept, and grave doubts had been cast on the psychologist's own moral authority.

The controversy around Arendt and Milgram was part of a seismic cultural shift that would come to full flower later in the sixties. Americans were increasingly suspicious not only of the authority of psychologists but of almost any institutional power, and the reputation of the Rorschach would be a casualty.

19

A Crisis of Images

IN THE LATE 1950S, DR. IMMANUEL BROKAW, PERHAPS THE GREAT-est psychiatrist who ever lived, disappeared without a trace from his prominent New York practice. He'd had a crisis of faith. One day, listening to tape recordings of his therapy sessions, he'd discovered that a patient had said her husband "loved the best in me," not, as Brokaw had thought, "loved the beast in me." A very different kind of marriage. Brokaw found he had been hearing wrong for years: hundreds of apparently successful treatments were all based on error and illusion. New contact lenses shook his worldview further, by revealing the dirt and ugliness in his formerly soft-focus surroundings, in his own face in the mirror. He might have been misperceiving reality all this time, but now he preferred not to see it.

Ten years later, a former close friend found Brokaw wandering up and down the aisle of a public bus in Newport, California. That was how he now spent his time, an old man in Bermuda shorts, an L.A. Dodgers baseball cap, black leather sandals, and a psychedelic shirt: brightly flowered, crammed with details, fluttering and swarming with line and color. All the great doctor had left to offer was a simple question about his shirt: "What do you see?" Men and women, adults and children, saw horses in it, clouds, big waves and super surfboards, lightning, Egyptian amulets, mushroom clouds, man-eating tiger lilies. Not a sunset but a beautiful sunrise! His shirt provoked laughter and delight, an answer of their own from everyone he asked, until a contented Dr. Brokaw would step out of the bus and disappear across the beach.

Brokaw is not often mentioned in histories of psychology because he is fictional. Ray Bradbury made him up in a story called "The Man in the Rorschach Shirt," published in *Playboy* in 1966 and in book form in 1969. Silly though the plot was, it captured the countercultural spirit of the sixties, increasingly suspicious of authority figures and heartless experts of all kinds, whether Nazi bureaucrats, Milgram's experimenters, nuclear Strangeloves, or just anyone over thirty. The story symbolized—and proposed the Rorschach as a symbol for—how rejecting singular truth could unleash a beautiful chaos of individuality.

In Bradbury's story, the Rorschach shirt let Dr. Brokaw escape his psychiatric dead end. In the real world, clinical psychology was undergoing its own crisis of faith. At least some practitioners were growing increasingly skeptical about their discipline's leading test. What if the Rorschachs being given all across the country were based on error and illusion too?

FOR ALL OF the Rorschach's prominence, the ambiguous inkblots had always fit somewhat uneasily into what American psychologists tend to think of as "the tough-minded attitude of the psychometric tradition." Proponents of the test who understood it as "projective" continued to claim that the inkblots revealed the unique personality in ways that made standardization irrelevant. But the Rorschach played both sides, with scientists still wanting to use it as a test. And so its validity and reliability remained the subject of extensive research.

In the early 1950s, air force scientists had set out to study how the military might be able to use personality tests to predict success as a combat pilot. More than 1,500 air force cadets were given group Rorschach tests, along with a background interview, the Feeling-and-Doing questionnaire, a sentence-completion test specially designed for the air force, a group Draw-a-Person Test, and a group Szondi Test, where test takers were asked to say which were the most appealing and most repellent out of a set of facial photographs. Some of these cadets would go on to shine, rated well by their teachers and considered leaders by their peers; others would have good flying skills but be kicked out of the service because of "overt personality disturbances"; most were average or would fail for other reasons.

In 1954, the scientists randomly selected fifty case files from among the most successful cadets and fifty from the disturbed personalities and randomly divided the hundred cases into five groups of twenty.

Each packet of twenty files was given to several assessment experts, among them Molly Harrower, the developer of the Multiple-Choice Rorschach, and Bruno Klopfer. Could they tell from the test results which category a cadet fell into? In other words, would a cadet's initial tests, in the hands of the country's foremost experts, have been able to predict his future psychological problems?

A coin toss would have been right an average of 10 times in each group of twenty cases. The psychologists were right an average of 10.2 times. Not a single psychologist did significantly better than chance. They were asked to say which evaluations they felt especially confident about, and even when counting only those cases, just two psychologists out of the nineteen did better than chance. Seven did worse.

Some of the psychologists said afterward that the air force modifications to the standard tests had skewed the results. Harrower had already pointed out, in response to similar negative findings, that maybe what makes a successful pilot "is not at present clearly envisaged in Rorschach terms"; maybe good soldiers don't have what we normally think of as "good mental health" at all. Rorschach tests showed an equal number of "frankly unstable or psychopathic personalities" among both decorated aviators and those who had failed to complete more than five missions—but these were psychopathic personalities "judged by our peacetime standards." A well-balanced personality in normal circumstances might not be the best suited for a dangerous and high-stakes environment like a fighter jet. Compelling counterarguments or not, "10.2 times out of 20" sounded pretty damning, if not of the Rorschach per se then certainly of the battery of personality tests on offer.

In other studies, the Rorschach proved worse at predicting job performance or academic success than more straightforward tools like report cards, employment records, or a short questionnaire. "Color shock"—Hermann Rorschach's term for being startled by colored cards, a sign of vulnerability to being overwhelmed by emotions—was discredited when it was found to be just as common when subjects were shown black-and-white versions of the colored inkblots. Still more studies, investigating the claim that the Rorschach should be used with other tests and never by itself, found that incorporating Rorschach information into a battery of tests actually made the diagnosis less accurate, not more accurate.

Multiple studies found that clinical psychologists consistently over-diagnosed mental problems in Rorschach subjects. In one 1959 study, tests were given to three healthy men, three neurotics, three psychotics, and three with other psychological disorders. "Passive dependent personality"—"Anxiety neurosis with hysterical features"—"Schizoid character, depressive trends": not one of the multiple Rorschach evaluators labeled *any* of the healthy subjects as "normal."

The most cutting criticism spoke to the Rorschach's great selling point: that the results depended on who you were, not on how you were trying to present yourself. The Rorschach was an X-ray, the test that couldn't be faked any more than a slide could fool a slide projector. By 1960, though, studies were showing that examiners could consciously or unconsciously influence the results and that test takers modified their responses depending on why the test was being given, what the examiner thought of them, or just the examiner's personal style. While some saw the interpersonal aspect of the test as part of its power, this did make the test less objective.

What psychological testers liked to call "clinical validity"—the fact that a skilled interpreter could use the Rorschach to gain insights that worked in practice and that could then be confirmed with the patient or checked against other sources—was starting to look very different to skeptics. They described these so-called insights as a combination of confirmation bias (overvaluing, even overperceiving, information one already agrees with), illusory correlations (deciding a connection exists that isn't there), and the kinds of techniques used by fortune-tellers and psychics (unconsciously using contextual information, making statements true of almost everyone but felt to be insightful, offering "push" predictions subtly modified or even totally reversed in follow-up questions, and so on).

Blind diagnosis eliminated some of these issues but by no means all. The test still had to be administered by someone in contact with the test taker. Any verification of the diagnosis required checking it against the judgments of someone like the subject's regular therapist, which only replicated the problem. Besides, for psychological truths, it was hard to say what outside confirmation could look like. If a clinician and a patient both felt that a description of the patient was true, what else was there? But these feelings would not satisfy a demand for hard proof.

Few claimed that Rorschach testers were consciously cynical frauds or quacks. Then again, a fortune-teller surrounded by customers amazed at the accuracy of his mind-reading might start to believe in his own astounding abilities, too—and some of the most forceful critics of the Rorschach drew just this analogy. At the very least, they expressed dismay at a "Rorschach culture" of orthodoxy, arguments from authority, and antiscientific bias.

Such criticisms, appearing in professional publications, had little effect on the Rorschach, which was in widespread use and central to the self-definition of clinical psychology. There was too great a demand for the access to the personality that the inkblots claimed to provide.

THE COLD WAR was running at its hottest in the sixties, demanding total ideological clarity in the battle between communism and capitalism, and there were moments when the fate of the world quite literally depended on how ambiguity was interpreted. In October 1962, President Kennedy was handed photographs of Cuba taken from America's most advanced U-2 spy plane, which either did or didn't show a Soviet medium-range ballistic missile launch site, and either were or weren't reason to start a nuclear war.

JFK saw "a football field" in one picture; RFK saw "the clearing of a field for a farm or the basement of a house." Even the deputy director of the National Photographic Interpretation Center—there was such a thing, established in 1961—admitted that the president would have to take "on faith" what the pictures showed. But what was needed was certainty. When JFK delivered a televised address to the nation on October 22, he called the photographs "unmistakable evidence" of a Soviet missile site; when they were reproduced around the world, the public found them just as unmistakable.

The combination of real ambiguity and an overwhelming need for visual and ideological certainty produced what has been called a "Cold War crisis of images" affecting both sides of the Iron Curtain. Capitalists and communists alike went looking for secret messages behind everything, and insisted they had found them. A new word for hiding specific meanings in material that seemed random and intentionless—

"encryption"—entered *Webster's Dictionary* in 1950. US Customs officials were confiscating abstract paintings sent from Paris because they thought the images contained communist messages. Ambiguities like the inkblots' now tended to be thought of no longer as fruitful methods for exploring individual personalities but as codes to be deciphered.

Efforts to read minds were inseparable from attempts to control them—a link clearest in the research and debates on so-called "brainwashing" that rocked American behavioral sciences around the time of the Korean War. (These were the techniques immortalized in popular culture by *The Manchurian Candidate*: novel 1959; movie 1962.) The US government heavily promoted efforts to plumb the recesses of "the Soviet mind," "the African mind," "the non-European mind," and so on, both in anthropology and more generally. It funded ventures like the Fulbright Fellowship, promoting cultural exchange and infiltration, and the creation of Area Studies ("Latin American" or "Far East" departments in prominent universities).

Psychology was seen as intrinsically linked to national security and the cause of democracy, and even outside of specific hotspots like Latin America or the Soviet mind, the inkblots were widely deployed to penetrate foreign psyches. Bleuler's Moroccan farmers, Du Bois's Alorese, and Hallowell's Ojibwe had been just the beginning. Scholar Rebecca Lemov has counted five thousand articles published between 1941 and 1968 in what she calls the "Projective Test Movement": research using Rorschachs and other projective methods on peoples from the Blackfoot Indians in the American West to every last Ifalukan living on coral islands in Micronesia totaling half a square mile. These studies, too, were well funded by the government. "Cold War–era look-inside-your-head fantasies flourished," Lemov remarks.

In this technocratic context, the collected information was likely to end up as enormous stockpiles of data in archives and university libraries. The Vicos Collection at Cornell documented how the university leased a Peruvian village in 1952, expropriated it to the sharecroppers, and managed its transition into modernity, studying it and its inhabitants with projective tests every step of the way. The Microcard Publications of Primary Records in Culture and Personality in Wisconsin, known as the "database of dreams," contained thousands of miniaturized Rorschach protocols and life histories, slices of life such as the

Rorschach responses of one hard-drinking Menominee Indian from northeastern Wisconsin who had run aground on the transition to modernity. Card VI, he said, "*is like a dead planet. It seems to tell the story of a people once great, who have lost . . . like something happened. All that's left is the symbol.*"

Another Menominee, a peyote worshipper, found the inkblots more comforting: "You know, this Rorschach . . . is something like peyote in a way. It looks into your mind. Sees the things that aren't out in the open. It is like that with peyote. At a meeting you get to know a man in a few hours better than you would get to know him in a lifetime otherwise. Everything about him is right there for you to see."

Perhaps the low point of Cold War ambitions for psychology came when ARPA, the Defense Department's Advanced Research Projects Agency, sent teams of psychologists into the war-torn jungles of Vietnam. They tested more than a thousand peasants with a modified TAT (uncaptioned pictures, redrawn from the Harvard originals by a Saigon artist), looking for the values, hopes, and frustrations that motivated them. They then met with military and civilian officials eager to "convert a war of devastation into a 'welfare war'" that would bring "peace, democracy, and stability" to the region, and wanting to tailor their counterinsurgency propaganda to win over the hearts and minds of the South Vietnamese. As one historian puts it: "The Vietnamese psyche was a crucial policy target."

Simulmatics Corporation was a for-profit research company originally founded in 1959 to computer-simulate voter behavior before the 1960 presidential election. It had since branched out, and in 1966 it sent Walter H. Slote, a Columbia University lecturer and psychotherapist, to Saigon for seven weeks. His mission: uncover "the Vietnamese personality." He believed that one life could reveal the forces that shape others—the "deeper" a single person's motivation, "the more likely it is to represent universals"—and so he drew his conclusions from four people. After duly conceding that the sample was too small to generalize from, he generalized away.

A senior Buddhist monk and faculty member of three Vietnamese universities; a bombastic student demonstration leader who had brought down an interim government and lived for the glory of dramatic rebellion; a leading intellectual, the son of a poor village farmer who had made it to France at age sixteen, graduated at twenty, and returned as a dissident writer; and a Vietcong terrorist who had bombed the US Embassy and six other sites, "a thoroughly deadened man" who said "the only moments of happiness he had ever known were those when he was killing." What "character structure" had made these four "evolve into the kinds of persons they had become"? Slote used Rorschach and TAT tests and psychoanalyzed his four subjects for two hours a day, sometimes up to seven hours a day, five to seven days a week, to find out.

After repeatedly digging for personal details, despite his subjects' discomfort in talking about such matters, Slote concluded that family dynamics "held the key" to the Vietnamese psyche. In Vietnamese culture, authoritarian parents were idealized and all hostility toward them was repressed. This left the Vietnamese feeling unfulfilled, incomplete. They were really just "looking for a kind, loving father figure"—they had "the desire, at times almost wistful, to be embraced by authority," and they cast the United States in the role of "the all powerful, all giving father image." That meant, "in essence," that the Vietnamese were not anti-American at all, they were pro-American! Unfortunately, such thoroughgoing repression also built up "monumental amounts of rage" that had to be channeled somewhere. This explained "their very volatile and confused perspective in regard to the role of America."

Slote noted a strategy he found especially paranoid: his subjects' tendency to "start in the middle of an incident and totally disregard the precipitating antecedent events" in assigning blame. For instance, the Vietcong fighter had the obviously delusional idea that American soldiers wanted to kill innocent Vietnamese civilians. Americans had shot at a bus full of farmers. Slote pointed out that the bus was passing a building where a bomb had just gone off; the Americans had reason to think this busload of civilians might be enemies; "under the immediate circumstances the Americans might understandably not have used their best judgment," he suggested. Yet for some reason, these facts were "completely disregarded" by the Vietcong member as he interpreted the Americans' gunfire. "A profound lack of critical self evaluation," in Slote's view.

With hindsight, it is easy to see the profound lack of critical self-evaluation in Slote himself. He ignored any political, historical, or military reasons the Vietnamese might have had to hate America. To the extent that the United States was responsible at all for "fostering this unhappy situation," it was only because we were just too big and powerful. But this was apparently what Americans wanted to hear: a 1966 front-page article in the *Washington Post* called Slote's work "almost hypnotically fascinating"; officials in Saigon found it "extraordinarily perceptive and persuasive."

BY THE END of the sixties, the rising tide of antiauthoritarianism was bringing exercises such as Slote's to an end. There were students in the streets, revolution in the air. Academics were increasingly uneasy about being associated with murky government funding, and the idea that any technique could give curious and tolerant American investigators nearly perfect access to otherwise inaccessible souls was starting to seem a lot less plausible.

Anthropologists had promised that projective tests could give voice to the people being tested, but it was increasingly hard to ignore that, in Lemov's words, such tests purported to "provide a kind of instamatic psychic X-ray that, by its very workings, allocated *to the expert* the task of discerning the true meaning of what was being said, what the native was thinking." It was the same ethical dilemma raised by any notion of the unconscious: If you claim that there are things about people that they are unaware of, you are claiming to speak for them better than they can speak for themselves, usurping their right to their own life stories. Third World locals, politicians, and revolutionaries were making it increasingly clear that they wanted their own voices heard.

In anthropology, there was a growing emphasis on biology and a move back toward behavior-based theories, which saw social interactions as more significant than unconscious mental states. Culture and Personality studies, and especially the projective test movement, quickly collapsed into total irrelevance, neither practiced nor taught nor read. Even its old champion, Irving Hallowell, now looked back on his Ojibwe studies and doubted that the Rorschach had made any valuable contribution—it had only supplemented what he'd already learned in other ways.

Analogous shifts were under way in the mental health professions.

Newly discovered psychopharmaceuticals—antidepressants, lithium, Valium, LSD—were prompting a swift turn away from psychoanalytic psychiatry toward the "hard science" psychiatry we know today. With the rise of community-based mental health treatment focusing on external socioeconomic and cultural forces, and the return to prominence here too of behavior-based theories, it started to seem relatively pointless to pay attention to the mind or to inner motivations.

Within clinical psychology in particular, criticisms of the Rorschach were gathering force. Surveying the situation in 1965 for the most highly respected reference work in the field, *The Mental Measurements Yearbook*, distinguished psychologist Arthur Jensen was as blunt about the Rorschach as anyone before or since: "Put frankly, the consensus of qualified judgment is that the Rorschach is a very poor test and has no practical worth for any of the purposes for which it is recommended by its devotees."

It was Jensen in this essay who called the Rorschach test "as closely identified with the clinical psychologist as the stethoscope is with the physician," but he didn't mean it as a compliment. The test was not merely useless: it could "lead to harmful consequences in nonpsychiatric settings, such as in schools and in industry," because of its tendency to overpathologize. "Why the Rorschach still has so many devotees and continues to be so widely used is an amazing phenomenon," he concluded, whose explanation requires "greater knowledge of the psychology of credulity than we now possess. Meanwhile, the rate of scientific progress in clinical psychology might well be measured by the speed and thoroughness with which it gets over the Rorschach."

In the widespread, decentralized use of the Rorschach at midcentury, even such a forceful indictment from a prominent voice in the field was lost. No single authority, however well credentialed, was trusted to give the last word. The year after Jensen's article saw the publication of both Walter Slote's report and Ray Bradbury's story—paternalistic Cold War testing taken to an extreme and the reaction against it. In the unlikely event that Slote or Bradbury ever heard of Jensen, they wouldn't have cared in the least about his critique.

And yet clinical psychology did, in Jensen's words, "get over" Freud with a "speed and thoroughness" that was downright startling. Beginning in the late sixties, Freudian psychotherapy tumbled from undisputed centrality to being an embattled, sometimes cliquish enclave. The Rorschach—its validity under question, the trustworthiness of the people administering it under suspicion—could easily have met the same fate.

In some countries it did. But in America it survived, both in the culture at large and within clinical psychology.

The inkblots had already emerged as a metaphor for the same antiauthoritarian relativism that was calling the test into question. Your reaction to a blot, or shirt, now delightfully interpreted itself, no doctor in a white coat or puffing a cigar behind a couch required. The free self-expression that the culture was demanding was just what the inkblots offered, at least in the popular imagination.

Precisely when Dr. Brokaw was taking his shirt to the people, the Rorschach was becoming a symbol in real life for anything that elicited different, equally valid opinions. In 1964, a reviewer confronted with ten books about New York summed up: "Composing a New York City book is a kind of projective psychological test, a Rorschach, say; the five boroughs are only a stimulus to which the observer responds according to his personality." In the *New York Times* at least, this was the first of thousands of Rorschach clichés to come. Charles de Gaulle would soon be "a Rorschach test" for biographers; the loose plot ends of Stanley Kubrick's *2001: A Space Odyssey* were a Rorschach test too.

In a culture-wide crisis of authority, it was easier for arbiters to stop claiming authority at all. Opinions differed, and calling something "a Rorschach test" meant there was no need to take a side and risk alienating anyone. Journalists and critics no longer saw it as their job to tell readers which possible reaction to New York City or *2001* was correct: everyone had the right to their own opinion, and an inkblot was the indispensable metaphor for that freedom.

A resonant metaphor alone, though, would not have been enough to save the Rorschach as an actual psychological test. The fact had to be addressed that, by this point, there was no such thing as "the" Rorschach test at all.

20

The System

THE MAN WHO WOULD CHANGE THAT WAS JOHN E. EXNER JR., born in Syracuse, New York, in 1928. After a stint in the air force during the Korean War, serving as an airplane mechanic and physician's assistant, he came back to the States and went to college at Trinity University in San Antonio, Texas. He first saw the inkblots in 1953 and knew at once he had discovered his life's work. He enrolled at Cornell and began his PhD in clinical psychology.

What he found was chaos. Klopfer's and Beck's approaches had continued to diverge since the forties. Hertz had her own methods, while two other systems were gaining prominence in the United States, the psychoanalytic Schafer-Rapaport and Zygmunt Piotrowski's idiosyncratic "Perceptanalysis," not to mention various other approaches abroad. All of these used the same ten inkblots in the same order, although some added an additional sample blot, shown at the start to explain to test takers what they were going to be asked to do. But the administration procedures, scoring codes, and follow-up questioning were often incompatible, and even what the test was fundamentally testing *for* varied widely.

None of these methods was used by a clear majority of psychologists, although Klopfer maintained his plurality, with Beck in second. Professors didn't know which system to teach; practitioners themselves combined them ad hoc. As Exner would later describe it, they operated "by intuitively adding a 'little Klopfer,' a 'dash of Beck,' a few 'grains' of Hertz, and a 'smidgen' of Piotrowski, to their own experience, and calling it *The Rorschach*."

Even the pettiest details proved bedeviling. When administering a Rorschach test, where should you sit? Exner had read in Rorschach and Beck that you should sit behind the test taker; Klopfer and Hertz said sit to the side, Rapaport-Schafer said face-to-face, and Piotrowski said wherever was "most natural." This range of views was not because the seating arrangement didn't matter but because of contradictory, well-worked-out reasons in favor of each approach. But you had to sit somewhere.

A generation after Marguerite Hertz had tried and failed to heal the "rift in the family" of Rorschachers, Exner took up the challenge. It was Exner who, as a twenty-six-year-old graduate student in 1954, had turned up at Sam Beck's house in Chicago accidentally carrying Klopfer's book, and was asked: "You got that from *our* library?" When he later told his committee about the faux pas, one of them suggested: "Why don't we call old Klopfer and you can go out and work with him next summer?" Exner did, and, he later recalled, "fell in love with *both* those guys."

Klopfer and Beck remained implacable, but at Beck's suggestion and with Klopfer's approval Exner decided to write a short paper comparing the two systems. Each thought his system would "win." That short paper grew into a long book that took Exner nearly a decade to write: a detailed history and description of the five main Rorschach systems, with biographies of the various founders and a full-length sample interpretation using each method. In 1969, at age forty-one, he published *The Rorschach Systems*.

Exner found that the five systems generally overlapped on key concepts Hermann Rorschach had discussed explicitly, such as the significance of Movement responses or of the sequence of Whole and Detail responses. But in the many areas of the test where Rorschach was vague or had offered no guidance before his early death—administration procedures, theoretical underpinning, codes beyond the few he proposed—later Rorschachers had gone their own ways.

It was clear what needed to come next. Drawing on thousands of published studies and surveys of hundreds of practitioners, Exner started compiling a synthesis. Five years later, in 1974, he published *The Rorschach: A Comprehensive System*—five hundred pages long, with numerous further volumes, revisions, and spinoffs to follow. Its stated goal: "to present, in a single format, the Best of the Rorschach."

Methodically moving through every aspect of the test, Exner

brought it all into a single framework. He eventually decided on side-by-side seating, incidentally, to reduce the influence of any nonverbal cues from the examiner, and noted that seating for all kinds of psychological tests should probably be reconsidered given the research on how behavior can be influenced. He provided numerous sample results and interpretations, and far more complete lists of common and uncommon responses—the crucial "norms" that were used to determine whether a test taker was normal or abnormal. Ninety-two Whole responses for Card I:

> Good: Moth
> Good: Mythological creatures (on each side)
> Poor: Nest
> Good: Ornament (Xmas)
> Poor: Owl
> Good: Pelvis (skeletal)
> Poor: Pot
> Poor: Printing press
> Poor: Rocket
> Poor: Rug
> Good: Sea animal . . .

There followed 126 more things found in nine typically interpreted details areas of the card, and 58 more responses covering ten rarely interpreted areas, all shown on diagrams. Then on to Card II . . .

The Comprehensive System was more complex than any Rorschach method yet, packed with new scores and formulas. Hermann Rorschach's dozen or so codes had now mushroomed to some 140 in total, including

$$\text{Present Distress (eb)} =$$
$$\text{Unmet Internal Needs (FM)} + \text{Situation-Determined Distress (m)} /$$
$$\text{Shading Responses (Y + T + V + C')}$$

or

$$3 \text{ X Reflection (r)} + \text{Pair (2)} / \text{Total Responses (R)} =$$
$$\text{the "Egocentricity Index"}$$

In plain English: If John Doe gave two answers for each card on a Rorschach test, his total number of responses (R) would be 20. Any answer describing the inkblot as something and its mirror image or reflection—*"A woman looking at herself in a mirror"*; *"A bear stepping across rocks and water, and here's his reflection in the creek"*—had to be coded in Exner's system as a Reflection response, "r," along with its other codes. (The stepping bear would be a Movement response, and a Color response too if the "water" was a blue part of the card, and Whole or Detail, et cetera.)

Let's say Mr. Doe gave both of those Reflection responses, as well as four Pair responses, each coded "2"—this kind of response describes two things, *"A couple of donkeys"* or *"A pair of boots,"* symmetrically located on either side of the card but *not* parts of a single whole such as two eyes on a face or two blades of a scissors. Plugging those numbers into Exner's formula would produce an Egocentricity Index of $([3 \times 2] + 4) / 20 = 10/20 = 0.5$: a bad sign for Doe, since anything higher than 0.42 suggested "intense self-focus which may contribute to reality distortions, especially in interpersonal situations." A number below 0.31 would suggest depression. But all was not lost for John Doe: a host of other scores and indexes coming out of his test might modify the significance of this high number.

In some cases, Exner's new scores enabled the test to measure conditions and mental states that Rorschach had not considered, or that were not even defined in his day: suicide risk, coping deficits, stress tolerance. In other cases, the codes seemed to attach numbers for numbers' sake. The important Exner score WSum6, for instance, measuring the presence or absence of illogical and incoherent thinking, was simply a weighted sum of six other scores dating back to the 1940s: Deviant Verbalizations (now coded DV), Deviant Responses (DR), Incongruous Combinations (INCOM), Fabulized Combinations (FABCOM), Contaminations (CONTAM), and Autistic Logic (ALOG). The new score provided a measurable threshold: research eventually concluded that WSum6 = 7.2 was average for adults, while WSum6 ≥ 17 was high, resulting in another point on the nine-variable PTI (Perceptual Thinking Index) that came to replace the earlier SCZI (Schizophrenia Index) with its high false-positive rate. A score of PTI ≥ 3 "usually identifies serious adjustment problems attributable to ideational dysfunction."

All of this was an extraordinarily elaborate way to restate the fact that *If you say a lot of crazy things, you might be crazy.*

But this kind of quantitative framing was just what the times demanded. Exner was the Rorschach champion for an era after Klopfer's: not a flashy showman but a collegial, solid technocrat whose expertise seemed to rise above the feuds. The Rorschach had to be standardized, stripped of its intuitive, emotionally powerful, and arguably beautiful qualities, to fit into the data-driven new era of American medicine.

IN 1973, A year before Exner's synthesis was published, President Richard Nixon signed into law the Health Maintenance Organization (HMO) Act. "Managed care"—a shorthand term for a complex new system of insurance rules and payment plans—aimed at efficiency by eliminating "unnecessary" hospitalizations and imposing cost-effective therapies at fixed rates. The family doctor was now a "primary care physician," responsible for guiding the HMO member through a maze of specialists and authorizations, and increasingly caught between pressures to cut costs and the need to satisfy the consumers formerly known as patients.

While managed-care policies provided better access to health care (more people had health insurance), the resulting cost increase (more people used health insurance) forced insurance companies to clamp down. In mental health care, the shift away from traditional personality assessment that had begun in the sixties accelerated. The need to establish "medical necessity" for a treatment naturally put pressure on any approach that didn't involve prescribing a pill. Psychological assessment was less often reimbursed; preauthorization requirements and other paperwork made it harder to use assessment flexibly. Even in narrow utilitarian terms, one would expect that better initial assessment and diagnosis would lead to cost savings, but in fact it was likely to be one of the first things to go unless psychologists could prove it provided "treatment-relevant and cost-effective information" and was "relevant and valid for treatment planning." National surveys of psychological practice in the managed-care era confirmed a widespread feeling among doctors that "marketplace-driven demands" had "created obstacles . . . that threaten[ed] the very existence of traditional psychological practice."

For better and for worse, Exner recast the Rorschach for this modern world. He couldn't make the test quick and easy, any more than Molly Harrower had been able to in the forties, but he could make it numerical. This had always been part of the Rorschach test's appeal, going back to Rorschach himself, who considered it "quite impossible to obtain a definite and reliable interpretation without doing the calculations." Compared to psychoanalysis, what someone saw in the inkblots really was easier to code, count, and compare than their dreams or free associations on an analyst's couch. There were times, such as when the inkblots were largely used as a projective method to uncover subtleties of the personality, that a more intuitive or qualitative approach would come to the fore, but whenever the pendulum in psychology swung back toward privileging numbers, the quantitative side of the inkblot test could always be emphasized. That said, Exner's system was numerical like none before. And as the punch cards from Harrower's era developed into ever more powerful computers—an integral part of the growing managed care bureaucracy—quantifiability was more important than ever.

As early as 1964, four years after the term *data science* was coined, researchers had run the Rorschach responses of 586 healthy Johns Hopkins medical students through an early computer-indexing program and produced a 741-page large-format concordance. By the mid-1980s this corpus, plus the life histories available from long-term follow-ups with the test takers, made it possible to sidestep traditional Rorschach interpretation altogether. Computers simply counted up every occurrence of every word spoken in the tests and went looking for correlations between answers and later fates. An unnerving article from 1985, "Are Words of the Rorschach Predictors of Disease and Death?" claimed that those who mentioned "whirling" in any of the ten cards were five times as likely to commit suicide as those who didn't, and four times as likely to have died of other causes.

Exner brought computers into his own methodology as well. Beginning in the mid-1970s, he explored ways to "increase computer utilization as an aid in interpreting the test," eventually resulting in the

Rorschach Interpretation Assistance Program (1987, with numerous updates to follow). After an examiner coded all the patient's answers, the program would do the math, generate complex scores, and highlight significant deviations from statistical norms. It would also offer a printout of "interpretive hypotheses" in prose form:

> This person appears to compare himself unfavorably to other people and consequently to suffer from low self-esteem and limited self-confidence.
>
> This person demonstrates adequate abilities to identify comfortably with real people in his life and appears to have opportunities to form such identifications. . . .
>
> This person gives evidence of limited capacity to form close attachments to other people . . .

Exner disavowed the computer approach by the end of his life, but the damage had been done. The Rorschach, once hailed as the most sophisticated window into human personality, could now be read by machine.

Even when used exclusively by human beings, Exner's system had a downside. Its rigorous empirical emphasis minimized what many advocates found most valuable in the Rorschach: the test's open-ended ability to generate surprising insights. Strategies that generations of clinicians had found helpful and revealing—such as the idea that a person's first answer to the first card says something about his or her self-image—found no place among Exner's flurry of codes and variables. As a result, psychologists who had used the inkblots as a starting point for talk therapy or other open-ended explorations tended to either reject Exner or drift away from the Rorschach altogether.

Yet Exner gave the test new respectability in the field, especially after 1978, when the more rigorous Volume 2 of his manual came out. His accommodating, synthesizing approach won over most holdouts practicing the earlier Rorschach systems, and even leading assessment psychologists who had long criticized projective methods as subjective started praising the rigor Exner brought to the Rorschach.

Exner also pressed the reset button on the history of Rorschach controversies: Arthur Jensen's 1965 critique and all the other earlier attacks could now be dismissed as being directed at "earlier, less scientific versions" of the test.

Exner's private Rorschach Workshops in Asheville, North Carolina, starting in 1984, taught a generation of clinicians, and his textbooks replaced Klopfer's and Beck's throughout clinical psychology graduate programs. One exception, the City University in New York, remained die-hard Klopferian, but students there had to learn Exner's system too, since they would be expected to use it in residencies and internships elsewhere. As thousands of Rorschach articles and studies continued to proliferate, Exner's centralized Rorschach became the only source most practitioners ever had to look to.

Bruno Klopfer had died in 1971, Samuel Beck in 1980; Marguerite Hertz passed the baton to Exner in 1986, calling his research "the first serious and systematic attempt to confront some of the unresolved issues that have plagued us through the years." "Best of all," she added, "Exner and his colleagues have brought discipline into our ranks and a sense of optimism to our field."

OVER THE YEARS, as Exner fine-tuned his formulas, the Rorschach test came to produce increasingly correct results—"correct" in the sense of labeling as, say, schizophrenia exactly what other tests or criteria labeled as schizophrenia. The inkblots were being used and judged as a standardized measure of known quantities, not an exploratory experiment.

For all the benefits of integrating the Rorschach with the findings of other psychiatric methods, this tended to make it a more cumbersome, less cost-effective way to do what psychiatrists had other techniques for already. As with computerization, Exner increasingly denounced the search for "generalized truths" and criticized psychiatric reference works such as the *Diagnostic and Statistical Manual of Mental Disorders* (the DSM) as "bookkeepers' manuals for classifying people in distress" and generating cookie-cutter treatment plans. He may have had reservations about how such standard classifications were used, but they were what his system provided—and what other tests and evaluations provided faster.

The move toward more efficient tests predated Exner's system. A

1968 survey of academic clinical psychologists, while showing that the Rorschach was still widely used, found that more than half the respondents felt that "objective," "non-projective" methods were increasing in use and importance. One of these methods, in particular, was rapidly gaining ground.

The Minnesota Multiphasic Personality Inventory, or MMPI, first published in 1943, pulled ahead of the Rorschach in 1975. It consisted of 504 statements—567 statements in the modified MMPI-2—that subjects were asked to agree or disagree with, ranging from the apparently trivial ("I have a good appetite"; "My hands and feet are usually warm enough") to the obviously alarming ("Evil spirits possess me at times"; "I see things or animals or people around me that others do not see"). It could be administered to a group by a clerical worker and was easy to score. Each MMPI scale—the Depression Scale, the Paranoia Scale— had two lists of question numbers associated with it: the number of items from the first list that had been answered True, plus the number from the second list marked False, was the result. It was quick and it was "objective."

Technically, this meant only that it was not "projective." A person's True/False answer to "Some people think it's hard to get to know me," "I have not lived the right kind of life," or "A large number of people are guilty of bad sexual conduct" could not be objective in any meaningful sense. People are not willing or able to evaluate themselves objectively—self-descriptions were often found to correspond only partially, at best, to what friends and family said about the test taker, or to what their behavior showed. Answers were not even meant to be taken at face value: Responding "True" to a lot of depressing statements and "False" to a lot of happy statements didn't necessarily mean a person was depressed. There were scales to measure whether a person was likely to be exaggerating or lying; there were other ways one scale could affect the others. Interpreting MMPI results, too, was an art, requiring subjective judgment. But the slanted terms *objective* and *projective* certainly helped the MMPI's fortunes.

In the decade after 1975, the Rorschach fell from being the second most commonly used personality test in clinical psychology to fifth. It was now behind both the MMPI and several other projective tests:

Human Figure Drawing (used primarily with children), Sentence Completion, and the House-Tree-Person Test.

Results from these more limited tests were relatively self-explanatory. Drawing a human figure with a big head might suggest arrogance. Leaving out key body parts was a bad sign. Completing sentences with hostile, pessimistic, or violent words: not good. These tests were thus more vulnerable to "impression management"—subjects could know how to stage the impression they wanted to make, present themselves as they wanted to be seen. One New York City cop, given the House-Tree-Person Test during his hiring process, said that his buddies had told him beforehand: "The house has to have a chimney with smoke coming out, and whatever you do, make sure you put leaves on the tree." That's what he did. Whatever their weaknesses, though, these tests were quick and cheap, and so increasingly preferred.

Popularity rankings among tests, usually based on sporadic surveys with small and unrepresentative samples, are not as precise or reliable as they sound. But the trend lines were clear—the ink was on the wall.

IN THIS NEW landscape, assessment psychologists were starting to find the education system more welcoming than health care. Insurance companies were unwilling to shell out three or four thousand dollars for comprehensive testing in a hospital setting—in fact, psychiatric patients were rarely allowed longer hospital stays at all—but schools would still pay for evaluations. These were not the kind of blanket programs that Sarah Lawrence College had instituted in the thirties—for that there were thriving industries of their own, such as IQ and aptitude testing. Instead, these were psychological tests given to individual troubled teens or children who turned up in school counseling centers or were referred for evaluation.

And so, as Exner continued to develop his Comprehensive System, he widened its range of applications. In 1982, he devoted a whole additional volume of his manual to children and adolescents. A child's Rorschach responses usually meant much the same as an adult's, Exner argued (for example, pure C and CF answers implied little emotional control), but the norms would often be different (lots of such answers would be normal in a seven-year-old boy but immature for an adult, while an adult's mature profile would indicate "a probable maladaptive overcontrol" in a child).

Exner emphasized that Rorschach testing was of limited use in cases of behavior problems, because the test's conclusions did not translate directly into information about behavior. No specific Rorschach scores could "reliably identify the 'acting out' child or differentiate the delinquent from the nondelinquent." In such cases, especially where there were environmental factors causing the child's behavior, the test merely suggested the kinds of psychological strengths and weaknesses that might affect treatment. In the most common cases youth psychologists faced, though—students having academic problems—the Rorschach could help distinguish between limited intelligence, neurological impairment, and psychological difficulties.

Many of the same market forces pushing clinical psychologists into education in the seventies and eighties also pushed them into the legal system. "Forensic assessment" boomed: evaluating parents in custody disputes, children in abuse cases, psychological harm in personal injury lawsuits, competence to stand trial in criminal cases. Exner's 1982 volume included several cases serving as double illustrations of how to use the Rorschach with children and in legal settings.

One of these cases involved Hank and Cindy, high school sweethearts who had gotten married in the midsixties when Hank was twenty-two. After a two-week honeymoon, he shipped out for Vietnam, where he served for a year and was decorated for heroism at Da Nang. The first three or four years after he returned were happy ones for the couple, but not the years that followed. By the late seventies, their thirteen-year marriage had ended in separation and a custody battle. Hank charged that Cindy was psychologically unfit to have custody of their twelve-year-old daughter; Cindy filed a counterclaim that Hank had been "mentally brutal" to both her and their child and that to evaluate only her would be unfair. Evaluations were ordered of both parents, and of the child as well.

Their marital problems showed up crystal-clear in interviews— Cindy complained about Hank's "bitchiness," admitted to spending sprees "out of spite"—while the Exner system findings were complex and technical. In the daughter's Rorschach, "if the magnitude of the *ep:EA* relation has existed for very long" that would explain her recent problems in school. "*Afr* is quite low for her age," so she might well be significantly withdrawn. Hank's "extremely disproportionate *a:p* ratio suggests that he is not very flexible in his thinking or attitudes. . . . The high Egocentricity Index, .48, suggests that he is much more self-centered than most adults, and this may have some negative effects on his interpersonal relationships."

Cindy seemed more disturbed. Her first answer to Card I was a spider, "which she later distorts even more by adding wings to it. If this is, in fact, a projection of her self-image, it leaves much to be desired. . . . All three of her *DQv* responses occur to [colored] cards, [indicating] she is a person who does not handle emotional provocation very well." Conclusion: "She is strongly influenced by her feelings and does not control them very well. . . . It is probable that she does not experience needs for closeness in ways that are common for most people." It was easy to understand how Cindy's overemotional immaturity and Hank's self-centered inflexibility, as revealed on their Rorschachs, might have caused conflicts in their marriage.

In the end, the psychologists' recommendations were modest. The child was "in considerable distress," they wrote. Whoever got custody, "the child's current state indicated a need for some form of intervention" and both parents should be involved. The report on the mother "stressed that while she might benefit from psychotherapy, this did not signify unfitness, nor did it indicate that she might be a less capable parent than the father." Despite lawyers repeatedly pressing the psychologists to take a side, there was "no specific recommendation concerning custody" or evidence of either parent being unfit. As a result, their input fell short of what the court had expected, and the judge had to reach his own conclusion. He awarded split custody and ordered the mother to seek therapy for herself and arrange intervention for the child.

Exner included Hank and Cindy's case precisely because it wasn't sensational or earth-shattering. This was what Rorschach findings in legal contexts were supposed to look like. Since the book was Exner's manual on how to use the Rorschach, that was naturally what it went into detail about, giving all three family members' full Rorschach transcripts, scores, and interpretations. In the case itself, the psychologists had combined the Rorschach results with other information not published in such detail. Still, the combination of cryptic codes with sweeping judgments of character and psychology could not help but look like repellent mumbo-jumbo to skeptics, especially those less familiar with Exner's version of the test. To practitioners, it was just another day at the office.

Like the medical system, the legal system had found the version of the Rorschach test it needed—one supporting an ever more impressive superstructure of codes, scores, and cross-checks. American psychology had made two Faustian bargains: asking to be paid for as a medical service justifiable to insurance companies, which required meeting their standards, and going into the courtroom, which required the psychologist to claim the same kind of impersonal authority as a judge. In theory, psychology didn't have to be used to answer narrow questions— Sick or healthy? Sane or insane? Guilty or not guilty?—any more than art or philosophy did. It could be open-ended, leading to truths but no answers. But now more than ever, that was how it was used, in contexts pushing for either-or verdicts, results in black and white.

John Exner's most important contribution was to sweep away the moving target of multiple Rorschach systems. In so doing, he made it easier to criticize the test, too: a unified Rorschach only sharpened the polarization between skeptics and believers. As the twentieth century drew to a close, the story of the Rorschach would fall apart into the controversies around it. No evidence would be equally accepted on both sides, no instance of applying the test would be any more emblematic than thousands of others, and nothing seemed able to change anybody's mind.

21

Different People See Different Things

I N THE FALL OF 1985, A WOMAN NAMED ROSE MARTELLI MARRIED Donald Bell; six months later, pregnant, she left him. After their son was born, Bell sued for custody and visitation rights. Rose claimed he had been violent during their marriage, and Rose's eight-year-old daughter by a previous marriage suddenly claimed to remember that Donald had sexually abused her three years before. But the judge, apparently finding the timing of the accusations suspicious, awarded Donald full parental rights and unsupervised contact. The boy started coming home with unexplained bruises, and Rose eventually called Child Protective Services, claiming physical and sexual abuse but with no decisive evidence. CPS requested that both parents be evaluated by psychologists.

Donald's test results came back normal. Rose's psychologist reported that she "was seriously disturbed and probably lacked genuine concern for her two children" and also that "Rose's thinking was so impaired that she distorted reality and the actions of other people." The CPS caseworker told Rose to drop the case and seek therapy herself, and refused to act on her subsequent reports. Eight months later, the boy, now five, said his father had hit him and "poked him in the butt" and asked to be taken to a doctor. The swab from a rape kit tested positive.

A new review of the case by a psychologist specializing in child abuse turned up numerous pieces of evidence that Rose's and her daughter's allegations should have been believed. Donald had a violent record; Rose had a reputation for honesty in her community; all of her "so-called bizarre stories" that he investigated turned out to be "meticulously accurate." Yet CPS had taken the original psychologist's report as the last word. In fact, the second psychologist was shocked to realize, Rose had been labeled untrustworthy and emotionally disturbed solely because of one test: the Rorschach.

The examiner had drawn conclusions from Rose's Rorschach using Exner scores that had little proven validity, or that commonly over-diagnosed normal test takers, while neglecting other, more positive findings in the test results. Rose had seen *"a Thanksgiving turkey already eaten"* in one inkblot: this "Food response" had contributed to her evaluation as clingy and dependent. But the examiner might have taken into account that Rose had been given the test on her lunch break without having eaten since breakfast, or that it was December 5, a week after Thanksgiving, when just such a carcass had been sitting in her fridge.

One of the examiner's most damning conclusions, that Rose was "self-centered and without empathy for her children," was due to a single Reflection response (mirrors or seeing reflections), which elevated the Egocentricity Index, indicating narcissism and self-absorption. But what Rose had seen in the inkblots was *"a paper snowflake, like you make by folding a piece of paper and cutting it out."* This was not a Reflection response—the examiner had coded it wrong. By the time the reviewing psychologist realized all of this, it was too late. The father had custody.

With cases like Rose Martelli's in mind, Robyn Dawes, a former member of the American Psychological Association Ethics Committee, wrote in the late eighties that "the use of Rorschach interpretations in establishing an individual's legal status and child custody is the single most unethical practice of my colleagues." Despite the Rorschach being "unreliable and invalid," in his words, "the plausibility of Rorschach interpretation is so compelling that it is still accepted in court proceedings involving involuntary commitment and child custody, with psychologists who offer such interpretations in these hearings being duly recognized as 'experts.'" Dawes's 1994 book *House of Cards* later used the Rorschach as its central example of psychology built on myth rather than science.

Exner's reinvention of the Rorschach had not persuaded everyone.

MEANWHILE THE INKBLOTS continued to capture the popular imagination. Many young people at the end of the twentieth century would have gotten their first glimpse of Rorschach's name in *Watchmen* (1987), the psychological superhero comic book that made it onto *Time* magazine's list of the hundred best English-language novels published between 1923 and 2005. Its noirish antihero, named Rorschach, hid a dark soul behind his inkblot mask. Due to the mask's special properties, its symmetrical black shapes shifted but never mixed with the white background, symbolizing the black-and-white, no-gray-area moral code that the character took to brutal extremes. The two colors would never come together.

In 1993, Hillary Clinton too used the inkblot metaphor to evoke irreconcilable extremes: "I'm a Rorschach test," she told an *Esquire* reporter, an image that would stay with her for years. (Annotating his classic article in 2016, the original reporter, Walter Shapiro, wrote: "I believe this was the first time Hillary said this oft-repeated line." And it is repeated still: In an anthology of articles about Clinton's career published for the 2016 election season, the introduction called Clinton "a Rorschach test of our attitudes—including our unconscious ones"; the collection "won't answer all the readers' questions, but at the very least it brings the Rorschach blot into clearer focus.") In this metaphor, people's reactions to Hillary defined them, not her; she bore little or no responsibility for which side they were on. This was the Rorschach as divider. Shapiro's article went on to debunk various myths and show that some interpretations of Hillary were simply false. And yet, he wrote, "She's right. Hillary Rodham Clinton the real person is largely unknown. We look at her visage on television and magazine covers— and we see what we want to see."

Outside of a polarized political context, "we see what we want to see" could sound like a shrug of indifference, and no one welcomed this indifference, even raised it to an art form, more than Andy Warhol. He had started manufacturing images of manufactured consumer products in the sixties, mechanically silkscreening images of Campbell's Soup cans like ones he had earlier painted, or having carpenters make plywood boxes the same size as supermarket cartons, with other people painting the silkscreened designs of Brillo soap-pad cartons on them. The result was a mass-produced series of objects that looked almost indistinguishable from the real products. "The reason I'm painting this way is that I want to be a machine," he famously said. "If you want to know all about Andy Warhol, just look at the surface of my paintings and films and me, and there I am. There's nothing behind it."

Beyond coolly undercutting the bombast of Abstract Expressionists such as Pollock, Warhol was denying the inner self altogether. Artists didn't express anything. Like Rorschach's blots, Warhol artfully concealed any trace of intentions. In one scholar's words, "Is the work merely a readymade, or does it communicate something more? Is there intentional significance in these marks on canvas?" Probably no other major artist's "actual, physical work matter[ed] as little as Andy Warhol's"—your reactions to a Warhol really *did* matter more than the Warhol itself.

The aspiring machine who hired others to make his Brillo boxes, do his silkscreens, and give his artist talks for him returned only once in his late career to making expressive marks of his own with paint on paper. In 1984, Warhol poured paint onto large, sometimes wall-sized white canvases, folded them in half, and ended up with a series of some six dozen symmetrical inkblot paintings. Most used black paint, some were in gold or multiple colors. They were first exhibited as a group in 1996. Every one was called *Rorschach*.

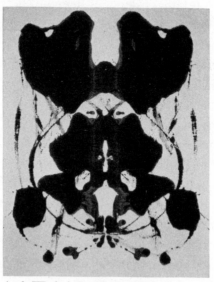

Andy Warhol, *Rorschach,* 1984

The project started with a mistake: Warhol thought, or claimed he'd thought, "that when you go to places like hospitals they tell you to draw and make Rorschach tests. I wish I'd known there was a set" of standard images, he said, so he could have just copied them. Instead, he made his own blots to see what he'd find. He quickly grew bored by the interpretation part of the process and said he'd rather hire someone to pretend they were him and say what they saw. That way the results would be "a little more interesting," he deadpanned. "All I would see would be a dog's face or something like a tree or a bird or a flower. Somebody else could see a lot more."

It was a classic Warhol provocation, and the blots looked great—Warhol could more than match Rorschach's sense of design and "spatial rhythm." He even admitted it: the *Rorschach* paintings "had technique too. . . . Throwing paint on, it could just be a blob. So maybe they're better because I was trying to do them."

Warhol brought the inkblots firmly into the artistic mainstream and in so doing transformed their significance. His blots didn't dance at the edge of interpretability like Rorschach's; as one critic wrote on the occasion of the 1996 show, "These are abstract paintings without the heavy air of cryptic obscurity and vague profundity that hangs around a lot of abstract art. There's a democratic, do-it-yourself quality to the Rorschach paintings: you can read whatever you want into them, there are no wrong answers." Above all, the blots were not psychological—not trying to penetrate into the viewer's mind, not designed to call forth Movement responses, a "feeling-into" the images. None of that would be, in Warhol's word, "interesting." Just look at the surface, they said: here I am.

In the history of the Rorschach, Warhol marks the point of greatest distance between the test in psychology and the inkblots in art and popular culture. Unlike the scientific and humanistic interests of Hermann Rorschach, or the work of Bruno Klopfer and influential anthropologist Ruth Benedict, or the fifties content analysts and the makers of *Rebel Without a Cause,* or even Dr. Brokaw's fictional crisis of faith and Arthur Jensen's real one, Warhol's *Rorschach* and Exner's Rorschach had practically nothing to do with each other. Warhol had no idea how the real test worked; Exner had entrenched the test in quantitative science rather than pushing for wider relevance to art or the culture at large.

In literature, too, the Rorschach could be flattened out into pure surface. A surprisingly gripping 1994 book called *The Inkblot Record,* by experimental poet Dan Farrell, gathered the answers from half a dozen Rorschach textbooks and simply alphabetized them—all the cards, all the test takers, jumbled together into a free-form Coltrane solo of things seen, occasionally letting out cries from the soul:

> . . . Wings here, head could be here or here. Wings out flying. Wings outstretched, ears, can't tell which side is facing, a diagrammatic representation. Wire-haired fox terrier, the head is here, the shape and little furry around nose. Wishbone. Wishbone. Wishes never came true, but it was fun to pretend. Wishing I really had a mother, I don't I never did. Witchy hats. With a large beard, large eyes. . . .

Answer after answer, stripped of all efforts to get behind them.

BY THE TIME the polarization around the Rorschach came to a head in psychology, the Rorschach meant Exner. By 1989, twice as many psychologists were using the Exner System as were using Klopfer's or Beck's; since it was taught in 75 percent of graduate courses on the Rorschach, its dominance only increased over time. And Exner seemed to be turning the Rorschach's fortunes around. Having slipped to fifth place in the late 1980s, the Rorschach at the end of the twentieth century was solidly in second again: still behind the MMPI, but administered hundreds of thousands of times a year or more in the United States, an estimated six million times a year worldwide.

In legal settings, too, Exner had prevailed. He and a coauthor published a short 1996 article, "Is the Rorschach Welcome in the Courtroom?," which surveyed the psychologists on Exner's mailing list and found that in over four thousand criminal cases, over three thousand custody cases, and close to a thousand personal injury cases across thirty-two states and the District of Columbia their Rorschach testimony had almost never been challenged. Thus, Exner concluded, "Contrary to whatever different opinion may be voiced, the Rorschach is welcome in the courtroom." While that certainly seemed to raise the big question of whether it should be, the law has real-world standards for what is admissible as evidence in court, and the Rorschach test met them. The adoption of the Daubert standard in 1993—mandating that evidence be "objectively scientific," not just common practice—led to increased, not decreased, use of Exner in the courts.

As the APA's Board of Professional Affairs wrote, honoring Exner with a lifetime achievement award in 1998, he had "almost single-handedly rescued the Rorschach and brought it back to life. The result [was] the resurrection of perhaps the single most powerful psychometric instrument ever envisioned." Exner was seventy, having devoted his life to the inkblots that had struck him so forcefully back in 1953. His name, according to the citation, had "become synonymous with this test."

This was true on both sides of the Rorschach wars.

Along with Robyn Dawes, a group of naysayers had published a series of articles in the eighties and nineties denouncing Exner's Rorschach as unscientific. The first peak of this wave came in 1999, only a year after Exner's award, when Howard Garb, a member of the VA Healthcare System—a stronghold for psychological testing since the forties—called for a moratorium on the use of the Rorschach in both clinical and forensic settings until the validity of its scores was established. His article opened with the rhetoric that dominated discussion of the test, and of practically everything else: "Trying to decide whether the Rorschach is valid is like looking at a Rorschach Inkblot. The results from research are ambiguous just as Rorschach Inkblots are ambiguous. Different people look at the research and see different things."

The second peak came in 2003, when the four most vocal critics of the test, including Garb, published a book that collected in one place all the attacks on Exner's reunified Rorschach. The book's lead author was the psychologist who had reexamined Rose Martelli's Rorschach test, James M. Wood, and *What's Wrong with the Rorschach? Science Confronts the Controversial Inkblot Test* opened with Rose's case.

The book presented the most thorough history of the Rorschach yet written, wrapped in a sensationalist package that started with the title. Three of the four coauthors published an article that same year called "What's Right with the Rorschach?" concluding that "the virtues of the Rorschach are modest but genuine," but that's not how the book was presented. A chapter on the future of the test was called

"Still Waiting for the Messiah." An account of Hermann Rorschach's strengths and weaknesses as a scientist appeared in a section called "Just Another Kind of Horoscope?" even though the section's own answer to that question was apparently "No": Rorschach was criticized for various failings but praised as having been right about the connection between personality and perception, and ahead of his time in insisting on group studies and quantitative validation.

It wasn't all sensationalism, though. The book pulled together decades of criticism from throughout the test's history, reframing earlier figures like Arthur Jensen not as isolated voices but as neglected champions of scientific objectivity. Wood also reviewed the new wave of research critical of Exner's system, such as fourteen studies from the 1990s that attempted to replicate Exner's findings about his Depression Index score. Rose Martelli had been found to have a high one of those, too. But eleven of these studies, according to Wood, found no significant relationship between the score and diagnoses of depression, with two other studies reporting mixed results.

A more systematic problem with Exner's system, which others had known about but Wood highlighted, was that the total number of responses a person gave on the test skewed many of the other scores. Giving a lot of answers made a person more likely to be found abnormal in other ways—it changed scores and results that were not supposed to have anything to do with how much the test taker liked to talk. Exner's system had no way to control for these variations.

Most dramatically, Wood publicized a problem known about since 2001. The credibility of Exner's 1989 norms had taken a brutal hit when it was revealed that hundreds of the cases used to calculate them were figments of a clerical error. Someone had apparently pressed the wrong button, and 221 records out of the 700-person sample were counted twice, another 221 records not counted at all. Exner seemed to have known about the mistake for at least two years, but he revealed it only in the middle of a paragraph on page 172 of the fifth edition of his *Rorschach Workbook*, offering a new set of norms that he claimed was valid this time. Whether or not the norms were vastly different, Wood called this "an error of enormous magnitude" and was appalled at Exner's cavalier treatment of a dozen years of potentially invalid diagnoses.

Wood had general criticisms to make, too. He pointed out that many of Exner's conclusions rested on hundreds of unpublished studies conducted by his own Rorschach Workshops, whose data had never been made available to outsiders and which had rarely been replicated. He accused the Comprehensive System of having a large component of what we might call science theater, with a blizzard of codes and an avalanche of mutually reinforcing publications wowing a generation of clinical psychologists less trained in statistics and a legal profession unaware of the controversies in clinical psychology.

These relatively technical attacks on Exner's system were followed, though, by speculation about why psychologists still "clung to the wreck"—explanations that came across as condescending, even demeaning, to professional readers. For example: It's hard to change one's mind. When asked about the book's split tone, James Wood admitted to "exasperation and open-mouthed disbelief at what's going on in the Rorschach movement." The aggressive messaging was justified, he and his coauthors felt, in reaction to sixty years of Rorschach true believers dodging and weaving, dismissing or ignoring inconvenient evidence.

It probably comes as no surprise that practicing assessment psychologists and Rorschach experts almost unanimously disagreed. Several reviews pointed to Wood's and his colleagues' own confirmation bias, selective and slanted presentation of information, reliance on anecdotal evidence (which the book itself criticized), and refusal to distinguish between poor clinical practice and inherent weaknesses in the test. They were not necessarily the impartial scientific arbiters they were claiming to be. One representative review called the book "useful and informative" but cautioned that "each and every study cited by the authors must be carefully scrutinized for selective abstraction and bias to see if it is portrayed accurately." More than one review pointed out that Rose Martelli's case, while heartbreaking, had little or no relevance to the value of the Rorschach test when used properly: Rose's responses had been coded wrong and interpreted badly; her lawyer had apparently requested expert reexamination of the test too late.

Meanwhile, the critics' call for a moratorium on the Rorschach in the courts went unheeded. Building on Garb's 1999 article, Wood's book had ended with a chapter of advice for lawyers, forensic psychologists, plaintiffs, and defendants, called "Objection, Your Honor! Keeping the Rorschach Out of Court." But a 2005 statement "intended for psychologists, other mental health professionals, educators, attorneys, judges, and administrators" countered by citing numerous studies to reaffirm Exner's argument from the nineties. It concluded that "the Rorschach Inkblot Test possesses reliability and validity similar to that of other generally accepted personality assessment instruments and its responsible use in personality assessment is appropriate and justified." While the article was authored by the not entirely neutral Board of Trustees of the Society for Personality Assessment, the fact remained that the test was still in use. It was cited three times more frequently in appellate cases between 1996 and 2005 than in the previous half century (1945–95), and such testimony was criticized less than a fifth as often, with not one instance of the Rorschach being "ridiculed or disparaged by opposing counsel."

Ultimately, the task of grappling with the complex controversy around the Rorschach was left to each individual psychologist or lawyer. While Wood doubted that what he called the "Rorschach cult" would suddenly come around, he hoped that the American public would force them to. "Increased public awareness may be the key to ending psychologists' long infatuation with the Rorschach," he wrote, and "word is beginning to leak out."

22

Beyond True or False

THE TEST HAD REACHED AN IMPASSE, WITH TWO DIVIDED CAMPS and onlookers resigned to the fact that different people see different things. When John Exner died in February 2006 at age seventy-seven, he must have thought that this would be his legacy.

The natural choice to be his successor was Gregory Meyer, a Chicagoan thirty-three years younger than he. Meyer's 1989 dissertation had raised several of the key failings of Exner's system that would gain prominence in the late nineties. But he had come to improve the test, not to bury it. He began publishing numerous, densely quantitative papers arguing for updates to the system, and in 1997, when Exner set up a "Rorschach Research Council" to decide what adjustments to his system were necessary, prompted by Wood's earlier articles, Meyer was on it, able to fight the Rorschach's scientific battles on the critics' terms.

Yet Exner left control of the Comprehensive System—the name, the copyrights—to his family, not to anyone in the scientific community. Exner's widow, Doris, and their children decided that the system had to stay the way it was: after all the decades of reconciliation and revision on Exner's part, further updates would no longer be incorporated. The phrase "frozen in amber" comes up often when talking about the decision, and the move seemed so bizarre and counterproductive that conspiracy theories have sprung up to explain it. Whatever the rationale, the Comprehensive System now faced precisely the kind of feud it had been created to overcome.

Meyer would diplomatically minimize any conflict, saying that negotiations with the Exner heirs were long and the final decision was amicable—that it would be "inaccurate" to call it a "schism" or "warring camps." But a schism is effectively what it was. He and other leading researchers—four of the six members of Exner's Rorschach Research Council (Meyer, Donald Viglione, Joni Mihura, and Philip Erdberg), along with a forensic psychologist named Robert Erard—felt they had no choice but to split off and create what is now the latest version of the Rorschach test, first published in 2011: the Rorschach Performance Assessment System, or R-PAS.

Essentially an update outside the boundaries of Exner's now-frozen system, R-PAS incorporated the new research and made countless other adjustments, large and small, to bring the real-world Rorschach into the twenty-first century. Ongoing edits to the manual are available online. Abbreviations for codes are simplified to make the system easier to learn. Test results are printed out with information displayed graphically, since printers today are more advanced than typewriters—for example, scores are marked along a line and color-coded either green, yellow, red, or black, depending on how many standard deviations they are away from the norm. The system is a product of consensus, not any one person's the way the Comprehensive System was Exner's.

To solve the problem that more or fewer answers skewed the other results, which Meyer's dissertation had discussed, he and his colleagues proposed a new approach to administering the test. Test takers would now straightforwardly be told: "We want two, maybe three answers." If you gave one answer or none, the fact would be noted down but you would be prompted for more: "Remember, we want two, maybe three answers." If you got carried away, you'd be thanked after your fourth answer and asked for the card back.

This meant giving the test taker a subtly different experience than in years past: the test was more of a concrete task, a little less open-ended and mysterious. It marked another step farther away from Rorschach himself, who privileged the open-ended test-taking experience over standardization. For example, Rorschach had argued in 1921 that measuring reaction times with a stopwatch was "not advisable, because doing so alters the attention of the subject and the harmlessness can be lost. . . . Absolutely no pressure should be exerted." Now constraints on the test and pressure on the test taker were acceptable prices to pay for better statistical validity.

In general, examiners administered the test in a more up-front way.

They were instructed to avoid saying that there's no right or wrong answer, for instance, since that's not entirely true and since thinking in
those terms might make people emphasize certain answers. The manual's suggestions for what to tell a curious test taker were noticeably
friendlier in tone than Exner's scripts (quoted on page 4):

How can you get anything meaningful from inkblots?
*We all see the world a bit differently and this task allows us to understand
some of how you see things.*

What does it mean to see a . . . ?
*That's a good question. If you'd like, we can talk about that when we're
done.*

Why am I doing this?
It helps us get to know you better so that we can help you more.

Finally, it was time to get realistic about exposure to the inkblots in
the internet era. The Separated Parenting Access and Resource Center, or SPARC, a support group primarily for divorced fathers founded
in the late nineties, felt that the Rorschach was inappropriate in custody cases. They seem to have been the first to put the inkblots up online, on one of the site's first web pages, so that members could refuse
to take the Rorschach on the grounds that they had already seen the
images. The site even discussed specific responses to each card, while
disclaiming that these were "not necessarily 'good' responses to the
Rorschach. . . . We don't advise anyone to use the sample responses.
What we advise is that you DO NOT take a Rorschach test for any
reason."

SPARC brushed aside ethical complaints from Rorschach proponents as well as legal complaints from the Swiss publisher, which
claimed that the images were copyrighted. In fact they were out of
copyright, though the term "Rorschach" has been trademarked since
1991 (it is illegal to call something "a Rorschach test" or "Rorschach
cards" and sell it). When the inkblots turned up on Wikipedia in 2009,
the Swiss publisher e-mailed, "We are assessing legal steps against
Wikimedia," but there was nothing they could do. The *New York Times*

asked, on the front page: "Has Wikipedia Created a Rorschach Cheat Sheet?"

The inkblots had long been out in the world, of course. Exner's books were available in libraries or for purchase; so too was Rorschach's own. The eye chart for DMV vision tests is online too: people can theoretically memorize the sequence of letters and get a driver's license despite poor eyesight, but in reality this rarely if ever happens. Yet for decades psychologists had tried to keep the inkblots a secret. That battle was now lost.

The R-PAS manual took a pragmatic approach: "Because the ink-blot images are on Wikipedia and other web sites, and also on clothing and household items like mugs and plates," examiners should know that "simply having previous exposure to the inkblots does not compromise an assessment." Studies showed that Rorschach results were "reasonably stable over time." Rorschach himself had used the same inkblots on the same people more than once. Rather than pretending the blots were still secret, examiners should be taught how to recognize if a test taker had been coached about what to say, and how to deal with intentional "response distortion."

In a preliminary 2013 study of what this new world of inkblot accessibility might mean, twenty-five people were shown the Rorschach's Wikipedia page and asked to "fake good"—to try to make their test results more positive. Compared to a control group, the fakers gave fewer answers overall, more of them standard Popular answers, and so several scores were on average more normal. But this raised red flags in the protocol, and controlling for the inflated number of Popular answers largely eliminated the other effects. The study concluded on a tentative note, calling for much more research.

Alongside relatively cosmetic changes to the Comprehensive System, Joni Mihura, an R-PAS coauthor and former member of the Research Council (who married Meyer in 2008), was spearheading a herculean project to go through all of Exner's variables and every existing study on any of them. As Wood and others had pointed out decades before, you can't, strictly speaking, ask if a test with multiple metrics is valid, only whether each individual metric is valid. Whether or not Movement responses indicate introversion and whether or not the Suicide Index can predict suicide attempts are two very different questions—and neither one is equivalent to deciding if "the Rorschach works." Since most research considered different scores at the same time, the task of combining all the earlier studies was one of dizzying statistical complexity. It took Mihura and her coauthors seven years.

They isolated each of the sixty-five core Exner variables and threw out the ones with weak or no empirical evidence for their validity, or that were valid but redundant—a good third of the total. This was a far more rigorous vetting than other tests such as the MMPI, with hundreds of different scores and scales of its own, had ever been subjected to. The variables that passed Mihura's meta-analysis were the ones accepted into R-PAS; unlike everyone else in the history of Rorschach systems, the creators of R-PAS added no new and untested variables of their own.

In 2013, Mihura's findings appeared in *Psychological Bulletin,* the top review journal in psychology, which hadn't published on the Rorschach in decades. Her work stood out from the avalanche of other articles and rebuttals, opinions and counterarguments: it put the Rorschach test on a truly scientific footing. And with that, the existential struggle with Wood and the other leading detractors seems to have come to an end. The critics called Mihura's work "an unbiased and trustworthy summary of the published literature" and officially lifted their call for a moratorium on the Rorschach in clinical and forensic settings "in light of the compelling evidence laid out" by the article, recommending that, yes, the test can be used to measure thought disorders and cognitive processing. The Rorschach had won; many of Wood's criticisms were addressed, so in a sense the critics won too.

After building a better Rorschach, the R-PAS creators then had to get people to use it. Mihura's article gave the baseline: shortly before the introduction of R-PAS, 96 percent of Rorschach clinicians were using Exner's system. Since then, R-PAS has made headway, but slowly; it will probably prevail, just as Exner's system eventually did over Klopfer's and Beck's, but it hasn't yet. Most psychologists outside of the theoretical vanguard seem to be sticking with Exner for now; many of them, busy in their practices and not necessarily following the latest research, have never heard of R-PAS. Forensic psychologists have largely stuck with Exner, whether or not they should, since it has years of precedent; three of the R-PAS creators have made the legal case for the new system, but it does not seem to have penetrated far into actual practice yet.

The conceptual differences between the systems may be relatively minor, but in concrete terms the problems of the era before Exner's synthesis have returned. Professors have to choose which system to teach, or else teach both and spend less time on either one. As of 2015, more than 80 percent of doctoral programs offering courses on the Rorschach taught Exner, and just over half taught R-PAS. Exner is still what students are most likely to need to know; R-PAS is finding favor in some internship and clinical settings but not all. Research conducted using one system may or may not remain valid when carried over to the other.

The compromise of R-PAS, like that of Exner's system before it, was to try to shrink the test down to what could be proven with iron-clad validity. This narrowed the terms of debate to the point where both sides could agree but may have narrowed the test in other ways as well. Another approach would be to open the test back up, not by making sweeping unscientific claims for its magic X-ray powers but by reconnecting it to a fuller sense of the self, putting it back into the wider world. The test could be revitalized by reimagining altogether what it might be used to do.

DR. STEPHEN FINN, based in Austin, Texas, seems like central casting's idea of a sensitive psychotherapist: gentle face, white beard, wide open eyes, earnest soft voice. Today, when assessment is most often used to label people for others to then treat, young assessment psychologists admire Finn like no one else in the field—thrilled at the prospect of using their skills in a less secondary role. With his approach, they get to ask not an impartial "What is this person's diagnosis?" but "What do you want to know about yourself?" Or, even more directly: "How can I help?"

The set of practices Finn has worked out since the midnineties is known as Collaborative/Therapeutic Assessment, or C/TA. *Collaborative assessment* means approaching the test session in a spirit of respect, compassion, and curiosity—with a desire to understand the test taker, not primarily to classify or diagnose. Test takers are generally seen as "clients," not "patients." *Therapeutic assessment* means using the process to help clients directly, not just provide information to other decision makers or service providers in the legal or medical system. Both goals—trying to understand clients and trying to change them—go against what Finn has called the "information-gathering" model, which aims to learn facts in order to label people with a diagnosis, an IQ score, or some other preexisting classification.

One day around the turn of the twenty-first century, a man came into Finn's office wondering why he always tended to avoid conflict and criticism. When prompted to turn that abstract why-question into a focused goal, the client spelled out: "How can I become more comfortable with other people's displeasure?"

His Rorschach scores indicated a tendency to avoid or flee emotional situations (Afr. = 0.16, C = 0), but Finn didn't talk scores. Instead, he read back to the man one of his responses to Card VIII, the colored card with the pink bearlike shapes on the sides: *These two creatures are scurrying away from a bad situation. . . . It looks like an explosion could happen at any minute and they're running like hell to save their lives.*

Finn: "Do you identify with those creatures at all?"

The man smiled. "I sure do! That's what I'm doing all day long at work. I guess I think I'll get killed if I stick around. The explosion these two are running from is a bad one."

"And is that true for you?"

"Not that bad, really. But I never really realized before that it feels like I'll die."

"Yes, that seems like an important insight into why you avoid confrontation," Finn said.

"I'll say. No wonder I've had such a hard time with this."

Treatment was concluded after just a few sessions. In their last meeting, Finn returned to the original assessment question: "So from what we've discussed so far, do you see any way to get more comfortable confronting other people?"

The man replied, "I guess I just need to learn that I won't die if other people are mad at me. . . . Perhaps I could start with some people who aren't that important to me. That would make it less scary."

All the decades of debate about the Rorschach's validity were irrelevant here—those terrified creatures on Card VIII gave Finn a way to see what the client was feeling and present it in a way that helped him learn about himself. This was Brokaw's do-it-yourself Rorschach shirt brought back into the doctor's office, with a therapist experienced in standard Rorschach scoring able to home in on which answers were most telling—in this case, shapes usually seen as sluggish animals *running like hell for their lives.*

Finn has argued that a good therapist has to both adopt the patient's perspective and then step back to take a more distanced, objective view of the patient's problems. Failure in either direction can be damaging, whether the therapist overidentifies with patients, to the point where their destructive or pathological behavior seems normal, or is so intent on diagnosing abnormal behavior that she cannot recognize its significance in the patient's life or culture and intervene effectively. Psychological tests, Finn argued, can help a therapist with both of these movements: "Tests may serve both as *empathy magnifiers*—allowing us to step into our clients' shoes—and as external *handholds*—allowing us to pull ourselves back out of those shoes to an outside perspective."

In practice, then, Finn's approach means presenting test results as theories to be accepted, rejected, or modified by the client. People are "experts on themselves" and need to be involved in interpreting their own responses to any test. The therapist shares the results in nontechnical language, in personal letters instead of reports, or as fables for children. And instead of trying to answer a referral question—"Is X suffering from depression?"—therapists agree with clients on assessment goals and real-life questions to address, such as "Why do women call me emotionally unavailable? I think I'm just self-sufficient and self-controlled, but are they right about me?" Or from children: "Why do I get so mad at my mom?" "Am I good at anything?"

The idea is that when test results are connected to personally felt questions or goals, a client will be more likely to accept and benefit from them. A client's "coming for a psychological assessment is very different than their coming for a blood test or x-ray," Finn writes: it is an "interpersonal event," depending on the relationship that develops between client and therapist to make sense of what comes out.

Needless to say, this kind of "client-centered" model is not typically used in the courts, or in other contexts where an outside view on the person is called for. But as an increasing number of controlled stud-

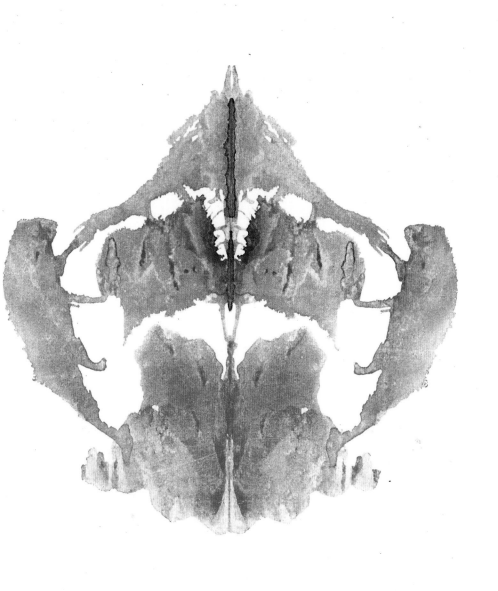

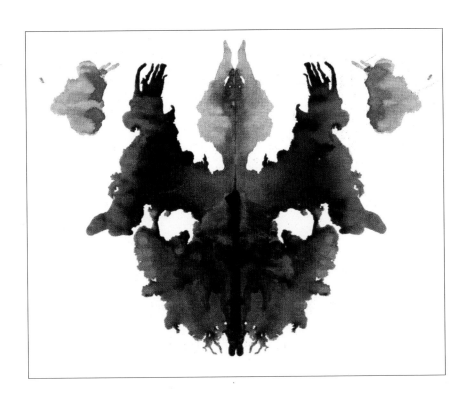

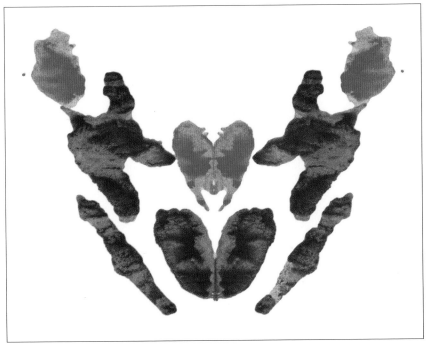

Previous page: Rorschach Test, Card VIII
These pages: Draft versions and (*opposite, bottom*) final Card III

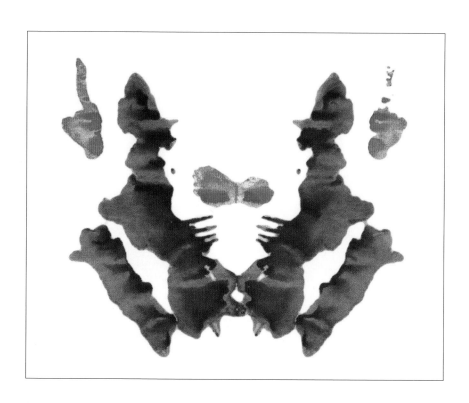

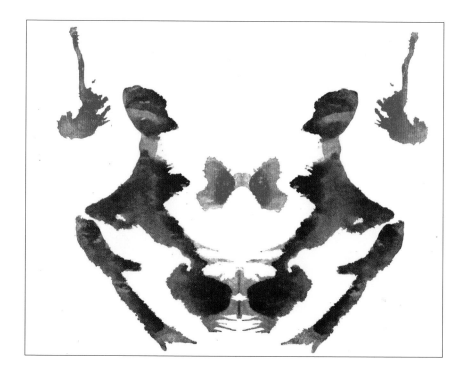

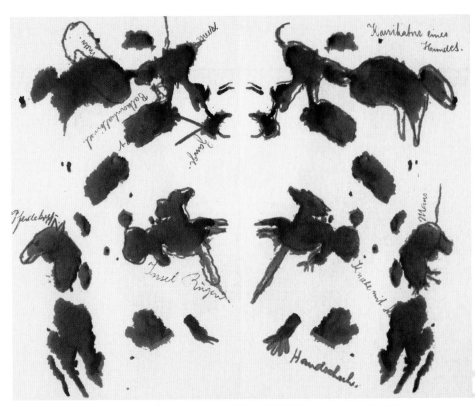

An inkblot Rorschach made for his work with Konrad Gehring (1911/1912), with interpretations marked on the page (probably responses from Gehring's students recorded by Gehring). *Left side:* "Balkan peninsula" (white space, upside-down caption) surrounded by "Adriatic," "Aegean," and "Black Seas," "tongs," "horse's head," "Island of Rügen." *Right side:* "cartoon of a dog," "boy riding hobby horse," "mouse," "glove."

Supplemental color test: see page 122.

Rorschach's painting of his apartment, 1918. The new baby, Lisa, is playing with her toys, including wooden animals Hermann made for her; some of the pictures visible through the door are hung low on the wall for the baby to look at.

Rorschach's depiction of life with baby Lisa. *Top left:* "The thing that always works"; *top right:* "Going out for a trip"; *lower right:* Rorschach seems to be taking notes on the baby's response to a symmetrical puppet, also visible hanging over the bed in top center.

Painting made for Lisa's first birthday

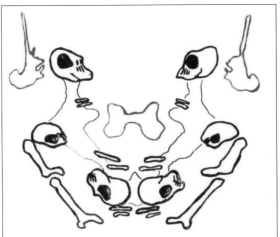

From Manfred Bleuler's 1935 article on Moroccan Rorschachs. *Top:* Common European interpretation of Card III: two waiters bowing. *Bottom:* Common Moroccan interpretation: unconnected parts of skeletons, a cemetery.

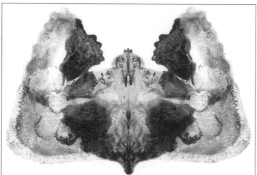

Roemer images, ca. 1919, published 1966. More artsy than Rorschach's, but their artistry was precisely the problem: "Roemer tries hard and does his best, but he likes very imaginative images, rich in fantastic figures, which spoils everything" (letter to Emil Oberholzer, January 14, 1921).

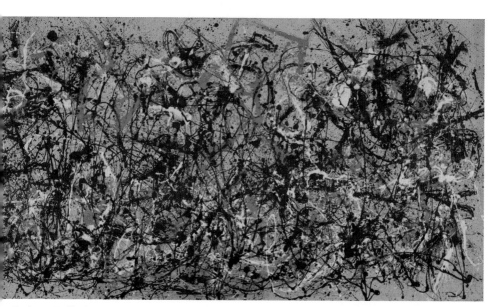

Jackson Pollock, *Autumn Rhythm (Number 30)*, 1950, which looks nothing like Rorschach's inkblots but accomplishes a similar feat: prompting the viewer to see and feel movement.

Above: Rorschach's program for the Carnival celebration at Münsterlingen (1911), including a portrait of himself in a wizard's costume holding calipers in place of a magic wand. The elegant lady next to him, holding the handbag, is Olga, and in the top left corner is Paul Sokolov, the other assistant doctor at Münsterlingen.

Rorschach in his apartment, dressed in wig and wizard's garb and holding calipers

ies demonstrate that C/TA is effective—that such brief assessments actually can accelerate treatment, or even give people life-changing insight into themselves, sometimes more incisively than traditional longer-term therapy—insurance companies are starting to pay for it. A 2010 meta-analysis of seventeen specific studies showed that Finn's approach has "positive, clinically meaningful effects on treatment" and "important implications for assessment practice, training, and policy making." (A skeptical response to the article was also published—written by three of the coauthors of *What's Wrong with the Rorschach?*)

Sometimes just the process of taking a test could be therapeutic. One woman in her forties who came in for assessment was an overachiever who had worked hard her whole life but had burned out at a demanding job several years before and had not recovered. On the Rorschach, she strove to give Whole responses to all the cards; the assessment team discussed this with her, and she agreed that she always avoided "taking the easy way out." They assured her that responses about parts were "just fine" and asked her to look back over several cards, just to see what it was like to answer that way. After tentatively offering some Detail responses, with continual reassurance from the assessors that the answers were okay, she finally sighed, looked relieved, and said, "This is so much easier." They had a long discussion about how she might have exaggerated ideas of what was expected of her and how this approach to life came out of her childhood.

Such nonstandard use of the test clearly makes those Detail responses scientifically invalid—but it helped the woman see things in a new way. Does that mean the test "worked" or not? Her initial test, with its high number of W's and lack of D's, was conducted scientifically, and in fact gave Finn valid information about her and prompted a therapeutic intervention that proved effective—but what about the follow-ups?

Tests are supposed to detect something; treatments are supposed to do something: this is the perspective Exner, Wood, and the R-PAS creators shared. A score on a test works if it gives valid and reliable information about a person. Results are true or false. But Hermann Rorschach had called his invention an inkblot experiment—an exploration, not a test. Taking a test *is* doing something. In Finn's words: "We would not necessarily consider our work in vain if the results of an assessment were not used by outside professionals to make decisions or to shape their interactions with clients. If a client felt deeply touched and changed by an assessment and was able to maintain that change over time, we would consider the assessment to have been well worth our time and effort."

Finn has trained thousands of psychologists in his methods over the years, and at personality assessment conferences C/TA is considered the most important development to have come along in a generation. Of course its roots go back further—Constance Fischer pioneered "collaborative psychological assessment" in the seventies; in 1956 Molly Harrower described "projective counseling," where people discuss their own Rorschach answers with examiners to "come to grips with some of their problems." Rorschach himself used his inkblots in much this way, with Greti and Pastor Burri and many others. C/TA is both the latest thing and the original.

THERAPEUTIC ASSESSMENT, AS an open-ended method to get to insights that feel right, may seem to occupy a kind of parallel universe from the R-PAS creators' efforts to improve and validate a scientific test. In fact, though, the R-PAS and Finn's C/TA reframe the nature of the Rorschach in similar ways.

Gone is reference to projection, much less X-rays. Instead, just as Finn focuses on the "interpersonal event" of the test, R-PAS—the Rorschach *Performance* Assessment System—treats the test as a task to be performed for an examiner. As the R-PAS manual lays out: "At its core, the Rorschach is a behavioral task that allows wide latitude" for responses and behaviors expressing "one's personality features and processing style": "Rorschach scores identify personality characteristics that are based on what people do, which is a complement to the characteristics they consciously recognize and willingly endorse on a self-report instrument. As such, the Rorschach is able to assess implicit characteristics that may not be recognized by the respondent him or herself." Taking a Rorschach means showing your stuff: problem solving under stress, nothing Freudian about it. People's actions are framed not as "projections" of their psyche but simply as behavior in our shared objective world. Unlike an audition or a time trial, though, it isn't obvious to the test taker how this task relates to life outside the testing situation. The fact that we're not quite sure what's being asked of us is what makes the test work.

Although Meyer and Finn rarely cite him, their emphasis on inter-personal performance returns to the insights of Ernest Schachtel, the philosopher of the early Rorschach. Both R-PAS and collaborative assessment, in their different ways, reiterate Schachtel's point that "the Rorschach performance and the experiences of the testee in the Rorschach situation are an interpersonal performance and interpersonal experiences." As he elsewhere says more evocatively, "the encounter with the inkblot world" is a part of life. The act of responding to blots for an examiner can be artificially seen in isolation from this human context, but it doesn't truly exist there.

This is especially clear when C/TA is used to help people that other therapies often cannot reach—people other than educated, white, upper- or upper-middle-class clients already familiar with the language and worldview of traditional psychotherapy. The WestCoast Children's Clinic in Oakland, California, provides services to thousands of vulnerable and often abused children, many of them living with foster parents, most from families without the financial or transportation resources to make use of other services. The clinic was founded with the conviction that these children have to be seen in the context of their often extreme situations, not simply classified with standardized measures of, say, "behavioral problems." From the start, the clinic tried to take a flexible and respectful approach; in 2008, it started to apply Finn's C/TA in particular.

Lanice, an eleven-year-old African American girl, no longer lived with her mother, who had mild to moderate intellectual disabilities. She lived instead with her aunt, Paula, and Paula's adult daughter. Lanice was acting out in school and at home; one time, she poured nail polish into her cousin's drink and sat quietly waiting to see what would happen when she drank it. Paula tended to minimize Lanice's problems at home and to focus on her increasing problems at school. When Lanice was in third grade, her teachers had urged Paula to request an evaluation, but when the school finally tested Lanice—a year and a half after Paula's request—they determined that she did not qualify for services, despite the fact that she was reading at a kindergarten level. Paula brought her to the WestCoast Children's Clinic for help.

The assessment questions, arrived at in collaboration with Paula and Lanice's mother, included "Does Lanice really not have a learning disability?" and "Why is she so angry?" The crucial breakthrough came about because of the C/TA practice of encouraging caregivers to observe a child's testing sessions, to help them better understand how the child operates. After a rapport-building first session, in which Lanice was mostly allowed to act out, she was given a Rorschach and other tests the next day. This time, when she squirmed in her seat, sprawled across the table, or spun the Rorschach cards on her finger like a basketball, the examiner set firmer limits than before. Paula watched it all on a live video feed.

Having spent the day in testing, Lanice went straight to afterschool, where her behavior seemed worse than ever: angrily pulling away from the teacher, refusing to follow instructions. When Paula picked her up, she was told that Lanice had acted out and was in danger of being expelled. Paula felt blindsided—everything had been fine earlier that afternoon.

The third day, when Paula and Lanice's mother returned to check in before the last session, it was Paula who blew up. She blamed the therapists for Lanice's behavior, insisting that by letting Lanice act out they had ruined her sense of how to behave in public. The therapists were then able to talk through not only Lanice's problems but Paula's expectations and anger. The therapists said they would try to support Paula and would talk to the afterschool teacher to explain the situation; they "acknowledged that the previous day's session was rather intense and that we would do more to plan for Lanice's transition from the testing session to school."

By the end of the session that day, Paula was able to see the extent to which Lanice's behavior was due to feeling overwhelmed and how Paula's own expectations were contributing to Lanice's problems. The acting out was a form of communication; Lanice hadn't known how to verbally communicate her feelings, including shame about her mother and anger at feeling abandoned by her, but those feelings had showed up in the assessments, as Paula watched on live video and started to understand.

In a joint storytelling task afterward, where Lanice and her aunt and mother had to come up with a story together, the family "began to listen, tolerate, and identify Lanice's anger and frustration." The treatment had worked by expanding the assessment process to include Lanice's family and the community—to help Lanice, the therapists had needed to understand her mother, support her aunt, reconsider their own approach, and talk to the people making decisions at her school. Insight into her psychology meant insight into her wider life context.

IN THE R-PAS framework, the Rorschach works as a performance challenge because it's mysterious. The inkblots and the task of interpreting them are unfamiliar and disorienting, forcing people to react without their usual self-presentation strategies or "impression management." As collaborative therapy, the Rorschach works because what you see in the inkblot is *not* mysterious: that explosion or screeching bat is concrete, vivid, ready to be shared and meaningfully discussed with a therapist.

From both of these perspectives, the Rorschach moves beyond the dichotomy between objective and subjective. The test is not just a set of images, not just a wolf that we either find in the cards or put there, but a process of grappling with a complex situation, acting in a confusing environment fraught with expectations and demands.

If Finn and Meyer's findings are any indication, this vision of the test as a task we perform, or as a possible way for a client and therapist to connect, may capture its complexity better than either alleged objectivity or purely subjective projection. That is why Meyer has proposed to scrap the old labels for "objective" and "projective" tests and instead call them "self-report tests" and "performance-based tests." Both kinds yield real information, and both are subjective, too, but in the first kind of test you say who you are; in the second kind of test you show it.

Framing the difference this way is a subtle move to highlight what the Rorschach has to offer. After all, in the skeptics' view, "to rely heavily on the Rorschach, even when it conflicts with biographical information and MMPI results," simply "puts the weakest source of information first (the Rorschach)" and is "forty years behind the times and out of step with scientific evidence." For Meyer and Finn, who have each extensively studied the relationship between Rorschach and MMPI results, both kinds of test are valid, but they work differently. A conflict between the results is meaningful information, not reason to reject either approach.

The MMPI is highly structured, noninteractive, and taken in schoolroom fashion by filling in bubble sheets or pressing buttons. Its True/False answers reflect a person's conscious self-image and conscious or unconscious coping mechanisms. In Finn's view, if someone is functioning reasonably well—perhaps showing up for counseling or with relationship problems but not in acute crisis—he is likely to do well on such structured tasks. The Rorschach can then reveal his underlying problems, emotional struggles, or propensities to act "crazy" that otherwise turn up only in private, or in intimate relationships that are as unstructured, interpersonal, and emotionally charged as the inkblot experiment. These may be difficulties he is unaware of, so can't express on an MMPI questionnaire—and yet the reason why he turned up seeking mental health services in the first place might be that he is having problems in his life that don't fit with his self-image. A Rorschach that finds things other tests don't may be "overpathologizing," or it may be getting at real issues that we can usually keep under control.

Finn found the reverse scenario, of someone producing a normal Rorschach protocol and a disturbed MMPI test, to be much less common. It usually meant one of two things: Either a test taker was faking, perhaps to claim disability benefits or as a "cry for help," and could consciously exaggerate on the MMPI but didn't know how to exaggerate on a Rorschach. Or else the more emotionally challenging and potentially overwhelming task of a Rorschach made him or her "shut down" and produce a dull but unremarkable protocol with few and simple responses. In the first case, the Rorschach was "right"; in the second, the MMPI was more accurate.

From this perspective, the MMPI's basis in self-reporting is both its strength and its weakness. Such tests show how you try to present yourself. The strength and weakness of the Rorschach is that it sidesteps these conscious intentions. You can manage what you want to say, but you can't manage what you want to see.

23

Looking Ahead

TODAY, EVEN AS THE INKBLOT TEST RESTS ON A FIRMER SCIENtific footing than ever before, both as diagnostic tool and as therapeutic method, it is being given less often. Usage has tumbled from its sixties peak of an estimated million times a year in America to a fraction of that—no more than a tenth, perhaps a twentieth. The Rorschach had stayed the most used personality test in the United States for decades until the emergence of the MMPI, and then was second except for a dip in the eighties. Not anymore.

Chris Piotrowski, a psychologist who has been tracking Rorschach usage for decades, estimated in 2015 that the Rorschach ranked ninth, perhaps lower, among personality tests used by assessment psychologists. It was behind several self-report tests (the MMPI; the Millon Clinical Multiaxial Inventory, or MCMI; and the Personality Assessment Inventory), short checklists (such as Symptom Checklist-90, the Beck Anxiety Inventory, and the Beck Depression Inventory), structured interview scripts targeting specific psychiatric diagnoses, and other quicker projective methods such as Human Figure Drawing and Sentence Completion. Anecdotal evidence suggests a gradual decline in usage, rather than a bombshell effect from *What's Wrong with the Rorschach?*, but there are no studies that reveal exactly when and why the shift happened and whether the introduction of R-PAS in 2011 and Mihura's article from 2013 have hastened, slowed, or reversed the trend.

Wood's book seems to be a plausible cause of the decline, but it is hard to gauge its real impact. Most psychologists and evaluators went right ahead doing what they were already doing. Those who disliked the Rorschach welcomed the takedown; those who knew and used the test largely dismissed the book, or used its criticisms to prompt narrow but real improvements. It is also impossible to disentangle Wood from wider dynamics in the field. The Rorschach had become, after Freud, a symbol for everything people didn't like about psychotherapy: too much unprovable inference, too much room for bias, not enough hard science. Many critics of the Rorschach were also critics of Freud, making the same kinds of argument against both. And so Rorschach researchers had to defend what they were doing far more than other assessment psychologists, even though most of the same problems affected other kinds of testing as well. Many chose to pick other battles.

In the popular media, at least, skepticism dominates. Whenever *Scientific American* or *Slate* has cause to mention the actual Rorschach test and quote an expert, that expert has almost always been one of the coauthors of *What's Wrong with the Rorschach*, who invariably says that the test has been scientifically debunked but is still in use. The criticisms brought up are those that were leveled at Exner's system in the early 2000s, and no one mentions any of the developments since.

Information about how often the test is taught, rather than used, is more mixed. Whether due to skepticism or to wider shifts in the field such as increased specialization, accredited graduate schools and internships have reduced their emphasis on projective, or "performance-based," techniques. The Rorschach was not among the top ten most covered tests in a 2011 survey of clinical psychology programs; Piotrowski called the decline "precipitous," concluding that the Rorschach would soon "become non-existent in clinical psychology training in the USA." A more recent study suggests that this prediction was too stark: while course coverage of the Rorschach dropped from 81 percent of programs in 1997 to 42 percent in 2011, it bounced back to 61 percent in 2015 (or perhaps the 2011 figure was too low). And almost all "practitioner-focused" programs, as opposed to "research-focused" programs, continue to teach the Rorschach, even though such training has declined in graduate schools overall.

Then there is the quality of Rorschach instruction. The APA requires clinical psychologists to be competent in psychological assessment, but doesn't say what that means: Students used to take five semesters on personality assessment but are now likely to have a one-semester course on theories of personality, which also covers how to establish rapport in testing situations and a wide range of specific tests. In 2015, the whole Rorschach test, history and theory and practice, Exner or R-PAS or both, might get two three-hour class sessions.

Eugen Bleuler worked to bring Freud's costly methods to the people who needed them most—the poor, the hospitalized, the psychotic. Rorschach, too, aspired to create a method that could be used with everybody. But the wider forces of inequality and specialization seem to be working against that vision. Assessment and psychotherapy in general are becoming more like pay-out-of-pocket counseling or coaching: exploratory and improvisational, with less of an emphasis on a specific diagnosis. The very ethos of assessment—trying to get a view of the whole person—seems not to fit into the managed-care system that we still have today. Maybe the technocratic Rorschach test will simply be unable to compete in the marketplace, and the more exploratory Rorschach will go the way of Freudian analysis and other open-ended client services, a luxury for those who can afford it. This more artisanal approach is likely to last as long as people want to know more about themselves.

"Even for sympathizers like me," in the words of Chris Hopwood, a young psychologist active in the assessment community, the Rorschach "is sort of like vinyl: you only use it if you really want the music to be good." If the Rorschach were merely one nuanced but inefficient test in a battery of assessments, this would be the end of the story.

THE DECLINE OF the Rorschach in clinical psychology should not be exaggerated: R-PAS is gaining ground, and a fraction of a million times a year is still a lot. The inkblots are used as a test all over the world, sometimes to assign a diagnosis, sometimes to less measurably change how a therapist understands a client. If a woman comes to see a psychologist for help with an eating disorder and then has a high Suicide Index score on the Rorschach, her psychologist might talk to her differently: "There are ways that you have your world organized that are a lot like people who go on to kill themselves. Should we talk about that?"

Examples like this will seem suspect to psychologists or laymen who think the Rorschach finds something crazy in everyone. But the test is also used to find mental health. Recently, at one state psychiatry facility in the criminal justice system that houses people declared to be Not Guilty by Reason of Insanity or Incompetent to Stand Trial, a violent man had been undergoing extensive treatment. (This story has to be kept vague for confidentiality.) The treatment seemed to have worked—the man's psychotic symptoms were gone; to all appearances, he was no longer a danger to himself or others—but the team of doctors on his case was divided over whether he had really improved or was faking health to get out of the facility. So they gave him a Rorschach test, which turned up no sign of thought disorders. The test was trusted enough as a reliable and sensitive indicator of such problems that the negative finding convinced the team, and the man was released.

The Rorschach also continues to be used in a research context. It is often hard to distinguish between Alzheimer's-type dementia and other effects of age and mental illness—could the inkblots tell them apart? In a 2015 conference, a Finnish scientist presented his analysis of Rorschach tests given to sixty patients in a Paris geriatrics unit, ages fifty-one to ninety-three (average age: seventy-nine). Twenty of the patients had mild or moderate Alzheimer's and forty had a range of other mood disorders, anxiety, psychosis, and neurological problems. The test found many common elements between the two groups but also a range of distinguishing features. Half a dozen Rorschach scores showed that Alzheimer's patients were less psychologically resourceful, with less cognitive sophistication, creativity, empathy, and problem-solving ability; they distorted information and did not integrate ideas and perceptions. Most intriguingly, despite putting a normal amount of effort into processing complex and emotional stimuli, Alzheimer's patients gave fewer Human responses—a kind of content response still generally accepted as an indication of interest in other people. The Alzheimer's patients, more than their peers, had checked out of the social world. This finding was new in Alzheimer's research, with implications for treatment and care.

Outside of clinical psychology, the fact that there is so much data about how the inkblots are perceived makes them useful in a range of applications. In 2008, when a team of Japanese neuroscientists wanted to study what happens when people see things in original ways, they needed recognized, standardized criteria for whether something a person sees is common, uncommon, or unique. So they took what they called "ten ambiguous figures that have been used in previous studies" and projected them inside an MRI tube equipped with a voice scanner, tracking brain activity in real time as subjects gave typical or atypical answers to the inkblots.

The study demonstrated that seeing something in a standard way uses more instinctive, precognitive brain regions, while original vision, requiring a more creative integration of perception and emotion, uses other parts of the brain. As the Japanese scientists pointed out, Rorschachers had long argued precisely that Original responses "are produced from the interference of emotion or personal psychological conflicts . . . on perceptual activities." The MRI study confirmed Rorschach tradition, just as the inkblots had made the MRI experiment possible.

Another conclusion from this research was that people who see forms less well have larger amygdalas, a sign that this region of the brain, which processes emotions, has been activated more often. "This suggests that emotional activation greatly influences the extent to which one distorts reality," just as Rorschach had posited a century ago with his correlation of Color and poor Form (F–) responses.

Other recent studies of perception have used new technologies to investigate the test-taking process itself. Since typical test takers give two or three responses per card on average but can give nine or ten when asked, a team of research psychologists at the University of Detroit argued in 2012 that people must be filtering or censoring their responses. Maybe getting around this censorship would make a performance-based test more revealing. If only there were an involuntary reaction to an image, or at least a reaction "relatively more difficult to censor." There was: our eye movements as we scan an inkblot before we speak.

So, building on eye-movement Rorschach studies going back to 1948, the researchers put a head-mounted EyeLink tracker on thirteen students, showed them the inkblots, and asked, "What might this be?," then showed each blot again and asked, "What else might this be?" They quantified and analyzed the number of times each subject stopped and looked at one place on the image, how long they looked, how long it took to disengage from the whole image and start looking around, and how far the gaze jumped. They drew general conclusions, too, such as that we hold our gaze longer during second viewings, since reinterpreting an image is an "attempt to acquire conceptually difficult information." This is paying attention to how we see, not what we say, with a vengeance. Eye movements will never reveal as much about the mind as what we see in the inkblots, but researchers are exploring what they do reveal about how we see—and returning to Rorschach's original vision of the test as a way to understand perception.

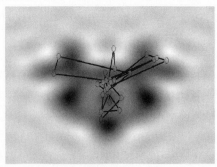

Not what you see, but how: Eye movements while looking at Card I. The blot is shown blurred by the researchers so as not to reveal the actual image. Lines are scan paths, and circles are pauses or fixations; this subject paid most attention to the central part of the blot.

THE MOST FUNDAMENTAL question about the test that Rorschach left unanswered at his death was how these ten cards could produce such rich responses in the first place. The mainstream trend in psychology, from Beck to the content analysts to both Exner and his critics, has been to leave this question of theoretical underpinning aside. Empiricists thought of the test as eliciting responses and spent decades fine-tuning how those responses should be tabulated. For Rorschach—and for only a few who came later—the inkblots elicited something deeper. Ernest Schachtel had argued that test results are not words that are spoken but ways of seeing. "It has to be emphasized that this is a test of formal things," Rorschach wrote in 1921, "*how* a person *perceives* and *absorbs*."

Today, we know more about the science and psychology of perception than ever before. As the test breaks free of the clinical psychology culture wars, it may at last be possible to integrate the inkblots into a full-fledged theory of perception, as Rorschach so wanted, or at least to sketch out what it is about the nature of seeing that gives the inkblots their power.

Look closely at this picture. There will be a quiz.

Imagine you are given all the time you want to study this picture, and then it's taken away and you are led to a dark room. Now imagine two different scenarios: In one, with your eyes closed, you have to answer a simple perceptual question about the image—*Is the tree wider than it is tall?* In the other scenario, you have to answer the same question, but your eyes are open and the picture itself is faintly shown on a screen so that you can look at it while you're being asked the question.

This experiment was tried on twenty people, with various images and analogous questions. The subjects' brain activity was measured during each scenario—that dark room was an MRI scanner. It turned out that the overlap in brain activity between the two scenarios was 92 percent, suggesting that almost all of what your brain does when you *see* something is the same—or is at least in the same area of the brain—as what it does when you *visualize* something. The retina actually picking up light or not is only 8 percent of what happens, so to speak. Perception is a mainly psychological, not physical, process.

When you look at something, you are directing your attention to parts of the visual field and ignoring others. You see the book in your hand or the baseball hurtling toward you, and choose to disregard all the other information that's reaching your eye: the color of your desk, the shapes of clouds in the sky. You are constantly cross-checking what's out there against objects and ideas you recognize and remember. Information and instructions are traveling along nerves from the eye to the brain, and also from the brain to the eye. In another experiment, Stephen Kosslyn, coauthor of the tree-visualization study and one of today's leading researchers into visual perception, monitored this two-way neural activity moving "upstream" and "downstream" during an act of seeing, and found that the ratio is 50-50. To see is to act as much as react, put out as much as take in.

Even what seem like completely straightforward optical tasks turn out not to be merely passive or mechanical. Our eyes may register wavelengths, but a lump of charcoal looks equally black whether it is in the bottom of a bag or out in the summer sun at your barbeque—the light it reflects is different, but we see it as black because we recognize it as black. In the same way, a sheet of white paper looks white regardless of the lighting in the room. Painters have to unlearn this way of seeing, so they can paint "black" or "white" things with different colors. As Kenya Hara, a Japanese designer, writes in a beautiful book called *White:* "Things like the rich golden yellow of the yolk from a broken egg, or the color of tea brimming in a teacup, are not merely colors; rather they are perceived at a deeper level through their texture and their taste, attributes inherent in their material nature. . . . In this regard, color is not understood through our visual sense alone, but through all our senses." In other words, the most perfect Yolk Yellow swatch in the biggest sample book in the world isn't pooled in its soft-boiled shell, or shimmering on a clear layer just hardening in a frying pan to the smell of olive oil starting to heat up, so it can't be the yolk-yellow color we actually see. Colors exist in connection with colored things that awaken our memories and desires. No objective system—no Pantone chart, no color wheel, no grid of pixels of "every" color—can truly represent *any* color. Even seeing a color is an act of the self, not just of the eye.

Here is how Rorschach made the same point in *Psychodiagnostics*, quoting his teacher Eugen Bleuler: "In perception, there are three processes: sensation, memory, and association." Bleuler's "associationist" theories are inadequate in various ways, as Rorschach himself came to recognize, but the basic fact remains: seeing is a combination of (1) visually registering an object; (2) recognizing the object, that is, identifying it *as* something by comparing it to known things; and (3) integrating what we see into our attitudes about these things and our worldview in general. This is not a three-step sequence but three inextricable parts of the same act. You don't *first* see a tree or a face or an ad, and *then* process it, and only *then* react: it happens all together.

That means it is possible to see impulsively, dreamily, hesitantly—not just see first and then act impulsively, dreamily, hesitantly. A psychologist can watch you seeing anxiously, not just watch you fidgeting anxiously or speaking anxiously. This is why it makes sense to call the act of seeing an inkblot a performance. It may seem obvious that perception happens on the inside, private and inaccessible, with the "performance" on the test coming after the act of seeing. Rorschach argued otherwise.

As he put it in a 1921 lecture to Swiss schoolteachers:

> When we look at a landscape painting, we feel a cluster of sensations that trigger processes of association in us. These processes call up memory images that then let us *perceive* the picture, both as a picture and as a landscape.
>
> If it's a picture of a landscape we know, we say: We *recognize* the image. If we don't *know* the landscape, we can then *interpret* it (or fail to interpret it) as the moors, a lakeshore, the Jura Valley, etc. Recognizing, interpreting, determining—all are kinds of perception that differ only in the amount of secondary associative work they involve.

In other words, every perception combines "the sensations coming in with the memory traces inside us that these sensations summon up," but in everyday life this "inner matching" happens automatically and unnoticed. *Interpretation,* Rorschach explained to his audience, is simply effortful perception, "where we notice and perceive the matching as it happens." We feel ourselves piecing together clues about that unknown landscape and arriving at an answer that feels like a more or less subjective interpretation. The inkblot is merely the case of the unfamiliar landscape taken to an extreme. But even then, interpreting the blot doesn't come after perceiving it. You don't interpret what you've seen, you interpret while you see.

Perception is not only a psychological process, it is also—almost always—a cultural one. We see through our personal and cultural "lens," according to the habits of a lifetime shaped by a particular culture, as the Culture and Personality anthropologists knew. One culture's trackless wilderness is full of detailed and meaningful information, specific plants and animals, for members of another culture; some people notice a friend's haircut, others don't; more than beauty is in the eye of the beholder. An enormous advantage of the Rorschach test is that it largely gets around these lenses—as Manfred Bleuler put it, it lets us strip off "the veils of convention."

Ernest Schachtel pointed out more than half a century ago that when we are asked to say what an inkblot might be, we are not in any context where we might reasonably expect some things to loom into view and not others—a dim living room, a foggy road, peering into an aquarium. As a result, interpreting the blot requires more of our active, organizing perception than we usually bring to bear; we are forced to dig through a fuller range of our experience and imagination for ideas about it. At the same time, a wolf in the blot is not a threat, unlike a wolf in a shadowy night, so whether we find it or not doesn't matter. Sane test takers know that the blot, unlike everything we physically come across in the course of our lives, is not anything "real" at all, other than a real printed card. The stakes are low—what we see has no immediate practical consequences. Our vision has room to relax and roam free, as much room as we are willing to give it.

This helps explain why the question Rorschach asked in the test is so crucial. If we're asked, "How does this make you feel?" or "Tell me a story about this scene," that task doesn't test our perception. The image on the TAT showing a boy with a violin is meant to look like a boy with a violin, whatever story we tell about him. We can free-associate thoughts or feelings from inkblots, but for that purpose they are no better than clouds, stains, carpets, or anything at all; Rorschach himself thought the inkblots were not especially well suited to free association. Being asked "What do you see?" or "What might this be?," though, gets at how we process the world on the most basic level—and in doing so calls upon our whole personality and range of experience.

To be free, for once, to perceive-as-such without any clues or guidelines—to see without the constraining filters of rigid conventionality—can be a powerful experience. Dr. Brokaw, offering this experience to bus riders with his psychedelic shirt, may have been onto something. Actual psychedelic drugs do not stimulate or overstimulate the visual parts of the brain, as one might expect; instead they suppress or shut down the "management layer" of mental functioning: the part of the brain keeping everything else separate—for example, keeping visual centers isolated from emotional centers. On such a drug, your perception is freed of management, filters and guidelines, "veils of convention." In the quote from William Blake that Aldous Huxley and Jim Morrison made famous, "The doors of perception are cleansed"—like the "windows" through which the abundance of the world flows in, in Rorschach's favorite line from Gottfried Keller's poem. Looking at a Rorschach blot is not as powerful an experience as taking a blot of acid, obviously, but they operate in analogous ways.

Perception is not only visual: "What might this be?" and "What do you see?" are not precisely the same question. But it was more than just personal preference, or technological limitations, that led Rorschach to make inkblots rather than an audio Rorschach test, or cypress knees, or smell-o-blots. Vision is the sense that both operates at a distance, unlike touch and taste, and can be focused and directed, unlike hearing and smell. We can pay attention to certain noises or odors, or try to ignore them, but we can't blink our ears or aim our nose: the eye is far more active, under far more control. Seeing is our best perceptual tool—our foremost way to engage with the world.

During the heyday of Freudianism, people thought that the unconscious was all-important and that a method to project the unconscious would reveal the true personality. Part of the reason there is so much anger about the Rorschach's use in real-world situations—the father in the shaken-baby case outraged that he's "being asked to look at abstract art"—is that people still widely think of it as a way to generate "projections." A test of seeing does far more, though. It reveals a person's grasp on reality, cognitive functioning, susceptibility to emotions. It shows how she approaches a task and gives her a chance to connect with an empathetic therapist and heal. Like any act of seeing, taking the Rorschach is a combination of shaping, thinking, and feeling, as Rorschach put it in his letter to Tolstoy.

The feelings are especially important. A range of research has shown that effective psychotherapy has to be emotional: talking in intellectual terms is not always enough. One 2007 meta-analysis showed that therapists who specifically draw attention to emotions, making comments like "I noticed that your voice changed a bit when we were talking about your relationship, and I wonder what you are feeling right now," get better results than therapists who don't. This focus on emotions turns out to have an even greater positive effect than good rapport between therapist and patient.

A visual test, Stephen Finn has argued, builds an emotional focus into the whole process. "Basically, I propose that tests like the Rorschach—because of their visual, emotionally arousing stimulus properties and the emotionally arousing aspects of their administration procedures—tap into material that is more reflective of right-hemisphere functioning. Other tests like the MMPI utilize more left-hemisphere functions because of their verbal format and nonemotionally arousing administration. (I don't want to overly simplify—obviously, both types of tests utilize both hemispheres to some degree.)" It's not just that Rorschach responses—bears, explosions—are easy to talk about. The mere fact that patients are asked to *look and see* allows therapists to measure "aspects of emotional and interpersonal functioning that are not well captured by other assessment procedures." It makes sense that Finn's key metaphor for testing would be visual: the Rorschach as an "empathy magnifier," not an empathy amplifier. A visual task can create the emotional bonds that help make healing possible.

Certainly compared to answering a questionnaire. In one collaborative/therapeutic assessment of a troubled eight-year-old girl, the mother told the psychologists afterward that the Rorschach was the most helpful part of the assessment for gaining new insight into her child, "because it demonstrated that she is not all drama and contrived and that really and truly she does not see things the way the rest of the world sees things." Follow-ups to the therapy showed real changes in their family, including both mother and daughter reporting a decrease in family conflict and decreased symptoms in the girl, and both parents reporting "feeling more patient, empathic, compassionate, and hopeful" toward their daughter and "less frustrated, less like they wanted to give up, less at their wits end." Seeing through her eyes brought them closer to the child than hearing what she said.

Along with its emotional power, seeing is also a cognitive process unlike any other. Rudolf Arnheim's classic *Visual Thinking* (1969) is still the most compelling argument for the radical notion that seeing doesn't precede thinking or give the mind something to think about, it *is* thinking. He showed how "the cognitive operations called thinking"—exploring, remembering and recognizing, grasping patterns, solving problems, simplifying and abstracting, comparing and connecting and contextualizing, symbolizing—do not take place somewhere above and beyond the act of seeing but are "the essential ingredients of perception itself." More than that, organizational problems such as grasping patterns or the character of a complex phenomenon can be solved *only* in the act of perception: a connection cannot be analyzed or thought about without it first being seen; the intelligence is in the seeing.

Interest in visual thinking, a relatively marginal but persistent tradition, is on the rise in our ever more image-saturated world. A passionate minority has continued to advocate for an emphasis on arts education and "visual literacy" as essential for making better citizens. Edward Tufte's *The Visual Display of Quantitative Information* and its sequels (1983, 1990, 1997) showed how much visual intelligence needs to go into the seemingly simple task of presenting information. Donald Hoffman's *Visual Intelligence: How We Create What We See* (1998) reiterated Arnheim's claims using decades of newer science. Effective visual thinking in a business context was championed in Dan Roam's *The Back of the Napkin: Solving Problems and Selling Ideas with Pictures* (2008), which proved its own point by becoming a huge bestseller, while Johanna Drucker's *Graphesis: Visual Forms of Knowledge Production* (2014) brought Arnheim into the online, smartphone age.

The point here is not that the inkblots should be used for the display of quantitative information or to sell ideas on the back of a napkin. It's that we can understand how the inkblots work as a psychological test only when we understand them as Rorschach did—in the broader context of vision, with all its emotion, intelligence, and creativity.

IN PRINCIPLE, THEN, the Rorschach test rests on one basic premise: Seeing is an act not just of the eye but of the mind, and not just of the visual cortex or some other isolated part of the brain but of the whole person. If that is true, a visual task that calls upon enough of our perceptual powers will reveal the mind at work.

A recent analysis by Gregory Meyer has helped quantify the inkblots' unique ability to activate our perceptions. It is not true that any formless shapes would work just as well; as Rorschach knew and some others have recognized, the blots are not "meaningless" or "random."

After all, over the course of a century spent looking at the inkblots—spent tallying, categorizing, and reframing what people see, everything you can imagine and quite a lot you can't—one truth has remained unassailable: Card V looks like a bat. Or maybe a butterfly.

In Rorschach tests given between 2000 and 2007 to six hundred nonpatient Brazilian men and women, 370 of those people saw a bat in Card V; most of the others saw a butterfly or moth. There were, as usual, a lot of bears in Card II. In fact, out of roughly fourteen thousand total responses, there were only 6,459 different responses, and a small pool of thirty answers were common enough to be given by fifty or more people. The inkblots objectively do look like certain things, while they also invite interpretation. It wouldn't be much of a test if everyone saw something totally different, or if almost everyone saw the same thing. In these six hundred tests, the long tail of personal variation consisted of about a thousand answers given by two people each, and fully 4,538 answers each given only once, including the "tragically misunderstood piece of cauliflower" seen by one depressed farmer.

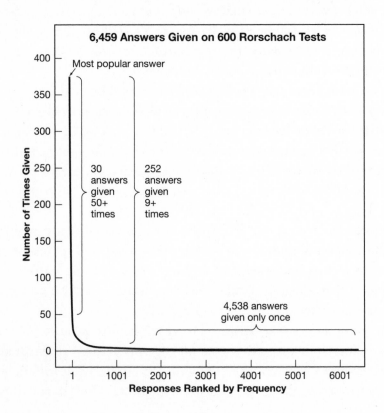

If you graph the responses, the near-vertical line on the left shows the inkblots' common ground—the obvious bats and bears—while the horizontal line shows the leeway for personal idiosyncrasy. Meyer called this the Rorschach test's structure and latitude. The graph also reveals a more specific pattern: the most common answer is twice as common as the second most frequent, three times as common as the third most frequent, all the way down.

This is what's known as a Zipf distribution, one of the mathematical ordering principles that structure the world. Other patterns are better known—the Fibonacci sequence in a nautilus shell, the bell curve of a random distribution—but the Zipf describes phenomena from earthquake size (there are very few huge ones and lots of little ones) to city populations, sizes of businesses, and word frequencies: in English "the" is twice as common as "of," three times as common as "and," on down to "cormorant" and "methylbenzamide." Rorschach answers in a large sample will follow the same pattern. The bat on Card V is the "the" of the Rorschach.

A single test also yields more than one data point. A person typically gives twenty, thirty answers over the course of the test, and a healthy test result won't be stuck on either side of the Zipf curve. Only obvious answers would suggest you're pretty guarded or rigid, or uninterested in the task, or boring, while too many unusual or bizarre answers might mean you have a poor grip on reality, or mania, or maybe you're a rebel trying to be different.

Finally, the Rorschach yields multiple data points in a sequence. The test is a fixed series of ten cards, but test takers have the freedom to give multiple answers per card in any order. A given person's answers move up and down the Zipf curve, so to speak, a movement that itself has structure and latitude. Do your answers fall apart in the colored cards at the end of the test, or come together? Do you start with something obvious on every card and then get quirky, or do you arrive at popular, common answers only gradually? Even if two test takers somehow gave exactly the same answers to each card, but in a different order, maybe only one of them would have a rigid compulsion to give one kind of answer first and another last on every card, a pattern meaningful to a sensitive examiner.

Using nothing but intuition, artistic skill, trial and error, and a few ideas about the power of symmetry, Hermann Rorschach created a set of pictures as inherently organized yet flexible as natural language or earthquakes. In this regard it is hard to imagine them bettered—psychologists have designed alternate series of inkblots over the years, but all fell more or less quickly by the wayside. Rorschach's inkblots are like the act of seeing, which itself has both structure and latitude. There's something really there, but not anything that constrains us completely. The visual nature of the world is objectively in things, but we see it there; we subjectively impose our view of the world onto things, but only if that view fits what we see. We're all looking at the same thing, even when we see it differently.

Rorschach's blots are unique in more than shape. The colors elicit emotion, even override the shapes, sometimes but not always. Putting movement into a still image is not easy—it takes an artist with real skill and, in Rorschach's words, "spatial rhythm" (like a Michelangelo, unlike a Futurist). It is even harder to *potentially* convey a sense of movement, to some people and not to others. Almost anyone will see movement in pictures like Rorschach's man struggling with a can (page 97), but, as Rorschach wrote in 1919, "A key point is that the experiment is set up to make Movement responses difficult. If you show someone good pictures, then everyone, even the intellectually disabled, will seem to be a movement type."

The symmetry of the blots, as Rorschach acknowledged, makes people see "disproportionately many butterflies etc.," but he was also right that "the advantages far outweigh the disadvantages." The blots' horizontal symmetry helps people connect with them, even identify with them. The blots are not mathematically symmetrical—they have variations in tiny protuberances, streaks, and shading—but neither are animals or people, which is precisely why the blots are seen as balanced and alive. In addition, since groups of people we encounter in real life are next to each other, not on top of each other, horizontal symmetry creates a "social" connection between the two sides of any image. It makes different parts of the inkblots interact, like pairs of people or other creatures. The inkblot test wouldn't have worked without horizontal symmetry: the blots wouldn't have been personal, psychological.

In all the changes to scoring systems, administration procedures, and understandings of the meaning of the test, Rorschach's inkblots have remained constant, for good reason.

AN ESSAY ON the Rorschach by the philosopher Jean Starobinski poetically opens: "'Every movement reveals us,' Montaigne wrote. Today we might add: every perception is likewise a movement and reveals us too." And today, Rorschach's insights about perceiving movement continue to be recognized as the most original and lasting aspect of his work. They have also been directly confirmed by some of the most talked-about neuroscience research in the past thirty years.

In the early 1990s, scientists at the University of Parma, Italy, made a seemingly simple discovery: some of the same brain cells in macaque monkeys fired both when the monkeys performed an action, like reaching for a cup of water, and when they saw someone else—another monkey, or a picture of a monkey, or a person—perform the same action. A series of ingenious experiments followed, showing that the cells didn't fire when the monkeys observed the same movement without the intention (the hand held the same way but not reaching for a cup), and did fire when performing a different action for the same purpose (using the left hand instead of the right hand, or using reverse-pliers, where fingers have to be spread apart instead of pinching together). It seemed that these neurons were reacting to the *meaning* of the actions. Rather than simply controlling mechanical or motor processes, they were reflexes that brought the intentions and desires of others right into the brain.

The problem of learning how to understand other people or decode their behavior—the philosophical problem of other minds—disappears if it's true that we neurologically mirror, literally feel, what others are trying to do. The scientists dubbed the cells "mirror neurons" and unleashed a torrent of research and speculation linking them to everything from the nature of autism to political opinions to kindness and the foundations of human society.

In 2010, another team of Italian scientists made the connection to the Rorschach. They hypothesized that if mirror neurons fire when a person sees intention in an action, perhaps they fire when a person sees movement in a picture: "We speculated that such mentalization is very close to what is thought to occur when an individual articulates the M response while observing the Rorschach stimuli." When they put EEG wires on the heads of volunteers looking at inkblots, they found "highly significant" mirror neuron activation when subjects were giving Human Movement responses, and not responses for animal movement, inanimate movement, Color, Shading, or Form. "For the first time to our knowledge," they concluded, Movement responses were proven to have a neurobiological basis. "This overall result is fully consistent with the century-long tradition of the Rorschach theoretical, as well as empirical, literature." Further studies of the Rorschach and mirror neurons followed, work that R-PAS cocreator Donald Viglione facilitated and that Finn and Meyer often cite.

The true significance of mirror neurons remains controversial—as does the whole idea that scanning technology such as MRI can straightforwardly read the brain, much less read minds. But whatever else they are or aren't, mirror neurons have reawakened scientific interest in what Rorschach's dissertation on reflex hallucinations described, and what the Movement responses in the Rorschach test show: that we feel, in our mind and body, what happens in the world, and that these literal or imagined movements are how we perceive in the first place.

Other recent experiments have shown that smiling when someone else smiles, or nodding in sync—behavior known as motor synchrony— not only produces emotional rapport, it *is* emotional rapport. We all know that if you see someone with a pained facial expression you feel their pain, but mimicry is a cause, not effect, of perception: in one study, participants holding a pencil between their teeth, thus unable to smile, frown, and so on, were much less adept at noticing emotional changes in other people's facial expressions. The mimicry, the physical movement, was needed to make perception possible. "It turns out that the perception of a face almost invariably implies motion. It is very difficult to look at a face and not to think about it in motion, making facial expressions."

Rorschach had already talked about visualizing a painting only after he held his arm the way the knight in the picture was holding his. Edgar Allan Poe gave the same strategy to his star detective, Dupin, in "The Purloined Letter": "When I wish to find out how wise, or how stupid, or how good, or how wicked is any one, or what are his thoughts at the moment, I fashion the expression of my face, as accurately as possible, in accordance with the expression of his, and then wait to see what thoughts or sentiments arise in my mind or heart, as if to match or correspond with the expression." It seems counterintuitive, but only from a framework that imagines the mind working like a computer, with the eye as a camera and the body as a printer or speaker: input—processing—output, perception—recognition—mimicry. That's not how it works.

The Movement response—in a sense, the entire inkblot experiment—rests on the premise that seeing includes the process of "feeling-in" to what you see, and that feeling is something that happens through seeing. This idea has come a long way since its origin in German aesthetic theory circa 1871, especially under its English name: empathy.

Empathy has been even more discussed in recent years than mirror neurons, with book after popular nonfiction book putting it at the center of what it means to be human. Some contrarians, such as Paul Bloom, even argue against it: if empathy is biased toward the familiar and the attractive, overrides quantitative facts (we feel more for a single baby in a well than for a thousand faceless casualties far away), indeed is downright "parochial, narrow-minded, and innumerate," then we may make better decisions about complex problems without it.

Discussions of the Rorschach test can bring useful perspectives to today's debates, since the whole history of the test, from its birth in the debate over whether psychiatry should define diseases or understand individuals, has been one of balancing the competing claims of "feeling into" other perspectives and keeping a distanced stance of rational objectivity. Stephen Finn's work, in particular, can be used to reframe the conversation around empathy. In reflecting on the C/TA approach, he argued that empathy does three different things. It is a way of gathering information: you come to understand someone by feeling their pain or standing in their shoes, not just by monitoring their behavior. It is an interactive process: while a therapist is trying to understand, a person eager to be understood is "at the same time tracking me and giving me information to help me understand her inner world better." Finally, empathy is a healing element in its own right: compassion can heal; many of Finn's clients tell him that feeling so deeply understood itself changed their lives. These three modes of empathy can point in different directions: a con man may be extremely sensitive and able to read people, "empathetic" in one sense, while sociopathically unempathetic in what he does with that information. From this perspective, arguments like Bloom's point to the weaknesses of empathy as an information-gathering tool but also overlook its value as a means of connection and healing.

Perhaps the most valuable reminder that the Rorschach can give is that empathy is a matter of more than words and stories. Empathy is vision: feeling into the world and then seeing out there something you connect to, in your body. Empathy is a reflex hallucination, a Movement response. It requires not just imagination, or a certain sensibility, but sensitive and accurate perception. You don't feel someone's feelings without seeing that person as they really are, which means seeing the world through their eyes.

24

The Rorschach Test Is Not a Rorschach Test

I CAME TO THE INKBLOTS FROM THE CULTURAL SIDE, NOT AS A practicing psychologist or crusader against personality testing. I had no ax to grind about whether the test, in whichever system, should be in second place or ninth; like most of the people I talk to, I was surprised to learn it was still used in clinics and courtrooms at all. "Rorschach" was a strange word to me, too—person, place, or thing?—and I knew nothing about Hermann Rorschach's life. What I did know was that I had seen everything under the sun called a Rorschach test. I had seen the inkblots, or thought I had, and I wanted to find out more.

My first step was to take the real test. That was when I learned that not just anyone knows how to give it, and the experts tend not to be inclined to indulge idle curiosity. I went looking for someone at least a little disillusioned, who knew all the techniques and formulas but who also still saw the test as an exploration, something you could talk about. I was eventually referred to Dr. Randall Ferriss.

In his office, he pulled his chair in front of mine, a little to the side, took out a legal pad and a thick folder, and handed me a cardboard card from the folder. "What do you see?"

In Card V, I saw, of course, a bat. In Card VIII, *"the witch of winter."* In what used to be called the Suicide Card, *"a big friendly dog with floppy ears."*

"Oh!" I gasped when handed Card II, startled by the red even though I had already read that not all the blots were going to be black and white. "Affect shock," Ferriss noted down.

I said Card III was *"people holding buckets,"* and that the gray streaks *"make it look like they're moving."* Later, when I knew enough to discuss the technical details with him, Ferriss told me that this might have been a Shading response: something gray that is moving or held in some kind of tension. Lots of Shading responses were thought to imply anxiety, Ferriss said. But there was also Cooperative Movement in my answer, and it was a Popular response. "So it's all good."

The whole thing took about an hour, and I came back at the end of the week to hear the basic interpretations and results. Did the test work? The exercise was not meant to diagnose me, settle a lawsuit, or kick-start therapy, so in that sense no. There was nothing for it to do. It seemed revealing, as these things go, and Dr. Ferriss's take on my personality seemed more or less insightful. What struck me most were the ten cards themselves, so rich and strange—enticing enough, in any case, for me to spend the next several years exploring their history and their power. Ferriss told me I was a little obsessive.

EVEN NOW, I don't quite know what to make of the color in the cards. "The multicolored blots are bad" and the colors "have a repellent effect on any painter": so said Irena Minkovska, a painter and neurologist's wife who knew Hermann and Olga Rorschach personally. Irena's sister-in-law Franziska Minkovska, another friend from Kazan in 1909, agreed. She had moved to Paris in 1915 and later wrote a major psychological study of Vincent van Gogh, and when she gave the Rorschach test to various modern artists in Paris—I wish I knew who—she said they all reacted badly to the colors.

Color may be the inkblot test's weak point, and it is telling that the new test Rorschach was starting to develop at the very end of his life, with his artist-psychologist friend Emil Lüthy, was specifically devoted to color. Still, once "color shock" was discredited as a diagnosis for "neurosis," Rorschach's bigger idea—that color is connected to emotion—was the baby thrown out with the bathwater. There has been almost no research on color in the Rorschach for half a century. The fact remains that people often do have startled responses to the colored cards, however that behavior is interpreted. I clearly did. Rorschach designed the colored cards to throw subjects off balance if they are disposed to be thrown, so maybe their troubling effect means they're working as planned.

In any case, it is the strong designs of the endlessly fascinating black and white blots, with or without red, that are obviously Rorschach's lasting masterpieces—not exactly art, but not not art either.

Some art historians are finally starting to take them seriously. Classic surveys had occasionally mentioned Rorschach inkblots but typically fell into the trap of simply listing precursors, especially Leonardo da Vinci's splotches on the wall and Kerner's klexography, whose influence on Rorschach was consistently overstated. A long essay published in 2012 was the first thorough treatment of the inkblots, drawing nuanced connections to Ernst Haeckel, Art Nouveau, and modernism. The catalog for a groundbreaking 2012 show at New York's Museum of Modern Art, *Inventing Abstraction,* included an essay discussing Rorschach's inkblots together with Malevich's abstract paintings, Einstein's thought experiments, and Robert Koch's Nobel Prize–winning visualizations of tuberculosis bacilli. There are countless visual connections still to be made.

Descended from artists on both sides of his family, Hermann Rorschach had a lifelong belief in perception as the point of intersection between mind, body, and world. He wanted to understand how different people see, and at the most fundamental level, seeing is, as the painter Cézanne said of color, "the place where our brain and the universe meet."

Alone among the pioneers of psychology, Rorschach was a visual person and created a visual psychology. This is the great path not taken in mainstream psychology, even though most of us today, even the talkiest or most bookish, live in a predominantly visual world of images on surfaces and screens. We evolved to be visual. Our brains are in large part devoted to visual processing—estimates run as high as 85 percent—and scientists are beginning to take that fact seriously; advertisers in quest of "eyeballs on the page" started to take it seriously a long time ago. Seeing runs deeper than talking.

Freud, though, was a word person. The whole tradition he founded, from noticing puns and "Freudian slips" to talk therapy itself, was designed to reveal the unconscious in what we say or don't say. It is psychology by the word people, for the word people. Modern psychology, meanwhile, worships at the altar of statistics—the revenge of the math people. Almost every field of knowledge is skewed to the verbal or the mathematical. Education is conducted in lectures and written tests and fetishizes statistical measures even more than psychology does. In intellectual life, these often seem like the only two choices: numbers or words, data or stories, science or humanities, hard or soft.

But that's not all there is. There are visual people, music people, athletes and dancers with brilliant physical intelligence, the enormous emotional intelligence of consolers and manipulators. Imagine if history essays were expected to include charcoal drawings of the main people or landscapes, not just sketches in words, and if historians were trained to draw as much as to write—every artist knows that that's a true and serious source of knowledge.

Love him or hate him, it changes things to frame Freud as a word person, because we all know that not everyone is one. I am a word person married to a visual person, a painter and art historian. Every day I come up against the fact that these two types of people see the world in often incompatible ways—or rather, visual people see it and word people read it. I've talked to a lot of word people who have visual types in the family, and vice versa: this fundamental difference is news to none of them. Hermann Rorschach was among the first to use that whole side of the human experience to explore the mind.

THE FACT THAT people come in different "types" raises the specter of relativism, which loomed into view with Jung's *Psychological Types* and came to the fore with the breakdown of authority in the sixties. Rorschach's fundamental insight was a visual version of Jung's types: we all see the world in different ways. But the fact that it's visual makes all the difference. Understanding the real inkblots and their specific visual qualities gives us a way to move beyond the relativism, at least in principle. It's not all arbitrary: there's something truly there that we're all seeing in our own way. Rorschach's insight can stand without forcing us to deny the existence of valid judgments, Truth with a capital T.

I've lost count of the number of times I've heard, after describing this book to someone: "It's like the Rorschach test is a Rorschach test! It can mean anything!" I want to say *No, it isn't.* However tempting it may be to "present both sides" and leave it at that, the inkblot test is something real, with a particular history, actual uses, and objective visual qualities. The blots look a certain way; the test either works in a given way or it doesn't. The facts do matter more than our opinions about them.

The Rorschach metaphor is changing, too. It first came to prominence in America with a culture of personality that privileged unique individual qualities and demanded a way to measure them. It became a symbol of the same antiauthoritarian impulses that brought down an earlier generation's psychiatric experts. For decades it was a symbol for irreconcilable individual differences. Now it often reflects a growing impatience with fragmentation, and the promise of sharing our worlds with one another.

I have started seeing it used to describe not something we react to, revealing our personality, but instead how we express ourselves. The writer of an August 2014 *Lucky* magazine story about owning eight nearly identical pairs of black skinny jeans said, "I call them my Rorschach pants. Whatever I want them to be, they'll be." That same year, the data-cruncher of the dating site OK Cupid published an analysis of self-descriptions in online profiles, revealing what words are most and least typical for different combinations of gender and ethnicity. "My blue eyes," "snowmobiling," and "Phish" are used most by white men compared to other groups; "tanning" and "Simon and Garfunkel" are used least by black women compared to others. The least used words, he wrote, are "the negative space in our verbal Rorschach"—a revealing picture of our self-presentation.

These are arguably just garbled metaphors, failing to realize that a Rorschach test consists of images we are shown, not ones we make. I don't see it that way. These particular mistakes, if that's what they are, would not have been made ten or fifty years ago.

Even when inkblots are used as a test, it's not so much our reaction that matters nowadays as what we do with it. On November 8, 2013, Rorschach's birthday, Google's doodle of the day was an interactive Rorschach test. As a glum but somehow likable Hermann took notes, you could click to see different blots, then share your answers on Google+ / Facebook / Twitter. "What do you see?" had turned into the onscreen instruction: "Share what you see."

In 2008, fifteen years after Hillary Clinton first called herself a Rorschach test, candidate Barack Obama did, too, but he meant something different. "I am like a Rorschach test," he said. "Even if people find me disappointing ultimately, they might gain something." Instead of labeling people as Red America or Blue America, Obama's use of the metaphor cast himself as collaborative/therapeutic: giving people a helpful glimpse into themselves and moving forward. Our different individual reactions did not need to separate us. The Rorschach test obviously won't bring us together any more than Obama did as president. Still, the metaphor has shifted in emphasis, from dividing to uniting.

The point of the cliché has traditionally been that there are no wrong answers—a blurry image from the Hubble telescope would never have been called "a Rorschach test of competing theories," because in that case one of the astronomical interpretations would be right and the others would be wrong. Now, though, the metaphor can be used that way, compatible with faith in a single, objective truth.

One recent article, on new technology that lets archaeologists fly over the Amazon compiling data in a day that would have once taken decades to collect, mentioned in passing that "in areas of dense forest those technologies yield Rorschach-like images that even experts cannot decipher." This is ambiguity without relativism: the truth is out there, and better technology will find it. Andy Warhol rejected self-expression and underlying meanings—"I want to be a machine"—but when Jay-Z used a Warhol *Rorschach* as the cover of his memoir, *Decoded,* both the title and the book itself, filled with explanations and backstories of the lyrics, put faith in the singular truth behind the code. Jeff Goldblum recently described a play he was acting in as "intended to be kind of like a Rorschach test or some kind of Cubist rendering so that simultaneously you get competing and equally viable narratives." A Cubist painting sees every side at once, so in Goldblum's metaphor we are all partly right, and all only partly, but the whole truth is there.

A handful of examples can't prove the zeitgeist, especially if one of them comes from Jeff Goldblum, but here's one more. In Verizon's "Reality Check" ad campaign from 2013, ordinary people in an art gallery of blotty images were asked: "How do you react when you first see this?" "It's kind of like a dancer," the first puzzled viewer answered, moving her arms (a Movement response!). Other gallery-goers said it was a witchlike shrew, or a bunch of berries. The images were actually cell-phone coverage maps—the ones in the background morphed to be symmetrical, Rorschach-style—and when faced with Verizon's map, everyone knew it was "clearly a picture of the United States." No latitude here. The last viewer, latte in hand, gave the only valid interpretation: "I should switch to Verizon *immediately!*" Personal interpretation was just an irrelevant distraction caused by technology's failure to deliver; a "Reality Check" relies on there being a reality to check.

Yet how can such shared reality be imposed on anyone who doesn't see it for themselves? This is the controversy about diagnosis, about "labeling people," about whether it's right to block someone's career or drastically intervene in his or her life because of a test. It's the Hannah Arendt question: *What gives someone the right to judge me?* Fifty years on, the question is more potent than ever. People seem to feel that they have the right to their own facts, not just to their own opinions. But there are situations where the stakes are too high, or we are otherwise unwilling to throw up our hands at the existence of different world-views and call it "a Rorschach test."

There is subjectivity in evaluating anyone, and in the end, people may disagree with and resent the evaluator. We don't have the solid information we want, yet we still have to make real choices—in clinics, in schools, in courts—relying on fallible judgment. We can improve that judgment over time, but only with practice and never to perfection.

We need to keep trying to put our decisions on as solid a basis as possible, as the decades of fierce fights over validity and standardization have tried to do. The widespread adoption of R-PAS, which addresses serious flaws in Exner's system and returns to the scientific principles of continued research and development, would be a change for the better. But the fantasy of being able to know, to perfectly know, whether someone should be allowed to be a schoolteacher, or needs therapy, or should have custody of a child, is just that: a fantasy. A person is going to make mistakes with any set of tools. When a jury produces a tragic miscarriage of justice, we don't conclude that trial by jury is wrong in principle.

Cases like Rose Martelli's are brutal anecdotal evidence against the Rorschach test, but anecdotal evidence is piled just as high on the other side, such as the nearly unbelievable story of Victor Norris with which I opened this book. As Norris's evaluator told me, it is each individual psychologist's job not to overpathologize, not the test's job. She is the first to admit that the Rorschach "ends up being given wrongly by *a lot* of people." Even if the Rorschach were a miraculously reliable and objective technique, there would still be an art in training people to use it properly, and countless ways human error might still creep in. A recent study found that judges regularly grant parole about two-thirds of the time when they hear a case first thing in the morning or after a food break, with the odds dropping to almost zero as the day wears on and their blood sugar drops. The Rorschach test is immune from none of these complications: nothing exists in isolation from our messy life in the world.

This is why humility about the test is key, on the part of both advocates and skeptics. Hermann Rorschach had a stronger sense than anyone of the test's concrete limitations, but also of the wider vistas it opened up onto the mind.

.

To END WITH: one last psychologist, and one last inkblot.

When Dr. Ferriss gave me the Rorschach, his inkblot cards had not been used for some time. He rarely gives the test anymore. He acknowledged that it had had to be standardized for use in diagnostic and legal settings. But it also seemed to Ferriss that Exner's system had "drained some of the life out of it": mere scoring "loses the human touch." Ferriss preferred to do content analysis, "the most interesting and psychoanalytical" approach, he felt, and just what the quantitative turn rejected.

There are other reasons, though, why Ferriss doesn't use the Rorschach. He works with defendants in the criminal justice system and doesn't want to find anything that might send them to jail. The last Rorschach test he gave before mine was in a prison. Most test takers there have a disturbed profile—no surprise, since prison is about as disturbing an environment as you can get. Ferriss was working with a young African American man on trial for carrying a gun. His brother had just been shot dead in South Central L.A. and he knew he was a target. He came across as "angry and hostile," as anyone would in those circumstances, so why give him a test? "You're trying to tell his story," Dr. Ferriss said. "You just don't want to know how disturbed people are unless you're diagnosing them in order to treat them." But no one was considering giving this guy any treatment, only whether to lock him up and throw away the key.

What would "perfecting the Rorschach test" look like for this defendant? Not tweaking the scores, compiling better norms, redefining administration procedures, or redoing the images, but using it to help, in a humane society, as part of a process of giving everyone who needs mental health care access to it. The argument can be made that Dr. Ferriss was concealing the truth by not giving his client the test, but truth exists in the context of what it is meant to be used for—which might be deciding whether someone needs help, or deciding whether to throw someone in jail.

To move past the dead-end Rorschach controversies of the past, and to use to the fullest the ways the test reveals our minds at work, we have to open up what we are asking of it. We have to return, in fact, to Hermann Rorschach's own broadly humanistic vision.

Finally, Card I.

In January 2002, it came to light that forty-year-old Steven Greenberg of San Rafael, California, had been sexually molesting twelve-year-old Basia Kaminska for more than a year. She was the daughter of an immigrant single mother who lived in one of his apartments. It later turned out that the abuse had gone on since she was nine. The police showed up at his house with a search warrant; hours later, he drove his new Lexus to Petaluma Municipal Airport, took off in a single-engine plane, and flew it into Sonoma Mountain, leaving behind a minor media frenzy about the abuse and suicide.

Here, unlike in the story with which I began this book, the names and identifying details have not been changed. Basia wants her story told.

When Basia was seen by a psychologist, her tendency to minimize and deny her problems made self-report tests basically useless. On the Trauma Symptom Checklist for Children, the Beck Depression Index, the Beck Hopelessness Scale, the Children's Manifest Anxiety Scale, and the Piers-Harris Children's Self-Concept Scale, as well as in talking to the psychologist, she underreported symptoms, said she had no feelings good or bad toward Greenberg, and claimed that she felt the events were behind her and she would rather not discuss them.

Only two tests gave trustworthy results. Her IQ, as measured by the

Wechsler Intelligence Scale for Children (WISC-III), was extremely high. And her scores on the Rorschach revealed emotional withdrawal, fewer psychological resources than one would think from how she presented herself, and a deeply damaged sense of identity.

Her first response to Card I, the answer often interpreted as expressing one's attitude about oneself, was something superficially conventional but actually quite crippled. The blot is often seen as a bat, though not as often as Card V is. What Basia saw was a bat with holes in its wings: "*See, here's the head, the wings, but they're all messed up, they've got holes. It looks like maybe somebody attacked them and that's sad. It looks very ripped right here and bat's wings are usually precise. The wings would normally go out here. It sort of disrupts what it would normally be.*" The rest of the test, both answers and scores, confirmed this first impression. The examining psychologist wrote in her notes: "Very damaged and hanging on by her fingernails with a shield of sophistication." Her report concluded that Basia was "clearly emotionally damaged as a result of traumatic circumstances, in spite of her cool exterior and protests to the contrary."

Basia eventually sued the estate for damages, and four years later, the case went to court. Greenberg's lawyers tried to use her earlier minimizing and denying against her. Then the psychologist read to the jury Basia's Rorschach response.

To be effective in a court of law, evidence has to be valid but it also has to be vivid. Forensic psychologists have had to master the technical debates around the Rorschach, to be able to respond to criticisms like the ones in *What's Wrong with the Rorschach?*, but they also need to avoid getting into those debates at all. Research shows that clinical opinions in clear everyday language are more persuasive than statistical or methodological minutiae. Paradoxically, the more impressively quantitative and expert the testimony is, the more a bored or mystified jury is likely to reject or ignore it.

Basia's sad, messed-up bat had the ring of truth—it let the jury feel they had reached through the fog of prosecution and defense to this girl's inner life, her real experience. It's not magic. Anyone who looked at Basia and felt sure that the girl was lying or faking would not have had their mind changed by this test result or anything else. But what Basia had seen in the inkblot told her story. It helped the people in the courtroom see her, deeply and clearly, in a way the other pieces of testimony couldn't.

No argument, no test or technique or trick, will get around the fact that different people experience the world differently. It's those differences that make us human beings, not machines. But our ways of seeing converge—or fail to converge—on something objective that's really there: interpretation, as Rorschach insisted, is not imagination. He created his enigmatic inkblots in an age when it was easier to believe that pictures could reveal psychological truth and touch on the deepest realities of our lives. And through all the reimaginations of the test, the blots remain. The question "What might this be?" has an answer, when you're looking, together, at something right in front of you.

APPENDIX

The Rorschach Family, 1922–2010

Olga, Wadim, and Lisa, 1923

After Hermann Rorschach's death in 1922, Olga was allowed to stay on in Herisau. She had worked as a doctor during Hermann's years in Herisau, but only while Director Koller was away. Now she was offered a position at the Krombach, but only as an administrator—the reasons given being her lack of Swiss credentials, her seeming "foreign" to the patients, and her "having less authority as a doctor" than a man would have. That position ended on June 24, 1924, shortly after her forty-sixth birthday.

According to Olga, Hermann had made a grand total of twenty-five francs from the inkblot test in his lifetime. With the modest sum paid out by Hermann's life insurance, Olga was able to buy a home in nearby Teufen, which she set up as a small residential clinic where she would house and care for two or three patients at a time. Hermann's contract with Ernst Bircher provided for royalties on *Psychodiagnostics* beginning with the second edition, which the book did not reach until 1932, partly because Ernst Bircher went bankrupt in 1927. A former employee, Hans Huber, who had helped with the original printing of Rorschach's inkblots, was able to buy up the rights and restart the business as Hans Huber Verlag, now Hogrefe, which continues to publish the Rorschach test today.

Olga led a lonely and precarious life, raising her two children and rarely able to practice medicine to her full potential. She never remarried, and she died in 1961 at age eighty-three. Lisa, forty-four years old in 1961, lived with Olga until the end, having studied English and Romance languages at the University of Zurich and worked as a teacher. She never married, and she died in 2006 at age eighty-five. Wadim studied medicine in Zurich, eventually had a psychiatric practice, and died in 2010 at age ninety-one. Rorschach had no grandchildren.

On June 26, 1943, at the Ninety-Ninth Conference of the Swiss Psychiatric Society in Münsterlingen, site of their first married home by Lake Constance, sixty-five-year-old Olga Rorschach-Shtempelin gave a lecture called "Hermann Rorschach's Life and Character." Biographical information from the first half of her lecture has been used throughout this book; the second half is translated here in full.

Hermann Rorschach's Character

H.R.'s DEVELOPMENT RESTED ON A SCIENTIFIC FOUNDATION, BUT his attitude toward life, toward people, toward the world, was emotional. He was very even-tempered, harmonious, friendly, and cheerful. He did not like problems and conflicts in human relationships—he almost instinctively rejected anyone and anything "dissatisfied" or "at odds with itself." He always looked for unity and clarity.

He was very modest and straightforward in daily life, frugal and unassuming, the "eternal student"; harmless and almost careless in practical things; not ambitious; a Parzival type. Throughout his life he kept a boyish sense of adventure, of being up for anything. He absolutely lived in the present, with a good sense of humor and liking humor in others.

Lively in his physical movements, he considered himself a movement type. He had very deep feelings for friends, which he tended to hold back. Only in the small circle of his family did he give himself completely. Very loyal in his feelings, not authoritarian. He considered the feeling of *deep respect* to be the foremost cardinal virtue of humanity, and judged people on the basis of whether this quality was present or absent in them. He was a religious person but not pious, and indifferent to the official church.

Above all, what interested him was the mind or spirit as it revealed itself in human dynamics. From this arose his great interest in religions, their founders and how they came to be; also myths, sects, and folklore. He saw in all these phenomena the revelation of the human creative/dynamic spirit. He saw in his mind's eye the subterranean river of humanity through the centuries, from the ancient Greeks through Romanticism to our own era—from Dionysus through Anton Unternährer to Rasputin—from Christ to Francis of Assisi. He loved this current of life in its multiplicity of appearances, in all its seeking and wandering. He often repeated the lines from Gottfried Keller: "Drink, oh eyes, all your lashes can hold / Of the golden abundance of the world." How he felt this abundance of the world! History, as the path of humanity in the struggle of ideas and the transformations of form, interested him as well. With his pronounced tendency to synthesize, he was always looking for the connecting idea.

He had no interest in, or understanding for, economic questions, and was indifferent to money, with no striving for worldly goods.

He loved nature, the world of the mountains. While certainly no Alpinist, he went hiking in the mountains at some point or another every year. He tended not to talk much in the mountains. He loved the colors; his favorite color was gentian blue. His attitude toward music was purely emotional: he loved *Lieder,* the Romantics. In painting, he on the one hand preferred the Romantics, such as Schwind and Spitzweg; on the other hand, he admired Hodler for his representation of movement, and Böcklin for his colors, though he found Böcklin "dead." He also appreciated the portraitists, especially the Russians. In the theater, he preferred cheerful comedies to tragedies and dramas. He liked going to the movies, which he found interesting primarily for the rich expressive possibilities of the faces and gestures.

He was not especially well read, except in the specialized literature of his field. But on quiet evenings when living in the clinic he read a lot with his wife: Zola, "the photographer of life"; he avoided Strindberg, though, for medical reasons. He loved Jeremias Gotthelf, Gottfried Keller, and Tolstoy, whom he considered the "greatest artists." He was especially interested in Dostoyevsky, with his spirited dynamism, his philosophical problems of life, his search for God, and the problem of Christ. He read the Russians in the original, of course. He planned to write about Dostoyevsky, but never did.

His attitude toward Freud was not an "orthodox" one: that is, he did not accept everything, and saw psychoanalysis simply as a medical treatment method indicated in certain situations and not others. He was decidedly opposed to the dominant tendency of the time, that of applying psychoanalysis to every question in life and even to writers, which he felt risked castrating the human spirit, dumbing down, and removing bipolarity, the necessary presence of any dynamism. He himself never underwent analysis, and always declined with a laugh any such suggestion from his psychoanalytical friends.

In women, what he valued par excellence was femininity, "nobleness of heart," goodness, a sense of domesticity, courage in everyday life, and cheerfulness. He disliked suffragettes and women with solely intellectual interests. He had not spent much time studying philosophy and saw this as a gap; he liked to say that he would start studying philosophy only after he turned forty. He did study gnosticism, though.

He was more drawn to the Bernese than to the other Swiss; he considered them very dynamically charged and liked their down-to-earthness and "rootedness." His favorite Swiss city was Zurich, both for having more to offer than any other Swiss city and for being the city of his youth. During vacations, he enjoyed Ticino to the fullest.

H.R. worked with amazing ease, as though playing, and was extremely productive. The secret of his productivity was his constantly moving between different activities. He never worked for hours at a time at one thing; he liked to move from intellectual work to manual labor and back. He never worked in the evenings, which he devoted to his family; likewise never while on vacation, which was meant solely for relaxation, for *dolce far niente*. This changing of task, this transition from intellectual creation to woodworking or reading, restored him, refreshed his mind and receptiveness. He also liked visitors, but not unannounced and not if they stayed too long. Hour-long conversations on a single topic tired him, even if it was one he found interesting.

He saw his book *Psychodiagnostics* as a key to knowing people and their capacities, and as key to understanding culture, the work of the human spirit. He took the large view and saw the possibility, in the future extension of the method, for fathoming *the connection* (a kind of synthesis), the human as such. He rarely spoke in these terms. For him, *Psychodiagnostics* was not an already finished crystal, it was only the beginning—he saw it *in statu nascendi,* in flow, as a probing and seeking. He hoped to find people to work with him, followers, but did not venture to say so openly, given his modesty. For him, his book was already "obsolete." With his perpetual inner creativity, he had already gotten much farther than the version preserved in writing there.

He knew that his method rested on no theoretical basis, hence his insistence, in the first publication of his book, on the "preliminary necessity" for "unassailable definitions" of his terminology and concepts. He had serious reservations about popularizing his method too widely, seeing the risk of it being dragged down to the level of a "fortune-telling machine." He was already deeply uneasy with the tendency of G. Roemer (who, incidentally, despite his claims, never "collaborated" with

H.R.) to lead his method onto other tracks. He saw that process not as one of *further development,* but as *variation and fragmentation* that would only provoke misunderstandings. Even three days before his death, he spoke about this topic and suffered from the thought of it.

After H.R.'s death, Eugen Bleuler wrote to me: "Your husband was a genius." It is not my place, as his wife, to claim such a thing, but I was always well aware that I was sharing a life path with a highly gifted, unique, uncommonly harmonious, and utterly lovable person, possessing great intellectual gifts and a rich artistic soul. He was steadily expanding his Experience Type from introversion toward ever-increasing extraversion. He thereby attained an enviable balance, and can properly be labeled as *ambiequal.* Obviously he was not conscious of this himself.

I would like to close with his own words (from a letter to G. Roemer) to convey how he understood this balance: "The person who is 'truly alive,' the ideal human being, is ambiequal: he can transition from intense introversion to extensive extraversion. This human ideal is the genius. That would seem to mean: Genius = Normal Human Being! But there is probably some truth in that." In that sense, Hermann Rorschach was a normal human being.

Rorschach's silhouette self-portrait

ACKNOWLEDGMENTS

_____

When I started writing this book, the biographical trail seemed to have gone cold. Rorschach's children, aged two and four when Hermann died, had passed away in 2006 and 2010. The family had protected their privacy, and a lot of personal material had been destroyed. The selection of Rorschach's letters published in 2004 omitted information thought to be "merely personal"; in the letters and diaries in the archive, pages were missing or blacked out.

The Hermann Rorschach Archives and Museum in Bern, Switzerland, was an exceedingly modest place, on the ground floor of an apartment building, with a handful of glass cases showing his cap labeled "Klex," draft inkblots, and a few drawings. They had managed to convince the heirs to donate all the material that remained, but there wasn't much apart from mementos and trinkets.

Before long, that cold trail started to seem almost cursed. In 2012, a fire destroyed the top floor of the building housing the Rorschach Archive, and the automatic sprinklers caused water damage throughout the building. The Archive was luckily spared but was relocated to the university library in Bern, and public access was closed off indefinitely. The author of the first history of the inkblots to use extensive archival material, Naamah Akavia, died of cancer in 2010; Christian Müller, coeditor of Rorschach's letters and author of numerous short articles on Rorschach, planning a future biography, died in 2013. In a far-flung corner of the internet I found a ten-page biographical sketch of Rorschach from 1996, claiming that "the first full length biography from unpublished primary source material" was "in preparation" by the author, Wolfgang Schwarz. The biography had never been published, and Schwarz had died in 2011.

I requested from the archive a folder labeled "Correspondence with Wolfgang Schwarz." The earliest letter establishing contact was from 1959, and a letter from Lisa dated September 4, 1960, set up a meeting between Schwarz and the family: Lisa, Wadim, and Olga. Schwarz, a German American born in 1926 who had discovered *Psychodiagnostics* at his university library in 1946 and stayed up all night reading it, had become interested in Rorschach's life. With the first grant from the National Institutes of Health in medical history, he tracked down and interviewed everyone he could find and organized and translated the material, all while working as a psychiatrist for sixty-two years and raising, eventually, eight children. He corresponded with Hermann's sister Anna, who lived until 1974. The most tantalizing document in the archive was a nineteen-page outline and table of contents for his tome *Hermann Rorschach, M.D.: His Life and Work,* with a handwritten note from Lisa dated 2006: "Finally finished in 2000/01, seeking a publisher."

One hot June evening in 2013, I sat down at Susan Decker Schwarz's living-room table in Tarrytown, a suburb of New York, with a large metal lockbox in front of me. It contained, she told me, her late husband's lifework. She hadn't gone through it and didn't know German. He had spent decades hunting down every fact about Rorschach's life but had shown the results to no one.

The box contained hundreds of Rorschach family photographs, letters, and drawings, both copies and originals; test protocols written in Hermann's handwriting; a first printing of the inkblots. Much of the material duplicated what I had already seen in the Bern archives, but much was new, including some of the most striking family photographs and the long letter from Olga to Hermann's brother describing Hermann's last days. Next to the metal box, stuffed into a shopping bag, was a thousand-page printout of Schwarz's manuscript. Schwarz used to say to his son about the archive in Switzerland that "they've got half and I've got half." By the end of that June evening, there were two Hermann Rorschach Archives: one in Bern and the other in my apartment.

Two large plastic bins Susan Schwarz found later contained the core of Wolfgang's research: 362 pages of notes from his interviews. He had found and spoken to Rorschach's colleagues, his best friend from school, his and Olga's live-in maid; the widow of Konrad Gehring, with whom Rorschach had made his first diagnostic inkblots; the woman who was in the room when Olga was told that Hermann had died. The manuscript, though, was almost entirely translations from Rorschach's letters and files. Schwarz had wanted to let Rorschach speak for himself, and the more he found, the less he could bear to leave anything out. It was not shaped into a biography, but it was an amazing cache of indispensable research.

I am deeply grateful to Wolfgang Schwarz's widow and children for giving me access to all this material, and their blessing to use it. It has now been donated to the Rorschach Archive, to be made available to others.

I would also like to thank the many other people and institutions that made it possible for me to write this book. The Leon Levy Center for Biography at the CUNY Graduate Center and the Doris and Lewis B. Cullman Center for Writers and Scholars at the New York Public Library gave me fellowships, and fellowship—I owe a great deal to Gary Giddins and Michael Gately at the Levy; Jean Strouse, Marie d'Origny, Paul Delavardac, Caitlin Kean, and Julia Pagnamenta at the Cullman; and my inspiring cohorts of other fellows. In Switzerland, Rita Signer and Urs Germann of the Hermann Rorschach Archive in Bern; Beat Oswald, Erich Trösch, and their colleagues at the Staatsarchiv of the Canton of Thurgau in Frauenfeld, Switzerland; Hans Ruprecht and Marianne Adank, gracious hosts in Bern in 2010; the 2013 Walser Weltweit conference that brought me and other Robert Walser translators from around the world to see Herisau; Raimundas Malašauskas and Barbara Mosca, who invited me to speak on Hermann Rorschach at the "HR" Summer Academy of the Paul Klee Center in Bern; and Reto Sorg, for kindness and generosity on many fronts. Editors Amanda Cook, Domenica Alioto, and Meghan Houser at Crown and Edward Orloff, my agent at McCormick Literary, put in a titanic amount of work on a first-timer's book of narrative nonfiction and made it what it is, for which I am very grateful; thanks too to Jon Darga and the rest of the Crown team, especially designer Elena Giavaldi, for making such a beautiful product. Jay Leibold, Scott Hamrah, and Mark Krotov read the work in progress—they and many other friends provided valuable help and encouragement.

This book is dedicated to Danielle and Lars, for a lifetime of teaching me how to see.

NOTES

All translations are mine unless otherwise noted.

Abbreviations

Archives

HRA: Hermann Rorschach Archive (Archiv und Sammlung Hermann Rorschach), Bern, Switzerland; the HR collection unless otherwise noted

StATG: Staatsarchiv Thurgau, Frauenfeld, Switzerland

WSA: Wolfgang Schwarz Archive, now donated to the HRA to be cataloged and accessible there

WSI: Wolfgang Schwarz's interview with [name], cited from notes in the WSA, emended for clarity and translation accuracy

WSM: Wolfgang Schwarz's unfinished manuscript, much of it consisting of quotations from Rorschach's letters translated into English

Key Writings by Rorschach

PD: *Psychodiagnostics: A Diagnostic Test Based on Perception* (Bern: Hans Huber, 1942; 6th ed., 1964), trans. Paul Lemkau and Bernard Kronenberg from *Psychodiagnostik: Methodik und Ergebnisse eines wahrnehmungsdiagnostischen Experiments (Deutenlassen von Zufallsformen)* (Ernst Bircher, 1921; expanded 4th ed., Hans Huber, 1941). The translation is poor and I have retranslated all quotations, but my notes give the page numbers in the English edition.

Fut: The only other text by Rorschach published in English to date is "The Psychology of Futurism," trans. Veronika Zehetner, Peter Swales, and Joshua Burson, in Akavia, pp. 174–86. Here, too, I have referred to the German and corrected the translations (HRA 3:6:2; I consulted Akavia's transcription, "Zur Psychologie des Futurismus," online: www.history .ucla.edu/academics/fields-of-study/science/RorschachZurPsychologiedes Futurismus.pdf).

IN GERMAN:

CE: [Collected Essays] *Gesammelte Aufsätze*, ed. K. W. Bash (Hans Huber, 1965).
Diary: September 3, 1919, to February 22, 1920 (HRA 1:6:6).
Draft: "Investigations of Perception and Apprehension in the Healthy and the Ill," with the title "1918 Draft" added later with a different typewriter, August 1918 (HRA 3:3:6:1).
L: [Letters] *Briefwechsel*, ed. Christian Müller and Rita Signer (Hans Huber, 2004). This selected edition, made while Rorschach's children were alive, omits letters and parts of letters judged to be "merely personal."

Smaller groups of letters are published in "Hermann Rorschachs Briefe an seinen Bruder," ed. Rita Signer and Christian Müller (*Luzifer-Amor: Zeitschrift zur Geschichte der Psychoanalyse* 16 [2005], 149–57); Georg Roemer, "Hermann Rorschach und die Forschungsergebnisse seiner beiden letzten Lebensjahre" (*Psyche* 1 [1948], 523–42); *CE*, 74–79; Anna R, 73–74. Some letters are translated in the WSM (translations emended by me), with the originals either in the WSA or missing.

All letters to and from Rorschach are cited by date, regardless of where and whether they have been published. The HRA is the source of these other publications and the single source for researchers now that it includes the WSA.

Key Writings About Rorschach

There is little useful nontechnical writing on Hermann Rorschach and the inkblot test. The major sources are:

Akavia: Naamah Akavia, *Subjectivity in Motion: Life, Art, and Movement in the Work of Hermann Rorschach* (New York: Routledge, dated 2013, actually 2012).
Ellenberger: Henri Ellenberger, "Hermann Rorschach, M.D., 1884–1922: A Biographical Study," *Bulletin of the Menninger Clinic* 18.5 (September 1954): 171–222, more easily available in *Beyond the Unconscious: Essays of Henri F. Ellenberger in the History of Psychiatry* (Princeton: Princeton University Press, 1993), 192–236, but the version there is abridged, with not all deletions indicated. My notes give page numbers from the *Bulletin* version. The German translation in *CE* (19–69), meanwhile, is "slightly altered and expanded by K. W. Bash based on remarks by Anna Berchtold-Rorschach, with the permission of the author." Material not in English is cited from *CE*.
ExCS: John E. Exner Jr., *The Rorschach: A Comprehensive System,* vol. 1 unless noted, year cited to indicate which edition.
ExRS: John E. Exner Jr., *The Rorschach Systems* (New York: Grune and Stratton, 1969).
Galison: Peter Galison, "Image of Self," in *Things That Talk: Object Lessons from Art and Science*, ed. Lorraine Daston (New York: Zone Books, 2008), 257–94.

Wood: James M. Wood, M. Teresa Nezworski, Scott O. Lilienfeld, and Howard
N. Garb, *What's Wrong with the Rorschach? Science Confronts the Controversial Inkblot Test* (San Francisco: Jossey-Bass, 2003).

IN OTHER LANGUAGES:

Anna R: Anna Berchtold-Rorschach, "Einiges aus der Jugendzeit," in *CE,* 69–74.
ARL: Anna Berchtold-Rorschach, "Lebenslauf," September 7, 1954 (HRA
Rorsch ER 3:1).
Blum/Witschi: Iris Blum and Peter Witschi, eds., *Olga und Hermann Rorschach:
Ein ungewöhnliches Psychiater-Ehepaar* (Herisau: Appenzeller Verlag,
2008), esp. essays by Blum (58–71, 72–83), Witschi (84–93), and Brigitta
Bernet and Rainer Egloff (108–20).
Gamboni: Dario Gamboni, "Un pli entre science et art: Hermann Rorschach et
son test," in *Autorität des Wissens: Kunst- und Wissenschaftsgeschichte im Dialog,* ed. Anne von der Heiden and Nina Zschocke (Zurich: Diaphanes,
2012), 47–82.
Morgenthaler: Walter Morgenthaler, "Erinnerungen an Hermann Rorschach:
Die Waldau-Zeit" (1954), in *CE,* 95–101.
Olga R: Olga Rorschach-Shtempelin, "Über das Leben und die Wesensart von
Hermann Rorschach," in *CE,* 87–95; the second half is translated in the
Appendix above.
Schwerz: Franz Schwerz, "Erinnerungen an Hermann Rorschach" (*Thurgauer
Volkszeitung,* in four installments, November 7–10, 1955).

Journals

JPA   *Journal of Personality Assessment,* a continuation of
JPT   *Journal of Projective Techniques,* itself continued from
RRE   Bruno Klopfer's *Rorschach Research Exchange*

Author's Note

ix **"simply having previous exposure"**: Gregory J. Meyer et al., *Rorschach Performance Assessment System: Administration, Coding, Interpretation, and Technical Manual* (Toledo, OH: Rorschach Performance Assessment System, 2011),
11. See chapter 22 below.

Introduction: Tea Leaves

1 **Victor Norris:** Caroline Hill, interview, January 2014.
4 **Any questions:** These are scripts taken from the standard Rorschach
manual of the time, instructing examiners how to deflect questions: ExCS
(1986), 69, quoted in Galison, 263–64.
6 **were "perverse":** Elizabeth Weil, "What Really Happened to Baby Johan?,"
Matter, February 2, 2015, medium.com/matter/what-really-happened-to
-baby-johan-88816c9c7ff5.

6 **One movie reviewer:** David DeWitt, "Talk About Sex. Have It. Repeat," *New York Times,* May 31, 2012.

8 **"spatial rhythm":** *PD,* 15.

8 **CeeLo Green remembered:** "Gnarls Barkley: Crazy," Blind website, www .blind.com/work/project/gnarls-barkley-crazy.

9 **"The method and the personality":** Walter Morgenthaler, "Preface to the Second Edition," in *PD,* 11.

9 **"a tall, lean, blond man":** Ellenberger, 191.

Chapter 1: All Becomes Movement and Life

11 **One late December morning:** This imagined scene is based on letters, photographs, and Rorschach's habits. Typical German-Swiss children's games: Reto Sorg, Robert Walser Center in Bern, personal communication, 2012.

13 **their ancestors:** Heini Roschach, 1437; Jörni Wiedenkeller, 1506; there are full details starting with Hans Roschach, b. 1556, and Balthasar Wiedenkeller, b. 1562 (HRA 1:3; Ellenberger, *CE,* 44).

14 **Hermann was born:** HRA 1:1.

14 **Ulrich did well:** WSM, quoting Anna and Ulrich's transcripts. Ulrich taught at the elementary school (ages seven to twelve) and *Realschule* (ages twelve to fourteen on the academic track leading to *Gymnasium,* for ages twelve to sixteen, which would then be followed by entry into a profession).

14 **Schaffhausen is a small:** Population 11,795 in 1880, roughly triple that today.

14 **"On the banks":** *Schaffhausen und der Rheinfall,* Europäische Wanderbilder 18 (Zurich: Orell Füssli, 1881), 3.

14 **"the spray fell thickly on us":** Mary Shelley, *Rambles in Germany and Italy in 1840, 1842, and 1843* (London: Edward Moxon, 1844), 1:51–52

14 **"A heavy mountain":** *Schaffhausen und der Rheinfall,* 28.

15 **The house was roomier:** This section from Anna R; WSM, citing interviews with Anna from 1960; Ellenberger, 175–77.

15 **"could look at something":** WSI Fanny Sauter.

16 **"I can still see this modest man":** Schwerz.

16 **a small compilation:** *Feldblumen: Gedichte für Herz und Gemüth* (Arbon: G. Rüdlinger, 1879), an anthology of local verse of a kind common at the time, with eight of the twenty-seven poems by Ulrich.

16 **a hundred-page "Outline":** HRA 1:7.

18 **symptoms more severe:** WSI Regineli. It is unclear what the disease was—in WSM, Wolfgang Schwarz conjectures Parkinson's or "a kind of encephalitis."

18 **When Ulrich died:** Ulrich's obituary attests: "He was not only a draftsman but also a philosopher, devoting much of his time to detailed consideration of the highest questions. . . . He had a true artist's spirit and would have probably found the greatest satisfaction in purely artistic work but did not have the means to pursue a general education and take study trips; he felt all too strongly bound by considerations of his family's material well-being. Despite his short time in school, self-study gave him a thorough base of knowledge and linked it to proficient creative ability. . . . The only thing Rorschach lacked was true self-assurance and artistic confidence, the abil-

ity to be nimble and sure in his outward demeanor; he did not know how to bring his knowledge and ability to fruition." Ulrich was "always ready to appreciate others' accomplishments; he was much too modest to recognize his own worth" (*Schaffhauser Nachrichten*, June 9, 1903).

19   **"I am afraid that"**: To Anna, August 31, 1911.

19   **"I think back"**: To Anna, January 31, 1910.

19   **"the Schaffhausen mind-set"**: To Anna, January 24, 1909.

Chapter 2: Klex

21   **Swiss-German fraternities**: WSM; WSI Theodor "Schlot" Müller and Kurt Bachtold; *100 Jahre Scaphusia: 1858–1958*, edited by the same Kurt Bachtold (Schaffhausen, 1958); *125 Jahre Scaphusia* (Schaffhausen, 1983); the Scaphusia log of its activities and 1903 scrapbook (HRA 1:2).

22   **Rorschach attended**: This section: Anna R; Schwerz; WSI Regineli and former schoolmates.

23   **a toothache**: *CE*, 133.

24   **"Women's Emancipation"**: HRA 1:2:1; see Blum/Witschi, 60.

25   **In one picture**: This picture shows Herbert Haug, a fellow Scaphusia member at the Schaffhausen *Gymnasium*, looking at a picture of a young woman while a black dog stares spookily at the viewer. Beneath the picture is a poem, which likewise suggests Haug's dreamy melancholy. He would drown a few years later, probably a suicide. (To Anna, October 31, 1906, and WSM.)

26   **Ernst Haeckel**: Robert J. Richards, *The Tragic Sense of Life: Ernst Haeckel and the Struggle over Evolutionary Thought* (Chicago: University of Chicago Press, 2008), 2–4; Philipp Blom, *The Vertigo Years: Europe, 1900–1914* (New York: Basic Books, 2008), 342. Haeckel also developed a wave theory of inheritance through the protoplasm, which would decisively influence Nietzsche's formulation of the will to power: "that life arose from the periodic vibrations stored within the minute material structures of the protoplasm . . . a thoroughly mechanical approach to heredity" (Robert Michael Brain, "The Pulse of Modernism: Experimental Physiology and Aesthetic Avant-Gardes circa 1900," *Studies in History and Philosophy of Science* 39.3 [2008]: 403–4 and notes).

26   **An aspiring landscape painter**: Irenäus Eibl-Eibesfeldt, "Ernst Haeckel: The Artist in the Scientist," in Haeckel, *Art Forms in Nature: The Prints of Ernst Haeckel* (Munich: Prestel, 1998), 19.

26   **Darwin praised Haeckel**: Richards, *Tragic Sense of Life*, 1, 262.

27   **visual vocabulary for Art Nouveau**: Olaf Breidbach, "Brief Instructions to Viewing Haeckel's Pictures," in Haeckel, *Art Forms*, 15.

27   **household showpiece**: The book was "brought out at every possible opportunity, presented, examined, even admired" by children and grandfathers alike (Richard P. Hartmann, preface to Haeckel, *Art Forms*, 7).

28   **the ultimate atheistic science**: Richards, *Tragic Sense of Life*, 385. He points out that biologists today have less faith in a personal God than scientists in any other fields: 5.5 percent, as opposed to 39.3 percent of elite scientists in general and 86 percent of American citizens, 94 percent if belief in a "higher power" counts. A survey from 1914 shows the same pattern.

28 **"Your misgivings":** From Haeckel, October 22, 1902.

28 **several people:** Anna R, 73; Olga R, 88; Morgenthaler, "Hermann Rorschach," in *PD*, 9; Ellenberger, 177. "This bold step of turning to a famous man for advice seems characteristic of Rorschach": *L*, 25n1. "It seems doubtful Rorschach would have put the entire choice of his future profession in the hands of a stranger. . . . Most of Rorschach's actions as revealed by his correspondence seem deliberate and premeditated": WSM. In 1962, the Ernst Haeckel House in Jena, Germany, told Schwarz that no letter from Rorschach to Haeckel could be found.

Chapter 3: I Want to Read People

29 **graduating from high school:** Rorschach graduated fourth in his class and was disappointed in his results, but his teacher told him he hadn't spoken up enough—Rorschach's friend Walter Im Hof, an outgoing good talker and future lawyer, had outperformed the quietly good listener and future psychiatrist (WSI Walter Im Hof; transcript, HRA 1:1).

29 **French lessons:** WSM.

29 **straight to Paris:** Anna to Wolfgang Schwarz, response to queries, ca. 1960, WSA.

29 **"nowhere stupider":** To Anna, February 18, 1906.

29 **private diary:** HRA 1:6:4.

29 **"Everyone knows"** and other quotes: To family, August 13, 1904.

29 **"They like to talk":** To Anna, May 26, 1908.

30 **the Dukhobors:** Orlando Figes, *Natasha's Dance: A Cultural History of Russia* (New York: Picador, 2002), 307; Rosamund Bartlett, *Tolstoy: A Russian Life* (Boston: Houghton Mifflin, 2011), 271; Andrew Donskov, *Sergej Tolstoy and the Doukhobors* (Ottawa: Slavic Research Group, University of Ottawa, 1998), 4–5; V. O. Pashchenko and T. V. Nagorna, "Tolstoy and the Doukhobors: Main Stages of Relations in the Late 19th and Early 20th Century" (2006), Doukhobor Genealogy Website, www.doukhobor.org/Pashchenko-Nagorna.html, last accessed August 2016.

30 **In 1895, Tolstoy called:** An 1899 visitor found that though Tolstoy "scorn[ed] discipleship" more than anyone, a group nicknamed "the College of Cardinals" had gathered around him: Vladimir Chertkov, Pavel Biryukov, and Ivan Tregubov (James Mavor, *My Windows on the Street of the World* [London and Toronto: J. M. Dent and Sons, 1923], 2:70; cf. Chertkov, Biryukov, and Tregubov's pamphlet *Appeal for Help* [London, 1897]). All three were soon kicked out of the country; Tregubov would return in 1905, where he fomented resistance before the 1917 Revolution and served in the Commissariat of Agriculture afterward, continuing to try to protect the Dukhobors' interests (Heather J. Coleman, *Russian Baptists and Spiritual Revolution, 1905–1929* [Bloomington: Indiana University Press, 2005], 200). He survived under Stalin until 1931.

In his diary (HRA 1:6:4), Rorschach first mentions Tregubov in a political context: "Dijon Socialist Workers Party. Evening meeting at Tréguboff

(Doukhobor)." Following quotes: To Anna, April 14, 1909, January 21, 1907; Anna R, 73.

31 **apparently mastering:** Olga R, 88–89; Ellenberger, 197.

31 **"I want to know":** Anna R, 73.

31 **"I never again want to read just books":** To Anna, February 19, 1906.

31 **go to university:** Matriculation October 20, 1904, registration number 15174.

31 **showed up in Zurich:** This section: Schwerz; to family, October 23, 1904; visit to Weinplatz, November 2012.

32 **"went to two art exhibits":** To Anna, October 22, 1904.

32 **an extra in the student theater:** Recalled by his son, Wadim (Blum/Witschi, 85).

33 **the Künstlergütli:** Details from Baedeker's *Switzerland* (1905 and 1907).

33 **Rorschach took the lead:** a recollection from Walter von Wyss, in Ellenberger, 211.

33 **"I was the only one":** To Anna, May 23, 1906.

34 **"the large number of revolutionary-minded young foreigners":** Including Herzen, Bakunin, Plekhanov, Radek, Kropotkin, Karl Liebknecht, and a young Benito Mussolini (Peter Loewenberg, "The Creation of a Scientific Community: The Burghölzli," in *Fantasy and Reality in History* [New York: Oxford, 1995], 50–51).

34 **the debates in Little Russia:** "Es wurde heiß debattiert und kalt gesessen," quoted in Verena Stadler-Labhart, "Universität Zürich," in *Rosa Luxemburg,* ed. Kristine von Soden, BilderLeseBuch (Berlin: Elefanten Press, 1995), 58.

34 **university students:** Stadler-Labhart, "Universität Zürich," 56, 63n2; Blum/Witschi, 74; Universität Zürich, "Geschichte," n.d., accessed July 8, 2016, www.uzh.ch/about/portrait/history.html.

35 **"It was simply unthinkable":** Deirdre Bair, *Jung: A Biography* (Boston: Little, Brown, 2003), 76. Emma, despite having served as her father's assistant for years, was sent to Paris for a year to be an upper-class au pair for her father's business friends and to pursue appropriate cultural interests in her spare time. Cf. Stadler-Labhart, "Universität Zürich," 56–57; John Kerr, *A Most Dangerous Method: The Story of Jung, Freud, and Sabina Spielrein* (New York: Knopf, 1993), 34.

35 **"semi-Asian invaders":** Stadler-Labhart, "Universität Zürich"; Blum/Witschi, 62–63.

35 **"the Christmas angel":** *Christchindli,* a little girl with a bell who flies to every house and delivers presents.

35 **presumably his looks:** Rorschach's roommate, Schwerz, who preserved the anecdote fifty years later, left such attractions out of his account, writing only that the "artistically inclined aesthete Rorschach" was interested in the Russian beauty and that up in their room it was "Tolstoy's letter [that] was admired by all." No letter from Tolstoy survives, but an autographed photograph of him was one of Rorschach's prized possessions.

35 **Some truly were revolutionaries . . . others were "thoroughly bourgeois":** Schwerz.

35 **Sabina Spielrein:** Bair, *Jung,* 89–91; Kerr, *Most Dangerous Method*; Alexan-

der Etkind, *Eros of the Impossible: The History of Psychoanalysis in Russia* (Boulder, CO: Westview, 1997). Spielrein and Rorschach likely met, since they had the same adviser, he hung out with Russians, and Spielrein "attended classes daily, was punctual everywhere, and felt honor bound to participate fully" (Loewenberg, "Creation," 73, quoting Jung).

35   **Olga Vasilyevna Shtempelin:** Штемпелин. The German spelling, "Stempelin," which has an initial *Sht-* sound, has often been brought over into English, where it wrongly suggests a *St-* pronunciation.

In 1910, Olga signed her middle name "Vil'gemovna" on a notarized document giving her consent to be married; in Hermann's correspondence with Swiss authorities about the formalities of his marriage, he likewise gave it as "Wilhelmowna" (I thank Rita Signer for this information). However, in the family tree Rorschach made later and many other Swiss documents, her middle name is given as "Wassiljewna."

36   **a perk:** According to Hermann and Olga's daughter Elisabeth (Blum/Witschi, 73–74 and 126n139).

36   **"My Russian friends":** To Anna, September 2, 1906. His letters mention her by name for the first time in 1908.

36   **"Dear Count Tolstoy":** HRA 2:1:15:25. Translated and included here by the kind permission of Yuri Kudinov of the State Leo Tolstoy Museum in Moscow.

37   **far from alone:** The book has not yet been written about the influence of Russian culture in the West before World War I. Russian novels and plays were astonishing readers from Woolf to Hamsun to Freud; Russian ballet was the toast of Paris; the country's physical immensity and combination of spiritual depth and political backwardness inspired awe and anxiety across the continent; "Tolstoyans" spread through Europe, opening vegetarian restaurants and preaching Christian brotherhood. The long list of indispensable novels on the subject begins with Joseph Conrad's *Under Western Eyes,* set in Russia and Switzerland around 1907.

Chapter 4: Extraordinary Discoveries and Warring Worlds

38   **The professor's compact silhouette:** Description by Auguste Forel, quoted in Rolf Mösli, *Eugen Bleuler: Pionier der Psychiatrie* (Zurich: Römerhof-Verlag, 2012), 20–21; Bair, *Jung,* 58; see note on p. 335 for Eugen Bleuler.

38   **Another lecturer:** Bair, *Jung,* 97–98; see note on p. 335 for Carl Jung.

39   **Zurich in the first decade:** The best single source on the rise of modern psychiatry, helpfully centered on Zurich, is Kerr's masterful *A Most Dangerous Method* (a.k.a. *A Dangerous Method*), whose twenty-two-page "Bibliographical Essay" is a library in itself. Henri Ellenberger, *The Discovery of the Unconscious* (New York: Basic Books, 1970), is still the most detailed, in-depth study. George Makari's *Revolution in Mind: The Creation of Psychoanalysis* (New York: HarperCollins, 2008) is a good, more recent general history.

39   **"medicine in Chekhov's day":** Janet Malcolm, *Reading Chekhov: A Critical Journey* (New York: Random House, 2001), 116.

40   **351 copies:** Sigmund Freud, *The Interpretation of Dreams* (John Wiley, 1961),

xx. In contrast, Théodore Flournoy's major work on the unconscious, also published in late 1899, went into a third edition within three months and received rave reviews throughout Europe and America in both academic journals and the popular press (*From India to the Planet Mars: A Case of Multiple Personality with Imaginary Languages* [Princeton: Princeton University Press, 1995], xxvii–xxxi). For a revisionist take on the "legend" that Freud's *Interpretation of Dreams* was largely ignored, see Ellenberger, *Discovery*, 783–84.

41   **"better known locally for the brothel"**: Kerr, *Dangerous Method*, 40.

41   **Eugen Bleuler**: Ellenberger, *Discovery;* Bair, *Jung;* Kerr, *Most Dangerous Method;* Makari, *Revolution in Mind;* Mösli, *Eugen Bleuler;* Daniel Hell, Christian Scharfetter, and Arnulf Möller, *Eugen Bleuler, Leben und Werk* (Bern: Huber, 2001); Christian Scharfetter, ed., *Eugen Bleuler, 1857–1939* (Zurich: Juris Druck, 2001); Sigmund Freud and Eugen Bleuler, *"Ich bin zuversichtlich, wir erobern bald die Psychiatrie": Briefwechsel, 1904–1937*, ed. Michael Schröter (Basel: Schwabe, 2012; hereafter cited as "F/B"). Bleuler has usually been described as somewhat overbearing and insufferable, mostly because that was how Jung saw him (though Kerr, *Most Dangerous Method*, 43, is more balanced). As more material on Bleuler is published, this view is starting to seem slanted.

41   **"We know now"**: Quoted in Loewenburg, "Creation," 47, emended.

41   **"The great mass"**: Kraepelin's textbook *Einführung in die psychiatrische Klinik*, 4th ed. 1921, quoted in Christian Müller, *Abschied vom Irrenhaus: Aufsätze zur Psychiatriegeschichte* (Bern: Huber, 2005), 145. Müller goes on: "What is it about this quote from the great, uncontested master of psychiatry that bothers me? Is it the style, the word choice? The brutality with which he labels a reality that to him was completely objective? This quote highlights the powerful transformation that has come to pass in our relation to human suffering as a whole. We have become more sensitive."

42   **six to eight hundred patients**: Mösli says 655 patients (*Eugen Bleuler*, 114), Makari "over eight hundred" (*Revolution in Mind*, 183).

42   **as an adjective**: Eugen Bleuler, "The Prognosis of Dementia Praecox," in *The Clinical Roots of the Schizophrenia Concept: Translations of Seminal European Contributions on Schizophrenia*, ed. John Cutting and Michael Shepherd (Cambridge, UK: Cambridge University Press, 1987), 59. One recent writer says that simply eliminating the term *dementia* played no small role in giving sufferers and their families hope for a cure (Daniel Hell, "Herkunft, Kindheit und Jugend," in Mösli, *Eugen Bleuler*, 25–26).

43   **One of Bleuler's assistants**: Abraham Arden Brill, quoted in Mösli, *Eugen Bleuler*, 153.

43   **"The way they looked at the patient"**: Brill quoted in Loewenberg, "Creation," 65–66.

44   **Carl Jung**: The literature on Jung is enormous and blazing with controversies; Sonu Shamdasani's *Jung Stripped Bare by His Biographers, Even* (London: Kamac, 2005) is a book about controversies about *biographies* of Jung. Kerr's *A Most Dangerous Method* is the best place to start; for an encapsulation of Jung's personality it is hard to beat the paragraph beginning: "It is important to emphasize the almost Rabelaisian nature of [Jung's] gifts"

(53). See also Bair, *Jung;* Sonu Shamdasani, *Jung and the Making of Modern Psychology: The Dream of a Science* (Cambridge, UK: Cambridge University Press, 2003).

44 **"complexes"**: As Jung explained in 1934: "The word 'complex' in its psychological sense has passed into common speech both in German and in English. Everyone knows nowadays that people 'have complexes.' What is not so well known, though far more important theoretically, is that complexes can *have us*" (*Collected Works of C. G. Jung* [Princeton: Princeton University Press, 1960–90], 8:95–96).

44 **"unprecedented and extraordinary"**: Kerr, *Most Dangerous Method,* 59; Makari calls it a "bombshell" (*Revolution in Mind,* 193).

44 **Independent of Freud**: At least in Jung's self-interested retelling—Jung had in fact read *The Interpretation of Dreams* by 1900.

45 **"that was how"**: Bleuler in 1910, quoted by Michael Schröter, introduction to F/B, 16.

45 **"opened up a new world"**: Ibid., 15.

45 **"Dear Honored Colleague!"**: F/B, letter 2B.

45 **asking for tips**: "Although I realized on first reading that your book on dreams was correct, I only rarely succeed in interpreting one of my own dreams . . . My colleagues, as well as my wife, a born psychologist, cannot crack the nut. So you will surely forgive me if I turn to the Master himself." Freud obliged, and Bleuler sent more. On November 5, 1905, sitting at his typewriter, he followed Freud's instructions and tried to free-write: "Will anything come out? . . . In my associations, too, only old things come up. Doesn't that contradict Freud's theory in a way, in his sense. The principle is undoubtedly correct. Do all the details apply in every case? Don't individual differences matter? . . . It's stupid for me to have doubts, with my limited experience. But it's also stupid that I can interpret my dreams so rarely. Stalemate. (Distracted by the sound of the rain, thoughts of upcoming visitors.)"

"If only I knew," Bleuler concluded rather sadly, "how I'm supposed to write more unconsciously" (F/B, letters 5B, 8B). The mail-order analysis quickly trailed off.

45 **"An absolutely stunning acknowledgment"**: To Fliess, quoted in Schröter, introduction to F/B, 15. "I am confident": F/B, letter 12F.

46 **"two warring worlds"**: *The Freud/Jung Letters: The Correspondence between Sigmund Freud and C. G. Jung,* ed. William McGuire (Princeton: Princeton University Press, 1974), hereafter cited as "F/J," 3F.

47 **It was Jung**: "Freud's Theory of Hysteria: A Reply to Aschaffenburg," a seven-page blast of superficial praise and cool superiority (Jung, *Collected Works,* 4:3–9); Jung vents his real feelings in F/J, letter 83J. Following quotes: F/J, letter 2J, 219J, 222J, 272J.

47 **"I am the city of Naples"**: This patient, a dressmaker, was one of Jung's favorite examples (*Collected Works,* 2:173–74; *Memories, Dreams, Reflections* (New York: Vintage, 1989).

47 **Jung's accusation**: Bair, *Jung,* 98, paraphrasing Jung, *Memories,* 114; see 683n8.

48 **running a large hospital**: Bleuler's key essay was published only in 1908— ten years after his return to the Burghölzli and more than twenty after start-

ing at Rheinau—and his celebrated book on schizophrenia appeared in 1911. He had devoted his time and energy to his patients and to improving conditions at the Burghölzli (doubling its staff, tripling its admissions, increasing its budget tenfold): "Publicizing his discovery took back seat to the problem of running the asylum" (Kerr, *Most Dangerous Method*, 43).

48 **"twenty years"**: Bair, *Jung*, 97.

48 **never met Rorschach**: A 1957 interview, in *C. G. Jung Speaking: Interviews and Encounters* (Princeton: Princeton University Press, 1977), 329.

49 **"in Vienna"**: To Morgenthaler, November 11, 1919. The 1916 lecture (see chap. 8 below) remarks that psychoanalysis is indicated for fewer types of illness now—"even Freud has gradually limited the indications somewhat"—and that there is usually no need to dig all the way down to childhood to cure a neurotic.

49 **word association test**: At one point, Rorschach set aside sixty francs, a third of all the money he had, for a watch with a 1/5-second indicator "to use in psychological experiments," no doubt the word association test (to Anna, July 8, 1909). It came in handy within a month, when a man discharged from the army was brought in for evaluation after stealing a horse. Rorschach used the test to establish a precise diagnosis and find him not legally accountable for his actions (*CE*, 170–75).

49 **"fascinated by archaic thought"**: Olga R, 90.

49 **"For this reason"**: Jung, *Collected Works*, 3:162.

49 **on the pineal gland**: "On the Pathology and Operability of Tumors of the Pineal Gland" was Rorschach's only essay that the editor intentionally excluded from Rorschach's *Collected Essays*, as "almost entirely unrelated to his other work and too long to be included" (*CE*, 11).

50 **none of these prejudices**: Mösli, *Eugen Bleuler*, 174. Bleuler worked closely with his wife and always credited her (and his mother's) psychological insight as indispensable.

50 **"if an old person"**: To Anna, July 7, 1908.

50 **pledge of abstinence**: To Anna, May 23, 1906.

51 **Johannes Neuwirth**: "The Association Experiment, Free Association, and Hypnosis in Removing an Amnesia" (*CE*, 196–205). Rorschach calls the soldier J.N.; expanded into pseudonym for readability.

Chapter 5: A Path of One's Own

53 **"Real work with real patients"**: To Anna, May 23, 1906.

54 **"The doctor meets with"**: To Anna, September 2, 1908.

54 **"two months busy being extraverted"**: To Hans Burri, July 16, 1920.

54 **"I know too many people"**: To Anna, September 2, 1906.

54 **"Berlin with its millions"**: Ibid.

54 **"I'm in total solitude"**: To Anna, October 31, 1906.

55 **"a little stone"**: To Anna, November 10, 1906.

55 **the modern metropolis**: See Peter Fritzsche's evocative *Reading Berlin 1900* (Cambridge, MA: Harvard University Press, 1996), esp. 17, 109, 192.

55 **"cacophonous blowing"**: Quoted in ibid., 109, from Walter Kiaulehn,

whom Fritzsche calls "Berlin's great twentieth-century chronicler" (17). Much of Fritzsche's book is suggestive for the Rorschach, e.g.: "The depiction of the city in an endless series of sharp, visually compelling images" meant that "men, women, and children, as well as newcomers, proletarians, and tourists, all imagined the city in different ways" (130–31).

55 **"In a few years"**: To Paul, December 5, 1906.

56 **"cold" and "boring"**: To Anna, October 31, 1906.

56 **the society "despicable"**: To Paul, December 5, 1906.

56 **the whole experience "idiotic"**: To Anna, January 21, 1907.

56 **"worship the uniform"**: To Anna, January 21, 1907; on the Captain of Köpenick, see Fritzsche, *Reading Berlin,* 160.

56 **"the land of unlimited possibilities"**: To Anna, January 21, 1907.

57 **"You can see and understand more"**: To Anna, November 16, 1908.

57 **"retracing our father's steps"**: To Anna, January 21, 1907.

57 **No one rereads *War and Peace:*** To Anna, January 25, 1909.

57 **"disappointed and a bit depressed"**: Olga R, 89.

57 **"Bern isn't bad"**: To Anna, May 5, 1907.

57 **Anna jumped at the chance:** Her stay in Russia was her own decision: Hermann had pushed for a governess position in England, preferring it over Russia as "a school for character, lifestyle, and insight into human nature," but Anna turned it down; a few months later, she eagerly accepted the job in Russia. (To Anna, September 17, 1907, and January 31 and February 6, 1908.)

58 **"When I read your first letter"**: To Anna, December 9, 1908.

58 **Russian paintings:** Rorschach specifically mentions a "very beautiful gray picture" called *Christ* by Ivan Nikolayevich Kramskoi, which he had hung above his desk in Bern; and Russian folklorist and Romantic modernist Viktor Vasnetsov's *God the Father,* which hung in his room. He also mentioned wanting a postcard of *Above Eternal Peace* by Isaac Levitan, master of the so-called mood landscape.

58 **"Do it"**: To Anna, November 16, 1908.

58 **"I'm enclosing one of my photos"**: To Anna, October 21, 1909. The next year he would write, "I've finally learned how to take photographs properly. I've enclosed some of our best ones, with descriptions. Tell me how you like them. How's your photography coming?" (August 3, 1910).

58 **"I could come to him"**: ARL, 2.

58 **"meat market" of Berlin streetwalkers:** To Anna, October 31, 1906.

58 **"Shockingly many men see women"**: To Anna, September 17, 1907.

59 **"The stork question"**: To Anna, June 15, 1908.

59 **"You will probably know more"**: To Anna, November 16, 1908.

59 **"see a country only when"**: To Anna, December 9, 1908.

59 **"You only learn to love"**: To Anna, September 17, 1907.

59 **"You have to write me"**: To Anna, May 26, 1908.

59 **"You know, Annali"**: To Anna, May 26, 1908.

60 **at age four:** Fut, 180.

60 **"My love"**: HRA 2:1:48. This is the consistent tone of the surviving letters; most were destroyed by Olga or their children, for privacy (HRA catalog note).

60 "She doesn't feel well": To Anna, November 27, 1908.
61 "Four people died on me": To Anna, September 2, 1908.
61 "I've had it up to here": To Anna, December 9, 1908.
61 "finally, finally! be done": To Anna, November 27, 1908.
61 his professional options were limited: Ellenberger, 180.
61 He hoped he could earn enough: To Anna, January 25, 1909.
61 "If science is not very far advanced here": To Anna, early July, 1909.
62 "I like Russian life": To Anna, April 14, 1909.
62 "This waiting!": To Anna, April 2, 1909.
62 "Kazan is not a large city": To Anna, April 2, 1909.
62 Hermann helped Olga study: To Anna, April 14, 1909.
62 "lacking in understanding": To Anna, early July 1909.
62 "and obviously we didn't want to": Ibid.
63 "No human society treats women": To Anna, May 26, 1908.
63 "trying to prove that Woman": To Anna, December 22, 1909.
63 "it *is* true and it *remains* true": Ibid.
63 "a doctor or engineer": Ibid.
64 one last maddening incident: To Anna, August 27, 1909.

Chapter 6: Little Inkblots Full of Shapes

65 These were a few: *CE,* 115 (another doctor's patient), 112–13, 118.
65 collection of psychiatric cases: HRA 4:2:1.
66 Münsterlingen Clinic: StATG 9'10 1.1 (reports), 1.6 (brochure), 1.7 (album).
67 spoke German and Russian: To Anna, September 24, 1909.
67 "The director is very lazy": Ibid.
67 "It's totally natural": To Anna, October 26, 1909.
67 "At last": To Anna, September 24, 1909.
67 "a very nice little town": Olga to Anna, August 3, 1910.
68 the same route: Mikhail Shishkin, *Auf den Spuren von Byron und Tolstoi: Eine literarische Wanderung* (Zurich: Rotpunkt, 2012). Olga R, 89: "He loved Münsterlingen and felt utterly happy there, almost like a king in his two-room 'home of his own' with a view of his beloved Lake Constance that he enjoyed in all kinds of weather."
68 "Lola and I are doing well": To Anna, November 14, 1910.
68 "There is a fair": Olga and Hermann to Anna, August 3, 1910.
69 a large cargo ship: 1913 Annual Report, p. 11.
69 her "perfect" gift: To Anna, late December 1910. "Of all the Russian writers," Hermann wrote, "the one I most like reading is Gogol, because of his beautiful language."
69 "to give her something": Ibid.
70 sent his sister Goethe's *Faust*: To Anna, December 22, 1909.
70 art therapy: Blum/Witschi, 92–93; John M. MacGregor, *The Discovery of the Art of the Insane* (Princeton University Press, 1989), 187 and n8. At a sanitarium near Berlin "sports, gardening, and art therapy were in full operation" in 1908, and the patients had pets, including a donkey (Ellenberger, *Discovery of the Unconscious,* 799).

70   **got hold of a monkey:** Ellenberger, 192.

70   **from a troupe of traveling players:** Urs Germann, personal communication, 2014. The name "Fipps" survives only in a handwritten caption to a photograph of the monkey: StATG 9'10 1.7.

70   **eleven articles:** Three were short notes on sexual imagery he had come across in his reading or practice, simply published for the record; others were psychoanalytical essays applying Freudian theory directly, such as "Failed Sublimation and a Case of Forgetting a Name," "The Theme of Clocks and Time in a Neurotic's Life," and "A Neurotic's Choice of Friends," which explored the unconscious elements at work in the choice. One article was forensic along Jungian lines, using the word association test: "The Theft of a Horse in a Fugue State" (all in *CE*).

71   **"For a period":** Roland Kuhn, "Über das Leben . . . ," StATG 9'10 8.4. He praises Rorschach's essays and dissertation for being "well written and interesting, and particularly attentive to the human qualities in people, skillfully portraying their personalities and destinies and highlighting their abilities."

71   **a patient's drawing:** "Analytical Remarks on a Painting by a Schizophrenic" (*CE*, 178–81).

71   **about a wall painter:** "Analysis of a Schizophrenic Drawing" (*CE*, 188–94).

72   **would take the patient's hand:** WSI Mrs. Gehring (first name not recorded) .

72   **"I'm glad":** To Paul, December 8, 1914.

72   **"Mother gave me nothing":** To Anna, May 23, 1911.

72   **"despite everything he went through":** To Anna, November 14, 1910.

72   **Swiss and German newspapers:** Rorschach's work as a columnist—"his desire to communicate, to formulate ideas, and to take up important matters of the day"—was "truly unusual" (Müller, *Abschied vom Irrenhaus*, 107, 103).

72   **"Russian Transformations":** *März* [March], issue 12 (1909); HRA 6:1. "The new Russian society is undergoing rapid transformations. Like the individual during puberty. First, the recent political activities; then, after the onset of reaction, persistent and aggressive political repression—repression in the psychological sense . . ."

73   **Andreyev was considered:** His plays were widely performed and made into movies, including *He Who Gets Slapped* (1924). "The Thought" is in Leonid Andreyev, *Visions* (San Diego: Harcourt Brace Jovanovich, 1987), 31–78.

73   **"This writing for the papers":** To Anna, early July 1909.

73   **"his constantly moving":** Olga R, 94; translated in the Appendix.

73   **"fanatical":** Rita Signer and Christian Müller, "Was liest ein Psychiater zu Beginn des 20. Jahrhunderts?" *Schweizer Archiv für Neurologie und Psychiatrie* 156.6 (2005): 282–83. His excerpts of Jung's *Symbols and Transformations of the Libido* ran to 128 pages; in his studies of sects, mythology, and religion, he took notes on books such as Paul Max Alexander Ehrenreich's *General Mythology and Its Ethnological Foundations* and *Myths and Legends of the Primitive Peoples of South America*, Ludwig Keller's *The Reformation and the Older Reform Parties*, Karl Rudolf Hagenbach's seven-volume *Lectures on Church History*, and Jacob Burckhardt's *The Civilization of the Renaissance in Italy*.

74   **Justinus Kerner:** Ellenberger, *Discovery*; Karl-Ludwig Hoffmann and Christmut Praeger, "Bilder aus Klecksen: Zu den Klecksographien von

Justinus Kerner," in *Justinus Kerner: Nur wenn man von Geistern spricht,* ed. Andrea Berger-Fix (Stuttgart: Thienemann, 1986), 125–52; Friedrich Welt-zien, *Fleck—Das Bild der Selbsttätigkeit: Justinus Kerner und die Klecksografie als experimentelle Bildpraxis zwischen Ästhetik und Naturwissenschaft* (Göttingen: Vandenhoeck und Ruprecht, 2011).

74 **botulism, the bacterial food poisoning:** Erbguth and Naumann, "Histori-cal Aspects of Botulinum Toxin: Justinus Kerner (1786–1862) and the 'Sau-sage Poison,'" *Neurology* 53 (1999): 1850–53.

74 **"curiously gifted":** Afterword to a 1918 edition of Kerner's early novel *The Travel-Shadows of Lux the Shadow-Player,* quoted in Kerner, *Die Reiseschatten* (Stuttgart: Steinkopf, 1964), 25.

74 *Klecksographien:* Project Gutenberg, gutenberg.spiegel.de/buch/4394/1. The opening stanza of the first poem is typical: "Everyone carries his death in-side him— / When all outside is laughing and bright / You roam today in the light of the morn / And tomorrow in the shadow of night."

75 **"daguerreotypes":** Kerner to Ottilie Wildermuth, June 1854 (quoted in Weltzien, *Fleck,* 274): "In some ways, the images remind me of the new pho-tographic pictures, even though one does not need a special apparatus for them and they rely on a very old material: ink.... The strangest images and figures are formed entirely from themselves, without any contribution from me, like the pictures in a photographic camera. You can neither influence nor guide them. You can never bring forth what you want; you often get the exact opposite of what you expected. It is remarkable that these pictures often resemble those from the bygone eras of the dawn of mankind.... For me they are like daguerreotypes of the invisible world, even though, since they are tied to the blackness of the ink, they can only make visible the lower spirits. But I would be very surprised if the higher spirits too, the spir-its of light from the middle realm and heaven, were unable to arrange the chemical processes of photography in their own way so as to shine forth in it. What are those spirits, in the end, if not wanderers in light?"

75 **many historians:** Ellenberger, 196; E. H. Gombrich, *Art and Illusion: A Study in the Psychology of Pictorial Representation* (New York: Pantheon, 1960); H. W. Janson, "The 'Image Made by Chance' in Renaissance Thought," in *De Artibus Opuscula XL: Essays in Honor of Erwin Panofsky* (New York: New York University Press, 1961), 1:254–66; "Chronological and geographico-cultural proximity makes a direct link more than likely" (Dario Gamboni, *Poten-tial Images: Ambiguity and Indeterminacy in Modern Art* [London: Reaktion, 2002], 58). Olga R, 90, says that her husband knew these images by Kerner from early on, but she described them in the context of imagination, not perception (see chap. 10 below for why this is misleading): "He had always been interested in 'imagination,' and viewed it as the 'divine spark' in hu-manity.... It was like a half-conscious premonition inside him that maybe these 'accidental forms' could serve as a bridge to *test the imagination.*"

75 **Rorschach was asked:** From and to Hans Burri, May 21 and May 28, 1920. These were personal letters, written before the publication of the test; Ror-schach had no reason to lie about Kerner's influence.

The Rorschach test is sometimes also linked with graphology, but Rorschach knew nothing about graphology as late as 1920 and was not very interested when told about it (WSI Martha Schwarz-Gantner).

75 **child's game:** Jung, *Memories,* 18. Henry David Thoreau, *The Journal, 1837–1861* (New York: New York Review of Books, 2009), February 14, 1840, with a page of inkblots slipped in, unpublished but preserved in the Morgan Library, New York. WSI Irena Minkovska.

76 **used before:** Alfred Binet and Victor Henri, "La psychologie individuelle," *L'Année Psychologique* 2 (1895–96): 411–65, quoted in Franziska Baumgarten-Tramer, "Zur Geschichte des Rorschachtests," *Schweizer Archiv für Neurologie und Psychiatrie* 50 (1942): 1–13, 1; cf. Galison, 259–60.

76 **It reached Russia as well:** F. E. Rybakov, *Atlas dlya ekspiremental'no-psikhologicheskogo issledovaniya lichnosti* (Moscow: Sytin, 1910), excerpted in Baumgarten-Tramer, "Zur Geschichte," 6–7.

76 **an American, Guy Montrose Whipple:** See his *Manual of Mental and Physical Tests* (Baltimore: Warwick and York, 1910), chap. 11, "Tests of Imagination and Invention," Test 45: Ink-Blots.

76 **Binet's own inspiration—Leonardo da Vinci:** Baumgarten-Tramer, "Zur Geschichte," 8–9, quotes Leonardo's "Treatise," speculating that Binet got the idea from this passage. The Leonardo scene was fictionalized by Dmitri Merejkovski in his well-known novel *The Romance of Leonardo da Vinci* (1902; repr., New York: Random House, 1931), 168, which Hermann and Olga read together (Ellenberger, 198, quoting the scene). George V. N. Dearborn, "Notes on the Discernment of Likeness and Unlikeness," *Journal of Philosophy, Psychology, and Scientific Methods* 7.3 (1910): 57.

77 **early blots:** HRA 3:3:3; WSI Mrs. Gehring.

Chapter 7: Hermann Rorschach Feels His Brain Being Sliced Apart

78 **"In my first clinical semester":** Rorschach's dissertation (*CE,* 105–149), 108–109. Quotes and examples in this chapter are from his dissertation unless noted.

81 **Robert Vischer:** "On the Optical Sense of Form" (1873), in *Empathy, Form, and Space,* ed. Harry Francis Mallgrave and Eleftherios Ikonomou (Santa Monica, CA: Getty Center for the History of Art and the Humanities, 1994), quotes from 90, 92, 98, 104, 117, emended in places. See editors' introduction to Ibid.; Irving Massey, *The Neural Imagination* (Austin: University of Texas Press, 2009), esp. "Nineteenth-Century Psychology, 'Empathy,' and the Origins of Cubism," 29–39. Carol R. Wenzel-Rideout, in a diligent dissertation, discovered no direct link between Rorschach and Vischer's theory of empathy but convincing circumstantial evidence of his familiarity with the literature, and "at the very least a strong kinship" between their ideas ("Rorschach and the History of Art: On the Parallels between the Form-Perception Test and the Writings of Worringer and Wölfflin," PsyD diss. [Rutgers University, 2005], 199–207; 70–74 are on Worringer).

82 **"gift for entering":** Richard Holmes, "John Keats Lives!," *New York Review of Books,* November 7, 2013.

83 **a medical student:** Massey, *Neural Imagination,* xii and 186–89, reading

Keats's poem "Ode to Psyche" as a fable of neuroscience that advocates for Psyche's place in the Pantheon and evokes such neurological details as dendrite brain cells ("the wreath'd trellis of a working brain") and neuroplasticity ("branched thoughts, new grown with pleasant pain").

83 **Since Freud wanted:** He told André Breton in 1937 that "the superficial aspect of dreams, what I call the manifest dream, holds no interest for me. I have been concerned with the 'latent content' which can be derived from the manifest dream by psychoanalytical interpretation" (letter, December 8, 1937, quoted in Mark Polizzotti, *Revolution of the Mind: The Life of André Breton* [Boston: Black Widow Press, 2009], 406, cf. 347–48).

84 **Karl Albert Scherner:** 1825–89. Freud especially appreciated Scherner's attention to wish fulfillment, experiences from the day before the dream, and erotic longing as the substance transformed by the dream (Vischer, "On the Optical Sense," 92; Freud, *Interpretation of Dreams,* 83, 346, passim). One recent scholar calls Scherner "an interesting but mysterious figure, heavily buried under the sands of intellectual history," even though "Scherner has by far the most justified claim to being Freud's major forerunner, taking what was primarily an aesthetic theory and making it the basis of his dream psychology" (Massey, *Neural Imagination,* 37, and Irving Massey, "Freud before Freud: K. A. Scherner (1825–1889)," *Centennial Review* 34.4 [1990]: 567–76).

84 *Abstraction and Empathy:* Wilhelm Worringer, trans. Michael Bullock (1953; repr., Chicago: Ivan Dee, 1997). Rudolf Arnheim called *Abstraction and Empathy* "one of the most influential documents in art theory of the new century," whose effect "upon the modern movement was prompt and profound" (*New Essays on the Psychology of Art* [Berkeley: University of California Press, 1986], 50, 51).

84 **no more valid or more aesthetic:** Worringer takes as representative Theodor Lipps (1851–1914), the father of the "scientific" psychological theory of empathy, who stripped away Vischer's mystical, pantheistic overtones and defined empathy simply as "objectified self-enjoyment." For Lipps, reality distortion was "negative empathy," a.k.a. "ugly." Worringer rightly counters that distortions of reality give other cultures, other individuals, the same "happiness and satisfaction which the beauty of organic-vital form affords us" (*Abstraction and Empathy,* 17).

85 **"valuable parallel":** "A Contribution to the Study of Psychological Types" (1913), Jung, *Collected Works,* 6:504–5. In *Psychological Types* Jung devotes an entire chapter to Worringer.

85 **proposed five ideas:** October 17, 1910; Ellenberger, 181; Akavia, 25ff.

85 *Reflexhalluzination:* The German psychiatrist Karl Ludwig Kahlbaum, who coined the term *paranoia* (F/J, 29n10), also created this term in the 1860s; it has always been translated literally.

87 **John Mourly Vold:** 1850–1907; *Über den Traum: Experimental-psychologische Untersuchungen,* 2 vols. (Leipzig: J. A. Barth, 1910–12). "One can hardly imagine two dream theories so totally opposed to each other": Ellenberger, 200–201; Akavia, 27–29.

87 **stepping on the foot:** HRA 3:4:1, dated March 18–19, 1911. The patient was named Brauchli.

87   **forced to drastically shorten:** To Bleuler, May 26, 1912, July 6, 1912, July 16, 1912; *L,* 120n3. Rorschach's essay "Reflex Hallucinations and Symbolism" (1912) contains material deleted from the dissertation linking it with psychoanalysis (*CE*; Ellenberger, 182; Akavia, 29).

Chapter 8: The Darkest and Most Elaborate Delusions

88   **In 1895:** "Zwei schweizerische Sektenstifter (Binggeli–Unternährer): Eine psychoanalytische Studie" [Two Swiss sect-founders (Binggeli–Unternährer): A psychoanalytic study], published in Freud's journal of psychoanalysis and culture, *Imago* 13 (1927): 395–441, and as a fifty-page book (Leipzig: Internationaler Psychoanalytischer Verlag, 1927); two earlier essays are "On Swiss Sects and Sect-Founders" and "Further Considerations on the Formation of Swiss Sects" (all in *CE*).

89   **Hermann Wille:** WSI Manfred Bleuler.

89   **Rorschach followed Brauchli:** As it happens, one of the canonical crime novels in German, *In Matto's Realm* (1936), takes place in "Randlingen," a barely disguised Münsingen, and is about the murder of the asylum's director, one "Ulrich Borstli." Friedrich Glauser (1896–1938) was a patient there in 1919—where he instantly loathed Brauchli (uniformly remembered by others as warm and kind)—and again later. His novel vividly conveys the atmosphere, rooms and corridors, patients and treatments, and look and feel of life at a Swiss asylum, and "captures Brauchli so precisely," according to the real asylum's second in command, Max Müller, "not only in his outward appearance but in all his weaknesses, that it would be the death of him if he ever got his hands on a copy." Müller started censoring Brauchli's mail to make sure he never heard about the book. (*Matto regiert* [Zurich: Unionsverlag, 2004], 265n; the German edition has wonderfully evocative notes and photographs of Münsingen. *In Matto's Realm,* trans. Mike Mitchell [London: Bitter Lemon Press, 2005].)

89   **was fascinated:** Morgenthaler, 98; see Ellenberger, 186; Blum/Witschi, 112.

89   **his lifework:** Ellenberger, 185; Rorschach said this to Karl Häberlin, a philosophy professor at the University of Bern.

No less dramatically deranged than Binggeli was a paranoid schizophrenic patient, Theodor Niehans, hospitalized in 1874 and in Münsingen from 1895 to 1919. His symptoms included stabbing his attendant and setting fire to the asylum woodworking shop on orders from God; Akavia gives a full description. Rorschach drafted a long case study (HRA 4:1:1), in the mode of several key Zurich School texts published between 1910 and 1914 in *Yearbook for Psychoanalytic and Psychopathological Research,* Bleuler and Freud's short-lived journal edited by Jung. He also compiled a twelve-page table comparing Niehans to Schreber, Freud's paradigmatic schizophrenic, "following in the footsteps of Jung and Bleuler" but also taking them farther and "anticipat[ing] present-day critiques of Freud's reading of Schreber" (HRA 3:1:4; Akavia, 111ff.; Müller, *Abschied vom Irrenhaus,* 75–88).

90   **"a thick book":** To Pfister, October 16, 1920.

91   **Russian state medical exam:** *L,* 128n4; Olga R, 90.

91   **Silver Age:** Etkind, *Eros of the Impossible*; Irina Sirotkina, *Diagnosing Literary Genius: A Cultural History of Psychiatry in Russia, 1880–1930* (Baltimore: Johns Hopkins University Press, 2002); Magnus Ljunggren, "The Psychoanalytic Breakthrough in Russia on the Eve of the First World War," in *Russian Literature and Psychoanalysis,* ed. Daniel Rancour-Laferriere (Amsterdam: John Benjamins, 1989), 173–92; John E. Bowlt, *Moscow and St. Petersburg, 1900–1920: Art, Life and Culture of the Russian Silver Age* (New York: Vendome Press, 2008), 13–26, quoting Alexandre Benois, designer for the Ballets Russes under Diaghilev and founding member of the World of Art movement.

92   **"to heal":** Sirotkina, *Diagnosing Literary Genius,* 100, emended.

92   **Osipov, for instance:** Sirotkina, *Diagnosing Literary Genius,* 112; Ljunggren, "Psychoanalytic Breakthrough," 175.

92   **sanatorium gave preferential treatment:** Sirotkina, 104; Etkind, *Eros of the Impossible,* 131.

92   **a number of themes:** Bowlt, *Moscow and St. Petersburg,* 29, 68, 90, 184.

92   **advertising brochure:** Nikolai Vyrubov, quoted in Ljunggren, "Psychoanalytic Breakthrough," 173. That same year, Vyrubov launched the reception of Freud in Russia with an article on his experiences using Freudian psychotherapy at Kryukovo.

92   **"rational therapy":** Sirotkina, 102.

93   **Tolstoy, the wise, humanistic soul-healer:** This is the theme of Etkind's *Eros of the Impossible.* "There could hardly have been a better way to facilitate the reception of psychoanalysis in Russia than to link it with Tolstoy's teachings" (Sirotkina, *Diagnosing Literary Genius,* 107). Another common foundation was the incalculable influence of Friedrich Nietzsche in Russia, on Freud, and on Jung (Etkind, *Eros,* 2). Overviews not centered on Freud's reception in Russia describe German-style biomedical psychiatry as dominant: the line from Emil Kraepelin (who worked in Russia between 1886 and 1891) to Pavlov and beyond. In this view, the psychoanalytic Kryukovo psychiatrists were "noteworthy" exceptions (Caesar P. Korolenko and Dennis V. Kensin, "Reflections on the Past and Present State of Russian Psychiatry," *Anthropology and Medicine* 9.1 [2002]: 52–53).

93   **Freud had joked:** F/J, 306F.

93   **"censorship," an explicit allusion:** quoted in Etkind, *Eros,* 110.

93   **a tale of Russian culture:** Etkind, *Eros;* Ellenberger, *Discovery* (e.g., 543, 891–93); Sonu Shamdasani, intro to Flournoy, *From India.* It was not "mere chance" that Freud's "favorite patient, like his favorite author [Dostoyevsky], was Russian"—Freud, with a Galician mother, was half-"Russian" himself (Etkind, *Eros,* 110–12, 151–52; James L. Rice, *Freud's Russia: National Identity in the Evolution of Psychoanalysis* [New Brunswick, NJ: Transaction, 1993]).

93   **In a lecture:** The talk is published in Christian Müller, *Aufsätze zur Psychiatriegeschichte* (Hürtgenwald: Guido Pressler, 2009), 139–46; it is largely devoted to a few rather racy cases of psychoanalytic intervention in Rorschach's own experience.

94 **journalistic opening:** Fut, 175. Probably in 1915: Akavia, 135.

94 **modernist pressure-cooker:** *Russian Futurism,* by Vladimir Markov (Berkeley: University of California Press, 1968), is still the best source.

95 **"walk with painted faces":** 133. Rorschach almost certainly saw the great poet Vladimir Mayakovsky—the astonishing orange-eater—in person: Mayakovsky was famous for his bright yellow or multicolored shirts, occasionally with accessories such as an orange jacket, a whip in his hand, or a wooden spoon in his lapel, and Rorschach's Niehans case study compares Niehans's "childishness" to "a phenomenon that I had the opportunity to observe in Russia last winter: a group of Russian *Futurists*: They paint their faces, walk around in fantastically colored blouses, and behave as far as possible in an uncouth manner" (quoted in Akavia, 133).

95 **Mikhail Matyushin:** Bowlt, *Moscow and St. Petersburg,* 310; Markov, *Russian Futurism,* 22; fullest account in Isabel Wünsche, *The Organic School of the Russian Avant-Garde: Nature's Creative Principles* (Farnham, UK: Ashgate, 2015), 83–139.

95 **Nikolai Kulbin:** Markov, *Russian Futurism,* 5 and passim; Wünsche, *Organic School,* 41–49; an evocative description of Kulbin appears in Victor Shklovsky's *Third Factory* (1926; trans. Richard Sheldon [Chicago: Dalkey Archive Press, 2002], 29). Rorschach mentions in his essay: "In a proclamation we read that P is red and III is yellow [Cyrillic for *R* and *Sh*—perhaps coincidentally, Rorschach's and Shtempelin's initials]; Kulbin spoke in his lecture of a blue C [Cyrillic for *S*]" (Fut, 179). This claim also appears in Kulbin's manifesto "What Is the Word" (Markov, *Russian Futurism,* 180).

95 **Aleksei Kruchenykh:** Markov, *Russian Futurism,* 128–29. Rorschach quotes Kruchenykh's "Poem from Single Vowels"—"o e a / i e e i / a e e i"—and a nonsense phrase by him as an example of Futurist language (Anna Lawton and Herbert Eagle, *Words in Revolution: Russian Futurist Manifestoes, 1912–1928* [Washington, DC: New Academia, 2005], 65–67; Akavia, 143; Markov, *Russian Futurism,* 131).

95 **"bring about movement and the new perception":** Markov, *Russian Futurism,* 128, paraphrasing Kruchenykh.

95 **the poet is in a movie theater:** Markov, *Russian Futurism,* 105; the poem is by the leader of the Mezzanine of Poetry, Vadim Shershenevich.

95 **"the time has now passed":** Fut, 175–76.

96 **In the most original analysis:** Fut, 183–84. His ingenious explanation of the "error" is that the Futurist, painting one leg after another and feeling, in consequence, a sequence of attitudes in his body as he paints, is left with "an impression of succession" that he attributes to the painting itself—"It appears to him to be a real movement. But only to him."

96 **"A picture—The rails":** Fut, 183. This might be something he heard in person—it does not appear in any known Futurist writing (John Bowlt, personal communication, 2014).

97 **ahead of his time:** Although apparently a certain Russian, Dr. E. P. Radin, wrote *Futurism and Madness* in 1914, comparing pictures by children, madmen, and avant-garde painters: "Dr. Radin's excursions into literary analysis are inept, and his ability to critically interpret paintings and drawings is

limited, to say the least. At the end he is overcome by scientific objectivity and states that there is not enough data to declare the futurists mentally ill, but he warns that theirs is a dangerous road" (Markov, *Russian Futurism*, 225–26). Other than a short book from 1921, *How Soviet Power Protects Children's Health*, I have not found any further trace of Radin.

97 **Freud would freely admit:** "The revolutions in painting, poetry, and music exploding all around him left Freud untouched; when they obtruded themselves on his notice, which was rarely, he energetically disapproved" (Peter Gay, *Freud: A Life for Our Time* [New York: Norton, 1988], 165).

97 **Jung would write:** Jung was "unread in current fiction, contemptuous of contemporary music, and indifferent to modern art," and both of these essays met with a "lambasting by press and public. . . . The public ridicule was humiliating" (Bair, *Jung*, 402–3).

97 **German surrealist Max Ernst:** MacGregor, *Discovery of the Art*, 278.

98 **"bevies of girls":** Hans Arp, quoted in *Movement and Balance: Sophie Taeuber-Arp, 1889–1943* (Davos: Kirchner Museum, 2009), 137.

98 **Alfred Kubin:** *PD*, 111–12; see Akavia, 127–32. Kubin (1877–1959) was associated with the Blue Rider group and also wrote a moving fantasy novel, *The Other Side* (1909). Rorschach took extensive notes on Kubin's book (HRA 3:1:7; Diary, November 2, 1919; Akavia, 131), especially around synesthesia, and in *PD* he traces changes in Kubin's introversion and extraversion across his career, connecting them to his different artistic productions.

98 **"chronic question":** To Paul, May 1914.

98 **"European longing":** Olga R, 90–91; "He remained, and wanted to remain, a 100 percent European."

98 **"It's very hard to work":** April 2, 1909. Another time, he had half-jokingly defended his Swiss restraint against expectations of Russian effusiveness, signing off a letter to Anna: "You recently wrote to ask me why I don't send you kisses. Kisses are cheap in Russia, and there are lots more kinds of kisses. Here there are fewer, and very few indeed with me, did you forget that? You'll have to make do with regards, but they are Warm regards from Your brother, Hermann" (January 25, 1909).

98 **Anna later recalled:** *CE*, 32n.

99 **"after our endless gypsy wanderings":** in Morgenthaler.

99 **end of Olga's six weeks:** Olga to Paul, May 15, 1914.

99 **by choice:** Regineli (WSI) said of Olga's staying that "maybe it was a test of will."

99 **hard work:** He had about a hundred male patients and did his twice-daily rounds quickly to keep time for his other interests. "Everything was extraordinarily quick and easy for him. . . . He quickly connected with the patients, saw what needed to be done, and gave his instructions. . . . He wrote the case records fast too—for typical cases, a few sentences touching on the essential features." He spent more time on patients who interested him, and "the director as well as certain grumbly staff members would sometimes complain that he didn't care enough about the patients' laundry, shoelaces, nightstands, and so on," which deeply annoyed Rorschach, although after a few minutes and a joke or two, he would be back in form (Morgenthaler).

100 **pioneering study of art and mental illness:** Walter Morgenthaler, *Madness and Art: The Life and Works of Adolf Wölfli* (Lincoln: University of Nebraska Press, 1992); see MacGregor, *Discovery of the Art.*

The other pioneering work on the subject was Hans Prinzhorn's *Bildnerei der Geisteskranken* [Image-making by the mentally ill] (1922; repr., New York: SpringerWienNewYork, 2011), and Rorschach was directly connected with him as well. In 1919, Prinzhorn praised Rorschach's 1913 article on a schizophrenic's drawing as "highly instructive," and Rorschach sent him artwork he had collected from patients. In 1921, he wrote to ask if Rorschach's book would be published in time for him to cite it along with Jung's and Morgenthaler's, as he wanted to; the publishers' delays made this impossible (from Karl Wilmanns, December 13, 1919; to Bircher, February 12, 1921).

100 **schizophrenic named Adolf Wölfli:** Wölfli (1864–1930) "could serve as Exhibit A in a study of the outsider phenomenon. . . . His achievement is a revelation" (Peter Schjeldahl, "The Far Side," *New Yorker,* May 5, 2003).

100 **André Breton grouped:** André Breton, *L'écart absolu* catalog (Paris: Galerie l'Œil, 1965); see José Pierre, *André Breton et la peinture* (Paris: L'Âge d'Homme, 1987), 253.

100 **"will help us someday gain":** Rilke, letter to Lou-Andreas Salomé, September 10, 1921.

100 **visually interesting material:** Morgenthaler later said that many of the artworks in his collection "were obtained through [Rorschach's] persevering efforts" with patients (Ellenberger, 191). Rorschach's work on sects also helped encourage Morgenthaler to devote his time to Wölfli. Morgenthaler had been interested in sects too: his earlier research on the history of treating insanity in Bern had led him to Unternährer, and he had collected an archive of material intending to return to the topic. But when he found out what Rorschach had already done, and realized that Rorschach would make quicker and better use of his archive, he handed it over and abandoned the topic (Morgenthaler, 98–99).

Chapter 9: Pebbles in a Riverbed

102 **early autumns:** To Paul, September 27, 1920; Ellenberger, 185–87. One August, Hermann wrote to Paul: "Alas, the summer vacation was summer's end. Here in Herisau, winter is almost upon us, and a few days after our sunbathing we already had to fire up our stove and walked around sniffling" (August 20, 1919).

103 **The Krombach:** Koller, reminiscences, quoted in WSM; Ellenberger, 185–87; *Historisches Lexikon der Schweiz,* ed. Marco Jorio (Basel: Schwabe, 2002–), "Herisau."

103 **Rorschach identified more closely:** Morgenthaler, 96; WSI Regineli.

103 **When the moving van arrived:** WSI Sophie Koller; to Paul, ca. late November 1915.

103 **his son remembers telling:** WSI Fritz Koller.

103 **"somewhat small-minded":** To Paul, March 16, 1916.

103 **"Statistics Week"**: To Roemer, January 27, 1922; to Oberholzer, January 8, 1920; to Oberholzer, January 6, 1921.

104 **Koller's son Rudi remembered**: WSI Rudi Koller.

104 **Rorschach's workdays began**: WSI Martha Schwarz-Gantner and Bertha Waldburger-Abderhalden.

104 **"More or less exactly at midnight"**: Diary, 75.

104 **Rorschach was personally responsible**: To Morgenthaler, October 11, 1916; Diary, 54.

104 **Koller was afraid that his superiors**: From Koller, June 28, 1915.

105 **"As you can see"**: To Morgenthaler, March 12, 1917.

105 **Swiss Psychoanalytic Society**: This group was created to be more Freudian than the Swiss Psychiatric Society and yet independent of Freud's own party-line International Psychoanalytic Society. "Even if Freud appears here and there with an all too papal nimbus," Rorschach wrote to Morgenthaler, encouraging him to join the new group, "the danger of hierarchicalization is best avoided when people come together and create a counterweight, representing different points of view" (to Morgenthaler, November 11, 1919; see also *L*, 139n1 and 175n5, and to Oberholzer, February 16, 1919). Ernest Jones wrote to Freud that its "best members are Binswanger, a psychiatrist Rhorschach, and Frau Dr. Oberholzer" (March 25, 1919, quoted in *L*, 152n1).

105 **"It's too bad"**: To Morgenthaler, May 21, 1920.

105 **"Here in the provinces"**: To Oberholzer, May 3, 1920.

105 **While his friends said they were jealous**: From Oberholzer, January 4, 1922.

105 **"interesting people"**: To Roemer, January 27, 1922.

105 **"if you put a piece of paper**: Morgenthaler, 98.

106 **Rorschach had tried to volunteer**: Morgenthaler, 97.

106 **He and Olga volunteered**: To Paul, March 16, 1916.

106 **"There was a sudden reversal"**: To Paul, December 15, 1918.

106 **"in defiance of all truth"**: To Paul, December 15, 1918.

107 **"Have you read or heard about"**: To Burri, September 27, 1920.

107 **"I'm only just beginning"**: To Paul, September 27, 1920.

107 **"What do you think"**: To Burri, December 28, 1920.

107 **financial situation**: WSI Bertha Waldburger-Abderhalden. "Everything costs a lot," Rorschach wrote to Paul. "Wages are rising, so the tailor makes about as much as I do. . . . It's total madness. Everyone thinks he would live better if only he were paid more, and then everyone is shocked when the prices rise for everything" (April 24, 1919). Months later: "Our salary circumstances have improved somewhat but only to the point where we can now and then replace the clothes we have worn out in recent years. It doesn't go much further than that" (July 22, 1919).

107 **"At least we have always gotten"**: To Paul, August 20, 1919, slightly modified.

108 **"I am constantly in the woodworking shop"**: To Paul, April 24, 1919. Bookshelves: Diary 83, January 28, 1920.

108 **His great joy in Herisau**: See WSI, esp. Bertha Waldburger-Abderhalden

and Anna Ita; to Oberholzer, May 3 and May 18, 1920, and to Paul, May 29, 1920.

108 **"one genuine Swiss name"**: To Paul, May 6, 1919.

108 **Anna made it out of Russia**: To Oberholzer, August 6, 1918.

108 **married soon afterward**: Anna's husband was a widowed father of three named Heinrich Berchtold, and Rorschach perceived the family dynamics at once: "It won't be easy to raise the three boys, of course," he wrote to Paul. "But one good thing is that the oldest is mostly out of the picture since he won't be living there much longer. The youngest is a darling, and she will probably be able to make him completely her own. The middle one is the one who will definitely give her the most trouble." In any case, "Annali will do well with the groom. . . . He may bump up against certain bohemian attitudes here and there, which she has picked up from her Russian student circles, but I'm sure they'll wear off soon enough" (To Paul, April 24, 1919).

108 **Paul was married, too**: He had met Reine Simonne Laurent in Amboise and taken her to Brazil; they got married in Paris, and their daughter, Simonne, would be born in Bahia in 1921. *PD*, Case 6 (136–137), "Introverted Predisposition in an Extravert Career," is Paul, presenting Hermann's view of his brother in the language of diagnosis: "The subject comes from a talented family and became a businessman more for external reasons than to follow his own impulses. . . . He has marked introversive traits that he has not had time to cultivate because of the heavy demands for disciplined thinking life has placed upon him. Well-ordered affect, good capacity for both intensive and extensive rapport, especially good emotional adaptability. . . . Taken together, these qualities form the basis for a certain gift for humor. He is a good observer and original reporter of what he has seen."

These births and weddings awakened Hermann's interest in his family history, and his genealogical researches resulted in a calligraphed thirty-two-page book elaborately hand-drawn on heavy paper, written in the archaic style of an ancient chronicle, and richly illustrated with pictures including the ruin of the castle of the Counts von Rorschach, escutcheons, silhouettes, scenes of family members' hometowns, and imagined scenes from the lives of his ancestors. He would give the document to Paul in 1920 as a belated Christmas present (HRA 1:3; cf. Diary, late 1919).

108 **She later remembered Hermann**: WSI Regineli.

108 **His cousin remembered him**: WSI Fanny Sauter.

109 **licked it**: Priscilla Schwarz, Wolfgang's daughter who remained closest to Lisa Rorschach, interview, 2013.

109 **For Christmas one year**: Diary, September 15, 1919.

109 **"I'm hoping to send you"**: To Paul, April 24, 1919.

109 **But not all was well**: WSI Fritz Koller, Sophie Koller, Regineli, Martha Schwarz-Gantner.

109 **The Kollers**: Rorschach felt particularly close to the oldest Koller child, Eddie, an artist who planned to attend the same art school in Zurich where Rorschach's father had studied. Eddie suffered increasingly from depression—a development Rorschach predicted, and followed with concern—before committing suicide in 1923, at age nineteen.

110 **On a boat ride with family:** WSI Fanny Sauter; see also to Paul, March 16, 1916; *L* 139n3; Ellenberger 187.

110 **staging plays:** Blum/Witschi, 84–93.

110 **"He could instantly":** Rorschach was "particularly masterful in observing, capturing, and recording movement" (Miecyzslav Minkovski, obituary for Hermann Rorschach, in *CE,* 84).

111 **"My wife would like":** To Oberholzer, December 12, 1920.

112 **In mid-1917:** Olga would write much later that "in 1917" her husband "returned to his interest in 'chance-form inkblots' that he had left aside for years (perhaps inspired by S. Hens's dissertation, which obviously reminded him of the experiments he had conducted in Münsterlingen in 1911)" (Olga R, 91). "There can be little doubt that the stimulating impulse came from the research work of Szymon Hens" (Ellenberger, 189). In three interviews in 1959, Hens said he met with Rorschach twice, six months apart, then said three or four months apart; the meetings were in 1917, then he wasn't sure if the first mightn't have been in 1916, then he wondered if it was 1918. He also said it was when he was twenty-five years old (December 1916 to December 1917) and before the publication of his dissertation (December 1917). The most likely date for the decisive meeting is in mid- to late 1917.

112 **Hens used eight crude black blots:** Szymon Hens, *Phantasieprüfung mit formlosen Klecksen bei Schulkindern, normalen Erwachsenen und Geisteskranken* (Zurich: Fachschriften-Verlag, 1917). He is sometimes described as having tested subjects' "fantasies," but this is a mistranslation of *Phantasie,* "imagination."

Hens spent the rest of his life convinced that Rorschach stole his idea, and he passed down this claim to fame to his daughter and granddaughter ("to put it delicately, my father's ink blots were 'adopted' by Rorschach": "Honorable Joyce Hens Green," Oral History Project, Historical Society of the District of Columbia Circuit, 1999–2001, pp. 4–5 [www.dcchs.org/Joyce HensGreen/joycehensgreen_complete.pdf]; "my grandfather was the author of the Rorschach Ink Blot Test ... Dr. Rorschach conveniently got the credit for it as he used my Grandfather's research in his presentations and studies": Ancestry.com, Surname: Hens, thread "Western New York Hens," message posted November 4, 2010 [boards.ancestry.com, last retrieved August 2016]). One still finds mention of Hens's priority, especially in accounts trying to impute plagiarism or intellectual dishonesty to Rorschach.

Rorschach cited Hens in a February 1919 lecture (HRA 3:2:1:1), in letters, and in *PD*: "Hens suggests some of the questions of form investigated here, although he cannot go into them more deeply" because of his exclusive concern with content. Elsewhere: "I have to emphasize that my own work did not proceed from Hens's. I was exploring a perceptual-diagnostic form-interpretation experiment for years already, and conducted experiments with the Altnau secondary school as early as 1911, while based in Münsterlingen, in connection with my dissertation on reflex hallucinations." The starting point for the test was the investigation of reflex hallucinations in his dissertation, though "of course the whole psychiatric approach and psychological mind-set goes back to the influence of Bleuler and his writings" (*PD,* 102–3; to Hans Maier, November 14, 1920; to Roemer, June 18, 1921).

Hens himself (WSI) alternately said that he hadn't contributed much to the test, that the test was inadequate, that "people will attack me if I say the Rorschach test is not scientific," and that "it was wrong" for an academic conference to have the biggest round table on Rorschach: "Maybe I'm envious that it's Rorschach and not Hens. It should be Hens-Rorschach." He also admitted that "maybe Rorschach did have the idea four or five years earlier than 1917," before saying that Rorschach got everything from him: "Where else would Rorschach have gotten the idea from?"

Szymon Hens immigrated to the United States, changed his name to James Hens, and was later sentenced to five years in jail for trying to help would-be draft dodgers during World War II (Harry Lever and Joseph Young, *Wartime Racketeers* [New York: G. P. Putnam's Sons, 1945], 95ff.). In 1959, Wolfgang Schwarz tracked him down for three dramatic interviews (WSI). Schwarz claimed to observe him manipulating and flirting inappropriately with patients, "a total abuse of his role as a physician," and found him paranoid, repeatedly worrying about "making enemies" if he said what he really thought, and simultaneously "obsessed with feelings of omnipotence," to the point where Schwarz felt he "seemed insane."

112 **purely by content:** Hens, *Phantasieprüfung,* 12.

112 **"his girlfriends":** WSI Hens.

112 **"The mentally ill do not interpret":** Hens, *Phantasieprüfung,* 62.

Chapter 10: A Very Simple Experiment

114 **The blots had to not look "made":** Galison calls the inkblots "an exquisite art of artlessness" (271, cf. 273–74); the test's "neutrality" is central to Galison's fine essay, which I read early in the process of writing this book and which influenced my thinking more than is explicitly reflected in these notes. Gamboni expands (65–72). For the importance of the blots as having "made themselves," see note on page 386 "countless visual connections."

114 **After "spending a long time":** To Roemer, March 22, 1922. Specifically, "in the interest of better comparisons between results, more reliable calculations, and a greater likelihood of Movement responses."

115 **"conducted either like a game":** Draft, 1.

115 **an *experiment*:** It was originally intended as a "perceptual-diagnostic *experiment* and dynamic tool for the further development of psychological and psychiatric theorizing," not "the ossified psycho-technology 'test' it has since become" (Akavia, 10).

115 **The choice to make the blots symmetrical:** Later, he read Ernst Mach on symmetry and praised him as "an independent thinker!" but found nothing in it to add to his own ideas (Diary, October 21, 1919).

115 **from Vischer's essay:** "On the Optical Sense," 98 (see chap. 7 above).

116 **to use red:** See Ernest Schachtel, "On Color and Affect: Contributions to an Understanding of Rorschach's Test," *Psychiatry* 6 (1943): 393–409.

116 **Anthropologists would discover:** Brent Berlin and Paul Kay, *Basic Color Terms: Their Universality and Evolution* (Berkeley: University of California Press, 1969); Marshall Sahlins, "Colors and Cultures" (1976), in *Culture*

in Practice: Selected Essays (New York: Zone Books, 2000), gives more facts about red and puts these seemingly biological findings back in the context of culture.

116 **"to come up with an answer"**: *PD,* 104.

117 **whether or not he told**: *PD,* 16.

117 **Two responses**: Draft 24–25; *PD,* 103, 137–39.

117 **"Barack Obama"**: Quoted by James Choca, "Reclaiming the Rorschach from the Empiricist Pawn Shop," Society for Personality Assessment conference, New York, March 6, 2015.

118 *Interpretations of chance images*: *PD,* 16.

119 **on August 5**: To Miecyzslav Minkovski, August 5, 1918. *PD* uses cases from Draft, and since comparisons require use of "the same series of plates" or "an analogous series suitably standardized" (*PD,* 20, 52), the images must have been finalized by 1918. At some point his cards had gaps in the numbering after the current III and VI, but the letter to Minkovski mentions ten cards, as does his letter to Bircher, May 29, 1920. The claim that Rorschach's publisher "accepted only ten cards" from "the manuscript with 15 original cards" is false (Ellenberger, 206, see *L,* 230n1).

Summary in the rest of the chapter taken from Draft unless noted.

121 **"The resurrection"**: By *PD* (163) he would call the answer "a very complex contamination" and score it more fully: the whole statement is "DW CF– Abstract Original–" ("DW" = a Whole confabulated from a Detail); the *"resurrection"* (pointing to the red animals being resurrected) is "DM + A" ("A" = animal); the color-naming is "DCC"; the *"veins"* is "Dd CF– Anatomy Original–"; and "Other determining factors of the interpretation cannot be obtained."

123 **"Maybe we'll soon reach the point"**: To Burri, May 28, 1920.

124 **Whole responses could be a good sign**: Draft, Case 15; *PD,* Case 16.

125 **"It concerns a very simple experiment"**: To Julius-Springer Verlag, February 16, 1920.

Chapter 11: It Provokes Interest and Head-Shaking Everywhere

126 **Greti Brauchli**: Diary, October 26 to November 4, 1919; letters to and from Greti and Hans Burri, cited below; WSI Hans Burri and Greti Brauchli-Burri.

126 **"He understood it!"**: Diary, October 6, 1919.

126 **"who truly understood the experiment"**: Brauchli was "the first person after Oberholzer" to understand—see note for Emil Oberholzer on page 354.

126 **"Thank you for your report!"**: From Greti Brauchli, November 2, 1919.

127 **Rorschach wrote a warm reply**: To Greti Brauchli dated November 5, 1919, written November 4.

128 **"my compulsive neurotic clergyman"**: To Oberholzer, May 6, 1920.

128 **"An analysis must never be"**: To Burri, January 15, 1920.

128 **Burri's seventy-one responses**: *PD,* 146–55, and Diary, 77–83; see Diary February 7, 1920, and to Burri, May 20, and from Burri, May 21, 1920.

129 **"Thank you for everything"**: From Greti, May 22, 1920.

129 **Four months later:** To Burri, September 27, 1920. Fifty years later, in 1970, Burri called Rorschach's death a catastrophe as tears welled up in Greti's eyes (WSI).

129 **a journal:** Constantin von Monakow's *Swiss Archives of Neurology and Psychiatry,* where Rorschach often published (*L,* 148n2). See to Monakov, August 28 and September 23, 1918; to Morgenthaler, January 7, 1920. Monakov (1853–1930), an internationally renowned Russian neurologist who held the first chair in neurology at the University of Zurich Medical School, reappeared many times in Rorschach's life. He may have been the first to interest Rorschach in Russia. He treated Rorschach's father, Ulrich. Rorschach took courses with him starting in 1905 and did his work on the pineal gland under him. By 1913, they were close colleagues—when Rorschach left for Russia, Monakov wrote a notice for a local newspaper that called it "regrettable in the highest degree that the institution [at Münsingen] was not able to keep him here." "Don't stay too long in Moscow," he wrote directly to Rorschach. "You can do better in Switzerland, whether as a neurologist or a psychiatrist." Rorschach joked at one point that it might be better to discourage Monakov from attending his lecture on sects, "because otherwise he might undergo another collapse, which would weigh on my conscience. Someone needs to tell him that the subject is psychoanalytical through and through— i.e., for him, so to speak, life-threatening." In 1922, he was considering returning to work with Monakov, "the way I had planned to in Münsingen"; intellectually, he felt that "Bleuler's concept of perception is outdated," and he stated that "not only my personal inclination, but also the facts, are pushing me in a Monakovian biological direction" (Anna R, 73; WSM; *L,* 127n1, 128n4; to Mieczyslav Minkovski, August 5, 1918; to Monakov, August 8 and December 9, 1918; to Oberholzer, June 29, 1919; to Max Müller, January 6, 1922).

130 **a version where buyers would color:** To Monakov, September 23, 1918 (more literally: "Such archaic thoughts one has nowadays").

130 **"happy that it hadn't been printed":** To Morgenthaler, January 7, 1920.

131 **"Subjectively, I feel":** Lecture to the Pedagogical-Psychological Society of St. Gallen, February 1919, HRA 3:2:1:1.

131 **coined the term:** Ellenberger, 225.

131 **Emil Oberholzer:** 1883–1958. His wife was the Russian Jewish psychiatrist Mira Gincburg (1884–1949), an important psychoanalyst in her own right who had analyzed Oberholzer before sending him to Freud in 1913. In 1919, they opened a practice together (*L,* 138–39n1; Müller, *Abschied vom Irrenhaus,* 160).

131 **"the control experiments were as follows":** To Julius-Springer Verlag, February 16, 1920.

131 **a bit ambivalent:** *PD,* 121.

131 **"it looks so much like":** To Oberholzer, June 15, 1921.

131 **"Where in Herisau":** To Roemer, March 15, 1922.

132 **when he was able to explain:** Diary, November 4, 1919.

132 **handed his blots over:** Morgenthaler, 100.

132 **already intrigued:** "After 1918, there was only one analyst whose work

Bleuler took a lively interest in: Hermann Rorschach. He praised the Rorschach test publicly and in private" (Schröter, introduction to Freud and Bleuler, *"Ich bin zuversichtlich,"* 54).

132 **"Hens really should have explored":** Diary 63, November 2, 1919.

132 **tests of all his children:** To Oberholzer, June 3, 1921.

132 **future psychiatrist Manfred Bleuler:** "Der Rorschachsche Formdeutversuch bei Geschwistern," *Zeitschrift für die gesamte Neurologie und Psychiatrie* 118.1 (1929): 366–98; see Müller, *Abschied vom Irrenhaus,* 164.

132 **"You can easily imagine":** To Roemer, June 18, 1921.

132 **"Amazingly positive":** Quoted in Rorschach to Oberholzer, June 28, 1921.

132 **"confirmed his results":** *CE,* 254.

132 **"a certain plan":** To Paul, August 20, 1919.

132 **"All dark things, you see!":** To Roemer, September 21, 1919.

133 **"An analysis that goes well":** To Roemer, January 27, 1922.

133 **from normal subjects:** Nine were from healthy subjects, four from people with neuroses but not serious mental illnesses such as schizophrenia. To call this a shift is perhaps an overstatement: "From the beginning, even from the first experiments ten years ago, I have always tried the experiment on normals of all kinds. That is clear from the book—first and foremost, it's about normals" (to Roemer, June 18, 1921).

133 **By February 1919:** Quotes in this paragraph and next from Lecture in St. Gallen (see note "Subjectively, I feel" on page 354, and *L,* 182–84n).

134 **"the trickiest problem":** Quotes from *PD* unless noted: 25–26, 31, 33–36, 77–79, 86–87, 94–95, 107, 110–13.

134 **A colleague:** Georg Roemer, *Vom Rorschachtest zum Symboltest* (Leipzig: Hirzel, 1938). In one case, their discussion changed the total number of M responses in a test from seven to two.

135 **"Color":** Diary, October 21, 1919.

137 **ever more daring:** In *PD* (see note "the trickiest problem," above) and Diary, early September and December 12, 1919.

138 **earliest childhood memories:** Rorschach speculated that movement memories were linked to early childhood, so the number of M's indicated the age of one's earliest memories—or was a sign of repressing those memories if the ages didn't match (Diary, November 3, 1919). He quickly abandoned the theory as too simple, but not before collecting several people's first memories and recording his own:

> EARLIEST CHILDHOOD MEMORIES
> self: 6–7 years old—dim memory of playing together with Mother's youngest sister, Brother, and Sister in the hallway of the silk-weaving school—a long hallway, whose rear end is appropriately dim—I feel that this is connected to the "dim" memory—the game is 'Witches': Aunt runs after us with a broom—everything very faded and blurry—

As he surely realized, this memory weaves together different periods of his childhood. He must have been seven or eight, since Paul was born when Hermann was seven. Another of his mother's sisters, not the youngest, was to play a crucial role in his life as his stepmother. The silk-weaving school was doubtless the famous one in his birthplace, Zurich. There are those brooms again, as in his strange insistence on *"New Year's mummers with brooms"* as a Movement response (HRA 3:3:14:2).

138 **missionary from the Gold Coast:** H. Henking.

138 **Emil Lüthy:** 1890–1966. *L,* 208–9n6; WSI Lüthy; Diary, October 11, 1919.

138 **"In truth, every artist":** *PD,* 109. To Lüthy, January 17, 1922, includes more than a dozen color swatches and fascinating conjectures—such as purple being the most complicated and mysterious color because it oscillates between red and blue, warm and cold. Light violets can seem incredibly fresh and young, while "a dark heavy rich blue-purple looks mystical (the theosophist color!)."

138 **students, usually Bleuler's:** The flakiest was Hedwig Etter, who had proposed a dissertation on the inkblot experiment and contacted Rorschach in 1920. She was offered the volunteer position at Krombach, despite Rorschach's reservations, and left Koller and Rorschach in the lurch two days before her start date. After all the time Rorschach and Oberholzer put in collecting test material for her, she headed off to Vienna to see Freud and was never heard from again after September 1921 (*L,* 213–4n1, passim).

139 **Hans Behn-Eschenburg:** 1893–1934. *L,* 187n5 and passim; Müller, "Zwei Schüler von Hermann Rorschach," chap. 10 in *Abschied vom Irrenhaus.*

139 **"Whoever wanted to work":** Gertrud Behn-Eschenburg, "Working with Dr. Hermann Rorschach," *JPT* 19.1 (1955): 3–5.

139 **Behn gave the Rorschach:** His dissertation was "Psychological Examination of Schoolchildren with the Form Interpretation Test."

139 **"The fourteenth year":** To Burri, July 16, 1920.

139 **unassailable and make a good impression:** To Behn-Eschenburg, November 14, 1920.

139 **Rorschach wrote whole sections:** "He botched his dissertation about my experiment so miserably that finally I had to do almost the whole thing myself" (to Paul, January 8, 1921); "I just couldn't stand by and watch him mess up all that material so rich in problems and new perspectives" (to Oberholzer, December 12, 1920). To Behn's adviser Hans Maier: "I saw only too late that such projects actually do require much more than the simplicity of the method might suggest, and that they are not very well suited for beginners" (January 24, 1921). Behn's series of images was later publicized by child psychologist Hans Zulliger as the "Behn-Rorschach Test," but Behn himself published nothing further on the inkblots.

139 **"The experiment is very simple":** To Behn-Eschenburg, November 28, 1920.

140 **Georg Roemer:** 1892–1972. Müller, "Zwei Schüler"; *L,* 164–66n1 and passim; Blum/Witschi, 94–107. The most important of Roemer's many statements is "Hermann Rorschach und die Forschungsergebnisse seiner beiden letzten Lebensjahre" (*Psyche* 1 [1948]: 523–42).

Like Paul, Roemer appears anonymously in *PD;* Case 2: "The subject is a scientist, multitalented, draws and paints. A keen observer and clear thinker, well-rounded education, a bit inclined to get scattered and fragmented. Easily upset; very thorough in what interests him, but quickly jumps from one topic to the next. . . . Allows himself to be carried away by his emotions; his emotional instability is rather strongly egocentric."

140 **"I too think the experiment"**: To Roemer, January 11 or 12, 1921.

141 **making inkblot series of his own**: Diary, November 13, 1919.

141 **"the subject being taken"**: *PD*, 121–22.

141 **"I find your questions extremely interesting"**: To Roemer, January 11 or 12, 1921.

141 **Martha Schwarz**: later Schwarz-Gantner (b. 1894). WSI; *L* 322n2. Amusingly, she thought her job interview would be very competitive, but of course they were desperate to fill the unpaid position at Herisau. Rorschach asked her if she could act in the plays—she'd play the serious parts, he the comic ones. Could she sing? Play the piano? Dance? Good, she was hired. They became good friends, often strolling down to town together to buy tea or cake. She inkblot-tested her whole family and said that she learned a lot about people from his interpretations—"I could treat my parents much more fairly after that. Rorschach did this very quietly."

142 **Albert Furrer**: *L*, 284n3, quotes from to Roemer, May 23 and June 18, 1921, and to Paul, October 16, 1921.

142 **"The point is not to illustrate"**: To Bircher, May 19, 1920.

143 **"Trying the experiment"**: To Oberholzer, July 18, 1919.

143 **Oskar Pfister**: 1873–1956. If Bleuler and Jung were key figures in bringing Freud into the hospitals, Pfister was key to bringing him into the culture. The eventual author of more than 270 books, Pfister was a pastor who continued to believe that psychology was compatible with religious belief. He encountered psychoanalysis through Jung in 1908 and wrote the first textbook of psychoanalysis in 1913, with an introduction by Freud; his "thoroughly Christian outlook on psychoanalysis had proved unnerving but not completely indigestible" to Freud (Kerr, *Most Dangerous Method*, 210), and he remained a crucial figure in the story of Freud and religion. Freud asked Pfister to reply to his key book *The Future of an Illusion* (1927), which he did in "The Illusion of a Future: A Friendly Disagreement with Prof. Sigmund Freud" (1928; translated in *International Journal of Psychoanalysis* 74.3 [1993]: 557–79). Sigmund Freud and Oskar Pfister, *Psycho-Analysis and Faith: The Letters of Sigmund Freud and Oskar Pfister* (London: Hogarth Press, 1963); Alasdair MacIntyre, "Freud as Moralist," *New York Review of Books*, February 20, 1964.

143 **popular version**: Rorschach had put his sect studies aside for almost a year to work on the test, but in October 1920, thinking *PD* would be published any day, he planned to return to them. "Here is my advice," Pfister wrote: "Thick books are so expensive nowadays that no one buys them, and hence no one reads them. But publish monographs on the sect material! First, a piece for us, 'Sects and Mental Illness.' Accessible but well grounded scientifically—as goes without saying for you. . . . Even for a research scientist, it is excellent practice to write for a popular audience, and you can often reach a much wider audience that way." Rorschach quickly agreed—"It won't be hard to fill fifty pages on the topic. I think I can write the thing for you this winter"—although, as he told Oberholzer, "I naturally don't want to use up

my best material, Binggeli and Unternährer, in a little popular pamphlet, so
I have to pull together other material, which is taking a bit more work than I
had anticipated" (from Pfister, October 18 and November 3, 1920; to Pfister,
November 7, 1920; to Oberholzer, March 20, 1921).

143   **Walter Morgenthaler:** He much later set up a Rorschach Commission
(1945), founded the International Rorschach Society (1952), and established
the Hermann Rorschach Archive (1957). But he published nothing on the
Rorschach in the twenties and thirties, except for the second edition of *PD*
(Rita Signer's pamphlet *The Hermann Rorschach Archives and Museum* [Bern,
n.d.], 28ff.; Müller, *Abschied vom Irrenhaus,* 153).

143   **"the long wet Herisau spring":** To Morgenthaler, May 21, 1920. **"My manuscript is finished":** to Bircher, June 22, 1920. Drafts: HRA 3.3.6.2 and
3.3.6.3.

143   **he had mused:** In a diary that Rorschach kept for six months starting in
September of 1919—uncharacteristically for him, and further confirmation
of his introvert turn at ages thirty-three to thirty-five. The first entry pro-
tested that it was only "a kind of diary" because "keeping a diary is a pedantic thing to do."

143   **Bircher's first letter to Rorschach:** November 18, 1919.

144   **Rorschach wrote to his brother:** December 4, 1919.

144   **in a different font:** To Oberholzer, January 14, 1921.

144   **so many capital "F"s:** To Roemer, March 1921.

144   **One letter:** To Bircher, May 29, 1920.

146   **Morgenthaler argued in August 1920:** To and from Morgenthaler, August
9–20.

146   **"extremely arrogant":** To Roemer, January 11 or 12, 1921.

146   *Psychodiagnostics* **was published:** To Bircher, June 19, 1921.

146   **"I think that this research":** From Oberholzer, July 12, 1920.

146   **"Dear Doctor":** From Pfister, June 23, 1921.

147   **"All of them future ministers":** To Burri, November 5, 1921.

147   **he had plans to test:** Ibid.

147   **in November 1921:** *CE,* 254.

147   **"Well, it's made it—":** *CE,* 100.

147   **"Bleuler has now expressed":** To Martha Schwarz, December 7, 1921.

147   **Arthur Kronfeld's 1922 review:** *CE,* 230–33.

148   **Ludwig Binswanger:** *CE,* 234–47, originally published in 1923, but a letter
from Binswanger, January 5, 1922, expressed directly to Rorschach the same
praise of *PD* and criticism of its lack of theoretical basis.

148   **William Stern:** *L,* 218n4, 335n1.

148   **"approach was artificial":** Ellenberger, 225–26, who suggested that Stern's
reaction "depressed" Rorschach—even that this depression made Rorschach
fail to seek medical treatment the following year—but the evidence does not
bear this out.

148   **"proposing unnecessary modifications":** To Oberholzer, June 17, 1921.

148   **"Multiple different series":** To Roemer, June 18, 1921. "On the whole," Rorschach went on, before giving a long list of caveats and concerns, "you vastly

underemphasize the difficulties involved" in administering and interpreting the test.

148 **"more approachable":** To Guido Looser, July 11, 1921. See also his complaints about Roemer's behavior in a letter to Binswanger, February 3, 1922.

148 **A Chilean doctor:** Fernando Allende Navarro.

148 **"North America would obviously":** To Roemer, January 27, 1922.

149 **the only racial or ethnic difference:** *PD*, 97, 112. "It is, of course, nothing new to find that the Appenzeller is more emotionally adaptable, has greater rapport, and is physically more active than the reserved, stolid, slow Bernese, but it is worth pointing out that the test confirms this piece of common knowledge." Elsewhere, Rorschach attributed the high Appenzeller suicide rate to their being far more emotionally expressive than other Swiss, so that they acted out their depressions (1920 Health Commission meeting, WSA). A recent essay pokes gentle fun at the fact that, since Rorschach said so little in *PD* about cultural differences, Oberholzer had to bring in a comparison to Appenzeller Swiss in discussing the Indonesian Alorese in the 1940s (Blum/ Witschi, 120). For what it's worth, Jung, too, told his advanced students that when visiting the American Southwest he was "enormously struck by the resemblance of the Indian women of the Pueblos to the Swiss women in Canton Appenzell, where we have descendants of Mongolian invaders." This is one explanation he offers for "why Americans are closer to the Far East than Europeans" (*Introduction to Jungian Psychology: Notes of the Seminar on Analytical Psychology Given in 1925* [Princeton: Princeton University Press, 2012], 116).

149 **ethnographic and sect-related research:** Rorschach's last review summaries for Freud's journal *Imago* were about two comparative studies of drawings by European children and Dakota Indians, a nonpsychoanalytic book on indigenous child raising, and a study of Antonianer (*CE*, 311–14, all 1921).

149 **Chinese populations:** WSM.

149 **Albert Schweitzer's hotel room:** To Oberholzer, November 15, 1921; to Martha Schwarz, December 7, 1921; WSI Sophie Koller. Rorschach sent Burri further details (November 5, 1921): "Every color, down to the deepest dark blue, simply disgusts him. He is a rationalist through and through and yet he has become a missionary. He insists that the jungle Negroes know only the 'eternal disgusting green' of the jungle, and that they have never once had the chance to see red. Red birds, red butterflies, red flowers— there's no such thing, he said when I asked. Finally he did have to admit, with amazement, that the Negroes did at least see red when they bashed someone's head in or crushed their own finger."

149 **"There is a lot more":** To Roemer, June 18, 1921.

Chapter 12: The Psychology He Sees Is *His* Psychology

150 **One patient:** To Roemer, January 27, 1922; *L,* 403n1; *PD,* 207.

151 **"dynamic psychiatry":** Ellenberger's *Discovery of the Unconscious: The History and Evolution of Dynamic Psychiatry* is the authoritative account; definitions of *dynamic* on 289–91.

151 **one of these virtuosic performances:** *PD*, 184–216, included in second and all later editions. Quotes below are from 185 (Oberholzer's prefatory note) and 196–214 unless noted.

154 **"the Rorschach test must be liberated":** Roemer, *Vom Rorschachtest zum Symboltest*, quoted in *L*, 166n1.

154 **"more complicated and structured":** To Roemer, March 22, 1922, quoted in chap. 10 above.

154 **"My images look clumsy":** To Roemer, January 27, 1922. Roemer's embittered late years, after episodes of Nazi collaboration, were spent trying in vain to get recognition in Germany and America: despite decades of efforts, he could not find a publisher, eventually self-publishing his images in 1966. He continued to play up his three years of supposed "close daily collaboration" with Rorschach, and laid claim to the mantle of Rorschach's legacy, but at the same time constantly undermined Rorschach's own ideas and mischaracterized the test.

154 **"The essential thing":** To Roemer, January 28, 1922.

155 **Jung's *Psychological Types*:** *Collected Works,* vol. 6, 1976. Freud received a copy and called it "the work of a snob and a mystic, no new idea in it" (to Ernest Jones, May 19, 1921, in *The Complete Correspondence of Sigmund Freud and Ernest Jones, 1908–1939* [Cambridge, MA: Harvard University Press, 1993], p. 424).

155 **"Jung is now on his fourth version":** To Roemer, June 18, 1921.

156 **"hardly anything in common":** *PD*, 82. Rorschach's use of introversion and extraversion goes back to his sect studies; his successive understandings of Jung's ideas about introversion are a complicated development, which no one has clearly tracked (both Akavia and K. W. Bash, "Einstellungstypus and Erlebnistypus: C. G. Jung and Hermann Rorschach," *JPT* 19.3 [1955]: 236–42, and *CE*, 341–44, lacked access to some sources).

156 **In long, insightful descriptions:** For instance, Jung, *Psychological Types*, 160–63, on how an introvert might complain about how extraverts can't sit still, but only an introvert would be bothered—the extravert is simply living his life.

156 **When Jung was asked:** *C. G. Jung Speaking*, 342.

156 **Jung wrote in the epilogue:** Pages 487–495; quotes below are from these pages unless noted.

157 **"sprang originally from my need":** Quoted in Jung, *Psychological Types*, v; cf. 60–62 and *C. G. Jung Speaking*, 340–43, 435.

157 **it had taken Jung years:** In 1915, Jung recruited an extraverted psychiatrist colleague, Hans Schmid-Guisan, as a sparring partner who would not let him get away with his own prejudices. At the time, Jung still thought that extraverted thinking was intrinsically inadequate, that feeling was irrational, and in general that any traits the opposite of his own were "mere aberrations." The dialogue ends in mutual frustration, as each side proves unable to understand the other—Jung in particular comes off as an autocratic jerk, but then he is supposed to be, since he is playing the role of the imperious, introverted visionary against the other man's extraverted, socially adept collegiality. It worked, though: five years later, Jung had come to recognize the

existence and validity of other types. "The introvert cannot possibly know or imagine how he appears to his opposite type unless he allows the extravert to tell him to his face, at the risk of having to challenge him to a duel," Jung writes in *Psychological Types*—but that is just what Jung did, and came out the other side (*The Question of Psychological Types: The Correspondence of C.G. Jung and Hans Schmid-Guisan, 1915–1916* [Princeton: Princeton University Press, 2013]; Jung, *Psychological Types*, 164; Bair, *Jung*, 278–85).

158 **"I am reading Jung":** To Oberholzer, June 17, 1921.

158 **"I am now reading Jung's *Types*":** To Oberholzer, November 15, 1921.

158 **"I really want to have":** To Burri, November 5, 1921.

158 **"I have to agree with Jung":** To Roemer, January 28, 1922.

158 **"I thought at first that Jung's types":** To Burri, November 5, 1921. Rorschach found the Introverted Feeling, Introverted Sensation, and Extraverted Intuition types "especially dubious," and these are in fact less convincing than the other five—precisely as might have been predicted from Jung's personality. Jung, *C. G. Jung Speaking*, 435–46; Jung, *Introduction to Jungian Psychology*; Jung's letter to Sabina Spielrein, October 7, 1919, which diagrams his, Freud's, Bleuler's, Nietzsche's, Goethe's, Schiller's, Kant's, and Schopenhauer's positions on the axes of Thinking/Feeling and Sensing/Intuiting (Coline Covington and Barbara Wharton, *Sabina Spielrein: Forgotten Pioneer of Psychoanalysis* [New York: Brunner-Routledge, 2003], 57; important passages are quoted in Jung and Schmid-Guisan, *Question of Psychological Types*, 31–32).

159 **too inclined or too disinclined:** *PD*, 26, 75, 78.

160 **"My method is still in its infancy":** To Hans Prinzhorn (see in note "pioneering study of art and mental illness" on page 348), perhaps Rorschach's last letter.

160 **able to influence the content:** To Roemer, January 27, 1922.

160 **"A general view":** *PD*, 192, from the 1922 essay.

160 **"All my work has shown me":** To Roemer, June 1921.

160 **patients at the Deaf-Mute Clinic:** To Ulrich Grüninger, March 10, 1922; to Roemer, March 15, 1922.

Chapter 13: Right on the Threshold to a Better Future

162 **On Sunday, March 26:** Olga to Paul, April 8 and April 18, 1922; WSI; Dr. Koller's medical report (*L*, 441–42); Ellenberger.

163 **"He suddenly said to me":** April 8, 1922.

164 **"awestruck":** Rorschach had sent Pfister a detailed blind diagnosis, and he replied: "What fine work! I am awestruck at the accuracy of your judgment" (February 10, 1922).

164 **"yesterday we lost":** Pfister, *Psycho-Analysis and Faith*, emended. Freud replied with a certain ambivalence, on April 6 (in ibid.): "Rorschach's death is very sad. I shall write a few words to his widow to-day. My impression is that perhaps you overrate him as an analyst; I note with pleasure from your letter the high esteem in which you hold him as a man."

165 **"I found in him a seeking":** HR 1:4.

165 **When Ludwig Binswanger published an essay:** In *CE*, 234–47.

Chapter 14: The Inkblots Come to America

168   **David Mordecai Levy:** 1892–1977. See David M. Levy Papers, Oskar Diethelm Library, DeWitt Wallace Institute for the History of Psychiatry, esp. Box 1; the biography in *American Journal of Orthopsychiatry* 8.4 (1938): 769–70; David M. Levy, "Beginnings of the Child Guidance Movement," *American Journal of Orthopsychiatry* 38.5 (1968): 799–804; David Shakow, "The Development of Orthopsychiatry," *American Journal of Orthopsychiatry* 38.5 (1968): 804–9; obituaries in *American Journal of Psychiatry* 134.8 (1977): 934 and *New York Times,* March 4, 1977; Samuel J. Beck, "How the Rorschach Came to America," *JPA* 36.2 (1972): 105–8.

168   **stepping down for a year abroad:** Bruno Klopfer and Douglas McGlashan Kelley, *The Rorschach Technique: A Manual for a Projective Method of Personality Diagnosis* (Yonkers-on-Hudson, NY: World Book, 1942; 2nd ed., 1946), 6.

168   **Levy published Rorschach's essay:** Hermann Rorschach and E. Oberholzer, "The Application of the Interpretation of Form to Psychoanalysis," *Journal of Nervous and Mental Disease* 60 (1924): 225–48. The translator is not credited, but the timing, Levy's relationship with the journal, his fluent German and Rorschach expertise, and the notes in his copy of *Psychodiagnostik* (David M. Levy Papers) make it very likely that the translation was his. According to Exner, Levy in 1926 published a translation as "the first publication concerning the Rorschach to appear in an American journal": the description fits except for the date (ExRS, 7).

168   **first US seminar:** In 1925 (M. R. Hertz, "Rorschachbound: A 50-Year Memoir," *JPA* 50.3 [1986]: 396–416).

169   **champion in Switzerland:** Roland Kuhn (see also pages 70–71 and note on page 340 "For a period" above).

169   **advocate in England:** Theodora Alcock (see R. S. McCully, "Miss Theodora Alcock, 1888–1980," *JPA* 45.2 (1981): 115, and Justine McCarthy Woods, "The History of the Rorschach in the United Kingdom," *Rorschachiana* 29 (2015): 64–80.

169   **most popular psychological test in Japan:** Yuzaburo Uchida (see Kenzo Sorai and Keiichi Ohnuki, "The Development of the Rorschach in Japan," *Rorschachiana* 29 (2015): 38–63.

169   **on the rise in Turkey:** Tevfika İkiz, "The History and Development of the Rorschach Test in Turkey," *Rorschachiana* 32.1 (2011): 72–90. Franziska Minkovska, a pioneer of the French Rorschach, worked with Jewish children during and after the Holocaust; see note "Franziska Minkovska" on page 385 below.

169   **in the United States:** On the early history of the Rorschach in America, see ExRS; ExCS (1974), 8–9; John E. Exner, et al., "History of the Society," in *History and Directory: Society for Personality Assessment Fiftieth Anniversary* (Hillsdale, NJ: Lawrence Erlbaum, 1989), 3–54. Wood, 48–83, is thorough but polemical.

169   **Psychotherapists, having worked:** Ellenberger, *Discovery,* 896.

170   **"It comes out of two different approaches":** To Roemer, June 18, 1921.

170   **The two most influential:** Their initial feud is in Samuel J. Beck, "Problems

of Further Research in the Rorschach Test," *American Journal of Orthopsychiatry* 5.2 (1935): 100–115; Beck, *Introduction to the Rorschach Method: A Manual of Personality Study* (New York: American Orthopsychiatric Association, 1937); Bruno Klopfer, "The Present Status of the Theoretical Development of the Rorschach Method," *RRE* 1 (1937): 142–47; Beck, "Some Present Rorschach Problems," *RRE* 2 (1937): 15–22; Klopfer, "Discussion on 'Some Recent [*sic*] Rorschach Problems,'" *RRE* 2 (1937): 43–44, in an issue of Klopfer's journal that includes ten articles arguing against Beck; Klopfer, "Personality Aspects Revealed by the Rorschach Method," *RRE* 4 (1940): 26–29; Klopfer, *Rorschach Technique* (1942); Beck, review of Klopfer's *Rorschach Technique,* in *Psychoanalytic Quarterly* 11 (1942): 583–87; Beck, *Rorschach's Test,* vol. 1 (New York: Grune and Stratton, 1944).

Later reflections: Beck, "The Rorschach Test: A Multi-dimensional Test of Personality," in *An Introduction to Projective Techniques and Other Devices for Understanding the Dynamics of Human Behavior,* ed. Harold H. Anderson and Gladys L. Anderson (New York: Prentice-Hall, 1951); oral history interview with Beck, April 28, 1969, Archives of the History of American Psychology, University of Akron, Ohio; Beck, "How the Rorschach Came"; editorial, Silver Anniversary Issue honoring Bruno Klopfer, *JPT* 24.3 (1960); Pauline G. Vorhaus, "Bruno Klopfer: A Biographical Sketch," *JPT* 24.3 (1960): 232–37; Evelyn Hooker, "The Fable," *JPT* 24.3 (1960): 240–45. Also: John E. Exner's obituary for Beck, *American Psychologist* 36.9 (1981): 986–87; K. W. Bash, "Masters of Shadows," *JPA* 46.1 (1982): 3–6; Leonard Handler, "Bruno Klopfer, a Measure of the Man and His Work," *JPA* 62.3 (1994): 562–77, "John Exner and the Book That Started It All," *JPA* 66.3 (1996): 650–58, and "A Rorschach Journey with Bruno Klopfer," JPA 90.6 (2008): 528–35. Annie Murphy Paul, *The Cult of Personality* (New York: Free Press, 2004), has original material on Klopfer and Beck but is unreliable on Rorschach.

170 **fall of 1927:** Beck, *Introduction to the Rorschach Method,* ix.

171 **"I saw some of the best":** Oral history interview with Beck, quoted in Paul, *Cult of Personality,* 27.

171 **"by scientific method":** Ibid.

171 **"make up through his keen thinking":** Vorhaus, "Bruno Klopfer."

171 **popular weekly radio program:** Handler, "Rorschach Journey," 534.

171 **his eight-year-old son:** Paul, *Cult of Personality,* 25.

172 **In business-friendly Switzerland:** Ellenberger, 208.

172 **voluble conversations:** Molly Harrower, describing where she met Klopfer in October 1937, in Exner et al., "History of the Society," 8.

173 **a hundred subscribers:** "Retrospect and Prospect," *RRE* 2 (July 1937): 172.

173 **"does not reveal a behavior picture":** Klopfer, "Personality Aspects Revealed," 26.

173 **"a fluoroscope into the psyche":** Beck, "Multi-dimensional Test," 101 and 104; Beck, *Introduction to the Rorschach Method,* 1.

173 **"Once the response has been finally judged":** Beck, "Some Present Rorschach Problems," 16.

173 **Klopfer, while he agreed:** ExRS, 21.

173 **"combined, to a marked degree":** Klopfer, *Rorschach Technique,* 3.

174   **"knew the value of free association"**: Beck, "The Rorschach Test: A Multi-dimensional Test," 103.

174   **"Rorschach was able to handle"**: Beck, review of Klopfer, *Rorschach Technique*, 583.

174   **"a student trained in"**: Ibid.

174   **"does not seem consistent"**: Beck, "Some Present Rorschach Problems," 19–20.

174   **"little influence deriving from"**: Beck, *Rorschach's Test,* vol. 1, xi.

174   **Students at Klopfer's workshops**: Exner et al., "History of the Society," 22.

174   **In the summer of 1954**: Handler, "John Exner," 651–52.

175   **"awe those around him"**: Exner, obituary for Beck. Beck's later writing, especially the Experience Actual score, which reflects the subject's "inner state as total psychological vitality," enters quite speculative territory.

176   **One of her innovations**: ExRS, 158.

176   **she has since been called the conscience**: ExRS, 27, 42.

175   **Her first article in Klopfer's**: "The Normal Details in the Rorschach Ink-Blot Tests," *RRE* 1.4 (1937): 104–14.

176   **she cautioned Beck**: "Rorschach: Twenty Years After," *RRE* 5.3 (1941): 90–129.

176   **"far more flexible"**: In Exner et al., "History of the Society," 14.

176   **Her most dramatic effort**: Marguerite R. Hertz and Boris B. Rubenstein, "A Comparison of Three 'Blind' Rorschach Analyses," *American Journal of Orthopsychiatry* 9.2 (1939): 295–314. Technically, as she points out, her own analysis was "partially blind," since she administered the test in person, knowing only the subject's age. She offers all the necessary caveats: this exercise did not validate test procedures, or whether the Rorschach reveals personality structures, and of course many further studies are needed. But "the marked correspondence in these records can only be interpreted as positive findings." Within the field, this was a "famous confrontation" (Ernest R. Hilgard, *Psychology in America: A Historical Survey* [San Diego: Harcourt Brace Jovanovich, 1987], 516).

177   **Hertz got a phone call**: ExRS, 26–27 and 157, quoting personal correspondence from Hertz and reporting that "the manuscript was nearly completed." The date of the disaster is unclear—either 1937 or 1940 ("Hertz, Marguerite Rosenberg," *Encyclopedia of Cleveland History,* last modified 1997, ech.case.edu/cgi/article.pl?id=HMR; Douglas M. Kelley, "Report of the First Annual Meeting of the Rorschach Institute Inc.," *RRE* 4.3 [1940]: 102–3).

177   **apparently willing to let Klopfer**: ExRS, 44.

178   **By 1940**: Kelley, "Survey of the Training Facilities for the Rorschach Method in the U.S.A.," *RRE* 4.2 (1940): 84–87; Exner et al., "History of the Society," 16.

178   **At Sarah Lawrence**: Ruth Munroe, "The Use of the Rorschach in College Guidance," *RRE* 4.3 (1940): 107–30.

180   **"a permanent reservoir"**: Ruth Munroe, "Rorschach Findings on College Students Showing Different Constellations of Subscores on the A. C. E." (1946), in *A Rorschach Reader,* ed. Murray H. Sherman (New York: International Universities Press, 1960), 261.

Chapter 15: Fascinating, Stunning, Creative, Dominant

181 **a shift:** Defined by Warren I. Susman in "'Personality' and the Making of Twentieth-Century Culture," chap. 14 of *Culture As History: The Transformation of American Society in the Twentieth Century* (New York: Pantheon, 1984). His formulation, together with the examples in Roland Marchand, *Advertising the American Dream: Making Way for Modernity, 1920–1940* (Berkeley: University of California Press, 1985), have since been used across disciplines as the basis for a range of arguments; Susan Cain, for instance, uses them to argue that the culture of personality privileges extravert types (*Quiet: The Power of Introverts in a World That Can't Stop Talking* [New York: Crown, 2012], 21–25).

182 **One classic study:** Marchand, *Advertising the American Dream.*

183 **"As late as 1915":** Alfred Kroeber quoted in Hallowell, "Psychology and Anthropology" (1954), repr. in *Contributions to Anthropology* (Chicago: University of Chicago Press, 1976), 163–209.

183 **1939 essay:** Reprinted in *Rorschach Science: Readings in Theory and Method,* ed. Michael Hirt (New York: Free Press of Glencoe, 1962), 31–52; see also Frank, "Toward a Projective Psychology," *JPT* 24 (September 1960): 246–53.

183 **Lawrence K. Frank:** Obituary, *New York Times,* September 24, 1968; Ellen Herman, *The Romance of American Psychology: Political Culture in the Age of Experts* (Berkeley: University of California Press, 1995), 177. As president of the Macy Foundation, he agreed to sponsor the first academic conference that brought together academic psychologists and clinicians using the Rorschach, in 1941 (Exner et al., "History of the Society," 17).

184 **"The self does not know":** Markov, *Russian Futurism,* 5. Also quoted above on page 95.

185 **Thematic Apperception Test:** First published in Christiana D. Morgan and Henry A. Murray, "A Method for Investigating Fantasies: The Thematic Apperception Test," *Archives of Neurology and Psychiatry* 34.2 (1935): 289–306. The TAT still has its advocates today and is used relatively widely, subject to various multicultural updates including a "Black Thematic Apperception Test" and a set of images for the elderly.

185 **I see a wolf:** Galison makes a similar point: "In the world of Rorschach's inkblots, subjects make objects, of course: 'I see a woman,' 'I see a wolf's head.' But objects also make subjects: 'depressive,' 'schizophrenic'" (258–59).

185 **assumed that we have a creative:** The Rorschach "both reflected this new interiority [of the self] and, more actively, provided a powerful assessment procedure, a universally recognized visual sign, and a compelling central metaphor" (Galison 291).

186 **Prior to 1920:** This history is paraphrased from Hallowell, "Psychology and Anthropology," and "The Rorschach Technique in the Study of Personality and Culture," *American Anthropologist* 47.2 (1945): 195–210.

187 **"was the relation between":** Quoted in Hallowell, "Psychology and Anthropology," 191.

188 **second person to bring:** Beck, "How the Rorschach Came," 107.

188 **The Bleulers' 1935 essay:** M. Bleuler and R. Bleuler, "Rorschach's Ink-Blot

Test and Racial Psychology: Mental Peculiarities of Moroccans," *Journal of Personality* 4.2 (1935): 97–114. The journal itself is a revealing artifact of the time, filled with handwriting analyses, tests of twins separated at birth, and cross-cultural comparisons. It was originally a dual-language journal, called *Charakter* in German and *Character and Personality* in English, and the opening article of issue 1 (1932), William McDougall's "Of the Words Character and Personality," is rich in evidence for the shift from *character* to *personality* discussed above.

190   **easier said than done:** Samuel Beck criticized precisely this call for empathy, saying that what the test needed was fixed standards, not more subjectivity ("Autism in Rorschach Scoring: A Feeling Comment," *Character and Personality* 5 [1936]: 83–85, cited in ExRS, 16).

190   **Cora Du Bois:** 1903–91. *The People of Alor* (Minneapolis: University of Minnesota Press, 1944). There is now a biography: Susan C. Seymour, *Cora Du Bois: Anthropologist, Diplomat, Agent* (Lincoln: University of Nebraska Press, 2015).

192   **"The crux of matters":** Quoted in Seymour, *Cora Du Bois,* ebook.

192   **Could anything useful be learned:** Emil Oberholzer, "Rorschach's Experiment and the Alorese," in Du Bois, *People of Alor,* 588. Responses below from 638.

193   **Any such argument would be circular:** George Eaton Simpson, *Sociologist Abroad* (The Hague: Nijhoff, 1959), 83–84.

193   **An EEG:** John M. Reisman, *A History of Clinical Psychology* (New York: Irvington, 1976), 222.

193   **The figure usually credited:** E.g., Gardner Lindzey, *Projective Techniques and Cross-Cultural Research* (New York: Appleton-Century Crofts, 1961), 14; Lemov, "X-Rays of Inner Worlds: The Mid-Twentieth-Century American Projective Test Movement," *Journal of the History of the Behavioral Sciences* 47.3 (2011): 263.

193   **A. Irving Hallowell:** Jennifer S. H. Brown and Susan Elaine Gray, "Editors' Preface" to A. Irving Hallowell, *Contributions to Ojibwe Studies: Essays, 1934–72* (Lincoln: University of Nebraska Press, 2010); Hallowell, "On Being an Anthropologist" (1972), in ibid., 1–15. This volume contains all Hallowell essays cited below, unless noted. Hallowell used the older spelling "Ojibwa" in his essays; emended to "Ojibwe" in quotations. Many Ojibwe now refer to themselves as Anishinaabe (plural Anishinaabeg).

193   **summers along the Berens:** See especially "The Northern Ojibwa" (1955) and the evocative "Shabwán: A Dissocial Indian Girl" (1938).

193   **"a country of labyrinthine waterways":** "Shabwán," 253.

193   **"birchbark-covered tipis":** "Northern Ojibwa," 35.

194   **"In this atmosphere":** "Northern Ojibwa," 36.

194   **"the strange word Rorschach":** Quoted in "Note to Part VII" in Hallowell, *Contributions,* 467; cf. Hallowell, "On Being an Anthropologist," 7, and George W. Stocking Jr., "A. I. Hallowell's Boasian Evolutionism," in *Significant Others: Interpersonal and Professional Commitments in Anthropology,* ed. Richard Handler (Madison: University of Wisconsin Press, 2004), 207.

194   **"I am going to show you":** Quoted in Rebecca Lemov, *Database of Dreams:*

The Lost Quest to Catalog Humanity (New Haven: Yale University Press, 2015), 61. "Ojibwa" emended to "Ojibwe."

194 **dozens of Ojibwe Rorschach protocols:** The originals are in Bert Kaplan, *Primary Records in Culture and Personality*, vol. 2 (Madison, WI: Microcard Foundation, 1956). Hallowell eventually collected 151 protocols.

195 **different stages of Ojibwe assimilation:** Quotes and paraphrases from "Acculturation Processes and Personality Changes as Indicated by the Rorschach Technique" (1942), reprinted in Sherman, *Rorschach Reader*, and "Values, Acculturation, and Mental Health" (1950).

196 **two groundbreaking articles:** "The Rorschach Method as an Aid in the Study of Personalities in Primitive Societies" (1941); "The Rorschach Technique" (1945), see note "Prior to 1920" on page 365. See also "Some Psychological Characteristics of the Northeastern Indians" (1946), esp. 491–94, where he argues that the Rorschach does a better job of testing intelligence than other standard tests because it is less culturally biased toward Western modes of intelligence. His argument is very similar to Hermann Rorschach's in his 1920 letter to a prospective publisher.

196 **"since psychological meaning":** "The Rorschach Technique," 204.

196 **while "conceivable":** Ibid., 200.

197 **A 1942 study of Samoans:** Philip Cook, "The Application of the Rorschach Test to a Samoan Group" [1942], in Sherman, *Rorschach Reader*.

197 **"one of the best available means":** "The Rorschach Technique," 209.

197 **president of both:** Lemov, *Database of Dreams*, 136.

197 **"seemed like a mental X-ray machine":** Walter Mischel, who would go on to conduct the famous "marshmallow experiment" relating young children's self-control to later success, quoted in Jonah Lehrer, "Don't!," *New Yorker*, May 18, 2009.

Chapter 16: The Queen of Tests

198 **Within three weeks:** ExRS, 32; Exner et al., "History of the Society," 18–20.

198 **Army General Classification Test:** Thomas W. Harrell (who helped design it), "Some History of the Army General Classification Test," *Journal of Applied Psychology* 77.6 (1992): 875–78.

198 **Inspection Technique:** Ruth Munroe, "Inspection Technique," *RRE* 5.4 (1941): 166–91, and "The Inspection Technique: A Method of Rapid Evaluation of the Rorschach Protocol," *RRE* 8 (1944): 46–70.

198 **Group Rorschach Technique:** M. R. Harrower-Erickson, "A Multiple Choice Test for Screening Purposes (For Use with the Rorschach Cards or Slides)," *Psychosomatic Medicine* 5.4 (1943): 331–41; see also Molly Harrower and Matilda Elizabeth Steiner, *Large Scale Rorschach Techniques: A Manual for the Group Rorschach and Multiple Choice Tests* (Toronto: Charles C. Thomas, 1945).

198 **"the great difficulties":** "Group Techniques for the Rorschach Test," in *Projective Psychology: Clinical Approaches to the Total Personality*, ed. Edwin Lawrence and Leopold Bellak (New York: Knopf, 1959), 147–48.

200 **Harrower later commented:** Ibid., 148.

200 **a positive reception:** Ibid., 172 ff.

201 **standardized tests:** Reisman, *History of Clinical Psychology,* 271.

201 **"queen of tests":** Hilgard, *Psychology in America,* 517n.

201 **the turning point:** Reisman, *History of Clinical Psychology,* chap. 6–7; Jonathan Engel, *American Therapy: The Rise of Psychotherapy in the United States* (New York: Gotham Books, 2008), chap. 3; Wood, chap. 4–5; Hans Pols and Stephanie Oak, "The US Psychiatric Response in the 20th Century," *American Journal of Public Health* 97.12 (2007): 2132–42.

201 **1,875,000 men:** William C. Menninger, "Psychiatric Experiences in the War," *American Journal of Psychiatry* 103.5 (1947): 577–86; Braceland, "Psychiatric Lessons from World War II," *American Journal of Psychiatry* 103.5 (1947): 587–93; Pols and Oak, "US Psychiatric Response."

202 **"pitiful" physical health:** Engel, *American Therapy,* 46–47.

202 **When the war started:** Menninger, "Psychiatric Experiences"; Reisman, *History of Clinical Psychology,* 298.

202 **"practically every member":** Edward A. Strecker, "Presidential Address [to the American Psychiatric Association]" (1944), quoted in Pols and Oak, "US Psychiatric Response."

203 **designing complex instrument panels:** Reisman, *History of Clinical Psychology,* 298.

203 **By an accident of timing:** There was no textbook for the MMPI until 1951 (Wood 86 and n14).

204 **second most popular personality test:** C. M. Louttit and C. G. Browne, "The Use of Psychometric Instruments in Psychological Clinics," *Journal of Consulting Psychology* 11.1 (1947): 49–54.

204 **dissertation topic:** Hilgard, *Psychology in America,* 516.

204 **one first lieutenant:** Max Siegel, president of the American Psychological Association in the eighties, in Exner et al., "History of the Society," 20.

204 **operational fatigue:** Seymour G. Klebanoff, "A Rorschach Study of Operational Fatigue in Army Air Forces Combat Personnel," *RRE* 10.4 (1946): 115–20.

204 **Case review conferences:** Hilgard, *Psychology in America,* 516–17.

205 **status symbol:** Wood, 97–98; Engel, *American Therapy,* 16–17, 65–70.

205 **"at a time of emergency":** Klopfer, *Rorschach Technique,* iv.

205 **leading educational psychologist:** Wood, 175; **Lee J. Cronbach:** Quoted in Wood, 343n10.

205 **Ruth Bochner and Florence Halpern:** *The Clinical Application of the Rorschach Test* (New York: Grune and Stratton, 1942); see Wood, 85. I have found little information about Ruth Rothenberg Bochner (graduate of Vassar and Columbia) and Florence Cohn Halpern (1900–1981, PhD 1951, active in the civil rights movement and counseling the rural poor in the sixties).

205 **"a carelessly written work":** Morris Krugman, first president of Klopfer's Rorschach Institute, review of Bochner and Halpern, *Clinical Application,* in *Journal of Consulting Psychology* 6.5 (1942): 274–75. Samuel J. Beck's review is in *Psychoanalytic Quarterly* 11 (1942): 587–89.

206 *Time* **magazine:** March 30, 1942.

206 **on the double:** From a lively review by Edna Mann, *American Journal of Orthopsychiatry,* 16.4 (1946): 731–32.

Chapter 17: Iconic as a Stethoscope

208 **22.5 million:** Erika Doss, *Looking at Life Magazine* (Washington, DC: Smithsonian Institution Press, 2001).

208 **future novelist Paul Bowles:** His answers were "somewhat uncompromising and rather daring" and suggested a personality "amazingly complex and individualistic, little in common with 'ordinary' people" ("Personality Tests: Ink Blots Are Used to Learn How People's Minds Work," *Life,* October 7, 1946, pp. 55–60).

208 *The Dark Mirror*: See Darragh O'Donoghue, "*The Dark Mirror,*" Melbourne Cinémathèque Annotations on Film 31 (April 2004); www.sensesof cinema.com/2004/cteq/dark_mirror, last accessed October 2016.

209 **inkblot in print ads:** Marla Eby, in "X-Rays of the Soul: Panel Discussion," April 23, 2012, Harvard University, vimeo.com/46502939.

209 *Life* **magazine could look back:** Donald Marshman, "Mister See-odd Mack," *Life,* August 25, 1947; Siodmak was the director of *The Dark Mirror.* The sailor photo is from *Life,* August 27, 1945.

210 *Life* **headline about Jackson Pollock:** August 8, 1949.

210 **"Most modern painters":** 1950 interview with William Wright; Evelyn Toynton, *Jackson Pollock* (New Haven: Yale University Press, 2012), 20, 37, 52; T. J. Clark, *Farewell to an Idea: Episodes from a History of Modernism* (New Haven: Yale University Press, 1999), 308; Ellen G. Landau, *Jackson Pollock* (New York: Abrams, 2000), 159; John J. Curley, *A Conspiracy of Images: Andy Warhol, Gerhard Richter, and the Art of the Cold War* (New Haven: Yale University Press, 2013), 27–28. Rorschach had similar ideas: Emil Lüthy said Rorschach "wasn't interested in art per se, but art insofar as it is an expression of the soul. . . . He tended to judge artistic things as expressions of the mental, spiritual, emotional, or psychological state of its creator. He put the main weight on expression of the soul through the senses or the body, the hands, the movement for example" (WSI).

212 **"as closely identified":** Arthur Jensen, "Review of the Rorschach Inkblot Test," in *Sixth Mental Measurements Yearbook,* ed. Oscar Krisen Buros (Highland Park, NJ: Gryphon Press, 1965).

212 **One German dissertation:** Summarized by the author in Alfons Dawo, "Nachweis psychischer Veränderungen . . . ," *Rorschachiana* 1 (1952/53): 238–49. Dawo's methodology hardly inspires confidence—for instance, subjects were shown the Rorschach blots the first time and the Behn-Eschenburg "alternate series" the second time.

213 **Anne Roe:** *The Making of a Scientist* (New York: Dodd, Mead, 1953). C. Grønnerød, G. Overskeid, and E. Hartmann, "Under Skinner's Skin: Gauging a Behaviorist from His Rorschach Protocol," *JPA* 95.1 (2013): 1–12, gives all of Skinner's answers; my thanks to Greg Meyer for the reference. Other quotes: B. F. Skinner, *The Shaping of a Behaviorist* (New York: Knopf, 1979), 174–75.

213   **not to spend more of his weekends:** Joke stolen from Grønnerød, Over-
      skeid, and Hartmann, "Under Skinner's Skin."

213   **adopted this audio Rorschach:** Alexandra Rutherford, "B. F. Skinner and
      the Auditory Inkblot," *History of Psychology* 6.4 (2003): 362–78.

214   **Edward F. Kerman, MD:** "Cypress Knees and the Blind," *JPT* 23.1 (1959):
      49–56.

214   **A new theory:** Fred Brown, "An Exploratory Study of Dynamic Factors in
      the Content of the Rorschach Protocol," *JPT* 17.3 (1953): 251–79, quotation
      from 252.

215   **Robert Lindner:** "The Content Analysis of the Rorschach Protocol," in
      Lawrence and Bellak, *Projective Psychology*, 75–90 ("electroshock therapy"
      below is emended from the now obsolete term "convulsive therapy" in the
      original).

215   **Rorschach's own stance:** *PD,* 123, 207.

215   **David Rapaport:** David Rapaport with Merton Gill and Roy Schafer, *Diag-
      nostic Psychological Testing,* vol. 2 (Chicago: Year Book, 1946), 473–91, esp. 480,
      481, 485.

217   **Manfred Bleuler:** "After Thirty Years of Clinical Experience with the Ror-
      schach Test," *Rorschachiana* 1 (1952): 12–24, block quote from 22, emended.

217   **no conventions:** Lawrence Frank anticipated this argument as early as 1939,
      the same year as his groundbreaking essay on projective methods: the Ror-
      schach "reveal[s] the personality of the individual, *as an individual,*" rather
      than in relation to social norms, "because the subject is not aware of what he
      is telling and has no cultural norms for hiding himself" ("Comments on the
      Proposed Standardization of the Rorschach Method," *RRE* 3 [1939]: 104).
      Cf. Hallowell in 1945: "Because of the non-pictorial and unconventional
      character of the blots, they are open to practically an unlimited variety of
      interpretations" ("The Rorschach Technique," 199).

218   **Rudolf Arnheim:** "Perceptual and Aesthetic Aspects of the Movement Re-
      sponse" (1951), in *Toward a Psychology of Art,* 85 and 89; "Perceptual Analysis
      of a Rorschach Card" (1953), in ibid., 90 and 91.

219   **he too called into question:** Ernest Schachtel argued that "projection" in
      Frank's sense was so general as to be meaningless ("Projection and Its Rela-
      tion to Creativity and Character Attitudes in the Kinesthetic Responses,"
      Psychiatry: Interpersonal and Biological Processes 13.1 [1950]: 69–100).

220   **calling Klopfer's 1942 manual vague:** Review of Klopfer and Kelley's *Ror-
      schach Technique* in *Psychiatry: Interpersonal and Biological Processes* 5.4 (1942):
      604–6, followed by a dismissive one-paragraph review of Bochner and Hal-
      pern's book: "It shows traces of being hastily written . . . a simple description
      of the technical categories [and] some interesting case records." Schachtel
      had written a trenchant essay on Beck as early as 1937: "Original Response
      and Type of Apperception in Dr. Beck's Rorschach Manual," *RRE* 2 (1937):
      70–72.

220   **"not the words":** Ernest Schachtel, "The Dynamic Perception and the Sym-
      bolism of Form," *Psychiatry: Interpersonal and Biological Processes* 4.1 (1941):
      93n37 emended.

220   **"the test will become":** Review of Klopfer and Kelley's *Rorschach Technique.*

220 **took up Arnheim's 1951 call:** After Arnheim specifically criticized Schachtel, among others, for saying (in "Projection and Its Relation to Creativity," 76) that anything in the blot must have been projected into it, Schachtel took the lesson to heart. His book collecting and expanding his earlier essays approvingly cites Arnheim's article: Ernest Schachtel, *Experiential Foundations of Rorschach's Test* (London: Tavistock, 1966), 33n, 90n.

220 **He analyzed the blots' unity:** Ibid., 33–42; size: 126–130.

221 **discoveries in the science of perception:** Wolfgang Köhler, *Gestalt Psychology: An Introduction to New Concepts in Modern Psychology* (1947; repr., New York: Mentor, 1959), 118n8; Maurice Merleau-Ponty, *The Structure of Behavior* (1942; Pittsburgh: Duquesne University Press, 2002), 119, and *Phenomenology of Perception* (1945; London: Routledge, 2012), 547n3; Rudolf Arnheim, *Visual Thinking* (Berkeley: University of California Press, 1969), 71.

Chapter 18: The Nazi Rorschachs

222 **the Nuremberg Trials:** This chapter relies largely on Eric Zillmer et al., *The Quest for the Nazi Personality: A Psychological Investigation of Nazi War Criminals* (New York: Routledge, 1995); see also "Bats and Dancing Bears: An Interview with Eric A. Zillmer," *Cabinet* 5 (2001), and Jack El-Hai, *The Nazi and the Psychiatrist* (New York: PublicAffairs, 2013). Christian Müller supplements Zillmer with new primary material (see note "Kelley gave the Rorschach," below). Additional descriptions of Nuremberg from Douglas M. Kelley, *22 Cells in Nuremberg* (London: W. H. Allen, 1947); Gustave M. Gilbert, *Nuremberg Diary* (1947; repr., New York: Da Capo, 1995).

223 **"In addition to careful medical":** Kelley, *22 Cells,* 7.

224 **on no real authority:** John Dolibois, Gilbert's predecessor, said that Prison Commander Andrus "would not have known a psychologist from a bootmaker"; "Gilbert had pretty much a free hand and his book was foremost in his mind from the day he arrived" (quoted in Zillmer et al., *Quest,* 40).

224 **"could hardly wait":** Gilbert, *Nuremberg Diary,* 3.

224 **Some of the Nazis:** Zillner et al., 54 f. Gitta Sereny, *Albert Speer: His Battle with Truth* (New York: Knopf, 1995), records that Speer regarded the tests as "idiotic" and so responded with "total nonsense," especially on the Rorschach. Yet "it seems that he was rather irked when he found out that, as a result, the psychologist Dr. Gilbert had rated him twelfth in intelligence" (573).

225 **"chuckled with glee":** Gilbert, *Nuremberg Diary,* 15.

225 **"excellent intelligence bordering":** *22 Cells,* 44.

225 **"No Geniuses":** *The New Yorker,* June 1, 1946.

225 **"With but a short time":** Kelley, *22 Cells,* 18.

226 **except into other countries:** Geoffrey Cocks, *Psychotherapy in the Third Reich,* 2nd ed. (New Brunswick, NJ: Transaction, 1997), 306, emended; Zillmer et al., *Quest,* 49n.

226 **Kelley gave the Rorschach:** Zillmer et al. (xvii, 87, 195ff.) lists seven tests administered by Kelley: Rudolf Hess, Hermann Göring, Hans Frank, Rosenberg, Dönitz, Ley, and Streicher; in the appendix giving all the proto-

cols, he gives six—without Hess, whose test was not in the archive where the protocols were retrieved in 1992. However, Hess's results have been found among Kelley's papers (cited by El-Hai); another copy of Kelley's protocols, in the Marguerite Loosli-Usteri papers (HRA Rorsch LU 1:1:16), includes the same six without Hess's, plus one from Joachim von Ribbentrop, previously unknown (Christian Müller, *Wer hat die Geisteskranken von den Ketten befreit?* [Bonn: Das Narrenschiff, 1998], 289–304, esp. 300–301).

226 **The prisoners' results:** Zillmer et al., *Quest,* chap. 6.

227 **"lay on his cot":** Gilbert, *Nuremberg Diary,* 434–35, last ellipsis in the original.

227 **"essentially sane":** Quoted in Zillmer et al., *Quest,* 79.

228 **"not spectacular types":** Kelley, *22 Cells,* 195ff.

229 **More likely, they themselves didn't know:** Zillmer et al., *Quest,* 67.

229 **"We operated on the assumption":** Quoted in Zillmer et al., *Quest,* 60–61, quotation shortened here.

230 **The insults and retaliations:** Zillmer et al., *Quest,* 61–67.

230 **"only interested in gaining":** Quoted in El-Hai, *Nazi and the Psychiatrist,* 175.

231 ***Criminal Man:*** El-Hai, *Nazi and the Psychiatrist,* 190; cf. 188, 214.

231 **uncomfortably close bond:** Kelley, *22 Cells,* 10, 43.

232 **"Göring died":** Gilbert, *Nuremberg Diary,* 435.

232 **Kelley committed suicide:** Here El-Hai supersedes Zillmer et al. See also "U.S. Psychiatrist in Nazi Trial Dies," *New York Times,* January 2, 1958; "Mysterious Suicide of Nuremburg Psychiatrist," *San Francisco Chronicle,* February 6, 2005.

232 **the Nazi who had been in charge:** Zillmer et al., *Quest,* 239–40; Hannah Arendt, *Eichmann in Jerusalem: A Report on the Banality of Evil* (1963; repr., New York: Penguin, 2006); Alberto A. Peralta, "The Adolf Eichmann Case," *Rorschachiana* 23.1 (1999): 76–89; Istvan S. Kulcsar, "Ich habe immer Angst gehabt," *Der Spiegel,* November 14, 1966; Istvan S. Kulcsar, Shoshanna Kulcsar, and Lipót Szondi, "Adolf Eichmann and the Third Reich," in *Crime, Law and Corrections,* ed. Ralph Slovenko (Springfield, IL: Charles C. Thomas, 1966), 16–51.

232 **"The Mentality of SS Murderous Robots":** Quoted in Zillmer et al., *Quest,* 89 and n.

233 **"average, 'normal' person":** Arendt, *Eichmann,* 26.

233 **a joiner:** A term used in Roger Berkowitz's helpful "Misreading *Eichmann in Jerusalem,*" *Opinionator,* July 7, 2013, opinionator.blogs.nytimes .com/2013/07/07/misreading-hannah-arendts-eichmann-in-jerusalem/.

233 **"to think from the standpoint":** Arendt, *Eichmann,* 49. See xiii and xxiii on Arendt's term "thoughtlessness," a poor English word choice for "inability to think"; **"wreak more havoc":** 278; **"as if a criminal":** 289; **"from the Zeitgeist":** 297; **"one of the central moral questions":** 294; **"truly the last thing":** 295; **"about nothing does public opinion":** 296.

234 **Stanley Milgram:** "Behavioral Study of Obedience," *Journal of Abnormal and Social Psychology* 67.4 (1963): 371–78; *Obedience to Authority* (New York: Harper and Row, 1974).

234 **she never said he was an unwilling:** Berkowitz ("Misreading *Eichmann*") also writes that "the widespread misperception that Arendt saw Eichmann as merely following orders emerged largely from a conflation of her conclusions with those of Stanley Milgram."

235 **"half a dozen psychiatrists":** Arendt, *Eichmann,* 49. Kulcsar told Michael Selzer (see note "The Murderous Mind," below) that no other psychiatrist examined Eichmann. It now seems to be proven that Arendt misread Eichmann as well: A recent book of compelling historical detective work has shown that Eichmann was well aware of his crimes and enthusiastic about them, not banal and "unthinking" as Arendt had thought (Bettina Stangneth, *Eichmann Before Jerusalem* [New York: Knopf, 2014]). That Israeli soul expert may have been right after all.

235 **not until 1975:** Zillmer et al., *Quest,* 90 ff; "It is an oversimplified": Quoted on 93.

235 *The Nuremberg Mind*: New York: Quadrangle/The New York Times Book Co., 1975; see Zillmer et al., *Quest,* 93–96.

235 **"The Murderous Mind":** *New York Times Magazine,* November 27, 1977.

236 **a 1980 analysis:** Robert S. McCully, "A Commentary on Adolf Eichmann's Rorschach," in *Jung and Rorschach: A Study in the Archetype of Perception* (Dallas: Spring Publications, 1987), 251–60.

Chapter 19: A Crisis of Images

237 **"The Man in the Rorschach Shirt":** *I Sing the Body Electric* (New York: Knopf, 1969): 216–227, partly quoted in the paragraphs above.

238 **"the tough-minded attitude":** Wood, 128.

238 **air force scientists:** W. H. Holtzman and S. B. Sells, "Prediction of Flying Success by Clinical Analysis of Test Protocols," *Journal of Abnormal Psychology* 49.1 (1954): 485–90.

239 **Harrower had already pointed out:** Molly Harrower, "Clinical Aspects of Failures in the Projective Techniques," *JPT* 18.3 (1954): 294–302, and "Group Techniques," 173–74.

239 **In other studies:** Discussed in Wood, 137–53. Probably the most widely read of these studies at the time was J. P. Guilford, "Some Lessons from Aviation Psychology," *American Psychologist* 3.1 (1948): 3–11.

240 **In one 1959 study:** Kenneth B. Little and Edwin S. Shneidman, "Congruencies among Interpretations of Psychological Test and Anamnestic Data," *Psychological Monographs* 73.6 (1959): the entire issue.

240 **was starting to look very different:** Wood, 158–174.

241 **JFK saw "a football field":** Curley, *Conspiracy of Images,* 10.

241 **"Cold War crisis of images":** Ibid.; Joel Isaac, "The Human Sciences and Cold War America," *Journal of the History of the Behavioral Sciences* 47.3 (2011): 225–31; Paul Erickson et al., *How Reason Almost Lost Its Mind: The Strange Career of Cold War Rationality* (Chicago: University of Chicago Press, 2013).

242 **confiscating abstract paintings:** Curley, *Conspiracy of Images,* 17, 21–23.

242 **"brainwashing":** Lemov, "X-Rays of Inner Worlds," 266; Joy Rohde, "The Last Stand of the Psychocultural Cold Warriors," *Journal of the History of*

the Behavioral Sciences 47.3 (2011): 232–50, 238. Brainwashing had a capitalist counterpart uncomfortably close to these terrifying communist techniques for robbing us of free will with coded stimuli, the subject of great interest and anxiety in the period: advertising (Curley, *Conspiracy of Images,* 62–63, 131–33).

242 **five thousand articles:** Lemov, "X-Rays."

242 **"Cold War–era look-inside-your-head fantasies":** Lemov, *Database of Dreams,* 233.

243 ***"is like a dead planet":*** Ibid., 186.

243 **"You know, this Rorschach":** Ibid., 65.

243 **Perhaps the low point:** Rohde, "Last Stand," quotes from 232, 239.

243 **Walter H. Slote:** *Observations on Psychodynamic Structures in Vietnamese Personality* (New York: Simulmatics Corporation, 1966); see Rohde, "Last Stand," 241–43.

245 **"almost hypnotically fascinating":** Ward Just, "Study Reveals Viet Dislike for U.S. but Eagerness to Be Protected by It," *Washington Post,* November 20, 1966.

245 **"extraordinarily perceptive":** Rohde, "Last Stand," 242.

245 **"provide a kind of instamatic psychic X-ray":** Lemov, "X-Rays," 274.

245 **its old champion, Irving Hallowell:** Note to Part VII, in Hallowell, *Contributions,* 468–69.

246 **Arthur Jensen:** "Review of the Rorschach," esp. 501 and 509.

247 **in 1964, a reviewer:** Bruce Bliven Jr., *New York Times,* June 7, 1964.

247 **Charles de Gaulle would soon:** Stanley Hoffmann, December 18, 1966.

247 **Stanley Kubrick's *2001*:** Renata Adler, May 5, 1968, prompting a letter to the editor: "True, but what a Rorschach; and what a revelation. A searing inkblot."

Chapter 20: The System

248 **John E. Exner Jr.:** Obituary, *Asheville Citizen-Times,* February 22, 2006; Philip Erdberg and Irving B. Weiner, "John E. Exner Jr. (1928–2006)," *American Psychologist* 62.1 (2007): 54.

248 **Zygmunt Piotrowski's idiosyncratic "Perceptanalysis":** An experimental psychologist trained as a mathematician, Piotrowski (1904–85) approached the Rorschach from a very different angle. He emphasized the test's theoretical underpinnings and its use in diagnosing organic conditions (influenced by his close friend and fellow exile Kurt Goldstein, a Gestalt neuropsychologist, in New York in the thirties). His insistence on the tremendously complex interdependence of the scoring components led him to start working on a computer program to integrate the information. By 1963, his program was up and running, including some 343 parameters and 620 rules; by 1968, it had 323 parameters and 937 rules (ExRS, 121ff.). Partly because of his different concerns, partly because his synthetic book *Perceptanalysis: A Fundamentally Reworked, Expanded, and Systematized Rorschach Method* (New York: Macmillan) came out only in 1957, Piotrowski's influence on the main Rorschach debates remained relatively marginal.

248 **"by intuitively adding 'a little Klopfer'"**: ExCS (1974), x, emended.

248 **where should you sit?**: Ibid., 24–26.

250 **Present Distress (eb)**: Ibid., 147 and 315–16. **3x Reflection (r)**: The formula first appears in Ibid., 293; the name "Egocentricity Index" and cutoffs of 0.31 and 0.42 were added in later versions of the system.

251 **Exner score WSum6**: Irving B. Weiner, *Principles of Rorschach Interpretation* (Mahwah, NJ: Lawrence Erlbaum, 2003), 126–28; Marvin W. Acklin, "The Rorschach Test and Forensic Psychological Evaluation: Psychosis and the Insanity Defense," in *Handbook of Forensic Rorschach Assessment,* ed. Carl B. Gacono and F. Barton Evans (New York: Routledge, 2008), 166–68.

252 **data-driven new era**: Marvin W. Acklin, "Personality Assessment and Managed Care," *JPA* 66.1 (1996): 194–201; Chris Piotrowski et al., "The Impact of 'Managed Care' on the Practice of Psychological Testing," *JPA* 70.3 (1998): 441–47; Randy Phelps, Elena J. Eisman, and Jessica Kohout, "Psychological Practice and Managed Care," *Professional Psychology* 29.1 (1998): 31–36.

252 **Even in narrow utilitarian terms**: T. W. Kubiszyn et al., "Empirical Support for Psychological Assessment in Clinical Health Care Settings," *Professional Psychology* 31 (2000): 119–30.

252 **"treatment-relevant and cost-effective information"**: James N. Butcher and Steven V. Rouse, "Personality: Individual Differences and Clinical Assessment," *Annual Review of Psychology* 47 (1996): 101.

252 **"relevant and valid"**: Phelps, Eisman, and Kohout, "Psychological Practice," 35.

253 **"quite impossible"**: *PD,* 192.

253 **As early as 1964, four years**: Jill Lepore, "Politics and the New Machine," *New Yorker,* November 16, 2015, 42, dating the term to "1960, one year after the Democratic National Committee hired Simulmatics Corporation."

253 **large-format concordance**: Caroline Bedell Thomas et al., *An Index of Rorschach Responses* (Baltimore: Johns Hopkins University Press, 1964).

253 **An unnerving article**: C. B. Thomas and K. R. Duszynski, "Are Words of the Rorschach Predictors of Disease and Death? The Case of 'Whirling,'" *Psychosomatic Medicine* 47.2 (1985): 201–11.

254 **"This person appears"**: John E. Exner Jr. and Irving B. Weiner, "Rorschach Interpretation Assistance Program™ Interpretive Report," April 25, 2003, www.hogrefe.se/Global/Exempelrapporter/RIAP5IR%20SAMPLE.pdf; "his/her" and similar phrases emended.

254 **damage had been done**: The rather appalled-sounding Galison quotes "an excerpt from the advertised selling points of one popular" program, and excerpts from "an automatically produced case file" (284–86). Exner, "Computer Assistance in Rorschach Interpretation," *British Journal of Projective Psychology* 32 (1987): 2–19; his rejection of computers appears in the last text he wrote, a Comment on "Science and Soul" by Anne Andronikof, *Rorschachiana* 27.1 (2006): 3. "Excessive reliance on interpretive programs is bad psychology and simply reflects a sort of naivety or carelessness by the program user and ultimately does a grave disservice to clients and the profession." Cf. Andronikof, "Exneriana–II," *Rorschachiana* 29 (2008): 82 and 97–98.

254 **started praising the rigor:** Wood, 212–13.

255 **"Best of all":** Hertz, "Rorschachbound," 408.

255 **"bookkeepers' manuals":** Exner, "The Present Status and Future of the Rorschach," *Revista Portuguesa de Psicologia* 35 (2001): 7–26; Andronikof, "Exneriana–II," 99, emended.

256 **1968 survey:** M. H. Thelen et al., "Attitudes of Academic Clinical Psychologists toward Projective Techniques," *American Psychologist* 23.7 (1968): 517–21.

256 **not willing or able:** Gregory J. Meyer and John E. Kurtz, "Advancing Personality Assessment Terminology: Time to Retire 'Objective' and 'Projective' as Personality Test Descriptors," *JPA* 87.3 (2006): 223–25.

256 **the Rorschach fell:** N. D. Sundberg, "The Practice of Psychological Testing in Clinical Services in the United States," *American Psychologist* 16.2 (1961): 79–83; B. Lubin, R. R. Wallis, and C. Paine, "Patterns of Psychological Test Usage in the United States: 1935–1969," *Professional Psychology* 2.1 (1971): 70–74; William R. Brown and John M. McGuire, "Current Psychological Assessment Practices," *Professional Psychology* 7.4 (1976): 475–84; B. Lubin, R. M. Larsen, and J. D. Matarazzo, "Patterns of Psychological Test Usage in the United States: 1935–1982," *American Psychologist* 39 (1984): 451–54; Chris Piotrowski, "The Status of Projective Techniques: Or, Wishing Won't Make It Go Away," *Journal of Clinical Psychology* 40.6 (1984): 1495–1502; Chris Piotrowski and John W. Keller, "Psychological Testing in Outpatient Mental Health Facilities," *Professional Psychology* 20.6 (1989): 423–25; Wood, 211, 362n114, 362n115.

257 **One New York City cop:** Interview, November 2014.

257 **additional volume of his manual:** Here and below, ExCS vol. 3: *Assessment of Children and Adolescents* (New York: John Wiley, 1982), esp. 15, 342, 375–76, and 394–434 (case presented anonymously in the book; names supplied for clarity).

257 **norms would often be different:** Caroline Hill (see Introduction above) put it more vividly: "Every normal twelve-year-old boy I have ever seen sees explosions on the Rorschach, and less experienced psychologists tend to think this is a problem, but it isn't. They're boys" (interview).

260 **truths but no answers:** See the work of Adam Phillips, e.g., *On Flirtation* (Cambridge: Harvard University Press, 1994), 3–9.

Chapter 21: Different People See Different Things

261 **Rose Martelli:** Wood, 9–16; date of case from James M. Wood, interview, March 2016. The names are pseudonyms.

262 **"the use of Rorschach interpretations":** Robyn M. Dawes, "Giving Up Cherished Ideas," *Issues in Child Abuse Accusations* 3.4 (1991), excerpted from *Rational Choice in an Uncertain World* (San Diego: Harcourt Brace Jovanovich, 1988), and *House of Cards: Psychology and Psychotherapy Built on Myth* (New York: Free Press, 1994).

263 **Hillary Clinton:** Walter Shapiro, "Whose Hillary Is She Anyway?," *Esquire*, August 1993, 84, and "Editor's Notes: Whose Hillary Is She Anyway?," *Esquire*, January 7, 2016, classic.esquire.com/editors-notes/whose-hillary-is

-she-anyway-2/; *Who Is Hillary Clinton? Two Decades of Answers from the Left,*
ed. Richard Kreitner (London: I. B. Tauris, 2016).

264 **"Is the work merely a readymade"**: Curley, *Conspiracy of Images,* 18.

264 **"actual, physical work"**: Barry Gewen, "Hiding in Plain Sight," *New York Times,* September 12, 2004.

264 **inkblot paintings**: Robert Nickas, "Andy Warhol's *Rorschach Test,*" *Arts Magazine,* October 1986, 28; Benjamin H. D. Buchloh, "An Interview with Andy Warhol," May 28, 1985 (Warhol quotes below are from this interview), and Rosalind E. Krauss, "Carnal Knowledge," introduction to *Andy Warhol: Rorschach Paintings* (New York: Gagosian Gallery, 1996), both in *Andy Warhol,* ed. Annette Michelson, October Files (Cambridge: MIT Press, 2001).

265 **"These are abstract paintings"**: Mia Fineman, "Andy Warhol: Rorschach Paintings," *Artnet Magazine,* October 15, 1996, www.artnet.com/Magazine /features/fineman/fineman10-15-96.asp.

266 *The Inkblot Record*: Toronto: Coach House Books, 2000, esp. 102–103.

266 **By 1989**: Piotrowski and Keller, "Psychological Testing"; B. Ritzler and B. Alter, "Rorschach Teaching in APA-Approved Clinical Graduate Programs: Ten Years Later," *JPA* 50.1 (1986): 44–49.

266 **solidly in second again**: W. J. Camara, J. S. Nathan, and A. E. Puente, "Psychological Test Usage: Implications in Professional Psychology," *Professional Psychology* 31.2 (2000): 141–54. This ranking does not count IQ tests, two of which were used more often. The Rorschach was "the second most common personality assessment instrument in the U.S."

266 **estimated six million**: Wood, 2, calling this a "conservative figure."

266 **"Is the Rorschach Welcome in the Courtroom?"**: Irving B. Weiner, John E. Exner Jr., and A. Sciara, *JPA* 67.2 (1996): 422–24.

266 **real-world standards**: Gacono and Evans, *Handbook,* 57–60. In 1993, after *Daubert v. Merrell Dow Pharmaceuticals,* the Daubert standard superseded the weaker Frye standard from 1923 in most states. Expert witnesses' testimony would be admissible only if the judge determined it to be based on objective science. The criteria included: Is the theory or hypothesis testable and falsifiable? Have the findings been subjected to peer review and publication? Has the theory been generally accepted as valid in the relevant scientific community? The Comprehensive System was consistently found to meet the Daubert standard.

267 **"almost single-handedly"**: APA Board of Professional Affairs, "Awards for Distinguished Professional Contributions: John E. Exner, Jr.," *American Psychologist* 53.4 (1998): 391–92.

267 **"Trying to decide"**: James M. Wood, M. Teresa Nezworski, and William J. Stejska, "The Comprehensive System for the Rorschach: A Critical Examination," *Psychological Science* 7.1 (1996): 3–10; Howard N. Garb, "Call for a Moratorium on the Use of the Rorschach Inkblot in Clinical and Forensic Settings," *Assessment* 6.4 (1999): 313.

267 **four most vocal critics**: Wood, building on many of the coauthors' earlier articles. In the text I refer to the book's coauthors as Wood or "he" for convenience; "James Wood" refers to the individual.

267 **"What's Right with the Rorschach?":** By James M. Wood, M. Teresa Nez-worski, and Howard N. Garb, *Scientific Review of Mental Health Practice* 2.2 (2003): 142–46.

268 **fourteen studies from the 1990s:** Wood, 245 and 369 n1111.

268 **A more systematic problem:** Wood, 150–51, 187–88.

268 **a problem known about since 2001:** Wood, 240 f.

269 **hundreds of unpublished studies:** Wood, 219 f.

269 **James Wood admitted:** Interview, January 2014.

269 **Several reviews:** Gacono and Evans, *Handbook,* collects Hale Martin, "Scientific Critique or Confirmation Bias?" (2003), Gacono and Evans, "Entertaining Reading but Not Science" (2004; quotation from 571), and J. Reid Meloy, "Some Reflections on *What's Wrong with the Rorschach?*" (2005), which gives an example of checking Wood's references in detail and finding in Wood "distortions of detail, false imputation, and the construction of a straw man. . . . This is a tricky and crafty book which unfortunately sullies the scientific credibility of its authors" (576). The editors of *Handbook* list numerous other scientific articles responding to what they call the "pseudo-debates" engendered by Wood's attacks (5–10).

269 **But a 2005 statement:** Board of Trustees for the Society for Personality Assessment, "The Status of the Rorschach in Clinical and Forensic Practice," *JPA* 85.2 (2005): 219–37. A 2010 follow-up article reaches similar conclusions: Anthony D. Sciara, "The Rorschach Comprehensive System Use in the Forensic Setting," Rorschach Training Programs, n.d., accessed July 11, 2016, www.rorschachtraining.com/the-rorschach-comprehensive-system-use-in -the-forensic-setting.

270 **cited three times more frequently:** Reid Meloy, "The Authority of the Rorschach: An Update," in Gacone and Evans, *Handbook,* 79–87, which concludes (85) that either Wood's criticisms have "paradoxically resulted in a much firmer scientific footing for the Rorschach" or the debates "have largely gone unnoticed" by both forensic psychologists and the appellate courts. When, on the other hand, the test was misused, the psychologist's conclusions "were considered unfounded and speculative" and rejected by the court.

270 **"Rorschach cult":** Wood, 300, 318–19, 323.

Chapter 22: Beyond True or False

271 **densely quantitative papers:** One such article collated data from more than 125 meta-analyses on test validity and eight hundred samples examining multimethod assessment, concluding that: "(a) Psychological test validity is strong and compelling, (b) psychological test validity is comparable to medical test validity, (c) distinct assessment methods provide unique sources of information, and (d) clinicians who rely exclusively on interviews are prone to incomplete understandings" (Meyer et al., "Psychological Testing and Psychological Assessment: A Review of Evidence and Issues," *American Psychologist* 56.2 [2001]: 128–65).

271 **"inaccurate" to call it a "schism":** Interview, September 2013. The statement in print is in Erard, Meyer, and Viglione, "Setting the Record Straight: Comment on Gurley, Piechowski, Sheehan, and Gray (2014) on the Admissibility of the Rorschach Performance Assessment System (R-PAS) in Court," *Psychological Injury and Law* 7 (2014): 165–77, esp. the history on 166–68: "RPAS is not really competing with the CS; it is evolving beyond it and is designed to replace it."

272 **Rorschach Performance Assessment System, or R-PAS:** Meyer et al., *Rorschach Performance Assessment System Manual* (see note to my Author's Note, p. 329), hereafter *Manual*.

272 **"not advisable":** Lecture to teachers in St. Gallen, May 18, 1921 (HRA 3:2:1:7), 1.

273 **no right or wrong answer:** *Manual,* 11.

273 **"How can you get anything":** *Manual,* 10.

273 **SPARC, a support group:** They seemed to take the position that the Rorschach was unfair to men, while Rorschach opponents concerned about unfairness to women were just as vocal on the other side, e.g., Elizabeth J. Kates ("Re-evaluating the Evaluators" and "The Rorschach Psychological Test": n.d., accessed July 11, 2016, www.thelizlibrary.org/liz/child-custody -evaluations.html and www.thelizlibrary.org/therapeutic-jurisprudence /custody-evaluator-testing/rorschach.html). See the website for SPARC, especially the pages "The Rorschach Test" and "The Rorschach Test: Additional Information and Commentary" (www.deltabravo.net/cms/plugins /content/content.php?content.35 and . . . content.36). Interview with Waylon (SPARC's founder), November 2011.

273 **trademarked since 1991:** Silvia Schultius, Hogrefe Verlag, personal communication, 2016.

274 **"Has Wikipedia Created Rorschach Cheat Sheet?":** By Noam Cohen, *New York Times,* July 28, 2009.

274 **"Because the inkblot images":** *Manual,* 11.

274 **preliminary 2013 study:** D. S. Schultz and V. M. Brabender, "More Challenges Since Wikipedia: The Effects of Exposure to Internet Information About the Rorschach on Selected Comprehensive System Variables," *JPA* 95.2 (2013): 149–58: "Recent research aimed at investigating the Rorschach's ability to remain unaffected by conscious attempts at response distortion [has] yielded inconsistent results." See also Ronald J. Ganellen, "Rorschach Assessment of Malingering and Defensive Response Sets," in Gacono and Evans, *Handbook,* 89–120.

274 **test with multiple metrics:** Wood, Nezworski, and Stejska, "Comprehensive System," 5.

275 **In 2013, Mihura's findings:** J. L. Mihura et al., "The Validity of Individual Rorschach Variables," *Psychological Bulletin* 139.3 (2013): 548–605.

275 **seems to have come to an end:** Some of the usual critics pointed out ways the R-PAS didn't go far enough, calling it a half measure rushed into existence before a truly empirical, scientific groundwork could be laid (see next note, and interview with James M. Wood, January 2014). Meanwhile, oth-

ers criticized the R-PAS as going too far. They rallied to Exner's posthumous defense and founded an "International Rorschach Organization for the Comprehensive System," with the heartfelt cry that the developers of R-PAS had "confused and bewildered many in the psychological community" with their corrections. "Our goal should be to continue Dr. Exner's deliberate and methodical evolutionary process for a still better Comprehensive System," even though it is not clear how any of the actual materials can legally be updated, evolutionarily or not. Carl-Erik Mattlar, "The Issue of an Evolutionary Development of the Rorschach Comprehensive System (RCS) Versus a Revolutionary Change (R-PAS)," Rorschach Training Programs, 2011, www.rorschachtraining.com/wp-content/uploads/2011/10/The-Issue -of-an-Evolutionary-Development-of-the-Rorschach-Comprehensive-System .pdf. Squabbles aside, the scientific debates seem settled.

275   **The critics called:** James M. Wood et al., "A Second Look at the Validity of Widely Used Rorschach Indices: Comment," *Psychological Bulletin* 141.1 (2015): 236–49. They still had various complaints, but for a convincing rebuttal see Mihura et al., "Standards, Accuracy, and Questions of Bias in Rorschach Meta-analyses: Reply," *Psychological Bulletin* 141.1 (2015): 250–60.

275   **legal case for the new system:** Erard, Meyer, and Viglione, "Setting the Record Straight." I was not able to consult Mihura and Meyer, ed., *Applications of the Rorschach Performance Assessment System (R-PAS)* (New York: Guilford Press, forthcoming 2017), which has several articles on the topic.

276   **more than 80 percent:** 35 out of 43 programs, versus 23 out of 43 (Joni L. Mihura, Manali Roy, and Robert A. Graceffo, "Psychological Assessment Training in Clinical Psychology Doctoral Programs," *JPA* [2016, published online], 6).

276   **Collaborative/Therapeutic Assessment:** Stephen E. Finn and Mary E. Tonsager, "Information-Gathering and Therapeutic Models of Assessment: Complementary Paradigms," *Psychological Assessment* 9.4 (1997): 374–85, and "How *Therapeutic Assessment* Became Humanistic," *Humanistic Psychologist* 30.1–2 (2002): 10–22; Stephen E. Finn, *In Our Clients' Shoes: Theory and Techniques of Therapeutic Assessment* (Mahwah, NJ: Lawrence Erlbaum, 2007) and "Journeys Through the Valley of Death: Multimethod Psychological Assessment and Personality Transformation in Long-Term Psychotherapy," *JPA* 93.2 (2011): 123–41; Stephen E. Finn, Constance T. Fischer, and Leonard Handler, *Collaborative/Therapeutic Assessment: A Casebook and Guide* (Hoboken, NJ: John Wiley, 2012); Stephen E. Finn, "2012 Therapeutic Assessment Advanced Training," *TA Connection* newsletter 1.1 (2013): 21–23.

277   **a man came into Finn's office:** Finn and Tonsager, "How *Therapeutic Assessment* Became Humanistic."

278   **"empathy magnifiers":** Finn and Tonsager, "Information-Gathering."

278   **"coming for a psychological assessment":** Finn, Fischer, and Handler, *Collaborative/Therapeutic Assessment,* 11.

278   **But an increasing number of controlled studies:** Ibid., 13 ff.

279   **2010 meta-analysis:** John M. Poston and William E. Hanson, "Meta-analysis of Psychological Assessment as a Therapeutic Intervention," *Psycho-*

logical Assessment 22.2 (2010): 203–12. S. O. Lilienfeld, H. N. Garb, and J. M. Wood, "Unresolved Questions Concerning the Effectiveness of Psychological Assessment as a Therapeutic Intervention: Comment," and discussion, *Psychological Assessment* 23.4 (2011): 1047–55.

279 **One woman in her forties:** Finn, "2012 Therapeutic Assessment Advanced Training."

279 **"We would not necessarily consider":** Finn and Tonsager, "Information-Gathering," 380.

280 **its roots go back further:** Molly Harrower, "Projective Counseling, a Psychotherapeutic Technique," *American Journal of Psychotherapy* 10.1 (1956): 86, emended. For a history, see Finn, Fischer, and Handler, *Collaborative/Therapeutic Assessment,* chap. 1.

280 **"At its core, the Rorschach":** *Manual,* 1.

281 **"the Rorschach performance and the experiences":** Schachtel, *Experiential Foundations,* 269.

281 **"the encounter with the inkblot world":** Ibid., 51.

281 **people that other therapies often cannot reach:** B. L. Mercer, "Psychological Assessment of Children in a Community Mental Health Clinic"; B. Guerrero, J. Lipkind, and A. Rosenberg, "Why Did She Put Nail Polish in My Drink? Applying the Therapeutic Assessment Model with an African American Foster Child in a Community Mental Health Setting"; M. E. Haydel, B. L. Mercer, and E. Rosenblatt, "Training Assessors in Therapeutic Assessment"; and Stephen E. Finn, "Therapeutic Assessment 'On the Front Lines,'" all in *JPA* 93 (2011): 1–6, 7–15, 16–22, 23–25. Cf. Barbara L. Mercer, Tricia Fong, and Erin Rosenblatt, *Assessing Children in the Urban Community* (New York: Routledge, 2016).

281 **Lanice, an eleven-year-old:** Guerrero, Lipkind, and Rosenberg, "Why Did She Put Nail Polish?" Lanice and other names are pseudonyms.

283 **scrap the old labels:** Meyer and Kurtz, "Advancing Personality Assessment Terminology." Exner started the process of downplaying the unconscious and talking more about cognitive processes: "Searching for Projection in the Rorschach," *JPA* 53.3 (1989): 520–36. The most recent edition of the Exner system textbook puts it this way: "The nature of the Rorschach task provokes a complicated process, that includes processing, classification, conceptualization, decision making, and lays open the door for projection to occur" (ExCS [2003], 185). And even when a test taker *is* projecting something onto the image, that isn't entirely subjective or arbitrary. Different things call up different projections; different things ask, as it were, to be projected onto in different ways. As the psychoanalyst and essayist Adam Phillips writes, "Projection is often a relationship of considerable subtlety" because "people, and groups of people, call up different things in each other" (*Equals* [New York: Basic Books, 2002], 183).

283 **the skeptics' view:** Wood, 144; he assumes that the Rorschach as "an interpersonal situation" simply can't be reliable (151–53).

283 **For Meyer and Finn:** Gregory Meyer, "The Rorschach and MMPI," *JPA* 67.3 (1996): 558–78, and "On the Integration of Personality Assessment

Methods," *JPA* 68.2 (1997): 297–330; Stephen E. Finn, "Assessment Feedback Integrating MMPI-2 and Rorschach Findings," *JPA* 67.3 (1996): 543–57, and "Journeys Through the Valley."

Chapter 23: Looking Ahead

285 **Chris Piotrowski:** Personal communication, July 2015. In his view: "This all depends on the type of practitioner you survey—clinical psychologists versus counselors versus psychiatrists and so on. If you look at *all* mental health practitioners, then the Rorschach would probably more accurately rank 12th (as of late 2015, 2016)." Another survey, published in 2016 but conducted in 2009 and aiming to cover the field of psychology as a whole, found the Rorschach ranked below the MMPI, MCMI, and an unstated number of "symptom-specific measures" such as the Beck Depression Inventory (along with intelligence tests and measures of cognitive functioning), and slightly ahead of other performance-based or projective assessments (C. V. Wright et al., "Assessment Practices of Professional Psychologists: Results of a National Survey," *Professional Psychology: Research and Practice* [online, 2016]: 1–6; my thanks to Joni Mihura for the reference).

286 **The Rorschach had become:** Bruce L. Smith, interview, November 2011; Chris Hopwood, interview, January 2014.

286 **also critics of Freud:** See the review of Wood by Frederick Crews: "Out, Damned Blot!" (*New York Review of Books,* July 15, 2004), which concludes, predictably: "This test is a ludicrous but still dangerous relic."

286 **In the popular media:** The lone exception I have seen is "The Rorschach Test: A Few Blots in the Copybook," *Economist,* November 12, 2011.

286 **a 2011 survey:** Rebecca E. Ready and Heather Barnett Veague, "Training in Psychological Assessment: Current Practices of Clinical Psychology Programs," *Professional Psychology: Research and Practice* 45 (2014): 278–82.

286 **Piotrowski called the decline:** Chris Piotrowski, "On the Decline of Projective Techniques in Professional Psychology Training," *North American Journal of Psychology* 17.2 (2015): 259–66, esp. 259, 263.

286 **course coverage of the Rorschach:** Mihura et al., "Psychological Assessment Training," 7–8. As the authors note, it is hard to compare data across different studies, which might ask whether a topic is "taught," is "emphasized in required courses," is something "students should be familiar with," or other variations.

286 **almost all "practitioner-focused":** Ibid.

286 **The APA requires:** Ibid., 1.

287 **might get two three-hour class sessions:** Chris Hopwood, interview, March 2015.

287 **"Even for sympathizers":** Chris Hopwood, interview, January 2014.

287 **If a woman:** June Wolf, interview, August 2015.

288 **a Finnish scientist:** Emiliano Muzio, "Rorschach Performance of Patients at the Mild and Moderate Stages of Dementia of the Alzheimer's Type," Society for Psychology Assessment conference, New York, March 7, 2015; the

research goes back to his 2006 dissertation, and the tests were administered between 1997 and 2003.

289 **"ten ambiguous figures"**: Tomoki Asari et al., "Right Temporopolar Activation Associated with Unique Perception," *NeuroImage* 41.1 (2008): 145–52.

289 **"This suggests that emotional activation"**: Stephen E. Finn, "Implications of Recent Research in Neurobiology for Psychological Assessment," *JPA* 94.5 (2012): 442–43, referencing Tomoki Asari et al., "Amygdalar Enlargement Associated with Unique Perception," *Cortex* 46.1 (2008): 94–99.

289 **our eye movements as we scan**: Dauphin and Greene, "Here's Looking at You: Eye Movement Exploration of Rorschach Images," *Rorschachiana* 33.1 (2012): 3–22.

290 **"how a person perceives"**: Rorschach, St. Gallen lecture, May 18, 1921 (HRA 3:2:1:7).

291 **Look closely at this picture**: G. Ganis, W. L. Thompson, and S. M. Kosslyn, "Brain Areas Underlying Visual Mental Imagery and Visual Perception: An fMRI Study," *Cognitive Brain Research* 20 (2004): 226–41, building on S. M. Kosslyn, W. L. Thompson, and N. M. Alpert, "Neural Systems Shared by Visual Imagery and Visual Perception: A Positron Emission Tomography Study," *NeuroImage* 6 (1997): 320–34.

291 **Stephen Kosslyn**: "Mental Images and the Brain," *Cognitive Neuropsychology* 22.3/4 (2005): 333–47. See also "Cognitive Scientist Stephen Kosslyn: Why Different People Interpret the Same Thing Differently" (vimeo.com/55140758) and "Stanford Cognitive Scientist Stephen Kosslyn: Mental Imagery and Perception" (vimeo.com/55140759, both uploaded December 7, 2012).

292 **Kenya Hara**: *White* (Zurich: Lars Müller, 2007), 3.

292 **"In perception, there are three processes"**: *PD,* 17. Rorschach did not accept Bleuler's overall framework uncritically (see note "a journal" on page 354).

293 **impulsively, dreamily, hesitantly**: The adverbs are from Schachtel, who emphasized that how a person sees on the Rorschach "may be hesitant, tentative, groping, bewildered, anxious, unseeing, vague, impulsive, forceful, patient, impatient, searching, laborious, intuitive, playful, indolent, actively curious, explorative, absorbed, bored, annoyed, stymied, dutiful, spontaneous, dreamy, critical, and so forth" (*Experiential Foundations,* 16–17).

293 **"When we look"**: HRA 3:2:1:7.

294 **Ernest Schachtel pointed out**: *Experiential Foundations,* 15 f., 24 f.

294 **Being asked "What do you see?"**: Ibid., 73.

294 **psychedelic drugs**: Research into the therapeutic properties of LSD and other psychedelics, enormously promising in the fifties and sixties and shut down in the early seventies, has started up again with what look to be extraordinary results (Michael Pollan, "The Trip Treatment," *New Yorker,* February 9, 2015).

295 **One 2007 meta-analysis**: M. J. Diener, M. J. Hilsenroth, and J. Weinberger, "Therapist Affect Focus and Patient Outcomes in Psychodynamic Psychotherapy: A Meta-Analysis," cited in Finn, "Implications of Recent Research," 441.

296 **"Basically, I propose"**: Ibid., 442, condensed.

296 **a troubled eight-year-old girl**: Amy M. Hamilton et al., "'Why Won't My Parents Help Me?' Therapeutic Assessment of a Child and Her Family," *JPA* 91.2 (2009): 118.

296 **seeing doesn't precede thinking**: Arnheim, *Visual Thinking*, 13, 72–79; cf. "A Plea for Visual Thinking," in Arnheim, *New Essays*, 135–52.

297 **Interest in visual thinking**: Visual storytelling in books has also risen to full respectability, with milestones including Art Spiegelman's *Maus* (1992), Chris Ware's *Jimmy Corrigan, the Smartest Kid on Earth* (2000), and Alison Bechdel's *Fun Home* (2006); in nonfiction, Peter Mendelsund's much-praised *What We See When We Read* (2014) and Nick Sousanis's *Unflattening* (2015), a comic book on the principles of visual thinking, which quotes Arnheim among many others.

298 **Brazilian men and women**: Gregory Meyer and Philip Erdberg, conference presentation, Boston, October 25, 2013; Meyer also discusses this research in "X-Rays of the Soul Panel Discussion," vimeo.com/46502939.

300 **"A key point"**: Diary, November 3, 1919.

300 **a "social" connection**: Arnheim, *Visual Thinking*, 63.

301 **Jean Starobinski**: "L'imagination projective (Le Test de Rorschach)," in *La relation critique* (Paris: Gallimard, 1970), 238.

301 **continue to be recognized**: "Rorschach's most creative contribution to the study of personality" (Samuel J. Beck, *The Rorschach Test: Exemplified in Classics of Drama and Fiction* [New York: Stratton Intercontinental Medical Book, 1976], 79). "Since . . . Rorschach's monograph, human movement (M) responses to the test have been almost unanimously considered as one of the best sources of information about personality dynamics" (Piero Porcelli et al., "Mirroring Activity in the Brain and Movement Determinant in the Rorschach Test," *JPA* 95.5 [2013]: 444, quoting several examples from past decades). Akavia is the first book to set Rorschach's ideas about movement in their rich cultural context, linking them not only to Bleuler, Freud, Jung, and earlier psychiatrists of catatonia but to Futurism, Expressionism, and Émile Jaques-Dalcroze's "Eurhythmics," a Swiss system of teaching music through movement.

301 **In the early 1990s**: An enthusiastic overview of mirror neurons is Marco Iacoboni, *Mirroring People: The New Science of How We Connect to Others* (New York: Farrar, Straus and Giroux, 2009). Skeptical accounts include Christian Jarrett, "Mirror Neurons: The Most Hyped Concept in Neuroscience?," *Psychology Today*, December 10, 2012, and Alison Gopnik, "Cells That Read Minds? What the Myth of Mirror Neurons Gets Wrong About the Human Brain," *Slate*, April 26, 2007, who writes: "Mirror neurons have become the 'left brain/right brain' of the 21st century. . . . The intuition that we are deeply and specially connected to other people is certainly right. And there is absolutely no doubt that this is due to our brains, because everything about our experience is due to our brains. (It certainly isn't due to our big toes or our earlobes.) But it's little more than a lovely metaphor to say that our mirror neurons bring us together." The 2012 views of leading figures on different sides of the debates are usefully summarized in Ben Thomas,

"What's So Special About Mirror Neurons?," *Scientific American Blog,* November 6, 2012.

301 **connection to the Rorschach:** L. Giromini et al., "The Feeling of Movement: EEG Evidence for Mirroring Activity During the Observations of Static, Ambiguous Stimuli in the Rorschach Cards," *Biological Psychology* 85.2 (2010): 233–41. Robert Vischer, in 1871, had already pinpointed many phenomena that mirror neurons would be used to explain: "The suggestive facial expression [we see] is inwardly carried out or repeated"; "There is a very real and intimate connection between [touch and vision] . . . : The child learns to see by touching," etc. ("Optical Sense of Form," 105, 94).

302 **Further studies of the Rorschach:** J. A. Pineda et al., "Mu Suppression and Human Movement Responses to the Rorschach Test," *NeuroReport* 22.5 (2011): 223–26; Porcelli et al., "Mirroring Activity"; A. Ando et al., "Embodied Simulation and Ambiguous Stimuli: The Role of the Mirror Neuron System," *Brain Research* 1629 (2015): 135–42, all available on the R-PAS Library web page.

302 **remains controversial:** One critical account, by a coauthor of *What's Wrong with the Rorschach?* was positively reviewed by a cocreator of the R-PAS: Sally L. Satel and Scott O. Lilienfeld, *Brainwashed: The Seductive Appeal of Mindless Neuroscience* (New York: Basic Books, 2013); Dumitrascu and Mihura, review of Satel and Lilienfeld, *Brainwashed,* in *Rorschachiana* 36.1 (2015): 404–6.

302 **Other recent experiments:** Iacoboni, *Mirroring People,* 145 and passim.

303 **Empathy has been even more discussed:** Simon Baron-Cohen's *The Science of Evil* (New York: Basic Books, 2011) argued that the notion of evil should be replaced with "empathy erosion." Also Jon Ronson, *The Psychopath Test* (New York: Riverhead, 2011); Leslie Jamison, *The Empathy Exams* (Minneapolis: Graywolf Press, 2014).

303 **Paul Bloom:** "The Baby in the Well," *New Yorker,* May 20, 2013, and "Against Empathy," *Boston Review,* September 10, 2014, www.bostonreview .net/forum/paul-bloom-against-empathy, a forum with responses by Leslie Jamison, Simon Baron-Cohen, Peter Singer, and others.

303 **Stephen Finn's work:** Finn, "The Many Faces of Empathy in Experiential, Person-Centered, Collaborative Assessment," *JPA* 91.1 (2009): 20–23. This was an essay honoring Paul Lerner, who pioneered a psychoanalytic use of the Rorschach and himself saw empathy as the "heart" of the examiner's process.

Chapter 24: The Rorschach Test Is Not a Rorschach Test

305 **Dr. Randall Ferriss:** Name and identifying details changed.

306 **Irena Minkovska:** WSI. She said the other blots are "lively."

306 **Franziska Minkovska:** After working under Bleuler in Zurich and writing an important study of schizophrenia, she turned to the Rorschach test, developing an intuitive, emotional-centered system of her own (*Le Rorschach: À la recherche du monde des formes* [Bruges: De Brouwer, 1956]). The eulogy by her brother-in-law contains amazing details of her survival in Nazi Paris as a Polish Jew and her daily walks through the city, wearing the yellow star, to

the hospital where she administered the Rorschach to epileptics and children. "She used her own personal method of direct emotional rapport and empathy. . . . Along with scoring and quantitatively interpreting the answers according to Rorschach's classical method, Minkovska paid special attention to how the test subject picked up the card and held or moved it, as well as how he used language, his sentence constructions, use of time words, and the shifts in reactions and behavior during the test itself, and drew her conclusions from these elements." According to another eulogy, by her widower: "She always spoke reverently of Rorschach's ideas, his essential insight about exploring the world of visual forms, with the 'deeply held conviction' that she was staying true to them" (Mieczyslav Minkovski, *Schweizer Archiv für Neurologie und Psychiatrie* 68 [1952]: 413; Eugène Minkovski, talk at the Burghölzli, January 26, 1951, in *Dr. Françoise Minkowska: In Memoriam* [Paris: Beresniak, 1951], 58–74, 71).

306   **people often do have startled responses:** Schachtel suggested it likely had as much to do with "a sudden unexpected change" in the test as with color per se (*Experiential Foundations,* 48).

In Wood's telling (153–54, 289, 36–37), "The idea of Color Shock began to crumble" in 1949; several other studies in the fifties left the notion "discredited"; color shock was "shown to be useless" ("unimpressive," "generally dismal"), he concluded, citing the 1993 edition of Exner's manual. Exner, on the page cited, was actually addressing Rorschach's wider point—that Color responses are linked to emotional reactions. "Unfortunately, much of that controversy has not focused on" the general issue, "but rather on the concept of 'color-shock.'" Studies of the color-emotion theory as a whole, Exner claimed, "have generally been supportive of the concept" (ExCS, 421; cf. a 1999 overview of the research by Helge Malmgren, "Colour Shock: Does It Exist, and Does It Depend on Colour?," captainmnemo.se/ro/hhrotex/rot excolour.pdf.

307   *A long essay:* Gamboni.

307   *Inventing Abstraction:* The essay is Peter Galison, "Concrete Abstraction," in *Inventing Abstraction, 1910–1925: How a Radical Idea Changed Modern Art,* ed. Leah Dickerman (New York: Museum of Modern Art, 2012), 350–57. He is the author of "Image of Self" and co-organizer of a 2012 exhibition at the Harvard Science Center, "X-Rays of the Soul," connecting the inkblots in psychology to their role in the wider culture.

307   **countless visual connections:** Studies of the inkblots are flourishing elsewhere outside of science as well. A superb 2011 book on Justinus Kerner's inkblots, Friedrich Weltzien's *Fleck—Das Bild der Selbsttätigkeit* [Blot—The Image of Self-Making], links Kerner's claim that his blots came over from the other world to the idea of something that makes itself, which was central to nineteenth-century thought across a huge range of disciplines: photography as "the picture which makes itself"; self-registering instruments like seismographs; industrial automation (the dream of products that manufacture themselves) along with its dark double, automation out of control (the fable of the Sorcerer's Apprentice, written in 1797). Evolution was a theory

of "the life force"; in Hegel, the world-spirit unfolded itself through time, an idea recast by Schopenhauer's striving will and Nietzsche's will to power.

307 **"the place where our brain and the universe meet"**: Quoted by Paul Klee, in turn by Maurice Merleau-Ponty ("Eye and Mind" in *The Primacy of Perception* [Evanston, IL: Northwestern University Press, 1964], 180).

307 **85 percent**: Stephen Apkon, *The Age of the Image: Redefining Literacy in a World of Screens* (New York: Farrar, Straus and Giroux, 2013), 75, no source cited.

309 **"the negative space"**: Christian Rudder, *Dataclysm: Who We Are When We Think No One's Looking* (New York: Crown, 2014), 158–69.

309 **Barack Obama**: Quoted by Peter Baker in a postelection article, "Whose President Is He Anyway?," *New York Times,* November 15, 2008. Baker goes on: "The Rorschach part may fade with the end of the campaign but the test part is here."

310 **the metaphor has shifted**: Douglas Preston, "The El Dorado Machine," *New Yorker*, May 6, 2013; Lauren Tabach-Bank, "Jeff Goldblum, Star of the Off-Broadway Play 'Domesticated,'" *T Magazine, New York Times,* December 18, 2013.

312 **"ends up being given wrongly"**: Caroline Hill (pseudonym), interview, January 2014.

312 **judges regularly grant parole**: "I Think It's Time We Broke for Lunch . . . ," *Economist*, April 14, 2011; Binyamin Appelbaum, "Up for Parole? Better Hope You're First on the Docket," *Economix* (*New York Times* blog), April 14, 2011, economix.blogs.nytimes.com/2011/04/14/time-and-judgment.

313 **Finally, Card I**: Gary Klien, "Girl Gets $8 Million in Marin Molest Case," *Marin Independent Journal,* August 12, 2006; Peter Fimrite, "Teen Gets $8.4 Million in Alleged Abuse Case," *San Francisco Chronicle,* August 12, 2006; Dr. Robin Press and Basia Kaminska, personal communication, 2015.

314 **clear everyday language**: Gacone and Evans, *Handbook*, 7.

Appendix

317 **After Hermann Rorschach's death**: Blum/Witschi, 72–83.

318 **twenty-five francs**: Ellenberger, 194.

319 **H.R.'s development**: The second half of Olga R, © 1965, Verlag Hans Huber Bern. Translated and included here with the kind permission of Hogrefe Verlag Bern.

ILLUSTRATION CREDITS

page 212: Usage of "Rorschach" in English, from Google Ngram, accessed May 2016.

page 219: Figures 2, 3, 5, and 6 from Rudolf Arnheim, "Perceptual Analysis of a Rorschach Card" (1953), in *Toward a Psychology of Art* (University of California Press, paperback 1972), 92–94. © University of California Press.

page 264: Andy Warhol, *Rorschach* (1984). Synthetic polymer paint on canvas, 20 x 16 inches. © 2016 The Andy Warhol Foundation for the Visual Arts, Inc. / Artists Rights Society (ARS), New York. Courtesy Gagosian Gallery.

page 290: Figure 1 from Barry Dauphin and Harold H. Greene, "Here's Looking at You: Eye Movement Exploration of Rorschach Images." Reproduced with permission from *Rorschachiana* 33(1):3–22. © 2012 Hogrefe Publishing, www.hogrefe.com, DOI: 10.1027/1192-5604/a000025.

page 291: © Can Stock Photo Inc.

Color Plate 6: Figures 3 and 4 from M. Bleuler and R. Bleuler, "Rorschach's Ink-Blot Test and Racial Psychology: Mental Peculiarities of Moroccans," *Journal of Personality* 4.2 (1935): 97–114. © John Wiley & Sons, Inc. Reprinted by permission.

Color Plate 7: Jackson Pollock (American; Cody, Wyoming, 1912–1956 East Hampton, New York), *Autumn Rhythm (Number 30)*, 1950. Enamel on canvas. The Metropolitan Museum of Art, New York, George A. Hearn Fund, 1957 (57.92). © 2016 The Pollock-Krasner Foundation / Artists Rights Society (ARS), New York. Image © The Metropolitan Museum of Art.

INDEX

Page numbers in *italics* refer to illustrations.

About the Author

Damion Searls has written for *Harper's, n+1,* and *The Paris Review,* and translated authors including Rainer Maria Rilke, Marcel Proust, and five Nobel Prize winners. He is the recipient of Guggenheim, National Endowment for the Arts, and Cullman Center fellowships.